THE FIRM: MICRO-ECONOMIC PLANNING AND ACTION

THE FIRM: MICRO-ECONOMIC PLANNING AND ACTION

NEIL W. CHAMBERLAIN

Professor of Economics
Yale University

New York
San Francisco
London
Toronto

McGRAW-HILL BOOK COMPANY, INC.   1962

THE FIRM: MICRO-ECONOMIC PLANNING AND ACTION

10430

PREFACE

This book does not purport to be a complete treatment of the economics of the firm. It aims only to shift the focus of theorizing about the firm by providing an analytical framework which emphasizes three aspects of business behavior:

1. The planned manipulation of all the variables within the firm's control to achieve a given objective; the budget provides the integrating device for such plans.

2. The firm's preoccupation with the level and composition of its balance of inflows and outflows. These flows are always in *some* balance, but management is concerned with where and how. This concern with flows subordinates pricing, which has traditionally occupied the economist's principal attention, to the role, simply, of being one of the variables which management manipulates to achieve its objective.

3. The interplay between plan and actuality, between ex ante and ex post. A plan or budget is seldom (it might be said never) realized, and it becomes a critical management decision—really a stream of decisions—whether steps should be taken to conform activity to the original plan, or to maintain the planned objective but modify the means in the light of experience, or to conform plan (both objective and means) to experience.

These three present emphases have not, of course, been wholly absent from prior treatments of the firm, but they have tended to play secondary roles to rules for maximization. A shift from the traditional economizing principle to an empirical approach to the firm accords these three elements the status of major themes rather than minor embroidery. The economizing principle may inform certain managerial actions and decisions, but it is an inadequate basis for a theory of the firm.

One further significance of the present approach is worth noting, though it is not demonstrated in the present volume. (An earlier statement of it is given at some length in *A General Theory of Economic Process,* 1955.) In both its planning and its control activities, management is concerned with

v

tho flows of revenues and expenditures and with the level and composition of their balance. The significance of this concern is no less for the economist than for a firm's management.

For the manager, it emphasizes the manipulation of the variables of product, price, marketing strategy, technology, and organization to achieve objectives which have been validated either by his company's own experience or by that of other companies. For the economist, it provides a tie between the micro and macro levels of economic activity. In brief, the level of macro-economic activity depends on whether changes in the rate of flows within some micro units are offset or nonoffset in other units. If offset, the macro level of activity is unaffected. If nonoffset, the macro flows either swell or diminish. The income-flow approach to the firm, as to the household, provides the necessary link of micro- to macro-economic analysis.

My debts of gratitude for assistance in the execution of this work are numerous—to my profession, which nourished me intellectually; to my wife, who sustained me spiritually; to Columbia and Yale Universities, which encouraged me hopefully; and to the Ford Foundation, which supported me financially.

Neil W. Chamberlain

CONTENTS

volume. Break-even analysis. Other ways of increasing sales revenues. Manipulating costs. The budget as a product of bargains.

Introduction

THE SUBJECT

Relative Roles of Markets and Managers

This book deals with the business firm, which, along with households and governmental units, is perhaps the most characteristic organization of our society. It will be less concerned than is customary for an economics treatise with the market forces which mold the decisions of the firm's managers.

Certainly the lightness of treatment of this aspect is not due to any lack of belief in the importance of such market forces. All of us, whether businessmen or not, sometimes conform our decisions to circumstances which society forces on us. In the case of business operation this frequently means that prices and production within a company respond to influences arising outside the firm. If management "makes" a decision to raise or lower prices or to expand or curtail production, it does so because the market "dictates" the action. In these instances the businessman is as free in his judgment as a person is "free" to obey the law. To examine his decision-making process would perhaps be psychologically interesting, as an instance of the mental procedures by which a person reads external events in such a way that they have the same evitable and inevitable meaning for him that a sentence in a book might have. There would be little *economic* interest in his decision-making process under such circumstances, however.

As long as economists believed that this class of cases constituted a very high proportion of all business decisions, there was relatively little interest in the business firm except as a locus of these social and market forces. Business responses were predictable given the market forces prevailing. Business discretion was virtually nonexistent. There were simply varying degrees of business ability—ability to read the external forces so that one might act on them. There were good readers and poor readers, that is, good managers and poor managers, but this had nothing to do with discretionary decision making, any more than does the fact that some people are better readers of books than are others.

1

Although few economists today retain this view in any very pure sense, there are many who lean in its direction. Perhaps the most interesting and subtlest variant on it is one which can be best understood by contrasting its view of the business manager—the extent of his knowledge and discretion —with the view held by critics of market theory and businessmen themselves. Let us start with the critic.

The Case for Managerial Discretion and Control

The disbeliever in market theory typically argues as though control over the fortunes of a business firm lies with the managers of the firm. It is the quality of business decisions and the power which can be marshaled behind them which determine whether a firm survives or not, and if it survives how much profit it makes. The decisions which are important are actual ones, based on conditions which are real to the businessman—his costs, for example. There is little point in constructing an edifice of make-believe marginal decisions theoretically based on data which no businessman could possibly possess—the demand curve for his various products and services, for example, the amounts which customers would be willing to purchase at a schedule of varying prices.

It is such imaginary decisions founded on nonfacts, the presumed marginal calculations of businessmen seeking to maximize profit, which create the illusion of market dominance of the individual firm. In real life, according to this view, it is the judgments of flesh-and-blood businessmen, guided by a knowledge, imperfect though it be, of real conditions, and backed by consciously erected defenses against outside controls, which determine a firm's success or lack of it.

The critic is not always sympathetic with the businessman whom he endows with this measure of importance and power, but he has no doubts that it is the degree of personal ability to cope with such matters as competitive restraints which ranks a manager in some hierarchy among his fellows. Critics of market theory would restore the word "political" to the study of economy.

The Case for Mixed Market and Managerial Control

Despite the preeminence accorded them in this view, businessmen generally feel as uncomfortable about this version as they apparently do about the version which accords dominance to the market. For one thing, many businessmen act as though they do "know" and must use the data which critics of market theory have demonstrated are unknowable. The central fact confronting the business manager is that he cannot possibly know the future, but it is only data relating to the future which are relevant to his purpose. He knows that even with the most refined methods of market analysis the conclusions which he turns up about the demand for his products apply to yesterday and give him no assurance as to what his customers will do tomorrow, when their incomes and wants may have changed, when competing products may have come on the market, and when his rivals may have modified the prices they charge for products which substitute for his own. Nevertheless, he and his fellows go ahead assuming probable outcomes of particular decisions based upon assumed data. In planning advertising programs, for example, they are willing to state the expected results from a given campaign. In pricing a new product, they are likely to rest their judgment on an array of assumed price-quantity relationships in which they have considerable confidence.

In part, this willingness to assume data which cannot actually be known is due to the fact that some such guesses are necessary if a decision is to be made at all. Since guesses about the future are unavoidable, the manager is just as willing to guess about the variables which occupy the market theorists (even though these can never be isolated or measured) if they seem relevant (demand, for instance) as those which attract their critics.

Nevertheless, the businessman shares something of the critic's point of view. Although he does not go as far in asserting his independence of the market place, he does believe that his decisions can give him some measure of control over his environment. They are therefore important. He cannot and would not deny his responsibility for the success of his firm. At the same time he is also aware of an active and unpredictable world peopled by other businessmen, by an erratically fluctuating aggregate income, by prospects for war or peace, by a government which is more likely to be hostile than friendly. No matter how good any decision may be at the moment it is made, events beyond his control may convert it into a bad decision. Thus he shares the critic's view of the importance of his discretionary decision in explaining business success or failure, but he also shares the market theorist's notion of social forces which collectively determine the result. The responsibility for any outcome is mixed.

The Case for Market Control

The most sophisticated version of market theory pictures society as moving along evolutionary lines which Darwin would have understood and appreciated. The test is survival, in this case survival of the business firm. Businessmen make a variety of decisions, sometimes based upon careful research and analysis, sometimes based on hunch. There is no way of telling at the time whether any of these decisions are good or bad. The unfolding events of society at large—changes in the number of people, changes in their tastes and wants, changes in technology, and so on—will eventually make clear whether particular decisions did or did not contribute to the firm's survival.

Some business actions which might have appeared insane at the time they were taken may later turn out to be strokes of good fortune. Other business behavior which might at the time have seemed to be reasoned and warranted may later prove to have been mistaken and fatal. There is no way of knowing. The social forces of the unknown future are the active element in determining whether decisions have been helpful or hurtful to a firm's survival. To put the case in an extreme form, it might be entirely possible that a businessman who allowed a gypsy tea-leaf reader to guide his actions might turn out to have made, thus fortuitously, decisions which, in the light of unfolding events, proved far more fortunate than the decisions of a competitor advised by a corps of economists.

From this point of view it is obvious that business success cannot be predicted from business decisions. A business decision is comparable to the decision of a gambler to put his money on a number. There is no way of telling from that decision whether he will be successful, even though many gamblers have developed elaborate rituals, in which they firmly believe, for choosing a "good" number. Business success thus cannot be predicted ex ante.

But ex post it can be asserted that the decisions which would have led to business success—if all the facts could have been known at the time—would have been the same as those which the theory of markets posits on the basis of perfect knowledge. The basic condition of success in the short run is that a firm's marginal cost equal its marginal revenue, and over a longer period that its average cost equal its average revenue as well. Whether some firms achieve or approximate that condition by reasoned analysis and others by luck is immaterial. All those who do, however they do, find themselves in the most profitable possible circumstances and therefore have the best chances for survival.

On this approach, success is thus attributable not to a firm's actually making ex ante the decisions which are described in market theory, but to a firm's finding itself ex post in a position *as if* it had made such decisions. It is the degree of coincidence between a firm's profit position and the maximum profit position which market forces would have permitted that determines its potentiality for survival. Those which continue to meet the test, however accidentally, continue in existence. Others which do not do so well may lag along for a while. Those which fail to clear the profit hurdle are disqualified altogether and drop out of the race. Market theory thus describes the conditions of survival, but contains no "how-to-do-it" instructions to guide management decisions. It is not even particularly interested in these decisions.

This interpretation of the role of the firm in market theory is not widely held, but it is perhaps the soundest ground which can be put under that theory.

The Viewpoint of This Book: The Mixed Case

Of these three economic philosophies, the viewpoint which characterizes this book comes closest to that of the businessman. Unlike the critic of market theory, it does not deny the determining influence of social forces and collective decisions. Unlike market theory, it accords a role of greater importance to business decisions in determining business success. Without attempting to suggest relative degrees of significance, it can be loosely said that the area of discretionary control is considered in these pages to be as important as the area of external or nondiscretionary control, the social forces to which a firm must adjust because it cannot change them.

This book, then, does not deal with market forces, because these have been so ably and amply dealt with by economists for many years past. Regardless of the sharp distinctions made above, there is probably less dispute about the identity and reality of such influences than there is about the extent to which they control the decisions of managers in the business firm. This book makes no effort to assess the extent of that control. It does, however, start from the prior assumption that the degree of discretion which market forces permit to individual business firms is sufficiently significant that now the economist, not only the psychologist, must be professionally interested in the processes by which many decisions are made and carried out.

The Importance of Empiricism

An understanding of business procedures can only be achieved by empirical investigation. By and large, research of this nature has been undertaken by schools of business rather than by faculties of economics. On the whole, the business school researcher has been interested in particular decisions—the formulation of marketing policy with respect to a new product, the floating of a bond issue to acquire new capital for expansion, the choice of a new location, the determination of an appropriate depreciation policy. The relationship of these individual decisions to a more general theory of the firm, which ties into the economist's theory of markets, has not been a matter of much interest. At the same time, the economist has been peculiarly reluctant to involve himself in field research. While there has been a growing body of valuable statistical investigations of the business unit—and these may prove to be the more important—there has been relatively little examination of the business unit at first hand, to see for one's self how it operates, to discuss with its managers why they do what they do, and to try to hypothesize from what is found.

In part this reluctance stems from suspicion of such research. There are two principal doubts which many economists entertain. The first is that the evidence turned up by direct questioning is unreliable. What businessmen report they did is often a rationalization after the fact, having little to do with the actual circumstances of the case. The respondent puts on an impression of ratiocination because the questioner expects it of him, common decency demands it (after all, he *is,* or has been told that he is, a trustee for the stockholders if not for the larger society), and his own self-respect benefits from it. But it is all a myth, an improvisation.

The fact is that often events are sufficiently complicated, the number of people involved in a decision sufficiently large, and the time over which discussion takes place sufficiently protracted that it is very difficult for anyone to say just how even some important decisions were arrived at. An economist who was also a director of a Class I Eastern railroad once remarked that although he had sat throughout a lengthy afternoon board meeting having to do with a major matter of financing, he would be at a loss to say how the ultimate decision had actually been reached.

The other principal ground for suspicion of field research is that not enough cases can normally be included to give one confidence that he has an adequate statistical sample from which generalizations may be drawn. If a careful investigation is carried out, there simply are not time and resources to carry it out in enough firms to give one the right to say that the findings are statistically representative.

There is no point in disputing these criticisms. They are valid, but they are exaggerated. If it is true that one can never be sure of the accuracy or reliability of specific findings, it is no less true that there is a "cumulative weight of evidence" which, whether statistically justifiable or not, can help one to understand his subject. If it is true that one may not be sure of the correctness of his findings just because he has examined behavior in a few business firms, it is no less true that the person who bases his judgments on a complete absence of contact runs at least an equal risk of error. If exposure and experience do not confer infallibility, neither does innocence endow with knowledge.

This book is based on three primary sources of materials: interviews with management people in a number of companies; extensive perusal of the literature which management has itself created in its professional journals, in papers given before management audiences, and in internal documents; and replies to a questionnaire addressed to a select list of 1,000 corporate officials with approximately a 25 per cent response.

Chapter 1

THE GENERAL SETTING

Patterns of Relationships

Every business firm is the focus of a complex of relationships. It has lines which run to a number of suppliers of materials, to subcontractors, to employees, to financial backers (both lenders and equity holders), to customers, to competitors, to governmental agents. This web of relationships is largely of the firm's own weaving. While it is entangled in certain of these ties whether it wishes or not (as, for example, to government inspectors or regulatory agencies, or to unions chosen by a majority of its employees), on the whole it has fashioned its own web like some master spider.

The simile is not quite apt, however. The spider's web is something which the spider alone weaves. But every strand in the web of relationships over which a firm operates represents a joint weaving by itself and another. The strand which connects it with a supplier must be based on an agreement between the two. The link with a customer is a result of consent by each to a given set of terms. An employee forms part of the web because he has voluntarily caught the line which the firm has thrown out to him. The shape of the web in which the firm sits at the center has only in part been determined by it. All those with whom it holds relationships have also helped, in varying degree, to fashion its form.

Each of these—its suppliers and subcontractors, which are perhaps other business firms; its employees and customers, who are perhaps heads of households; its regulators, who are parts of governmental units whether Federal, state, or local—is in turn the center of its own web of relationships. Running from it are lines connecting it not only to the initial firm but to its own cluster of sellers and buyers, hired hands and hired capital, governmental and ownership controls, and so on. Perhaps a more appropriate pictorial analogy than the spider's web is a windowpane which a winter's frost has overnight covered with a pattern of stars, each one with a nucleus from which glistening lines radiate until they interlace with other lines which run into other nuclei, the whole forming a complicated mosaic. Each

7

of the nuclei is an economic unit—a business firm, a household, or a government—with lines of relationship connecting it to a large number of other economic units, in a tangle of alliances which is far too complex actually to identify even for the smallest of units. The whole fascinating and infinitely intricate design constitutes the economy.

Let us shift figures of speech again. The spider's web and the frosted pane are relatively fixed in shape, at least until the housewife or the winter's sun destroys them. There is no rearrangement of the web's filaments or the frost's crystals from one moment to the next. But each of the economic units which constitutes the focus of an involved combination of relationships is almost continuously modifying those relationships. Like a kaleidoscope, it changes patterns with great frequency, substituting one relationship for another, or discontinuing some relationship altogether, or spinning out a whole new complex mosaic. Yesterday's supplier has been replaced with a different one, or the same one continues but on different terms. Some of the firm's customers leave it to take their trade elsewhere, and others leave elsewhere to bring their trade to it. New products originate a whole new complex of relationships. Employees turn over with considerable frequency. New loans are floated and old ones paid off. New equity issues not only involve relationships with new stockholders but may also bring in new directors. Each of these changes always affects two economic units, the business firm and one other—another business firm, a household, a governmental unit.

Changing Patterns and Fortunes

As these changes occur, the fortunes of the economic units affected may also change, though this is not necessarily the case. The substitution of one supplier for another may merely be the result of, or touch off, a kind of game of musical chairs, in which supplier A shifts from firm A to firm B, while supplier B discontinues its tie with firm B and establishes one with firm X, substituting there for supplier C, who moves over to firm Y, and so on, with no one much differently off after all the changes have taken place. A few disgruntled customers leave one bank, but the same bank picks up a few new accounts from customers who have been disgruntled elsewhere. A certain amount of such change for change's sake is always going on; it does no one much economic good or harm but simply makes everyone a little better satisfied.

But at other times changes in the firm's web of relationships may affect its economic fortunes for good or ill. A company acquires a reputation as a bad employer, loses its best workers, and can replace them only with some of inferior ability. Another develops a name for high-quality products, and customers leave its competitors to flock to its brand, so that it grows while its rivals decline. A firm's principal product line becomes obsolete, and its mounting losses rob it of the credit it needs to gain a new start. A profitable company buys out another firm to diversify, and finds itself in difficulty in strange waters.

Sometimes a shock to the whole economy will profoundly disturb the relationships between most of the economic units whose interactions constitute the channels through which transactions take place. Recessions, inflations, and wars are probably the three most violent intruders. Major strikes may also affect a great many units. Orders are slowed down or expedited. Relations with some suppliers of materials or components, labor services, and capital are reduced or discontinued, or expanded or initiated. Changing relations with customers usually trigger such actions. The changes are sometimes to the advantage of companies generally, sometimes to their detriment generally, and almost always to the advantage and detriment of particular companies.

Management Reactions to Change

In the face of such changes, the management of a company can if it wishes simply sit back and allow whatever is happening to continue to happen, whether it is good or bad, and then seek to adjust to the impact. When orders and sales have fallen off and the flow of funds into the firm has dwindled, materials and direct labor can be reduced proportionately. When orders and sales expand, new workers can be hired and material purchases increased. But managements can, if they will, seek to control the impact of the change rather than merely react to it. This requires an analysis of what is happening, a projection or forecast of the future, and actions taken anticipatory of the changes which one sees coming. The impact itself is thus changed.

The difference between these two responses to altered circumstances can be sharpened by analogy. When a person is bathing in the ocean, he is conscious of the existence of waves which will disturb his physical equilibrium. He cannot escape their impact. He may, however, choose to pay little attention to their coming and simply recover his footing after they have buffeted him, floundering a little before he does so, or he may anticipate their coming and brace himself to offset their impact. Management is the bather in the sea of the economy. It knows it will be subjected to change. It can wait for change to strike and then seek to recover its position, or it can anticipate change and seek to prepare for its coming.

Having sharpened the difference between these two approaches, let us now blend them. No management ever wholly adopts one attitude in place of the other. Every management follows some mixture of the two. We may think of these as constituting the extremes of a continuum, along which managements and firms are distributed. Some do a good deal more reacting to experienced change than do others, floundering a little before recovering their footing before some heavy buffeting and at times going under. Even in these instances, however, there is—and almost inescapably—some measure of forecasting and anticipation. In every purchase of materials, in the continued employment of workers, in the payment of next month's or next year's rent, there is implicit at a minimum the expectation that things will continue pretty much as they are. Such an expectation may not even rise to the level of consciousness in the case of some small operations, usually exemplified by the "corner drugstore." In these instances, we are closest to the end of the continuum which represents "no planning." But as soon as such an expectation rises to the level of conscious thought, so that purchasing, hiring, renting, borrowing, and investing all proceed on the basis of such an assumption of continuity, an element of planning for expected future circumstances is present.

Other managements, and an increasing number of them, shape and tailor their operations with great care to the measurements of the future, as they foresee it. In the larger firms planning efforts are designed to encompass the total operations of the firm, and they occupy the time and attention of a good many staff and operating officials, the former sometimes set up as a special division or department.

Even in these instances, however, planning can never eliminate the element of chance, error, and surprise. The future turns out different than had been expected. Some aspect is overlooked. Thus some element of a firm's operations—and again, inescapably—always must consist in reacting to change after it has occurred, taking management by surprise, requiring some adjustment to compensate for the unforeseen.

Purposive Planning

Planning may consist not simply of anticipating changes which are expected to affect a firm's operations. It also commonly involves setting goals and then gearing the firm's operations to achieving them. It is purposive in nature. A business may plan to open new markets, offer a new product or service, expand its sales, improve the quality of its products, increase its efficiency, and so on. This effort to reach new positions is perhaps the clearest case of attempting to control the future. An objective is posed, the steps required to reach it are blueprinted, and the organization necessary to realize the purpose is put together. Even here, however, planning cannot encompass everything. A series of actions, set in motion, may precipitate events which had not been anticipated, requiring action after such events in order to accommodate the business to them.

Thus, inescapably, management must adjust—ex post—to changes which had not been expected and must lay plans—ex ante—to deal with expected future events or to realize future aspirations. The characteristics of different industries have some bearing on the extent to which adjustments are made ex post or ex ante. Some industries—electric utilities, for example—are much more susceptible to being planned than are others—the hotel business, by way of contrast. The temperament of managers and the size of their operations are also a factor. In general, the smaller and more personal operations are likely to react ex post; they do not have the facilities for extensive planning and are flexible enough to move quickly as they are affected by change. Larger operations, with personnel specialized to the task, less subject to the dominance of an individual's judgment, and with more at stake, are more likely to plan.

By and large the field of economics has neglected the planning characteristics of business enterprises. Planning is customarily wrapped up in the concept of "profit maximization." This neglect of the purposive nature of business, except for this assumed motivation, was less significant in the past, when it was more common for businesses to react ex post to market changes. If the market was viewed as dominant (except for a small class of monopoly cases), then businessmen could be expected to be dominated by it. They adjusted to changes in markets, in an effort to achieve or reestablish a position of maximum profit. But if one admits a larger area of managerial discretion, if he credits management with some capacity to make, build, affect, structure, or control markets, then the institutional mechanisms for planning become of greater interest. Conceivably they may affect the kind of planning which can be and is done and the results achieved. Organizational practices with respect to business planning become a fruitful field for analysis not only by the student of business, whose aim is to understand their relevance to the business's own performance, but by the economist, whose interest is in understanding their significance for the economy's performance.

Most of this study will be concerned with an examination of the planning and control mechanisms which have been developed by business managers. Before we proceed to that examination, however, it is desirable to spell out a little more clearly the relevance of these business procedures to the study of economics. The following represents the framework within which the present analysis is set.

Micro-economic Planning and the Economy

Micro-economic theory (which encompasses the theory of the firm and of the household) deals with individual factor and producer adjustments to conditions in the economy at large, chiefly demand and supply conditions but technically any conditions, and the effect of those adjustments on the conditions themselves. Its concern with the economy rather than with the individual units is epitomized in the concept of general equilibrium, a state of affairs in which all factors and firms are tied together in a network of counterpoised relationships. Micro theory is concerned chiefly with the allocation of factors and the distribution of income to competing ends.

Macro-economic theory is chiefly involved with levels of aggregate income. Micro and macro theory are related to each other through the flows of funds which the individual units generate in their relationships to each other and which, in the aggregate, become the national income. Households and businesses (and governmental units as well) do not simply respond to changes in their economic environment, as we noted earlier. They also attempt to anticipate and plan, to manipulate situations and their relationships with others to their own ends.

As we also noted earlier, this involves changes in the flows of income from one unit to another. Some of these changes are offsetting within the unit—a household or business receives less income from one source, but this is offset by more income from another source, the total remaining the same. Some of these changes are offsetting at the level of the economy even though not within the individual units—one household or firm receives more income, another receives less income, the one offsetting the other as far as effect on aggregate income is concerned even though the level of income in the individual units has changed.

Other changes are not offsetting even at the level of the economy. A number of households or firms receive more income, which is not offset by other units receiving less, or households and firms generally receive less income. These changes in the flow of funds between individual units which are nonoffsetting at the level of the economy are generated by a variety of factors, but they all reduce to changes in the aspirations characterizing the various units or in the ways in which they can satisfy their aspirations.[1] They constitute the causes of general business fluctuations.

In the present study we shall be concerned with only one of the micro units, the business firm. And with respect to the business firm, we shall focus principally on its purposive or planning activities. The heart of the analysis lies in its emphasis on the purposive, the planned, the anticipated, the ex ante. These plans do not always materialize, sometimes because of competitive factors (changes in income flows nonoffsetting at the level of the firm), and sometimes because of broad economic movements of a cyclical or secular nature (changes in income flows nonoffsetting at the level of the economy). As the ex post diverges from the ex ante, as performance deviates from plan, purposive adjustment is required.

[1] I have tried to spell this process out in considerable detail in an earlier book, *A General Theory of Economic Process* (New York: Harper, 1955).

The Interplay between Ex Post and Ex Ante

But I do not wish to overemphasize concern with the future. I do not wish to give any mystical importance to anticipated rather than actual events. Planning requires experience as a base. One cannot plan for a future without building on his past. It is the interplay between ex ante and ex post in which I am really interested. It is the relationship between past and planning which I want to emphasize.

Ex ante business planning involves forward decisions about product line, production processes, pricing and distribution, capital investment, and so on. In all these decision areas there is considerable scope for discretion, as to both ends and means. Even though the environment sets boundaries on decisions, it does not straight-jacket them.

Ex post, however, it may prove to be the case that the decisions reached by the planners set goals which cannot be reached by the operating people. Variances from plan occur, and adjustments in ex ante planning must then be made for the next period. The unfolding event affects the expected event. The extent of the firm's achievement influences the length of its grasp. Realization helps to shape aspiration.

This interplay between ex ante and ex post—the setting of goals which grow out of previous experience and the extent of whose realization affects a next set of goals, and so on, in a series of step movements into the future—is analytically useful. It helps to illuminate, for example, the postwar controversy between those who maintain that business follows average-cost (full-cost) pricing and those who plump for marginal-cost pricing. The inability of these two groups to come together lies in the unwillingness of each to admit that the validity of the other's position, and of its own, is limited to a time dimension.

Average-cost pricing is part of the planning process. It is not, of course, universally resorted to by businesses as a formula for pricing, but one does not have to scan the business literature very far before realizing that full-cost analysis is widely employed as a guide to price decisions. It is a useful concept in seeking to organize and project business activity purposively—toward given goals—over a period of time. Nor is it so illogical that business planners need feel embarrassed to use it; experience has demonstrated that under circumstances which repeat themselves frequently it is a workable basis for projecting prices into the planning future and estimating revenues which will be received on an expected volume.

This does not mean, however, that businessmen will stubbornly adhere to the full-cost price, refusing to adjust it as circumstances may dictate. Experience and not a priori logic, the ex post factor in the form of felt competitive forces and not the ex ante prevision of the future, may require modification of original pricing policy in the direction of marginal-cost pricing, as a limit. Again the literature is filled with discussions of the extent to which businessmen should be willing to adjust in this direction, and the dangers of doing so, but that they do so and will continue to do so is not in question.

Businessmen would seldom, however, *plan* on marginal-cost pricing where this would be less than average cost. Except in unusually straitened circumstances and depressed times, that would be taken as poor planning. Business operations would be guided by the purpose of realizing as close to full cost as possible, and managements would regard obstacles in the way of achieving that result as a challenge to their abilities and ingenuities. If their plans cannot be held to, however, they are prepared to move in the direction of shaving prices to meet competition or to win orders, if this does not seem to jeopardize other revenues.

The marginal-cost pricers argue as though it is only the modifications of price policy in the direction of marginal cost which are relevant and significant. The average-cost pricers argue as though the only important consideration is the original plan or purpose. Either position is tenuous. Plans are not self-fulfilling, and to the extent unrealized or unrealizable they will be modified. But at the same time, the modified policy, the adjusted price, the ex post action is likely to be different from what it would have been in the absence of any plan. The influence of purpose and goal on present activity is likely to affect the nature of that activity. The areas of discretion within which managements may move and manipulate in order to achieve as much of their objective as possible include more than automaton-like price adjustments to marginal cost.

The Interests of This Book

This study, then, has several distinguishing characteristics:

1. It focuses on planning.

2. It emphasizes, however, the interplay between experience and planning (control and adjustment).

3. While limiting its attention to the business unit, it seeks to carry through the analysis in conceptual terms which will permit its assimilation into a larger analytical system.

Chapter 2

BALANCE SHEET AND BUDGET

The Balance Sheet

A business firm's past is summarized in its balance sheet. Existence of this statement of assets, liabilities, and net worth can be traced back at least four centuries, but its general and periodic use is largely a product of the present century. Originally designed for the private information of the owners of a business, it was from time to time demanded by a banking house on the occasion of making a loan. It was not, however, until the spread of the modern corporation, the growth in the number of firms listed on the New York Stock Exchange, and the increasing resort to bank credit (spurred in part by rediscounting privileges under the Federal Reserve Act) that the balance sheet became a common instrument of business accounting.

Exhibit 1 presents a typical consolidated balance sheet. This financial statement is intended to serve two principal purposes. First, it indicates the *net worth* of the business. Second, it suggests the *financial viability* of the business. While it does each of these things imperfectly, it is the most convenient approximate summary that accountants have yet devised of where a firm stands financially at a point in time.

The net worth figure is presumed to represent the stockholders' equity. This is the value of the business to its owners. As one financial analyst has pointed out, however, the balance sheet can be said to perform this function only in a loose sense. Because a firm typically has a past stretching over a number of years and has acquired real property over that time span, at varying price levels, all of which have been lumped together at "cost," it would be more correct to say that the "net worth" figure really constitutes only "unamortized costs in year-of-purchase dollars." [1] No satisfactory alternative way of figuring shareholders' equity has yet been developed, however. The net worth figure is important at times when a company is

[1] E. Stewart Freeman, "Measuring Sales, Gross Assets and Invested Capital and Comparing Them to Profits," *The Controller,* February, 1955, p. 90.

15

seeking to raise new funds, whether through the sale of additional shares or through indebtedness. It is important in demonstrating to shareholders and lenders the results of management's past stewardship.

EXHIBIT 1

CONSOLIDATED BALANCE SHEET

ASSETS	LIABILITIES AND STOCKHOLDERS' EQUITY
Current Assets	Current Liabilities
Cash	Accounts payable
United States government and other marketable securities	Notes, loans, and debentures payable within one year
Accounts and notes receivable	Accrued salaries, wages, and other compensation
Inventories (at lower of cost or market)	Dividends payable
Raw materials and supplies	Accrued taxes, including taxes on income
Work in process and finished goods	Total current liabilities
Prepaid expenses, insurance, and taxes	
Total current assets	Long-term debt
Investments and Noncurrent Receivables	Reserves for specific purposes
Investments in unconsolidated subsidiaries	Stockholders' Equity
Notes and advances	Capital stock
Total investments and noncurrent receivables	Preferred, par value
	Common, par value
Property, Plant, and Equipment	Capital account in excess of par value of stock
At cost	Retained earnings
Less depreciation	Total stockholders' equity
Net property, plant, and equipment	Total liabilities and stockholders' equity
Total assets	

The balance sheet also suggests the capacity of the firm to surmount surprise shocks or to profit from unexpected advantage. The relationship to each other of the several items composing the statement indicates, though it does not establish, whether the firm is operating and growing in appropriate balance. In this respect it is guide to both management and investors. Evaluation of the relationship of the several items to each other is known as "ratio analysis." Good analysis requires a degree of background knowledge in addition to the figures themselves, but the statement represents the point of departure.

Ratio Analysis

One of the ratios most frequently examined by the managers or analysts of a firm is the current ratio. This is the relative magnitude of the current assets to the current liabilities. Current assets are not a sharply defined category, but in general may be said to consist of cash and securities which can be readily liquidated plus those assets which are in the process of being converted into cash in the normal short-run course of doing business. A year is the customary time limit. This includes, for example, inventories of raw materials and supplies which are in process of being converted into finished goods as well as stocks of finished goods themselves which presumably are in process of being turned over in sales to customers. The difference between current assets and current liabilities is referred to as "working capital."

The current ratio is important as an indicator of the resources available to a firm in carrying on its regular operations. If some product or service should catch on and sales should expand, its capacity to produce and market the additional output would depend on the adequacy of its working capital. Unless it could add to its lines of credit, it might actually have to refuse new business because of financial inability to increase purchases of the necessary materials and to meet a larger payroll.[2]

Even what appears to be a healthy working capital may turn out to be inadequate if its composition stresses illiquid assets. If there is a substantial increase in the volume of new orders, a company may find itself with suppliers pressing for payment of a higher materials bill and with payroll swollen, while its current assets—seemingly of sufficient over-all magnitude—are locked up in additional goods in process on which there can be no

[2] Although analysts with good reason contend that there is no "standard" or "normal" or desirable current ratio for all businesses, nevertheless there is a tendency to consider that a ratio of 2 to 1 of assets and liabilities is generally healthy. Some analysts have constructed current ratios for particular lines of activity, so that a firm may compare its position with others in the same industry. One set of five-year averages shows a range in manufacturing from 1.59 (airplane parts and accessories) to 3.78 (cotton cloth mills), in wholesaling from 1.94 (baked goods) to 3.70 (hosiery and underwear), in retailing from 2.72 (women's specialty shops) to 3.97 (installment furniture stores). Roy A. Foulke, *Practical Financial Statement Analysis,* 4th ed. (New York: McGraw-Hill, 1957), pp. 200–201.

A contrary point of view is offered by this comment of F. C. Dirks of the International Monetary Fund: "From the standpoint of the small businessman, the main job is to expand operations; the raising of funds is a subsidiary process to be determined by expediency. Where this is true, the patchwork way in which asset and liability patterns may develop during a period of aggressive growth reflects merely an historical conjuncture of each businessman's peculiar background, personal contacts, community institutions and the like. It follows that *average* behavior has little significance as a norm for sound or unsound development." *Conference on Research in Business Finance* (New York: National Bureau of Economic Research, 1952), p. 19.

Dirks' view is entirely valid, and the point he makes is an important one. At the same time it would be a poor exercise of discretion for a businessman to ignore the experience of other businessmen in circumstances which are similar enough to be instructive.

realization for some time. A firm might experience the unpleasant situation of being financially strapped even when its current ratio looked good. For this reason a secondary measure of business viability is the even more rigorous test known as the "quick ratio." This is the relation between those assets which are readily liquidated (cash and marketable securities, for example) and current liabilities.

Other balance-sheet ratios which managements and analysts sometimes examine, as clues to the viability of a firm, are current liabilities to net worth, total liabilities to net worth, funded debt to working capital, fixed assets to net worth, inventory to working capital, and (drawing on additional information not provided in the balance sheet itself) net sales to a number of these quantities. We are not here concerned with the significance of these various ratios.[3] We are only concerned with the fact that the balance sheet represents the financial state of affairs in which a business finds itself as of a moment in time, customarily the end of a fiscal year. It is a summary statement of past activity. It is an historical document. At the same time, as ratio analysis implies, it constitutes the basis for the firm's future activity. It reveals nothing, however, about the likely nature or shape or direction or magnitude of that activity, except as continuity may be inferred from examining a succession of balance sheets and changes from one to the next, over time.

The Income Statement

From one year to the next a firm's balance sheet indicates the changes in magnitude of its assets and liabilities. A second type of financial statement provides a summary of what contributed to the change in one of those items, retained earnings. This is the income, or profit and loss, or operating statement, a form of financial analysis which came into general use somewhat later than the balance sheet, probably owing in considerable part to the corporate income tax as well as to pressure from financial analysts in brokerage firms for more detailed information on corporate operations.

An income statement of the form shown in Exhibit 2 summarizes the total receipts of the business (principally from sales), categorizes total expenses incurred in obtaining its revenues, establishes the net income (both before and after income taxes), and subtracts dividend payments to arrive at the amount of earnings from the year's activities which have been retained in the business. These, when added to the previous year's balance-sheet total of retained earnings, show how the year's activities have affected the company's net worth.

The income statement does not show how the year's operations affected

[3] A useful volume in this connection is Foulke, *Practical Financial Statement Analysis.*

other asset and liability entries. Some portion of the year's production, entailing expenditures for materials and labor, may have gone to build inventories rather than directly to sales. The cost of such production would not appear in the year's income statement. It would affect the balance sheet, however, by increasing the asset item of inventories and balancing this either by a reduction in cash or by an increase in accounts payable. But the

EXHIBIT 2

CONSOLIDATED OPERATING (INCOME) STATEMENT

INCOME

Net sales and operating revenues
Dividends and remittances from unconsolidated subsidiaries
Income from securities and investments
Miscellaneous other income
Gross revenues

COSTS AND EXPENSES

Cost of goods sold, exclusive of items listed below (includes cost of materials and merchandise, subcontracted services, salaries, wages, and employee benefits)
Depreciation, depletion, and obsolescence
Interest expense
Selling, administrative, research, and general expenses
Provision for doubtful accounts
Contributions to profit sharing, bonus, or stock option plan
Total costs and expenses
Income before Federal and foreign income taxes
Less Federal and foreign income taxes
Net income
Less cash dividends
Retained earnings at end of year

change in the value of inventories is treated as an asset change, and the cost of the increase or decrease in inventories is not entered as a profit or loss item, since neither profit nor loss has been yet realized on their sale. Exhibit 3 gives an elaborated income statement incorporating total expenditures for all production, including that for inventory, but netting out those expenses which are incurred in effecting inventory changes.

The income statement, like the balance sheet, refers to the past. It is a brief summary of the factors contributing to a profit or loss for the current fiscal year. Its story deals with how much in the way of sales, involving how much in the way of expenses, led to what profit or loss for the owners on the year's operations, and how this profit or loss was divided between dividends and earnings retained for use in the business. It provides some notion of the scale of operations in a way that the balance sheet does not, but it gives much less information on how the firm financially faces its future. It shows the result of one year's operations, while the balance sheet sums the results of the lifetime history of the firm.

In the same way that the various elements of a balance sheet are compared to analyze how effectively management has been conducting the business, ratio analysis can be applied to the income statement. The ratio of greatest interest is that of profit to sales.

EXHIBIT 3

ELABORATED INCOME STATEMENT

INCOME
    Net sales and operating revenue   <u>XXXXX</u>

COST AND EXPENSES
  Raw materials cost
    Raw materials inventory at start of year
    Plus purchases during year
    Minus raw materials inventory at end of year
      Cost of raw materials used   XXX
  Direct labor cost   XXX
  Manufacturing overhead cost
    Indirect labor
    Factory heat, light, and power
    Insurance and taxes
    Interest expense
    Depreciation and obsolescence
      Total manufacturing overhead costs   <u>XXX</u>
        Total manufacturing costs   XXXX
  Plus goods in process inventory at beginning of year
  Minus goods in process inventory at end of year   <u>   </u>
    Cost of goods manufactured   XXXX
  Plus finished goods inventory at beginning of year   <u>   </u>
    Cost of goods available for sale   XXXX
  Minus finished goods inventory at end of year   <u>   </u>
    Cost of goods sold   XXXX
  Selling, administrative, research, and general expenses   XXX
    Total costs and expenses   <u>XXXX</u>
      Income before income taxes   <u>XXX</u>
    Minus income taxes   <u>XX</u>
      Net income   <u>XX</u>

The Flow-of-funds Statement

There is a third kind of financial statement which is in a less developed state than the two previously cited. This is the sources-and-uses or flow-of-funds statement. Its purpose is to disclose what were a firm's needs or uses for funds during the course of a fiscal year and the way in which it met those needs.

As customarily prepared, this analysis consists chiefly of rearranging the items on the balance sheet which show change from one year to the next (Exhibit 4). Those items which call for the absorption and application of funds are grouped under the heading of "uses." They consist of any increase in assets (larger cash holdings, an increase in inventories, expansion of plant and equipment); decreases in liabilities (payment of taxes out of a reserve for that purpose, repayment of a bank loan); or a decrease in stockholders' equity (principally the payment of dividends out of earnings, past or present).

Those balance-sheet changes which have provided the funds absorbed by these uses are grouped under the heading of "sources." These are the reverse of the changes noted under uses: decreases in assets, releasing cash (reduction of inventories, sale of securities); increases in liabilities, creating additional credit (a rise in accounts payable or bank loans, the floating of a bond issue); and an increase in shareholders' equity (an addition to retained earnings or the sale of additional shares).

EXHIBIT 4

SOURCES AND USES OR FLOW-OF-FUNDS STATEMENT

USES OF FUNDS

Increases in current assets
    Cash and marketable securities
    Accounts receivable
    Inventories
Increases in other assets
    Prepaid expenses
    Property, plant, and equipment
    Investment in unconsolidated subsidiaries
Decreases in current liabilities
    Notes, loans, and debentures of less than one year maturity
    Accrued salaries and wages
    Dividends payable
    Accrued taxes
Decreases in other liabilities
    Long-term debt
    Mortgages
Decreases in net worth
    Distribution of income or capital to stockholders

SOURCES OF FUNDS

Decreases in current assets
    Cash and marketable securities
    Accounts receivable
    Inventories

EXHIBIT 4 (continued)
SOURCES AND USES OR FLOW-OF-FUNDS STATEMENT

SOURCES OF FUNDS

Decreases in other assets
    Prepaid expenses
    Sale of property, plant, and equipment
    Investments in unconsolidated subsidiaries
Increases in current liabilities
    Accounts payable
    Notes, loans, and debentures of less than one year maturity
    Accrued wages and salaries
    Dividends payable
    Accrued taxes
Increases in noncash expenses
    Allowances for depreciation and obsolescence
    Special reserves
Increases in other liabilities
    Long-term debt
    Mortgages
Increases in net worth
    Sale of stock
    Retained earnings (surplus)

This rearrangement of balance-sheet items to reflect the flow of funds between asset and liability accounts of the firm, in the course of the year's operations, is the simplest form of the sources-and-uses statement. It is stated in *net* terms,[4] since the balance sheet is itself a summary statement in net terms. What is now generally lacking but what will surely come, as it has in the national accounts, is a flow-of-funds statement drawn from the items reflected in the income statement as well as the balance sheet, since the principal fund-flows through the firm relate to receipts from sales and payment of expenses in connection with production for sale no less than for inventory. It is a gross statement of all payments and all receipts which is wanted.

Whether on a net or gross basis, however, the flow-of-funds or sources-and-uses statement is, like the balance sheet and income statement, a product of past operations. It is an historical account. More than either of the other two statements, it does, or more correctly, it can, on a gross basis, contribute a picture of the firm's actual operations, and thus suggests in a rough sort of way the pattern of its future, since there is an element of continuity in most business activity, even though—unlike nature— it sometimes takes leaps.

[4] Except for capital expenditures, which are gross, since depreciation is included as a noncash expense which, to the extent realized out of the firm's operations, provides an offsetting source of funds.

Past and Plan

These three sets of accounts, then—the balance sheet, the income statement, and the flow-of-funds statement—contribute a picture of the effect of the firm's immediate past on its present, cumulative, financial position. The balance sheet shows the disposition as of the moment of its total assets and liabilities, the income statement shows how much of a change in the owners' equity position was contributed by the year's operations, and the flow-of-funds statement shows how that change in equity and other changes in the balance sheet came about. These three accounts attempt, however imperfectly, to reflect the firm's past-to-date position.

Nothing in these three statements relates to the future, except as continuity is implied or inferred. These are accountants' statements, and accountants work only with facts, with what is known, with the past. A businessman, however, is primarily concerned with the future. His use of the past is only as a springboard to reach some position in the time ahead. If the future is inescapably an unknown quantity, he can nevertheless do two things about it. He can analyze what is going on, not only in his own firm but in the national and international economy, to make informed guesses about the shape of the future. And he can lay his own plans for the future in such a way as to give him some measure of control over it. If a businessman did not do this, there would be little industrial research, little investment, little innovation.

Intuitive and Formal Planning

Even though businessmen cannot avoid planning, there is a difference among them in their methods of planning. One of the interesting economic phenomena of recent years has been the spread of a formal planning procedure in business which generally goes under the rubric of "budgeting." This formal procedure contrasts with an earlier period of personal and intuitive planning.

Even in an organization like General Motors, for example, if one goes back to management practices in the post-World War I period he finds a degree of personal control accompanied, interestingly enough, by lack of centralized planning of operations which it is difficult today to conceive. An associate once remarked of William C. Durant, who headed the company in the period 1916–1920, "No one knew how much money had been appropriated. There was no control on how much money was spent. Durant's executive committee consisted of the plant managers and when one of them had a project, he would get the vote of his fellow members; if they would vote for his project, he would vote for theirs. It was a sort of horse-trading.

In addition, if they didn't get enough money, when Durant visited the plant, he would tell them to go on and spend what they needed without any record being made." [5]

Such haphazard approaches to the future make difficult the organized effort to achieve specified goals. They permit the parts of a company to operate in ways which are inconsistent with each other. Particularly as a company expands does it become increasingly difficult for a single individual to coordinate the total operations. As the making of significant decisions gets dispersed among numbers of people, it becomes more and more necessary to institutionalize the planning process. This is what budgeting does.

One businessman has summarized the situation as follows: [6]

> Until more recent times there has been a native shrewdness that has served in place of carefully organized business knowledge. This shrewdness was based upon years of experience, a natural ability to observe the ways and reactions of people, and an intimate interest in men and their affairs, together with an abundance of common sense. This native ability was supposed to fit a man for any kind of enterprise. It dispensed largely with the need for formal education.
>
> There are many examples of men who have made notable success by their use of native business ability. . . . There will doubtless continue to be loose methods and controls in business. Too many managers or supervisors will continue to rely upon their ability to "size up" a situation rather than to analyze that situation on a basis of fact and determine a sound, far-seeing policy from the results of the analysis. But it is quite evident that it will become ever more difficult to carry on a business by such unscientific methods.

As this comment suggests, formalized planning is of quite recent origin. Professor James O. McKinsey of the University of Chicago, who was also a professional management consultant, wrote in the preface to his volume, *Budgetary Control,* published by the Ronald Press in 1922, "Although much has been written of budgetary control as applied to particular phases of a business, this is the first attempt, so far as the author is aware, to present the subject as a whole, and cover the entire budgetary program." A few pages later McKinsey comments, "Although practically all people who have given thought to the subject will admit that there should be budgetary control of public finances, very few have thought of budgetary control with reference to the individual business unit."

[5] Quoted in Ernest Dale, "Contributions to Administration by Alfred P. Sloan, Jr., and GM," *Administrative Science Quarterly,* vol. 1, June, 1956, pp. 33–34.

[6] G. W. Borman, divisional controller, Glass Container Division, Owens-Illinois Glass Co. of Toledo, "Measurement and Manpower," in *Control of Non-manufacturing Cost,* American Management Association Special Report 26, New York, 1957, p. 65.

The accounting literature of the 1920s contains occasional articles dealing with the subject as an innovation in business practice. Its spread was gradual in the following decade, picking up substantially in the 1940s, and extending rapidly throughout the business sector in the 1950s. A survey of 294 companies by the National Industrial Conference Board in 1931 revealed that only 55 per cent had budgets "of some kind." [7] A questionnaire survey conducted in 1958 found that 89 per cent of 389 respondent companies operated with a formal budget program.[8]

Commercial banks have been one agency responsible for this extraordinary spread of annual budgets. One bank reported in a 1952 study released by the National Industrial Conference Board (NICB) that "it is common practice for banks to require a small company borrower to prepare a budget in support of its application for a loan and to maintain the budget during the existence of the loan. Standard bank forms are provided for the purpose." [9] Increasingly, however, businessmen through their professional associations have themselves been the instrument for educating each other to the potentialities of the new procedures. Controllers Institute, the National Association of Accountants (formerly the National Association of Cost Accountants), the American Management Association, the National Industrial Conference Board, and the National Society for Business Budgeting have sponsored conferences, seminars, and institutes on the subject and have published a now sizable body of literature on the subject, largely authored by business practitioners.

[7] *Budgetary Control in Manufacturing Industry* (New York: National Industrial Conference Board, 1931), p. 17. Stanley Z. Bronner, assistant vice-president and director of production planning and inventory control at the Bridgeport Brass Co., writes (*N.A.A. Bulletin*, July, 1959, sec. 2, p. 37): ". . . based on my own observation in the early 'thirties' when I first became interested in the subject . . . , most of the companies using some form of budgeting limited their attempts to manufacturing expense budgets as aids to supervision of local operations. Only a very few managements embraced the concept of formalized operations planning on a company-wide basis as we know it today in its fully developed coordinated corporate form."

[8] Burnard H. Sord and Glenn A. Welsch, *Business Budgeting* (New York: Controllership Foundation, 1958), pp. 267–268. A study of "30 representative British firms" in 1958–1959 found that "19 of the 30 companies use complete systems of operating budgets for all income, costs and expense; while three make limited use of such budgets for sales, costs or overheads. Budget programs have been introduced only since the end of the Second World War in 17 of the 22 companies now using these budgets." J. R. Perrin, "Budgetary Planning and Control in Britain," *International Executive,* vol. 1, Fall, 1959, p. 25.

[9] *Budgeting Expenses in Small Companies,* NICB Studies in Business Policy, no. 58, New York, 1952, p. 22. In a survey conducted by Prof. Robert Eisner, one chief accountant commented that in soliciting a loan for expansion purposes his firm had prepared various statements, including projected balance sheets, to prove ability to pay off the loan. *Determinants of Capital Expenditure,* University of Illinois Bulletin, 1956, p. 68.

The Budget as Plan

What is a budget? In its simplest form, it consists of a forecast as of some future date of one or more of the accounting statements which we earlier examined—the balance sheet, income statement, and flow-of-funds statement. It differs from them in several important respects, however. The financial statements are prepared by accountants from records of what others have done. A budget is customarily the joint product of those who will be involved in carrying it out. The financial statements are ex post summaries of the firm's activities as they are reflected in its financial position. The budget is an ex ante statement of where the firm hopes to go, set out not only in financial terms but in the plans which are expected to lead to that position. The financial statements represent achievement. The budget represents aspiration. If a budget can even be described as an account or a financial statement, it can be said to be such only in being, a statement couched in future tense.

In some companies the budget has been termed a profit plan; in others, the operating plan. The National Management Planning and Control Committee of Controllers Institute was referring to budgeting when it adopted the following definition for its own guidance: "Management planning and control refers to the organization, techniques, and procedures, whereby long and short range plans are formulated, considered, and approved; responsibility for execution is delegated; flexibility to meet changing conditions is provided; progress in working the plan is reported; deviations in operation are analyzed, and corrective action required to reach the desired objective is taken."

Another definition has been supplied by James L. Pierce, vice-president and controller of the A. B. Dick Co.: [10]

> In the modern sense of an integrated planning and control system, then, planning refers to the construction of an operating program, comprehensive enough to cover all phases of operations, and detailed enough that specific attention may be given to its fulfillment in controllable segments. . . .
>
> All planning must ultimately be translated into dollar figures, which is the language in which business operates. The ultimate form of the programming therefore is, typically, a planned profit-and-loss statement for a forthcoming period of, say, 12 months, supported in detail by sales budgets or forecasts, expense budgets and so on, and also supplemented with detailed explanations.

The assistant controller of a bank writes: "The primary purpose of a sys-

[10] James L. Pierce, "The Planning and Control Concept," *The Controller*, September, 1954, pp. 2–3.

tem of budgetary control is to plan and establish a course of operations which will result in a satisfactory profit or return of investment. The goal is comprised of many separate objectives for functions, departments and individuals which, when consolidated, will produce the over-all objective." [11]

The budget manual of one company defines the process in the following way: [12]

> A budget is a plan of expected achievement based on the most efficient operating standards in effect or in prospect at the time it is established, against which actual accomplishment is regularly compared. The primary aim of budgets is to assist in assuring the procurement of the profits planned; and to provide a guide for assisting in establishing the financial control policies, including fixed asset additions, inventories, and the cash position. The adoption of a correctly constructed budget provides opportunity for: a regular and systematic analysis of incurred or anticipated expense, organized future planning, fixing of responsibilities, and stimulation of effort. In short, it provides a tool for more effective supervision of individual operations and practical administration of the business as a whole.

Form of the Budget

While financial statements tend to be similar in form, guided by standards which have been generally agreed on by the accounting profession, no such uniformity attends the construction of a budget. Each firm which relies on an operating or profit plan tends to create its own pattern. To some extent this is probably due to the newness of the field. It would be a reasonable prediction that greater standardization of budgeting practice is likely to come. Already, certain tendencies in this direction are discernible.

Generally a comprehensive or master budget is supported by a number of subsidiary budgets or budget schedules. The controller for the Armstrong Cork Company writes: "The operating budget is the coordinated plan of operations of a company for a budget period. It provides the profit budget for the company and for its units and product lines through consolidating the sales, factory cost, distribution expense, and administrative expense budgets and including all other items of income and expense which have not been reflected in the other budgets." [13] The treasurer's office of a ball and roller bearing company says, "We have a financial budget that is ex-

[11] T. W. Harris, "Control Budgeting in Commercial Banks," *N.A.C.A. Bulletin,* April, 1954, sec. 1, p. 981.

[12] *The Analysis of Cost-Volume-Profit Relationships,* National Association of Cost Accountants Research Report (undated, but reprinting Research Series 16, 17, 18 of 1949–1950), p. 47.

[13] I. W. Keller, *Management Accounting for Profit Control* (New York: McGraw-Hill, 1957), p. 298.

pressed in terms of a balance sheet, fed by an operating budget of income and expense items. Then we have our capital appropriations budget; a sales budget for factories and branches; and standard or budgeted costs for our manufactured products." [14]

One accountant who has been active in budgeting work has offered an illustrative but hypothetical budget taking the following form.[15]

> The budget report contains three sections. The first states the directives which governed the preparation of the budget, and comments on the extent to which the directives were achieved. The second section contains the following exhibits:
>
> Forecast Operating Statement
> Forecast Statement of Return on Capital Employed
> Forecast Sources and Applications of Funds
> Forecast Changes in Working Capital
> Forecast Balance Sheets
>
> These five exhibits summarize the planned results of the period's operations. The third section contains selected schedules to supplement the exhibits.
>
> I-*a*. Forecast Sales and Factory Cost of Sales
> I-*b*. Forecast Selling Expenses
> I-*c*. Forecast General and Administrative Expenses
> I-*d*. Forecast Other Income and Deductions

The appendix to this chapter lists the section headings of the operating budget for one power and light company.

Projected Statements

Where comprehensive budgeting is undertaken, the end result increasingly tends to take the form of projections of the three financial statements we earlier examined—the balance sheet, the income statement, and the sources-and-uses statement. These are frequently compiled not only for a fiscal year but also for shorter periods (monthly, quarterly, or semi-annually) and longer (five to ten years), and of course all are made consistent with and related to each other. Examples of the forms which these projections often take are given in Exhibits 5 and 6, which come from one company, and Exhibit 7 from another company.

The estimated or projected income statement details the operations which, if carried out as intended, will lead to an end-of-year profit of specified magnitude. The portion of this which is marked for retention in the busi-

[14] Private correspondence, Aug. 22, 1960. Future quotations from company officials without specific citation may be presumed also to have come from private correspondence in the summer of 1960.

[15] Herman C. Heiser, *Budgeting* (New York: Ronald, 1959), pp. 86–87, 89. On pp. 90–104 Heiser reproduces the text of this hypothetical budget report.

ness, along with any resulting or planned changes in working capital or capital investment, shows up in the projected balance sheet. The estimate of sources and uses of funds arising out of these statements provides an indication of the amount, form, and timing of the funds required to execute the plans embodied in them.

The "budget," then, comprises ex ante the set of three accounts which a firm expects or hopes to make ex post by the end of the year. It represents the firm's most preferred future position under all the circumstances prevailing or expected to prevail. As operating results depart from plan, the next phase of the plan must itself be altered. But at any moment of time the budget (or most recent variant of it, as we shall examine later) always remains as the shape of the future which a firm hopes to incorporate into its history.

From its present position, as expressed in its balance sheet, the firm hopes to move by plan to a future position expressed in its budget. As the future becomes past, the firm's success or lack of success in realizing its budget plans is written into its new balance sheet, which then becomes the base for a new budget, and so on, as long as the firm continues.

EXHIBIT 5

PROJECTION OF INCOME STATEMENT

COMPANY
_____
DIVISION

STATEMENT OF EARNINGS FORECAST FOR PERIOD ENDING			
Net Sales and Service Revenue			
Variable Cost of Sales			
Variable Margin			
Period Costs			
Manufacturing – Gross			
Less Absorbed and Redistributed			
Manufacturing – Net			
Direct Charges			
Selling			
Administrative and General			
Engineering			
Total Period Costs			
Operating Earnings			
Inventory Adjustment –			
Fixed Complement			
Other Income			
Interest Earned			
Royalties Received			
Miscellaneous			
Total Other Income			
Other Deductions			
Interest Expense			
Central Office Expense			
Miscellaneous			
Total Other Deductions			
Earnings Before Taxes			
Taxes on Income – Estimated			
Federal Normal and Surtax			
State Taxes			
Foreign Taxes			
Total Current Year			
Adjustment for Prior Years – Net			
Total Taxes on Income			
Net Earnings			
Income Retained at Beginning of Period			
Income Retained at End of Period			
SUPPLEMENTARY INFORMATION			
Depreciation and Amortization – Book Basis			
Provision for Contingencies			
Gross Earnings – Whole Cost Basis			
Operating Earnings – Whole Cost Basis			
OPERATING RATIOS			
Percent to Sales			
Variable Margin			
Total Period Costs			
Operating Earnings			
Earnings before Taxes			
Net Earnings			
Earnings before Taxes – % Invested Capital			

EXHIBIT 6

PROJECTION OF BALANCE SHEET

COMPANY

DIVISION

BALANCE SHEET FORECAST

FOR PERIOD ENDING   ,19

							DETAIL		ASSETS
									Current Assets
							Accounts Receivable – Net	1	Cash
							Accounts Receivable – Public	2	Notes Receivable – Public
							Less Allow. for Doubtful Accts.	3	Accounts Receivable – Net
							Accounts Receivable – Net	4	Accounts Receivable – Interco.
								5	Inventory – Variable
								6	– Fixed Complement
							Inventory	7	Total Inventory
							Finished Goods	8	
							Field Service Materials	9	Total Current Assets
							Work in Process	10	
							Raw Materials	11	Property, Plant and Equipment
								12	Less Allow. for Depreciation
							Less Allowance for Loss	13	Net Property
							Subtotal	14	
							Less Progress Payments	15	Intercompany Investments
							Total Inventory	16	
								17	Other Assets
								18	
							Property, Plant and Equipment	19	Deferred Charges
							Land	20	
							Buildings	21	Total Assets
							Machinery and Equipment	22	
							Leasehold Improvement – Net	23	LIABILITIES and CAPITAL
							Field Service Equipment – Net	24	Current Liabilities
							(Gross –)	25	Notes Payable
							Rental Equipment – Net	26	Accounts Payable
							(Gross –)	27	Accounts Payable – Interco.
							Construction in Progress	28	Advances Against Contracts
							Total	29	Payroll Liabilities
								30	Other Accrued Liabilities
								31	Taxes on Income – Estimated
							Intercompany Investments	32	Total Current Liabilities
							Stock of Subsidiary Companies	33	
							Intercompany Advances	34	Notes Payable – Intercompany
							Interdivision Control	35	
							Stock of Affiliates	36	Long-term Debt
							Total	37	
								38	Reserves
								39	
							Taxes on Income – Estimated	40	Capital Stock
							Federal – Prior Years	41	Excess Capital
							Federal – Current Year	42	Income Retained
							State	43	Total Capital
							Foreign	44	
							Total	45	Total Liabilities and Capital
							Working Capital		
							Current Ratio		
							Capital Expenditures		
							Total Payroll		
							Number of Factory Employees		

EXHIBIT 7

PROJECTED SOURCES AND USES OF FUNDS

Sources and Uses	Actual, 19—	Projected			
		1st quarter	2d quarter	3d quarter	4th quarter
Funds Came or Come From:					
Sales					
Less all expenses, including cost of goods sold					
Final net					
Add: No cash outlay expenses:					
1. Depreciation					
2. Net increase in reserves					
Add: Sale of stock to employees					
public sale of stock					
sale of assets					
Total Funds Provided					
How Funds Used or To Be Used:					
Dividends					
Expansion (fixed assets)					
Purchase of common stock (deferred compensation plan)					
Increases in sundry accounts and investments					
Working capital (balance)					
Total Funds Used					

Appendix to Chapter 2

OUTLINE OF ONE OPERATING BUDGET *

1. Conditions and assumptions on which this budget is based. . . .
   (b) Business activity in the area served will continue its upward trend at about the present rate and no major strikes in industry will materially affect the economy of the area.
   (c) Aggressive load building will be continued. . . .
   (n) No increase in wage rates has been provided for. . . .

* From the 37-page operating budget of a power and light company. Only section headings are given here, with one or two sentences from the earlier sections in the report to give some indication of its flavor.

2. Total Operating Revenues.

Total operating revenues for 1959 are estimated at $31,965,000, an increase of $3,391,000 or 11.9% over 1958 (11 months actual and 1 month estimated). Total kilowatt hours delivered are estimated at 2,703,000,000, an increase of 327,000,000 or 13.8% over 1958. The estimates for 1959 are predicated on normal weather throughout the year. During 1958 the unusually warm weather substantially reduced kilowatt hour sales and revenues.

A. General Comments

(1) Residential sales

Residential revenues for 1959 are estimated at $17,966,000, an increase of $1,811,000 or 11.2% over 1958. This estimate is based on the following assumptions:

new home construction will continue at about the same average level as prevailed throughout 1958;

the average kilowatt hour use by existing customers will increase at a higher rate than was experienced in 1958 (premised on normal weather prevailing throughout 1959);

increased revenue will continue to result from space heating customers added at about the same rate (2,500) as during 1958;

increased revenue will result in the residential classification due to projected sales promotion activities;

increased services were extended to 3,000 existing customers during 1958 and about 3,000 increased services are anticipated in 1959; . . .

(2) Commercial sales

Commercial revenues for 1959 are estimated at $8,337,000, an increase of $795,000 or 10.5% over 1958 (11 months actual and 1 month estimated). This estimate is based on the following assumptions:

the larger governmental account will continue to operate at approximately the prevailing level;

new business, involving loads in excess of 35 KW, now known and estimated to produce revenue in the amount of $227,000 annually, will be connected during the year; . . .

(3) Industrial sales

Industrial revenues for 1959 are estimated at $3,918,000, an increase of $626,000 or 19.0% over 1958 (11 and 1). This estimate is based on the following assumptions:

increased revenues amounting to $67,000 will result in the metalworking and defense activities classification due to (a) load growth ($28,000) of four existing airplane plants; (b) a new plant to be connected in the fall of 1959 ($12,000); (c) Blank Company ($11,800) due to subnormal operations during 1958, and (d) load growth ($15,100) from the remaining customers; . . .

(4) Public Street and Highway Lighting

Public Street and Highway Lighting revenues for 1959 are estimated at $360,000, an increase of $24,000 or 7.1% over 1958
(11 and 1). It is anticipated that this increase will result from the
City of K— ($7,500), and from the State (a) Toll Bridge Author-
ity ($2,500), (b) Highway Commission ($6,500), and the remainder from further modernization and expansion of public lighting.

(5) Other Sales to Public Authorities
(6) Sales to Electric Utilities
(7) Rent from Electric Property
(8) Miscellaneous Electric Revenues
(9) Prepaid Revenues

B. Estimate of Operating Revenues for the Coming Year Compared with
the Past Year

3. Operating Expenses

A. Operation—General Comments

(1) Production expenses
   (*a*) Steam power generation
   (*b*) Hydraulic power generation
   (*c*) Other production expenses
(2) Intercompany pool net purchases
(3) Transmission expenses
(4) Distribution expenses
(5) Customers accounting and collecting expenses
(6) Sales promotion expenses
(7) Administrative and general expenses

B. Maintenance—General Comments

(1) Steam power generation
(2) Hydraulic power generation
(3) Transmission expenses
(4) Distribution expenses
(5) Administrative and general expenses

C. Estimate of Operating Expenses for the Coming Year Compared with
the Past Year

4. Other Income—Net
5. Depreciation
6. Taxes
7. Interest and Amortization
8. Estimated Income Statement for the Coming Year in Comparison with the
Past Year
9. Cash Estimate for the Coming Year
10. Source of Construction Funds for the Coming Year
11. Net Utility Plant Investment.

Chapter 3

TIME AND THE BUDGET

The Time Dimension

Planning and budgeting range over a time spectrum that runs from the current day to a period sometimes as far as twenty-five years in the future. Practice on this score differs considerably. Certainly the most common form of budget is the annual operating or profit plan, commonly broken down into lesser time intervals, half years, quarters, and months being the most customary breakdowns for the master budget. Lesser divisions, particularly the shops, often operate on weekly and even daily budget schedules as well.[1]

The annual plan perhaps most frequently is geared to the firm's fiscal year, but some companies prefer a running budget. Thus Crucible Steel reports that its current budgeting practice "is to have a four-quarter budget

[1] In the meat packing industry, for example, workers who are called for the second day of work in a week are guaranteed work for the remainder of the week, under the terms of the collective agreements. This means that for that week labor must be viewed as a sunk cost.

The meat packers have little control over the price they pay for carcasses, and relatively little control over the price at which unpackaged meats are sold. They do have some discretion as to the way a carcass can be cut to realize the best return and the markets where cuts will be placed.

The question at the start of the week for each packer is, How much buying to do? Shall it be only enough to preserve position in the markets, because the return is insufficient to justify more, or as much more as can be undertaken without disturbing prevailing prices adversely? The answer to that question, and to the further question of how the best profit can be realized, requires several alternative estimates based on different carcass breakdowns and marketing patterns. Depending on the results, some workers may not be called up for work on the second day of the week, thus keeping labor costs variable, or the whole force may be put to work, in the expectation that although this commits the packer to definite labor charges for the week, it would expect to incur them anyway in the normal course of business.

This in effect requires weekly budgeting by each slaughtering plant and those branch plants which engage in processing as well as sales.

cover the current and three succeeding calendar quarters, and prior to the close of the current quarter the previously submitted three succeeding quarters are repeated and a new quarter added. This procedure gives us a continuous four-quarter budget period." A number of companies follow this practice or some variant on it.

Another steel company which employs three planning processes of different time dimensions represents another frequently encountered pattern. (1) First there is the familiar one-year operating budget. (2) This is supplemented (and to some extent grows out of) a "normal" five-year budget which projects the company's activities over that period, abstracting from business fluctuations or any extraordinary company actions. (On the strength of this planning the company estimates, for example, the sales and earnings which it expects to generate over the interval and how much of the earnings it can retain in the business. This, along with depreciation allowances, gives an indication of the sum which it can expect to invest each year in its "normal" operations, enabling it to determine whether this is adequate to preserve or improve its present share of the expected market for steel.) (3) Finally, the company has a products and planning committee which is engaged in a continuing study of new fields the company might enter, acquisitions it might make, and other such extraordinary activity. These actions may be undertaken at any time, but when undertaken usually require special financing arrangements. (A recent acquisition was carried out by an exchange of stock, for example.)

Long-term Budgets

More and more managements are adopting long-range budgets as well as the one-year operating plan. Five years seems to be the most common duration, but longer spans are by no means unknown. Such budgets are sometimes based on projected high, medium, and low levels of expected future activity.

The controller of Philco Corporation describes his company's five-year planning approach as follows: [2]

> The financial section of each five-year plan is, of course, the summary of the dollar evaluation of the combined [divisional and functional] plans. Included is a profit and loss plan, showing by years the sales objectives, profit contribution goals, anticipated fixed plant, administrative, and other expense levels, and the net operating profit results. . . .
> The financial section also includes a balance sheet plan showing by years the anticipated inventory levels, receivable balances, capital in-

[2] Ernst E. Bareuther, "Budgeting Policy and Practice in a Decentralized Company," *N.A.A. Bulletin*, October, 1957, sec. 1, p. 34.

vestment, liabilities, etc. Included is a capital expenditure schedule showing details of facilities and equipment required as a result of the planning. Included, also, is a statement of funds showing the cash flow plan over the five-year period.

The complete five-year budget financial data and written report is considered to be one of the most important of management's tools. Because it must review with top management its business for five years ahead, each division must determine the specific planning for its design, engineering, manufacturing and sales activities. Preparation of the five-year plan enables the division to coordinate the planning of these various activities and to make certain that all members of the divisional management team are pulling together to achieve the objective agreed upon. Top management becomes calibrated with divisional planning, determines whether that planning individually and collectively meets the company's objective, ascertains whether the over-all corporation volume and profits are satisfactory, and determines the financing needs of the company. Budgeting five years ahead allows sufficient time for either level of management to ensure a change in the planning of any segment of the business.

Two food companies, Campbell Soup and H. J. Heinz, also operate with long-term budgets. The latter reports: [3]

> A moving five-year plan and a far more detailed annual operating plan are the time-phased stages whereby company operations are sighted in on the ultimate long-range profit target and, of these, the practical working tool is the annual operating plan or budget. . . .
>
> Five-year plans (on a moving or rolling five-year basis) are made for each of the Heinz companies with reference particularly to sales, cost of goods and similar items relating to operations and capital expenditures, capital requirements, cash requirements and return on investment.
>
> The annual operating plans (or budgets) are prepared in considerable detail for each company, each sales region, territory, branch, each warehousing and other distributive facility, each factory or other processing facility, department, production or cost center in plant or office. Corresponding capital needs and sources are planned for such specific points and, of course, with reference to the merchandising side, plans and profit goals are set for major products, product groups, and product mixes.

The vice-president for administrative planning describes the practice at the Campbell Soup Company: [4]

[3] *Management Planning and Control: The H. J. Heinz Approach* (New York: Controllership Foundation, 1957), pp. 10–11.

[4] Oscar H. Curry, "Budgeting: The Art of Planning and Cooperation." *N.A.A. Bulletin,* September, 1958, sec. 1, p. 69.

At Campbell Soup Company, we establish our future growth objectives for ten-year periods in the future. We re-examine these objectives each two years. We do this in order that our planned growth objectives will correlate with our current performance and with general national and world prosperity. Such studies are the creation of staff management. They assist us in planning our organizational needs, the direction of our research activities, and our cash and plant expansion requirements. It may be of interest to describe briefly our long-range forecasting techniques.

We study continuously a group of economic statistics which have been discovered to have close correlation with the level of activity of our national economy. We also study population economics, that is, growth rates, age distribution and migratory trends and other pertinent economic fields such as weather, changes in living habits, etc. We plot the historic growth trends of our various product lines and check these with our economic history. We then project our future sales growth on a straight-line basis and correct this projection to the economic climate our studies indicate will exist through the next ten years. Our next step is to profit plan each of our product lines as indicated by history and our economic studies and, from these, to prepare estimated earnings statements for each of the ten years in the forecast. Based on the sales estimates, we plot the need for facility expansion and our engineering people estimate for us a ten-year forecast of capital expansion and improvement costs.

With this information, our balance sheet forecasts can be projected. These projections are all made at current dollar values with our estimates of the effect of dollar value fluctuations supplied in an appendix. Quarterly chart reports are presented to management showing the results of our economic studies, budget performance and long-term forecasts.

Another example is contributed by the director of development planning at the Lockheed Aircraft Corporation. That company prepares a master plan over a ten-year period.[5]

Our plan contains three essential elements. First is a detailed forecast of probable sales. By "detailed" I mean projection of specific models of airplanes and other products in units, time, and dollars. Injected into these data are the manifold considerations which associate not only with the levels of output but with the technical characteristics of our production. Second is a detailed projection of the fixed capital investment required to meet the projected sales level, as well as research and development facilities necessary to maintain a desired level of technical competence. Individual buildings and major pieces of

[5] L. Eugene Root, "Development Planning for Management Decision," *Organizing for Effective Systems Planning and Control,* A.M.A. Special Report 12, New York, 1956, pp. 92, 104.

equipment are specified. Dates for their construction or acquisition, as well as costs, are determined. Third is a detailed projection of balance sheets and profit and loss statements. For the first five years, these are made on a quarterly basis. For the last five years they cover a calendar year.

Ample opportunity is provided for setting forth and examining alternatives. Different patterns and projections are developed, based upon selected possibilities in such areas as sales, new models, financial capability, organization, plant location, technical manpower availability, general industry competitive conditions, and product diversification. . . .

High and low possible sales curves will be prepared to provide measures of risk in undertaking alternative courses of action. Since the general economic and international political situations are so important to our sales, there probably will be a detailed analysis of their impact on Lockheed. We will also make a detailed projection of the Federal budget for airborne weapons and from this estimate the demand for specific Lockheed products.

Another major group of conclusions relates to preferred fixed asset investments. The results here will suggest, for the short term, preferred facility decisions that the company ought to make. For the longer period, desired facilities of specified characteristics will be spelled out in terms of cost and timing of acquisition. For research and development facilities, this work will consider in much detail the desirable technical characteristics and cost of the facilities. As a part of this analysis, the recommendations and projections will be made in light of, and specifically reflect, such considerations as research policies, desirable organizational and locational patterns, financial policies, and other matters having an important influence on facility acquisition.

Third, the financial impact of our sales projections and alternative facility investment programs will be examined in detail. This will include not only studies of different important sales and investment program combinations, but explorations of the financial methods to resolve the main problems which the plan reveals.

Simulation of Operations

An even more specific illustration of the use of five-year budgets is provided by the president of Northwest Airlines, who describes a procedure followed as part of the program to finance acquisition of jet airliners: [6]

To determine our total financing requirements for presentation to the Banks and Insurance companies, [the treasurer's] staff prepared forecasted profit and loss statements, capital equipment purchase sched-

[6] Donald W. Nyrop, "Financial Planning in the Jet Age," *Business Budgeting*, vol. 8, November, 1959, pp. 19–20.

ules, cash flow exhibits, and balance sheets for the years 1958 through 1963. The earlier year forecasts were prepared by month and the later year forecasts by quarters.

Behind these forecasts were supporting schedules showing the acquisition and in-service dates of new aircraft and the retirement from service of present aircraft. Schedules of forecasted production and revenue statistics were also included. Loan and interest payment schedules were worked out in detail through the years ahead.

Because of the assumptions and judgment that must go into such forecasts, considerable supporting commentary was included with our long-range financing plan for the Banks and Insurance companies.

Forecasting operating revenues and expenses for jet aircraft over our route for future years could not be taken lightly. We were taking a very important step forward so this job required careful planning. The jet airplanes we were purchasing were still in the manufacturing stage and, of course, actual operational experience was not available on which to base actual operating cost figures.

Our budget and forecast people worked with the aircraft manufacturers' information, our aircraft engineers, and Operations people to gather and cross-check information about these aircraft.

In effect, we had to work out the airline operation on paper for the 5 years ahead. The airplanes were routed or scheduled between cities on this paper operation.

Flight schedule changes were made for the new jet aircraft added to the fleet and older aircraft retired. Schedules were adjusted for our winter and summer operations. Future schedule changes were made to take care of the forecasted future increases in business, etc.

Routing diagrams and aircraft utilization figures were continually checked as we went through these planning stages. Non-revenue flying estimates were added for crew training, aircraft testing, and aircraft ferrying.

From the information worked out, forecasted aircraft hours and aircraft miles were obtained. Further statistical information was prepared showing the production statistics expressed in available seat miles and available ton miles.

With this statistical information, plus the information obtained about the jet aircraft and known cost information on present aircraft, direct flying expenses were calculated for each type aircraft on our various route segments.

Depreciation, computed on the basis of the aircraft acquisition and disposal program, was added to the direct flying costs. Indirect expenses for each period were then calculated and added to the direct costs to complete the operating expense forecast.

Operating revenue forecasts which included passenger revenue, mail, freight, express and other revenues, were calculated and tested for sound reasoning for each of the five years ahead. . . .

Funds required for new capital equipment and the retirement of the outstanding loan we had for piston-type aircraft, can be summarized as follows:

Retirement of the outstanding bank loan	37½	million
New jet aircraft	53½	million
Spare parts and assemblies for new aircraft	14	million
Ground equipment	10	million
Total	115	million

Money for these requirements comes from the following sources:

Preferred stock issue—December, 1958	11	million
Long-term note purchase agreements with 12 insurance companies	40	million
Short-term credit agreement with group of 15 banks..	37½	million
Sale or trade-in of piston engine aircraft	10	million
Total	97½	million

The balance will come from cash generated through the operation of the airline.

The above illustration suggests that budgeting, when carried out in detail, becomes in effect an a priori simulation of the enterprise, against which its actual operations will be measured for fit.

Values of Long-term Budgeting

Obviously, the farther ahead a firm plans, the more opportunity is there for error to enter into forecasts. For this reason some firms have voiced skepticism over the value of long-term budgets. The vice-president for finance and the budget director of Clevite Corporation, which forecasts on a three- to five-year basis, offer this justification: Although the figures entered in the budget may have limited value, the process as a whole is advantageous in several respects. First, determinations concerning specific projects such as new plant and equipment investment can be given realistic estimates regardless of the dubious quality of other estimates in the budget. Second, the act of setting targets provides an incentive to those who carry responsibility for realizing them. Third, it encourages a systematic examination of all the variables relevant to growth.

Similar justification has been voiced by Mark Cresap, Jr., president of Westinghouse Corporation. "Specifically, the purposes of [long-term] business planning, as I see it, are five: first, to raise the sights of an organization; second, to provide an organization with the stimulating effect of concrete goals; third, to assure a teamwork effort toward uniform objectives; fourth, to provide the necessary preparatory lead time for the achievement of objectives; and, fifth, to furnish a basis for annual budgeting in a more purposeful manner than by reference to historical performance or static standards." [7]

Partial and Total Abstainers

It is not only the long-term budget which has encountered skepticism from some businesses, at least as far as its applicability to them is concerned. For a variety of reasons they have eschewed the annual operating budget as well. Some of these may, however, make use of partial budgets, such as for advertising, selling, or administrative expense. The following sampling of opinion may be instructive in this respect.

There are some businesses which believe their revenues or costs are too erratic to permit profit planning.

> We do not have any formal budgeting program of earnings and our sales budgeting program is more of a general sales forecast than a budget. With the multitudinous number of chemicals we manufacture, and buy and resell, we have found it most difficult to project our earnings—particularly because of the great change in product mix.— *Vice-president and treasurer of a chemical company.*

> We do use budgets but they are of the most general type. We are so susceptible to day-to-day conditions over which we have no control that we have to conduct our business on a "play-it-by-ear" basis. Our local executives are close enough to the details of operation to do this successfully. They are subject only to the basic policies of our executive office management.—*President of a hotel chain.*

> We hold contracts with the Air Force, the Navy, and other government organizations. These contracts cover hundreds of items and are subject to change on a moment's notice. This makes it practically impossible for us to establish an accurate and usable budget for our operations as a whole. We do forecast our probable sales for a given period, and, within the framework of this forecast, estimate related costs and expenses. The vagaries of the business make this forecast subject to considerable change. . . .
> As you can see, it would be impractical to try to operate under

[7] "Long-term Planning," *Advanced Management,* January, 1953, p. 34. In a discussion of budgeting during the 1954 Conference of the National Association of Cost Accountants the same general attitude was displayed. It was reported (*N.A.C.A. Bulletin,* September, 1954, sec. 3, p. 183): "A show of hands indicated that some 25 to 30 of the companies had formal long-term budgeting. In response to the statement that the rapidly changing economic conditions of recent years had made it difficult to forecast for more than a year in the future with any degree of accuracy, it was pointed out that the accuracy of the forecast was not as important as the impetus to long range planning provided by formal budgets for as much as five or ten years ahead."

even a fairly flexible budget. Of course, on the division level, and in some instances the departmental level, we have established budgets. Company funded research projects are budgeted in advance, and we have budgets for such things as advertising, public relations, and other such services.—*Official of an aircraft manufacturing company.*

We do not attempt to prepare a budget for our revenues. The price of lumber is too changeable to attempt a long-term forecast as to what the product will bring for any given year. The demand for lumber is largely dependent on the construction of new residences. When a large number of residences are being constructed, a high level of lumber prices can be maintained. When the demand declines, every lumber producer is fighting for his share of the lower volume of business and such competition always means lower prices.

We do prepare a budget at the beginning of the year for expenses, predicated on an established volume of shipments, which may or may not prove to be accurate. We do not attempt to adjust the budget during the year, but a comparison is made at the end of the year with actual expenses and the variances are explained.—*Controller of a lumber company.*

We do not budget income. Our income is substantially dependent upon loan demand and the prime borrowing rate over which we have no control. . . . We do not budget expenses representing the cost of money. These factors are interest which we pay upon savings accounts and interest that we pay for borrowed money. Our reasons for not budgeting these items are the same as the reasons for not budgeting income items.—*Executive vice-president of a bank.*

In contrast to the above experiences, one well-known company reported that it had not sought to construct an operating plan because of the degree of stability in the business.

The . . . Company has not had a complete consolidated budget program until the current fiscal year. Minor segments of the Company operated under budgets in the last few years but there was little need for the primary business to be budgeted. In a company with 75 years experience in a stable industry . . . , revenues and expenses did not vary widely from year to year. However, with the recent decline in demand for our major product and the embarking on a program of diversification, the Company felt a greater need for advance planning and budgeting.—*Budget manager of a food products company.*

Some companies engaged in expensive contract work of fluctuating volume tend to budget on a contract basis rather than on over-all operations.

Because the Company's business, consisting mainly of long-term contracts of large unit value, is in many respects unique, . . . our current budgeting and control procedures as well as our long-range forecasts and projections are based mainly upon the individual contracts. . . .—*Financial vice-president of a shipbuilding company.*

This Company does not have a total company budget, or even divisional operating budgets, on a fiscal year basis. Our internal operating controls are exercised through the use of budgets or "targets" established on each program or contract.—*Assistant controller of an aircraft manufacturing company.*

We have no annual budgets except those for mining explorations and charitable contributions. In our construction activities the bid on every project is in a sense a budget, and we of course make comparisons between our actual performance and our estimates on the bid.—*Executive vice-president of a construction and mining company.*

Some companies budget capital investment even though they do not engage in comprehensive budgeting.

Producing, refining, transportation, marketing and administrative expenses are not budgeted in the strict sense of the word, although we do make annual estimates of these expenses. Our experience has been that these expenses can be controlled satisfactorily and with less cost and paper work by "on-the-spot" control of operations and delegations of authority within limits at the field level. . . . We depend most for over-all planning on estimates of earnings and cash position, and strict budgeting of capital expenditures.—*Controller of a large oil company.*

The vice-president of a major insurance company reports, "We do not typically budget income, for example, although we do make forecasts as to funds available for investment." This approach seems to characterize the insurance industry generally.

Still other companies do not attempt to budget revenue but emphasize control of significant elements of costs.

Comprehensive budgeting in the popular sense is not utilized. Instead, we endeavor to forecast the general level of business activity in each segment of our business. . . . We then formulate indications of our manpower and capital requirements. Once the basic manpower and capital plans are established, they are used by our management as flexible guides.—*Controller of a financing company.*

Our income arises mainly from commissions on advertising placed for our clients and I am sure you are aware of the fluctuations which occur in advertising budgets. Since these fluctuations are generally not within our control, there is not much we can do about them. . . . In agencies of our size, payroll is the largest item of expense, averaging about 60% of income. It is this item which must be controlled if we are to make a profit for the other items of expense are pretty much fixed. . . . Since payroll is so significant, its ratio to income is watched constantly and we consider the steps we take to control it in the realm of day-to-day operating policy rather than the carrying out of a budget policy.—*Vice-president and controller of an advertising agency.*

Our organization does not use specific prepared budgets. . . . The capital expenditures are "budgeted" to the extent that they are discussed with the Board of Directors. The Board will authorize such expenditures usually within the realm of a loose generalization, i.e., "we will spend in the vicinity of one million dollars over the course of the next two years for new machinery in our mills." The General Manager then takes this directive, as authorized, to purchase and/or replace machinery as he thinks best, and reports to the Board at various times on such programs.

In actuality, our cost reports are our budgets. . . . Such budgeting, in essence, comes down to the cost per unit of production. In other words, a certain number of man hours should produce a certain unit of production. The same goes for raw materials, supplies, etc.—*Official of a textile company.*

Finally, comprehensive budgeting is less prevalent in small businesses. The comment of the president of a rubber company is indicative.

Budgeting has been used very little in our business until this year. . . . We did not have a sufficient number of budgets of any consequence to be the least bit concerned as to how we varied from them. In conversation with other executives of companies of comparable size (sales only slightly over $2,000,000), I find this is not too uncommon among small companies. Largely as the result of the literature on the value and utilization of budgets, more and more of us are joining in preparing and using them. . . .

Certainly the problems of budgetary control must increase in a geometric ratio as the business increases. A small organization such as ours is assisted by a budget but it is not absolutely necessary in order to operate such a small enterprise. The beginning golfer who plays his round with a mashie and a putter is sometimes mystified by the need of a caddy and perhaps a cart to carry the clubs of the pro. He has just never hoisted a bag containing the full contingent, along with the umbrella, the raincoat, the towel, etc., that are part and parcel of the professional's equipment. It's somewhat like this for the small businessman and his pondering the total utilization of budgets which are made in the larger organizations. Simultaneously, however, the duffer learns another thing that the caddy does is watch the ball for the pro so that he'll be sure to keep his head down when he's hitting it. This little lesson is one of the things that we small potatoes want to learn from the big boys and are in the process of doing.

In general, then, the firms which have so far abstained from adding the element of the formal operating plan to their set of accounts have done so for one of three reasons—a belief that special characteristics of their companies make budgeting impractical, a belief that the process is unnecessarily complicated and that a partial application suffices, and the fact that the small scale of some operations has limited the manpower available for the budgeting process and may in some instances have been responsible for a lack of understanding of its benefits.

Use of the ex ante account is, however, spreading. More and more firms concur with the judgment expressed by the controller of a foundry: "Personally, I believe that budgeting forces a company to think in terms of short and long range planning and policy. Without this policy and planning, the course or avenue a business takes is somewhat happenstance, hectic, confusing and risky. The concern without adequate planning and solid financial backing may be successful in the short range but find itself in an unfamiliar and nonreceptive environment in the long range period."

Similarly the president of a company specializing in the manufacture of fountain pens testifies that "without the use of a sales forecast prepared well in advance of the fiscal year, plus a complete operating financial budget, plus a cash flow statement built upon this budgeted profit, it would be impossible for us to operate a business in such a highly competitive and rapidly moving atmosphere as that in which all commerce labors today."

Chapter 4

OBJECTIVES AND TARGETS

Proprietors and Planners

Planning presupposes objectives.

In a previous chapter it was pointed out that the conduct of a business necessitates some element of planning, since business operations are directed to the future. The nature of the planning process differs among firms, however. One important respect in which differences emerge is the extent to which the planning process is formalized. Another important differentiating characteristic is in the objective.

Probably the preponderant majority of all business establishments in the United States, small in size as they are and closely controlled either by a working proprietor or a one-man management, have no intention or desire to expand beyond rather narrow limits. They are operated as a source of livelihood for one or a small number of households. If they provide a comfortable living, subject their owners or operators to a minimum of risk, and provide them with a maximum of security, this is all that is asked. The objective is halfway between that of the salaried or wage-earning employee and that of the professional person—a good income with a measure of personal freedom. Such businesses are extensions of the personality of their proprietors, akin to the firm as conceptualized by Adam Smith.[1] They are not institutions as much as they are aspects of individuals.

In contrast to the vast majority of business firms of this nature there are those—large, medium, and small—which are conducted by managements who are driven, in varying degree, by greater ambitions. They look upon the

[1] I choose Adam Smith because he, more than his successors, recognized that individuals operated with a complex of objectives and that the pecuniary objective emerged in economic affairs not because it was somehow more fundamental than others but simply because in the sphere of economic activity this was the appropriate motivation. Profit seeking was an organizing and systematizing mode of behavior in this important sector of society. It was not itself a basic drive but simply one expression of people's natural and instinctive search for unifying, order-creating, and systematizing principles, in every walk of life.

firm as an organization, not a proprietorship. Their actions are informed by a different logic from that which guides the small, closely held unit. These are the managements who pose objectives for their organizations different from, and supplementary to, any income objectives which they may hold for themselves. These are the managements who are most likely to formalize planning and budgeting procedures as an instrument of achieving the goals they have set for the organization.

Subgoals

Objectives have two dimensions—time and structure. Business objectives, as we have already noted, extend along a time stream or spectrum, running from the present into the indefinite future. For present purposes it is sufficient that we recognize only three stages of time with their accompanying objectives. Proximate goals are those governing actions in the immediate future—the very short run, a week, a month, possibly a quarter. These in turn are guided by their relationship to intermediate goals—in budgeting practice, customarily one to five years. The intermediate goals are, in their turn, linked to long-run ("ultimate") objectives—in terms of the business planning process, ranging from five to twenty-five years.

Just as time can be broken down into units, and targets set for each segment of time, so may the organization itself be broken down into units, with goals set for each segment of the organization. The shop, the department, the division, the plant, the subsidiary—all can be given their specific targets which cumulate into the over-all company objective. Granting adequate attention to the problem of suboptimization (avoiding objectives set for one unit which impede or, at a minimum, fail to contribute to accomplishment of another unit's target, to the detriment of over-all performance), the whole is the sum of its parts. We shall explore this more fully later.

The Budget as Objective

Objectives are not enough by themselves, however. The posing of a target involves as well the devising of how that target is to be achieved. This means drawing up an operating plan or budget. As soon as the plan or budget is constructed, in all its detail, for the duration of time it covers and for all the subordinate units which it encompasses, it can be said that the budget itself becomes the objective, having incorporated into it the end result contemplated. The target simply emerges, then, as the end product of the plan, if the plan is successfully executed.

Targets and objectives thus operate on two levels. First, there are the specific states or conditions or results which are aimed at and which inform the whole planning process. But once the plan has been prepared or the budget adopted, it becomes surrogate for the end result aimed at. Hence, the extent to which a company realizes its basic objectives depends in part on the degree to which these have been successfully incorporated into the plan or budget.

The Profit Objective

Recent literature has emphasized that the modern corporation operates with multiple goals, of which profit is only one, although an important one. Management people have themselves contributed to this conception by claiming multiple responsibilities, running not only to the owners of the business but also to its employees, its suppliers and distributors, and the public. These interests are not all equally served by striving for higher profits. The firm, therefore, must operate with a rainbow of objectives which includes but is not limited to profit.

This viewpoint probably represents a reaction from the old and now thoroughly tattered concept of profit *maximization,* employed theoretically in its literal sense. But it appears that the reaction has gone too far, and it is time for a swing back in the direction of the original notion. Most organizations, like people, have multiple goals, but it is precisely for this reason that it is important to identify the distinctive and distinguishing objectives. In the case of the business firm there can be no doubt that this is the drive for profit.

There are a variety of reasons why this simple fact should in recent years have become blurred. Perhaps two are dominant. The first is that it has become difficult to answer the question, Profit for whom? The second is that it has become equally difficult to locate the source of the legitimization of the power of corporate managers, so that they have sought to root that legitimacy (a cutting from the now desiccated legal doctrine of sole responsibility to owner interests) in the new soil of the multiple goals of "social responsibility." A third but probably less significant reason for the fuzzing of the profit objective may be the corporate income tax, which has tempted some managements into good-will expenditures or profit-sacrificing arrangements only because they looked like cheap (48-cent-dollar) ways of currying public favor.

The reasons need not now concern us, however. What does concern us is that the spread of budgeting in the business world has helped to reestablish and clarify the importance of the profit objective. A recent survey of more than four hundred companies established that more than 95 per cent of these engage in comprehensive planning for defined short-run profit objectives, and that of these about nine-tenths specify the objective concretely, in writing.[2]

[2] Sord and Welsch, *Business Budgeting,* pp. 70–74.

Of these firms, something more than one-half have long-range profit plans. While there is no clear indication, this normally implies a long-term profit objective toward the achievement of which each year's operating plan is intended to move closer. This idea of some long-term "fair" or "desirable" rate of return, to which operations are geared, is probably one reason why the larger corporations do not "profiteer" by taking momentary advantage of transient demand situations, such as that prevailing immediately after World War II. Such action would constitute an aberration in the light of the profit objectives which they have set for themselves. Smaller, more closely controlled firms, without institutional personalities expressed in operating plans or budgets, are in a more likely position to move mercurially to seize an advantage.

A Priori and A Posteriori Profit Goals

Profit goals may be set in two different ways. In the absence of some long-term objective of achieving a given rate of return, the profit target may come out of the budgeting process itself. Whatever profit can be expected to flow from operations under the circumstances expected to prevail becomes the goal which guides the organization during the budget period. This is an *ad hoc* type of target, unrelated to a long-term goal. The president of the Chrysler Corporation thus testified in 1958 that "we do not have any objective saying that we have got to earn this much. All I say is we have got an objective that we must do better, and we will do better." [3]

This is in contrast to the situation where management has adopted a long-term objective which instructs each annual operating budget, setting a target which it seeks to realize by planning directed to that end. [4] Thus one corporation with plants in a number of states and abroad writes:

> Our budget serves two basic functions. It is a Corporate and Divisional Program for the financial management of the business, and an operating tool for cost control and performance measurement. The

[3] L. L. Colbert in *Administered Prices, Hearings before the Subcommittee on Antitrust and Monopoly*, U.S. Senate, 85th Cong., 2d Sess., 1958, part 6, p. 2934.

[4] The profit goal may be one toward which a company works without expecting to achieve it in the immediate future. This is the case at H. J. Heinz Company, for example.

"The published statement of over-all company policies and objectives is supplemented by written statements setting out separately and specifically the profits goals for (a) each of the Heinz companies, and (b) the consolidated Heinz setup. . . . The Executive Committee and others directly concerned realize, too, that attainment of these specific profit objectives will have to be worked out over a period of years—perhaps from ten to fifteen years." *Management Planning and Control: The H. J. Heinz Approach*, pp. 9–10.

Program phase is both for short and long term periods; the operating phase of the budget would not contemplate a period exceeding one year, and generally is limited to a six-month period.

With respect to the Program concept, we deem the financial objectives to be obtainable goals from which we do not anticipate material deviations over an extended period of time.

That is, on a year to year basis, results may fluctuate from the Program, but we expect that over a five year period, we will have attained the predetermined goal.

As so often with categorization, however, these two approaches are seldom found in their pure states. They tend to be blended in varying approaches along a spectrum which ranges from "planning operations to achieve efficient performance and therefore as good a profit as possible under the forecast conditions," at one extreme, to "planning operations to achieve as close to the desired profit goal as possible, even perhaps trying to modify the forecast conditions," at the other extreme. The former is more passive, more pliant. The latter is more active, more manipulative.

Most large firms blend the two approaches and spot themselves somewhere along the spectrum rather than at either extreme. This is almost inescapable, since seldom do the conditions or projections work out as forecast. This means that even the more passive firms may find themselves forced to become active to achieve their original goals, while even the more active firms find realization of targets sometimes not feasible and have to bow before forces which they cannot control, adjusting their sights downward.

Moreover, even in the case of those firms which profess not to have any long-run goals to which they gear their operations, there appear to be standards which substitute for goals. The official of another automobile company which claimed to have no profit target added, "except perhaps comparison with historical performance." This attention to what a company has done in the past, and what its competitors are doing in the present, as well, helps to determine whether top management will approve the first draft of an operating plan or will send it back to the responsible officers and committees with instructions to do better. No specific profit figure may be held in mind as a polestar which guides management's efforts, but the alternative is not necessarily to accept whatever profit figure seems to emerge out of original estimates.

Similarly, the vice-president for finance of the Ford Motor Company testified in a congressional hearing that his firm was not influenced in its planning by a profit objective,[5] but this apparently is a situation in which

[5] "SENATOR O'MAHONEY. Testifying here, he [Harlow Curtice, President of General Motors] said very plainly that the objective of General Motors is to earn 15 to 20 percent on net worth. Is that your concept of it?

even if there is no over-all company rate of profit to which comprehensive budget planning is geared, there *is* nevertheless a specific profit goal. The Ford Motor Company's manager of the budget analysis department wrote, two years before the foregoing testimony by Mr. Yntema: [6]

> Profit performance can be measured without first establishing objectives, but it cannot be evaluated. In establishing objectives, the type of objective first must be selected; then the magnitude of the objective must be determined.
>
> Several types of objectives were considered and rejected at Ford. . . . Return on assets employed was finally selected. . . .
>
> The amount of the objective—the percentage return on assets—varies from Division to Division, according to the type of business it represents. The Company objective is, in terms of dollars, merely the sum of Divisional objectives and, in terms of return, the weighted average of Divisional objective returns.
>
> In arriving at Divisional objectives, the Central Staff Controller's Office attempts to determine the theoretical profit potential of each Division and proposes a profit objective. The Division then develops a 5-year profit improvement program; if this results in a return satisfactory to Central Staff, the plan is presented to the Board Chairman and President for approval. If the plan is below the theoretical potential, Central Staff works with the Division until a mutually satisfactory objective is reached.

Wherever they appear on the profit-objective spectrum, then, it would appear that most companies operate with a more or less definite profit expectancy which motivates their planning. If this is a valid finding, it is a significant one. The profit which (1) is a specified a priori objective, which guides the making of the budget, or (2) is viewed as acceptable as an a posteriori product of the budgeting process is the profit which is sought by the firm, not some hypothetical maximum. It becomes an empirically tested and experience-sanctioned objective which is considered feasible and acceptable by those whose approval is needed.

When we say, then, that a firm must seek and earn a profit as a condition of survival, we can add that it learns and establishes for itself (and continually relearns, reestablishes, especially at times of change of leadership) what profit is satisfactory. In some firms this may not be reduced to a specific goal, but may be related to their own past performance, to the performance of competitors, to some range of returns which others, such as the financial community, accept as satisfactory. In other cases it may be

---

"MR. YNTEMA. No; we do not have a goal of that kind. We just like to do better than we are doing. . . ."
Administered Prices, p. 2683.

[6] W. W. Booth, "Profit Control and Profit Measurement at Ford Motor Company," *Business Budgeting,* September, 1956, pp. 12–13.

sharply pinpointed, either for the company as a unit or as the sum of the objectives of its subordinate units.[7]

Profit as Return on Sales

There are three measures of profit which tend to be used (singly or collectively) to compare a firm's performance with its budget, with its past, and with other companies' records. These are the percentage profit return on sales, the percentage profit return on total assets, and the percentage profit return on net worth. The first is probably the most commonly encountered. This is perhaps due to the fact that it is derived directly from the income or profit-and-loss statement, which operating managements generally regard as the test of the year's performance. Net profit (before or after taxes) can be measured against net sales to derive the profit rate which shows how well the firm did during the year.

The chief advantage which return on sales has over the return on investment figures is that both profit and sales are measured in common dollars. Investment, which has taken place over a number of years, relates profit in current dollars to a dubious figure which is simply the unadjusted sum of capital expenditures made under fluctuating price levels. As a former controller of the Dennison Manufacturing Company commented:[8]

> The sales are a better guide than the conventional assets when the price level changes up and down. . . . The relation of profit to sales comes nearer to being a comparison of like with like. Except for

[7] The profit with which we are concerned is not the reported net profit but the real net profit. The two are not necessarily the same. There are a number of ways in which they may diverge, usually owing to management's desire to make a good showing. Thus Roy A. Foulke, vice-president of Dun and Bradstreet, writes (*Practical Financial Statement Analysis*, p. 522): "The profit or the loss assumed on the sale of a factory or a piece of unnecessary real estate, or the loss assumed on a charge-off on bad debts that occurred 2 years ago is just as much a credit or a charge against the judgment and the efficiency of the management as the sale of unit products on a high gross margin of profit. When a concern has an operating profit of $25,000 and suffers a loss of $35,000 on an investment in a bankrupt subsidiary, there is a net loss of $10,000 for the year from the point of view of the complete operations of the business enterprise. A business may conceivably show operating profits each year for a number of consecutive years and retain all the operating profits in the business, but subsequently become bankrupt through unfortunate extracurricular activity which involves losses that are greater than operating profits."

And on p. 562: ". . . it is the final net profit, after all possible charges, that indicates, year after year, how well the funds invested in a business enterprise may have been utilized. All other profit figures, while interesting, are of secondary importance."

[8] E. Stewart Freeman, "Measuring Sales, Gross Assets and Invested Capital and Comparing Them to Profits," *The Controller*, February, 1955, p. 59.

differences due to inherited costs the profits are customarily measured in the same current dollars as the sales.

Assets, however, are conventionally expressed in an unraveled tangle of anachronistic and obsolete dollars. Hence the relation of profits to assets is more like a comparison of the number of French francs to the number of Belgian francs or of the number of lemons to the number of grapefruit.

Despite this consideration and despite the prevalence of its use, there are obvious disadvantages to the return-on-sales measure. Perhaps the most damaging flaw is that it does not permit meaningful comparisons among firms with different investment bases, both between industries and within industries. Two companies may show the same return on sales, but if one requires twice as much investment to achieve the result, it would be stretching a point to claim that their performances were equally good. A company which discharges only a brokerage function—buying from a producer to sell to a distributor or user—would hardly contemplate making the same profit on sales as a company which produces as well as sells.[9]

A related weakness in the return-on-sales concept is that exclusive concern with the profit margin may actually jeopardize profits. A representative of the Eastman Kodak Company recounts the following situation: [10]

> The advantage of the return on investment ratio over profit margin was well illustrated by the effect of a sudden cancellation in 1954 of a large government contract at our Camera Works. We recognized that this would have a serious effect on the profitability of this plant and immediately prepared an analysis showing the effect of the loss of this business. We were rather surprised to find that the profit margin on sales actually showed an increase for the plant as a whole. Since this governmental business was contracted for at a profit margin lower than that realized on civilian business, the loss of the military business increased the forecast profit margin on sales for the plant slightly. The reduction in sales was proportionately greater than the reduction

---

[9] "In the aircraft industry, some electronics companies make a 10 per cent return on sales after taxes, while others make only a 4 per cent return. Companies in the aircraft industry, however, are not completely integrated; they must buy from outside sources more than 50 per cent of what goes into the airplane. This means that some other company makes the necessary investment and takes the risk in producing 50 per cent of the sales value of the end product of the aircraft company. The electronic company's figures thus are spread over the final cost, including a subcontract, so that a 4 per cent return on sales after taxes is actually twice as great a return as it would be for a completely integrated company which makes the whole investment and takes all the risk." Charles B. Thornton, president of Litton Industries, Inc., in "Keeping in Phase with Changing Business Conditions," *The Dynamics of Management,* A.M.A. Management Report 14, 1958, pp. 20–21.

[10] William R. Brunson, "Methods of Evaluating the Profit," *N.A.A. Bulletin,* September, 1957, p. 40.

in profit. However, because the investment could not be reduced in proportion to the reduction in earnings, the return on investment ratio dropped significantly, thus indicating the adverse effect of this loss of business. Of course, the total earnings showed a drop but . . . we do not ordinarily use total dollars as control measures.

The above relation would be equally true in reverse. Acceptance of orders which reduced the rate of return on sales might actually increase profit.

Profit as Return on Investment

Recognition of the deficiencies of the profit margin rate as a measure of performance has led to increasing use of return on investment as a measure, despite the price-level problem which it introduces. Of 127 companies replying to one questionnaire, 99 used return on investment as a measure of total company performance, and two-thirds of these (about one-half the total) used it as their sole measure. Some 76 employed it in setting specific profit goals.[11] A somewhat similar response was obtained in a study sponsored by the Controllership Foundation in 1958. Inquiries addressed to 386 "leading" companies revealed that 51 per cent set a definite return-on-capital figure as a corporate goal. An even larger proportion (59 per cent) used it as a measure of corporate performance.[12]

With those companies using the return on investment approach it has become common practice to break the formula down into its component parts of percentage return on sales and turnover:

$$\frac{\text{Profit}}{\text{Sales}} \times \frac{\text{sales}}{\text{investment}} = \text{return on investment}$$

The explanation is invariably given that by detailing the two components which go to make up the final measure, management is alerted to the importance of both the profit rate on sales and the turnover of capital. Keller, for example, states: [13]

[11] James H. Miller, "A Glimpse at Practice in Calculating and Using Return on Investment," *N.A.A. Bulletin*, June, 1960, p. 73. The questionnaire was addressed to 200 companies selected to give "a diversified list . . . as to size and geographic location, but excluding railroads and public utilities," from the "Manual of Excellently Managed Companies," published by the American Institute of Management, and the *Fortune* list of the 500 largest companies.

[12] Sord and Welsch, *Business Budgeting*, pp. 88–89 and 148.

[13] *Management Accounting for Profit Control*, pp. 316–317. Not only do profit rates and turnover rates differ between industries and companies but they also differ between product lines within companies, to which the company rate (target or actual) may be applied as a measure of profitability. Thus Mark W. Cresap, Jr., president of Westinghouse, has commented ("Long-term Planning," *Advanced Management*, January, 1953, p. 35): ". . . because of inherent characteristics, product lines will vary in their profitability ratios as between (1) 'margin' of profit and

The intensity of use of capital, turnover, is just as important as profit on sales in determining the return achieved. In a recent year a food-processing company had a profit on sales of 2.3% and a turnover of 3.90, giving them a return of 8.9%; a chemical company had a profit on sales of 12.0% and a turnover of 0.74, resulting in a return of 8.88%. Both were using their capital with approximately equal effectiveness but achieving their return differently because of the different nature of their business.

Use of return on investment as a long-run profit goal implies an average rate. In any given year, the actual return might be higher or lower than the target rate. This lessens the usability of a specific long-term profit objective as a basis for short-run planning, but does not altogether deprive it of its incentive effect. Moreover, the concept of return on investment is far from precise. There are at least seven ways in which companies compute it. One way is to measure profit against the net worth of the company. Probably a more prevalent practice, however, is to relate profits to total assets— the latter taken at original cost, or at book value, or at estimated replacement cost, or at original cost less current liability, or at book value less current liability, or at replacement cost less current liability.[14] For present purposes we shall simply contrast briefly the method of computing return on some variant of total assets with that of basing return on net worth.

Return on Total Assets

The explanation usually given by those who use total assets rather than equity as the base is that the former is a measure of business performance and the latter a measure of financial performance. The literature abounds with expressions of this view. For example: [15]

> By capital employed we mean the total of the assets used in the business, i.e., the cash, accounts receivable, and inventories, commonly referred to as current capital, and plant property and equipment, or fixed capital. It is the figure shown at the bottom of the left-hand side

---

(2) return on investment. Some lines with high margins produce a low return on investment because 'turnover' is low—that is, the volume of sales in relation to capital employed. Other lines with moderate margins are able to produce a good return on investment because of high turnover. Often heavy special purpose machinery is in the first classification and standardized mass production items (automobiles, refrigerators) in the second."

[14] Miller (*N.A.A. Bulletin,* June, 1960, p. 73) found examples of all these methods of computation. In his returns, eighty-nine companies used some version of total assets, as against fifty employing the net worth approach (some using both).

[15] F. J. Muth, now controller of the Armstrong Cork Company, in "Return on Capital Employed: A Measure of Management," *N.A.C.A. Bulletin,* February, 1954, sec. 1, p. 699.

of the standard balance sheet in its traditional form. Where the money for these assets comes from is not significant. It may have its source in varying proportions from vendors, accrued taxes, funded debt, and stockholders. Our concern is with how these funds are put to use, both for determination of trend within our own companies and for evaluation of our performance against competition.

Why should we select capital employed as a basic measure rather than stockholders' equity, i.e., total assets minus liabilities? By relating profits to stockholders' equity, we obtain the return on the owner's investment, an important measure. However, all businesses actually employ funds in excess of the owner's investment. These additional funds are obtained through vendors, bank borrowings, or funded debt. We are interested in testing the effectiveness with which management employs the total funds made available to it. Furthermore, capital employed supplies a common base or denominator for comparison of competitive results, regardless of the various methods through which the companies compared may have accumulated the funds they are using in their business.

Similarly, President A. Lightfoot Walker of the Rheem Manufacturing Company remarked: [16]

In our formalized statement, we place particular emphasis on specific objectives designed to develop and support plant operations which have the potential of returning pre-tax earnings of 30 per cent or more on investment. This approach provides a measure of the progress made toward general objectives. For example, we have defined "investment" carefully as (1) total fixed assets, less depreciation, plus (2) inventory, plus (3) accounts receivable. We chose this investment base in preference to net worth in the belief that management should be given an incentive to make all assets productive; in other words, our investment base is an integral part of our productivity thinking.

A company manufacturing fixtures for residential and commercial construction writes in its administrative manual:

It is the policy of the Corporation to plan and manage its operations to planned profit objectives. These objectives must be consistent with the position of the Corporation in the financial community. Investors judge the effectiveness and success of our Corporation by the earnings generated by their investment. It necessarily follows that the basic yardstick for measuring the performance of the Corporation, and therefore each Division, is "Return on Investment."

For internal purposes, since we must manage *all* of the assets entrusted to us, the "investment" represents total gross assets. The Corporation's standard of performance is 15% return on these gross

[16] Walker, "The Need for Productivity Thinkers," in *Ends and Means of Modern Management*, A.M.A. Report 30, 1959, p. 128.

assets, before taxes. Any Division or product line which does not generate this return will hinder the achievement of the overall goals.

A representative of the Ford Motor Company says succinctly: [17]

> Several types of objectives were considered and rejected at Ford.
> . . . Return on assets employed was finally selected because it embodies all balance sheet and income statement variables—sales, costs and assets. It provides incentive to increase sales, reduce costs, add assets only when they will yield a satisfactory return and get rid of useless assets.

And the president of Westinghouse sums up: [18]

> Some argue that return on net worth is preferable. The "total asset" basis is preferred because it measures management in terms of profits returned on total capital employed, without injecting consideration as to the *sources* of capital. A "net worth" basis of measuring profit return is pertinent to a financial evaluation, but the "total asset" basis is the best for appraising management's basic responsibility for earnings. I was interested to note that, in a recent survey of practice in this regard among a representative group of large companies, the measurement of return against total assets, with the fixed assets included at gross value, was the predominant approach.

Return on Net Worth

This weight of authority behind the total asset approach is impressive but not decisive. When it is said that return on net worth is a measure of financial management rather than of operating management, it is difficult to see any special significance in the terminological distinction which is being made. One might equally maintain that productivity is a measure of engineering efficiency rather than operating management, or that the inventory ratio is a measure of marketing management rather than operating management, or that manpower turnover is a measure of personnel management rather than operating management. The fact is that all these measures collectively are summed up in profit as a measure of the management of the total business.

Leverage—the ratio of assets to equity, the use of equity as a foundation for credit—is one instrument for improving profit position. It is not simply a matter of financial management when a firm uses its leverage to improve its earnings. It is good operating management.

In part the question of whether return on investment should be calculated on total assets or on equity is a reflection of our present confusion over the

[17] W. W. Booth, *Business Budgeting,* p. 13.
[18] Mark W. Cresap, Jr., *Advanced Management,* p. 35.

function and title of profits. Those who argue for the total asset approach have depersonalized ownership of the firm, so that profits are regarded not so much as accruing to ownership as arising from management. But the fact remains that a business operation must begin with equity, and that the ability to manipulate the given equity position into a larger asset position via loans, reserves, accounts receivable, and so on, is one of the qualities on which management is tested.

Just as return on sales may, if made the sole measure, actually sacrifice profit in the effort to avoid sales which lower the measure chosen, so may return on total assets have the same effect. The danger is contained in the following philosophy, which is in common currency in business circles: [19]

> One objection to the method [of relating profit to equity], however, is that it may tend to promote an excessive use of borrowed funds or credit at too low a rate of return on the invested funds, but yet at a high enough rate to cover the interest costs and add something to the net profit as an additional return on owners' capital. Thus, for example, a 10 per cent return on capital of $500,000, or $50,000, may be increased to $70,000, or 14 per cent, by the simple expedient of borrowing $500,000 at 4 per cent and investing it in facilities earning 8 per cent. This increase in return to the owners may make them happy, but it tends to obscure the fact that funds have been committed to a lower rate of return than the owners would have required on their own investment. The result conceivably could be that of encouraging an uneconomic use of borrowed funds. This is not meant to condemn a possibly wise resort to borrowing as a means of pyramiding the return on owners' investment, but it suggests that *all* funds available to the management, regardless of source, should be invested economically, that is, put to work only for a fair return on the *funds used*.

To an economist this is a peculiar bit of reasoning. As long as funds earn more than the cost of borrowing, they add to profit, and a management bent on increasing profit would put such funds to work. But it is axiomatic in business that funds are not borrowed for investment unless they will return at least the prevailing rate on total assets. Otherwise, the rate of return—the measure of management's operating ability—is lowered.

It is evident how such a principle applies to the rate of return on net worth. Additional equity financing would not be sought unless the funds secured earned a return at least equal to that prevailing. Otherwise, earnings per share—the shareholders' criterion for good management—would decline. But if additional funds can be obtained from nonequity sources at rates of interest lower than rates of return, total dollar profits, as well

[19] Heiser, *Budgeting,* p. 21. A few pages further he writes, ". . . a management should have some standard rate in mind, below which it will not invest new funds."

as return on net worth, will be enhanced. This will be the case even if the rate of return on total assets declines in consequence.

It would appear that the widespread regard for rate of return on total investment constitutes a potential limitation on management's search for profit improvement. Use of it as a criterion of managerial efficiency could rule out investments which might add to total profit. As long as one is willing to maintain that a firm's performance is better if it makes a larger rather than a smaller profit, then return on total investment is a misleading measure of managerial efficiency. For it could easily be the case that a management would add to profit at the same time that it lowered its rate of return on total assets.

If maximum dollar profit is considered the prize, then rate of return on total assets will not always secure it. Rate of return on net worth will often do a better job. In comparing interfirm performance, one firm could be rated superior to another only if its rate of return was higher for the same total asset figure, or equal or higher for a larger total investment. But a lower rate of return on a higher total asset figure might actually describe a profit showing that is superior to a higher rate of return on a lower total asset position.

The contrast between the two approaches can be readily shown by example. Assume first that a firm makes a profit of $500 on sales of $10,000, employing total assets of $2,000 and with a net worth of $1,000.

Using the return on total assets approach, we would calculate the return as

$$\frac{\$\ \ 500}{\$10,000} \times \frac{\$10,000}{\$\ 2,000} \qquad \text{or} \qquad 5\% \times 5 = 25\% \text{ return on total assets}$$

Using the return on net worth approach, we would calculate the return as

$$\frac{\$\ \ 500}{\$10,000} \times \frac{\$10,000}{\$\ 1,000} \qquad \text{or} \qquad 5\% \times 10 = 50\% \text{ return on net worth}$$

Now assume that profits increase to $600 on sales of $20,000, with an expansion of total assets to $4,000 and net worth remaining at $1,000. The addition to assets, we will suppose, has come from an increase in accounts receivable financed by bank loans. Now the return on total assets would show:

$$\frac{\$\ \ 600}{\$20,000} \times \frac{\$20,000}{\$\ 4,000} \qquad \text{or} \qquad 3\% \times 5 = 15\% \text{ return on total assets}$$

In contrast, return on net worth would be

$$\frac{\$\ \ 600}{\$20,000} \times \frac{\$20,000}{\$\ 1,000} \qquad \text{or} \qquad 3\% \times 20 = 60\% \text{ return on net worth}$$

Thus the increase in sales, financed from nonequity sources and contributing an additional profit, would indicate an inferior managerial performance on the total asset approach but a superior performance based on net worth. If increased profit is the objective, however, clearly the net worth criterion is a more accurate guide.

There is, however, one explanation for this management maxim which otherwise would remain inexplicable to an economist. If a management's focus was on long-run profit rather than the current year's income statement, and if it believed that to undertake investments now simply because they would return more than the cost of capital, even though less than the current rate of earnings, might foreclose it from undertaking investments with superior profit showings later, then its reasoning becomes clearer. It might entertain such a view either because it believed that by borrowing now it would be in a less advantageous position to borrow in the future, having already exercised its financial leverage, or because it was conscious of its own physical limitations in extending its control over wider operations. Under either supposition, or both, it might then believe it wise to hold in reserve its borrowing and supervisory capacities, confident that opportunities would before long present themselves which would earn more than opportunities now present, but which would be foreclosed if present opportunities were to be acted on.

A management which for this reason adopts return on total assets as its objective is taking the position: "Our experience has shown that, on the average, we are capable of making investments which give such-and-such a yield. There is no reason why we shouldn't continue to do as well. Why should we undertake investments returning less, even if they are the best we can do at the moment, when at any time something better is sure to come along, as our experience has shown us?" This "opportunity-consciousness" does indeed seem to motivate many managements, and it explains their reluctance to undertake operations yielding less of a profit than they have found to be possible—on the average—from experience. The cost of making an investment (which helps to determine the rate of return on assets) is thus something more than the cost of capital: it is the (*anticipated*) opportunity cost of the particular venture. Even if a given project may yield a net profit, adding something to earnings and hence appearing to justify its undertaking, if it displaces a more profitable project just "over the horizon" the costs of the project must include the additional profits which could have been earned. Hence management saves its financial leverage and its organizational slack for those activities which promise the higher rate of return over a time period which is more than the present moment.

This is at best, however, a rule of thumb. On the whole, a goal which is geared to a return on net worth seems more nearly related to the objective of higher profits, as long as a management is conscious of the opportunity-cost factor which is the only justification for the rule of thumb.

Assets at Original Cost or Less Depreciation?

One other consideration in connection with the measurement of profits need not detain us long. There is considerable controversy in the literature over the question of whether, when profit is measured against total assets, the latter should be taken at original cost or less depreciation.

Those who argue for original cost do so on several grounds: that the depreciation which is taken is available for reinvestment and hence should be included as part of the total assets which management is expected to employ wisely; that the subtraction of depreciation penalizes new investment in any comparisons which are made, since management with older assets which were substantially depreciated would have a constantly declining asset base against which profits would be measured while a company with new assets would have a large and almost wholly undepreciated asset base; that to use older investments at cost offsets to some extent the distortion which rising prices of capital assets has introduced into the investment base.

There is respectable business authority for this point of view. One of the most influential is the Du Pont Company, which has said: [20]

> Return on Investment . . . is based upon *gross* operating investment and earnings *net* of depreciation.
>
> Gross operating investment represents all the plant, tools, equipment and working capital made available to operating management for its use; no deduction is made for current or other liabilities or for the reserve for depreciation. Since plant facilities are maintained in virtually top productive order during their working life, the depreciation reserve being considered primarily to provide for obsolescence, it would be inappropriate to consider that operating management was responsible for earning a return on only the net operating investment. Furthermore, if depreciable assets were stated at net depreciated values, earnings in each succeeding period would be related to an ever-decreasing investment; even with stable earnings, Return on Investment would continually rise, so that comparative Return on Investment ratios would fail to reveal the extent or trend of management performance. Relating earnings to investment that is stable and uniformly compiled provides a sound basis for comparing the "profitability of assets employed" as between years and between investments.
>
> In the case of any commitment of capital—e.g., an investment in a security—it is the expectation that in addition to producing earnings while committed, the principle will eventually be recovered. Likewise, in the case of funds invested in a project, it is expected that in addition to the return earned while invested, the working capital will be recovered through liquidation at the end of the project's useful life and the plant investment will be recovered through depreciation accruals.

[20] *Executive Committee Control Charts*, E. I. Du Pont de Nemours and Company, 1959, p. 34.

> Since earnings must allow for this recovery of plant investment, they
> are stated net of investment.

It is hard to fathom the reasoning in this statement. If depreciable assets
were stated at net depreciated values, earnings in each succeeding period
would not be related to an ever-decreasing investment, as the company
asserts, as long as the funds accruing through depreciation were reinvested,
as is apparently contemplated. Moreover, if facilities are kept in "top productive order" (a condition made possible, theoretically, at least, through
the application of depreciation-accrued reserves), there is no need for recovering their value all over again, through depreciation, during the period
when they remain in top productive order. There is confusion when depreciation is written off as an expense in the income statement but retained
as a kind of invisible asset on the balance sheet when it comes to estimating
return on investment. Actually, of course, it does not so appear on the balance sheet since the sums accrued through depreciation charges have found
their way into other asset accounts (whether current assets or fixed) which
are also included in the asset base against which profit is measured—a form
of double counting. The result is to understate the return on investment.
If capital is considered gross of depreciation, then it seems clear that earnings should not be considered net of depreciation accruals, and vice versa.
Nevertheless, the practice of basing earnings, less depreciation, on original
asset cost is not uncommon.

Summary on the Profit Objective

Summing the argument to this point, we find that most firms which
budget have objectives toward which the budget, as operating plan, is
directed. In most firms this objective is a rate of profit (or rate range) which
arises out of experience or comparisons or expectations. It is this more or
less defined profit goal, rather than some hypothetical maximum profit,
which informs business planning. The profit rate may be computed against
sales or, with increasing frequency, investment. In the latter case, investment may be construed as total assets (gross or net of depreciation) or as
net worth. Return on net worth is more in keeping with traditional economic assumptions of profit maximizing, but return on total assets seems
to be the measure preferred by a number of major business firms. The latter
approach can be justified only on the assumption that opportunities for
investments of varying profitability are continually presenting themselves,
that the number of opportunities which can be taken up by a company is
limited by the availability of financing and by administrative stretch-out,
and that it is good business to restrict one's investment "plunges" to those
opportunities which promise a return at least as good as the firm is currently realizing from all the assets available to it.

Chapter 5

SECONDARY GOALS

If some rate of profit constitutes the primary goal toward which most business firms drive, at least those firms which engage in budget planning, there are frequently other goals which accompany this one. These secondary goals are of several kinds. Some are maintained jointly with the profit objective, even though viewed as subordinate to it. We shall speak of these as concomitant goals. Some are considered as deriving from the profit objective. We may label these subsidiary goals. Finally, there are those which are regarded as reasons why profit itself is sought. These we may term anterior goals.

Concomitant Goals

One concomitant goal which emerges frequently is the establishment or maintenance of a reputation for quality. This is often stated as an objective independent of profit, rather than as a means of achieving the desired rate of return. While obviously product or service quality would not be pursued past some point at which the adverse effect on profit could not be tolerated, it is sometimes accepted as an objective sufficiently important that it "must" be accommodated within the desired rate of return.

The H. J. Heinz statement of company policies and objectives thus asserts:

> The reputation we have enjoyed since 1869 is based upon a public recognition of "Heinz Quality." Yet quality is a relative term which acquires significance only when the kind of quality is defined and the standard of quality established.
>
> Our objective is to make products of maximum recognizable value and desirability to the consumer within a price structure she can be induced to pay [and presumably consonant with the profit objective].
>
> The pursuance of our quality objective requires—
> 1. Clear determination of Heinz standard of quality for each finished product.

2. Careful and continuous qualitative evaluation of ingredients, packages and processes.

3. Maximum uniformity of finished products.

Similarly, employee welfare is often mentioned as a separate company objective. The concomitant goal which is most frequently encountered, however, is the obtaining of some identified share of a firm's market. In the same questionnaire results which showed 51 per cent of the 386 companies surveyed seeking a specific return on capital, 41 per cent of the respondents said they also sought some specific share of their markets.

One controller replied: [1]

> We view the budgeting process rather broadly and use it as our basic instrument of planning and controlling. We have established two very distinct standards of over-all performance. One is a specified per cent earnings on assets employed before taxes, and the other is a per cent of total industry sales. With these two goals in mind each division has specific targets to work toward, and in drawing up their yearly plans they know exactly what their goals should be.

Share of the market as an objective, even when not made explicit, often becomes implicit in comprehensive budgeting. In a number of instances sales forecasts are first made on a product or industry basis, and then the company's own sales objectives are determined by applying the customary or desired proportion of the total. Here market share is built into the budgeting procedure.

For several reasons, however, this objective must be viewed as inferior to, even though held concomitantly with, return on investment. More is involved than simply the difficulties of defining what constitutes a "market," though that is no small problem.[2]

[1] Sord and Welsch, *Business Budgeting*, p. 149.

[2] In a case study of General Electric, *Planning, Managing, and Measuring the Business* (New York: Controllership Foundation, 1955), p. 33, a member of management noted:

"There may be wide variations in the interpretation of what constitutes the market for a given product line. Therefore, it is important that for each of their lines, our product departments identify such things as:

"1. Whether the market includes not only directly competing products but also indirectly competing products (electric ranges vs. electric ranges; electric ranges vs. all types of ranges—electric, gas, oil, and others).

"2. Whether the market includes sales by all domestic competitors or only those reporting to trade associations.

"3. Whether the market includes imports, if foreign sellers are competing in the domestic market.

"4. Whether the market includes export sales.

"5. Whether the market includes captive sales.

"6. Whether the market is considered to be represented by sales to distributors, or to retailers, or to ultimate users."

Two other more basic problems limit the usefulness of market share as an objective. One is that its too diligent pursuit may jeopardize profit, which still remains the primary test a company must pass to remain viable. The danger is indicated by the deleterious effect on the company's operations of Armour's earlier efforts to overtake Swift in the meat packing industry.[3] The other is that a too successful pursuit of this objective may lead to a degree of market dominance that invites Department of Justice investigation and possible antitrust proceedings. An objective which a company can attain only by possible risk to the sinews of its survival, or which it is fully capable of exceeding but must be careful not to, ceases to be by itself an adequate standard or measure of performance.

Subsidiary Goals

Unlike concomitant goals, which can be maintained independently of profit, even though subordinated to it, subsidiary goals grow directly out of the profit drive. They are built into the profit plan. They may be functional (that is, phrased in terms of marketing or financial or personnel objectives) or organizational (stated in terms of the unit divisions within the company). They may be aspects of either short-run or long-run planning.

As has already been noted, realization of the budget may itself be treated as the objective, so that sales and cost estimates which are the basis for profit projections become subsidiary goals. These may be mixed with other short-run objectives whose achievement is sufficiently in doubt that they have not actually entered into budget planning. One company thus stated its six months' objectives as follows, in its report to the executive committee:

> For the second six months of 1959 these will be the goals of the main plant organization:
> 1. Net shipments of $6,205,000 at a manufacturing cost of $4,570,-000.
> 2. An inventory reduction of at least $300,000.
> 3. Cost reductions on an annual basis of at least $300,000.
> 4. A concerted program to bring into the plant components for [two recently introduced products] now purchased outside.
> 5. A continuing program to refine and improve the layout of the new plant.

In more general terms, another company has stated, in laying out a budgeting program for a newly acquired subsidiary: "Planning considers all significant cost and revenue elements in the business and blends them into the best attainable profit result. This obviously implies complete meshing of sales, engineering, and manufacturing efforts. It suggests also that within

---

[3] The story is told in "Beat Swift and Go Broke," *Fortune*, October, 1959, p. 123.

each function broad goals be defined to specific sub-goals and individual responsibilities."

These functional goals (corporate subgoals) need not, however, be identical with those contained in the current operating plan. They may constitute bench marks drawn from longer-run plans against which the annual operating plan itself is judged for its contribution to fulfillment of the five- or ten-year goals.

Unit Objectives

Even more prevalent than detailed functional objectives, however, are goals which are set for units of the company—sometimes by top corporate management, sometimes by top divisional management, and sometimes in collaboration. Historically, perhaps the most commonly encountered form of unit target was the sales quota set for a marketing division. (Even this form has tended to undergo change; it is much less common now for a sales quota to be set without attaching to it a profit objective.) Subgoals for subunits apply to more than the sales organization, however.

One survey disclosed the following practice: [4]

> In most of the companies visited, return on investment goals are set for each major segment of the business—division, product line, or territory—as well as for the business as a whole. Some executives reported experimentation with individual product ROI [return on investment] computations, but the general consensus was that such extreme detail was not worth the effort required. . . .
>
> For example, the top management group of one of the firms interviewed believed that the ROI of a certain division should be in the neighborhood of 40% before taxes, although it had actually been experiencing an ROI of approximately 19%.
>
> New divisional management was instructed to plan divisional operations to yield the 40% return within five years. The divisional management set as its goal for the first year 25% ROI, and keyed its planning to a growth to 30% the second year, 35% the third, and 40% by the end of the fourth year. It should be emphasized that the divisional management was not allowed to merely "plug in" the ROI figures the corporate management wanted, but was required to present well-thought-out plans to boost sales and trim costs sufficiently to achieve 25% ROI in the coming year, and to continue product and market development work as well as cost reduction programs to increase ROI further in succeeding years.

Other examples come easily to hand. The Minnesota Mining and Manu-

[4] Leon E. Hay, "Planning for Profits: How Some Executives Are Doing It," *The Accounting Review,* April, 1960, pp. 234, 235. The survey was of fifteen companies "with a reputation for experience with profit planning."

facturing [3M] Company is organized by divisions, which are largely autonomous: [5]

> Each division is organized to make money. Each has an established long-range profit target. . . . Each operates on a system of defining objectives, forecasting sales volume, costs and profits on a quarterly, annual and five-year basis. Control procedures are utilized to gauge performance, to plan annual spending rates, and to communicate to division management and to 3M Co. top management the progress (or business health) of the operating unit. . . .
>
> First and foremost of the control mechanisms used by 3M is the establishment between company management (the management committee) and division management of profit targets for each of our 36 major divisions. These profit targets are expressed as a per cent of sales and are based on a review of the history of the division, markets to be served, competitive conditions in the market, unique contributions through technology (or patents), and return on capital employed for each division. In a new division or newly-acquired subsidiary, a planned approach to the ultimate profit target is provided by establishing a progressive target over a period of 3 to 5 years to gain experience and permit establishing the ultimate profit target on a sound and factual basis.

The situation at Westinghouse is similar: [6]

> As we practice this pattern in Westinghouse long-term objectives are established by each Division for each of its product lines and for the Division in total. The sum of the Divisional objectives becomes the objective for the company as a whole. They are intended to represent attainable goals for the fifth year in the future. . . . They are set in terms of the following factors: Market participation (share of market); sales billed—both customer and inter-divisional; costs and expenses; profits; assets required to support the volume, and return on assets.
>
> These fifth-year goals provide the target at which the sights will be aimed. There are several criteria which can be considered in setting these goals. The Company's standard Return on Assets goal is the basic yardstick. Other criteria could be the performance of best competitors in corresponding lines of business, or the best rate of performance in earlier years. While the yardsticks may vary, the objectives should always represent excellence in performance.

[5] C. W. Walton, division general manager, "Company and Division Planning and Control," in "How We Report to Various Levels of Management: A Case Study of Financial Planning and Controls in the 3M Company," *N.A.C.A. Bulletin,* October, 1956, pp. 310–311.

[6] Russell B. Read, "Long Range Planning," from *Proceedings of the 1954 Conference of the National Society for Business Budgeting.*

The nature of divisional planning to reach company-set goals at Philco is described by a divisional controller.[7]

> The five-year planning committee includes the department general, sales, and product planning managers, and the chief design engineer, together with the following divisional representatives: vice-president and general manager, vice-president for operations, vice-president for engineering and the controller.
>
> The planning committee does not set out to establish a budget but rather to evolve a plan. Its objective is to conceive and plan to manufacture, market, and sell merchandise at selling prices and costs which will permit the division to earn a satisfactory return on investment. Corporate management determines not only the required return but also fixes the investment base. So rigid is this investment concept, that use of funds in excess of those established is on a loan-at-interest basis. This forces recognition by the division and, consequently, by each department of the need to return not only a reasonable profit on sales but sufficient sales and profit combined to provide a satisfactory return on investment. The process is basically one of analytically planning what the department is going to make, how much, at what costs, to be sold at what prices, leaving how much in the till.

At Ford, "The 5-year profit plan shows, in a series of yearly steps, the levels of profits and returns that the Division expects to realize in the course of reaching its objective. It is not a projection of earning trends but a personal commitment by each General Manager to undertake a series of programs and other actions designed to increase dollar profits and return on assets." [8]

An example of the kind of instructions sometimes given to divisional managements to guide them in long-run planning to achieve company-set profit goals, as contained in one company's administrative manual, is given in the appendix to this chapter.

Goals within Goals

In this process of subdividing functions, units, and goals, objectives which have been stated for a given subunit may be further broken down along functional lines within that unit, taking goal-focused planning farther and farther down the operational ladder. A specialist in manufacturing budgets and measurements for the General Electric Company's Aircraft Gas Turbine Division at West Lynn, Massachusetts, provides one example,

[7] Bert E. Stromberg, "Divisional Budget Program," in "Budgeting Policy and Practice in a Decentralized Company," *N.A.A. Bulletin,* October, 1957, p. 37.

[8] W. W. Booth, *Business Budgeting,* September, 1956, p. 13.

adding the unusual touch of designating several levels of achievement with respect to the goals specified.[9]

MANUFACTURING SECTION GOALS FOR 1957 (SHEET METAL
OPERATIONS SUB-SECTION) *

Goal	Performance			
	Excellent	Good	Fair	Poor
1. Produce and ship a shop cost output of $600,000 by 12-31.........$	$600,000	$550,000	$500,000	$450,000
2. Reduce shop cost of inlet cover by 15% by year end...............	15%	12%	8%	5%
3. Maintain a ratio of indirect personnel to direct labor manpower below 30%..	25%	27%	30%	35%
4. Reduce manufacturing losses to below 20% ratio to direct labor............	10%	15%	20%	25%
5. Carry on an aggressive cost reduction program to exceed $40,000 by 12-31..$	60,000	$ 50,000	$ 40,000	$ 30,000
6. Maintain cost of quality at a level below 5.5% ratio to sales dollars.....	4.5%	5.0%	5.5%	6.0%
7. Keep overtime requirements to a level below 3% of total man hours worked.	2%	3%	4%	5%
8. Increase inventory turnover rate to 8 or above by year end.............	9	8	7	6

* The figures shown in this exhibit are for illustrative purposes only and have no reference to actual conditions.

Subsidiary objectives may thus be in the form of both functional and organizational subgoals. In some companies these ultimately come to the same focus in individualized goals or quotas or targets or "bogies."

Anterior Goals

Finally, we come face to face with the question of *why* managements seek profits. There is no need for spending any time with the once-prevailing belief that it is necessary for management to satisfy the stockholders, by a superior profit performance, in order to retain its job. The job security of the management of a publicly held corporation does not depend on whether the profit on sales is 4 per cent or 5 per cent, or whether return on investment, after taxes, is 10 per cent or 12 per cent. Yet managements do strive to improve their profit performance by such increments and gear their planning to such profit objectives. Why?

Some managements are satisfied to strive for better profit showings,

[9] Chester H. Sneider, "Setting Operating Goals and Measuring Achievements," *N.A.A. Bulletin,* July, 1958, p. 26.

year after year, simply because they take pleasure in bettering prior performances, in the same way that a runner strives to clip an extra second off his previous best time. There is a challenge simply in doing better than one has done in the past or better than one's nearest competitor. Where this kind of challenge motivates management, as it seems to in a great many cases, it is hardly necessary to look for anterior goals. The dollars of profit are sought not for what can be done with them but simply because they constitute the units by which business performances are measured and compared. They are the tallies in the "great game of business."

But there is another breed of management which is impatient with playing such games, to whom profit is important not because it keeps some kind of score but because it represents the means to achieve other ends. Managers of this type are the creators, the doers, the empire builders, the dreamers. The more barbaric of them are often obsessed with the notion of growth for its own sake. They want to expand their own facilities, acquire other companies, buy out competitors, penetrate other markets. This is the Napoleonic complex, with which many of our most lionized managers are tinged in varying degree. To carry on such expansion, to build business empires, takes money. Profits provide it.

The more sophisticated among those who are driven to achieve anterior goals are less concerned with growth for its own sake than with specific but grandiose achievements. They envision putting together a corporate complex which perhaps delights an artistic sense of symmetry. They take majestic and philanthropic pride in turning out from their industrial laboratories some product which represents not just mundane variation on a former design but a bold and imaginative conception which they "confer" on society like a princely gift. The construction of a headquarters building which commands architectural admiration gives flight to their fancy and a sense of soaring to their spirits. The overcoming of specific production or engineering challenges provides the solid contentment of calculated mastery over adverse circumstance. But to achieve these varying satisfactions, perhaps best exemplified in recent years by Adriano Olivetti, also takes money. Again, profit provides it.

The Managerial Function

To say that profit provides the funds for the Napoleons and the Leonardos of the business world to realize their objectives places emphasis on retention of earnings in the business and implies a particular way of looking at management, since it is management which puts retained earnings to work.

Management may be conceived as the function which coordinates all the internal bargaining between the participants of a business in such a way as to satisfy them all sufficiently to keep them (or replacements for them) adhering to the organization, always subject to the necessary limitation that, as far as the pecuniary element of the various bargains is concerned, the outgo must be covered by the income. From office boy to principal stockholder, from shopworker to vice-president in charge of production, everyone connected with the business makes certain demands on the business. In the upper management circles these "demands" may include urging the acceptance of certain policies believed important to the success of the business with which one has cast his lot, to which he has staked his future, or policies thought to be helpful to his success within that business. The sales manager may insist that certain credit policies be adopted which will permit the more effective discharge of his role in the business, while the vice-president for finance may object that this would endanger the financial security of the business and counter with a different policy which he regards as preferable, and in the adoption of which he feels he has a stake. Thus policies become internal bargaining issues. In addition, at all levels of business operation compensation and advancement become elements in the internal bargaining.

The function of top management is to coordinate all these demands on the company—to manipulate them against each other in such a way as to satisfy all sufficiently to retain their services and to do this within the financial restriction that somehow inflows balance outflows. This balance must be achieved at whatever level the business operates, but management will try to achieve it at some preferred level of operations (as given by the operating budget).

Whatever funds remain unallocated after all internal bargains have been satisfied are management's to apply in whatever ways it may choose, as long as it has not limited its freedom in the internal bargaining process. For this purpose, we may properly regard stockholders as simply another claimant on the business, like its employees and suppliers. The demands of stockholders too must be met and manipulated in the same way as those of other participants in the business, but once this has been done, whatever discretion management has not bargained away remains its to follow as it chooses, with whatever funds remain undistributed. This is where management may draw upon profits retained in the business as the instrument with which to pursue its anterior objectives.[10] In this sense, it may be said that management is the residual claimant in the business firm.[11]

---

[10] I have tried to describe the management function and its relation to business innovation at greater length in *A General Theory of Economic Process*, pp. 166–172.

[11] The definition of profit has plagued economists for some time. At least as far as incorporated business is concerned, I would like to put in a word for defining profit as the earnings retained in the business. On this approach, dividends would be re-

Anterior Goals and Profits

It may at times be the case, as has occasionally been suggested, that management's attempts to achieve anterior goals may jeopardize a firm's profit position. The effort to achieve some objective (growth, new products through industrial research, and so on) may be pursued to the point where profits are sacrificed in the quest. The objective becomes obsessive, and a normal business goal of a return on sales or investment takes second place to it.

This may indeed be the case in specific instances, but it is not typical. The notion of a firm's pursuing multiple objectives, of which profit is only one, with others being actually inconsistent with or competitive to the profit drive, has probably been overdone. There is no a priori reason why high profit should be inconsistent with most other goals. In fact, more often than not profitability facilitates rather than impedes the achievement of other objectives.[12] Low profit realization is very seldom explainable by multiple management goals. It is probably more consistent with poor management, failing to achieve the profit which it would like to achieve, than with good management diverted into paths of seeking objectives other than or in addition to profit.

This is not the same thing as saying that management is typically guided by profit maximization in the classical sense. As has been suggested sev-

---

garded simply as a return on capital, which is how managements today tend to regard them.

In an interesting article, "The Profit Concept and Theory: A Restatement," *Journal of Political Economy,* vol. 44, April, 1954, pp. 152–170, Prof. J. Fred Weston develops a view that profit is the consequence of uncertainty, the difference between what is planned and what is realized. He sees two classes of factors—those with rates of compensation fixed in advance (contractual returns) and those whose compensation depends on results (residual returns). The former become fixed costs, in a sense, while the latter are the uncertain returns. The difference between the expected outcome "defined by the basis upon which contracts are entered into and the results actually realized is a measure of profit."

One difficulty with this approach, if I have interpreted it correctly, is that it would lead to the conclusion that where plans were fully realized, but no more than realized (that is, where performance ex post equals performance ex ante), no profit would exist.

It seems much simpler to me just to identify profit as the unallocated return to the firm. It is not a functional return, unless it can be said to be a return to the planning function. It accrues to the "firm," to the organization, and in the absence of any limitations which may have been imposed by internal bargaining, it may be drawn upon by management in the attempt to realize its anterior objectives.

[12] The American Telephone and Telegraph Co. has argued this case at length in an interesting polemic, *Profit, Performance, and Progress,* 1959.

eral times, the evidence points to the fact that most managements—at least most managements which think about the matter—strive to realize some specific profit rate which they conceive to be feasible and desirable, taking all things into consideration—the pace and precision at which they expect themselves and their associates and employees to work, the performance of competitors, the expectations of the financial community. Achievement of the rate projected is considered satisfactory, even good. To do better is fine, but not expected. Secondary objectives are not generally permitted to stand in the way of realization of the profit rate sought, though occasionally and almost inadvertently this happens. Profit realization in this more or less precise meaning of the term is the primary objective motivating management.

This is true whether profit is sought in its own right, as the unit measuring performance, or as a means of pursuing anterior objectives.

Appendix to Chapter 5

PROFIT IMPROVEMENT PLAN *

A. Instructions

In order to focus attention of Division and Corporate management on the areas requiring profit improvement and to permit an organized and orderly approach to the solution of problem situations, it is necessary (1) to determine minimum standards of acceptable profit and return on investment; (2) to establish what the present situation is; (3) to plan future objectives and (4) to develop specific scheduled plans of action designed to improve the performance of the business from its present level of performance to one which is compatible with Corporate return-on-investment goals. "Product Improvement Programs," as defined in this way, should identify the problems which must be overcome, and should specify what action is required, who is responsible for the action, and when it will be initiated and completed.

(a) The problem should be approached by product group. The more the process can be narrowed to product lines, the more specific and effective it will be.

(b) Formulation and evaluation of a "Product Improvement Program" for each product group can generally be improved if projects are classified by purpose. The key objective of all planning is Return-on-Investment, a function of Margin and Turnover. These ratios are in turn determined by the three factors in the business equation—Volume, Costs and Assets. All projects therefore should be directed at one of the following:

To increase volume
To reduce costs and expenses
To minimize assets

* From one company's administrative manual.

(c) The projected effect of Product Improvement Programs can usually be expressed tangibly in terms of additional volume, reduced cost ratios and faster asset Turnover. Some of the projects (such as quality improvement, for instance) may not be subject to such measurement. In spite of this fact, the total sum of the effect of these projects must be judged against the tangible objectives, if the gap is to be closed between intention and reasonable profitability of accomplishment.

Each of the three factors—volume, costs and assets—are interrelated in their effect upon the other two. Further, the development of an integrated set of supporting programs requires that the programming effort of each of the several functions—Sales, Engineering, Manufacturing and Research —shall be co-ordinated. Therefore, orderly programming requires that some pattern of sequence of steps be adopted and that valid assumptions be established during the process as the basis for programming subsequent steps. Schedule 10 on page 79—"Profit Improvement Plan"—has been developed for divisions to assist them in the organization and evaluation of their programs. Each "Profit Improvement Plan" for a product group must be backed-up by detailed supporting programs. The organization of the supporting programs and the sequence of steps in completing them are outlined in detail below. Briefly, these steps involve (a) defining quantitatively the gap between present performance and the long-term objective (b) specifying the volume-increasing programs and translating the effect of the planned additional volume on income and assets (c) specifying the cost-reducing programs and translating their effect on income and assets and (d) specifying the asset-control programs and translating their effect on income and assets.

Schedule 10, and the supporting programs must be prepared and submitted for *each* product group, individually, which fails to meet the following minimum standards:

(a) 20% gross profit margin in current year.
(b) 15% return-on-investment in current year.

As a result of preparing these analyses and profit improvement programs, one of the following alternatives must develop:

(1) Programs *can* be planned to meet minimum profit standards.
(2) Division and Corporate management must determine whether or not to continue a product group if programs *cannot* be developed to meet minimum profit standards.
(3) Division and Corporate management must develop and present a plan of action to discontinue the product group.

The 20% gross profit margin goal established here as a criterion for Profit Improvement Programs does *not* meet Corporate objectives but has been selected as the first *minimum* step toward the accomplishment of these goals. Specific programs to be included in each of the profit improvement areas are (but not by way of limitation) as follows:

SCHEDULE 11. SALES INCREASING PROGRAMS

1) Unit Volume Increasing Programs (present, improved and new products).

2) Pricing Programs
(Programs docketed may involve the planned lowering of prices to increase sales of product units . . . or the planned raising of prices to increase product *margins.*)

3) Delivery and Service Improvement Programs.

4) Distribution Improvement Programs
(Programs docketed in this section should include not only those focused on distributors, jobbers, agents and dealers . . . but also those involving revised application of *company* sales manpower to cover product markets more effectively in terms of areas and industries.)

5) Sales Training Programs.

6) Advertising and Sales Promotion Programs
(Include in this section not only consumer promotional programs . . . but any major docketed action involving special motivation of sales personnel.)

7) Production Capacity Expansion Projects needed to support planned increases in sales volume.

SCHEDULE 12. COST DECREASING PROGRAMS

1) Product Design Programs
(Include in this section not only programs calling for major product standardization changes . . . but also those involving other product re-design for lower cost.)

2) Manufacturing Method Programs
(Include in this section not only programs involving major planned improvements of equipment and tools . . . but also docketed action aimed at more efficient layout and handling methods.)

3) Programs to Reduce Direct Labor and Direct Material Costs within the framework of lowest cost design and method specifications.

4) Expense Reduction Programs
(Include in this section action aimed at reducing Factory Indirect Labor and Expenses and Operating Expenses.)

SCHEDULE 13. ASSET MINIMIZING PROGRAMS

1) Line "Pruning" Programs.

2) Manufacturing cycle improvement programs to minimize work-in-process inventories.

3) Programs to minimize inventories of parts and finished products (purchasing policy, reduced lead time, controlled deliveries).

4) Programs to insure optimum utilization of Fixed Assets.
For each project docketed, indicate degree of accomplishment expected in the budget year and in the second year.

B. *Comments*
If Profit Improvement Programs for any product group do *not* produce at least 15% R.O.I. and 20% gross profit margin by the end of the second year submit either:

a) Reasons for continuing the product group, or

b) Plans for discontinuing the product group.

PROFIT IMPROVEMENT PLAN: PRODUCT GROUP

	Current year	Sales increasing programs Budget	2d yr.	Cost decreasing programs Budget	2d yr.	Asset minimizing programs Budget	2d yr.	Goals Budget	2d yr.
Net sales..............									
Cost of sales.........									
Gross profit.........									
% of net sales.......									
Operating expense....									
Pre-tax income.......									
Margin (% N.S.)......									
Inventory............									
Other working capital....									
Fixed assets.........									
Total............									
Asset turnover (net sales ÷ gross assets).									
R.O.I. (margin × turnover)....									

NOTE: Amounts shown for "Budget" and "2d yr." represent only incremental profit and asset improvement for that year.

Schedule 11   Sales Increasing Programs
Schedule 12   Cost Decreasing Programs
Schedule 13   Asset Minimizing Programs
       Product Group

_____
(Name)

Description of programs to follow

Chapter 6

THE PLANNING PROCESS: INTRODUCTION

The Argument to This Point

As we have seen, the use of budgets as an instrument for business planning extends over a time spectrum ranging from the near present to the distant future. It encompasses all units of the business organization, from the elemental production shop or sales department on up to the consolidated corporation. This makes for a procedure for planning which is relatively simple for a small establishment but which becomes highly complicated and intricately articulated in the large corporation.

Long-run strategical planning, which takes place for the most part at upper management levels, requires leaps of imagination from the operating people, translated into money terms by the financial people and confined within projected long-term balance sheets. Short-run tactical planning calls for a more precise and calculated statement of intentions and capabilities, converted into projected short-term income statements and balance sheets. Finally, the balancing of inflows and outflows of the funds which a realization of plans will provide and which are required for the realization of plans is charted in projections of the sources and applications of funds. Behind or underlying these structural mainstays of the planning process there are numerous additional supporting schedules such as the schedule for sales, manpower, materials, administration, research, and capital investment.

Motivating and guiding the fashioning of each of the pieces of this planning structure and their final assembly into the finished whole are the profit objective and secondary goals of the business. If these objectives have been clearly stated and widely disseminated within the firm to the responsible members of management, they will inform every phase of the planning process. Prices and volumes will be proposed to yield the planned sales receipts. Sales receipts will be planned to provide, relative to costs,

80

the planned return. Costs will be engineered, relative to the necessary production volume, to return the percentage on investment which has been set as target. Capital investment will be undertaken only when the profit to which it gives rise matches or exceeds the profit goal (assuming a stream of investment opportunities over time among which enough can be anticipated to meet this criterion to warrant foregoing investments which are simply profit-yielding rather than target-realizing).

It is the exceptional firm which states its targets so precisely and impresses its management hierarchy so emphatically with the relation of planning to goal. But even in the larger number of firms which leave the goal implicit (a profit better than last year, or as good as the best previous year, or equal to the competitor chosen as bench mark), the planning process is guided by these understood or assumed objectives.

Participants in the Planning Process

With respect to the pieces of the budget which apply to subunits in the organization, the principle which is generally stated, though frequently not followed, is that each supervisor should participate in the development of that part of the budget plan for which he has actual responsibility. As set forth in one company's guide:

> Each supervisor should establish his own budget based on knowledge of the job to be done. It may not be possible to approve each supervisor's budget in its entirety, but agreement can be reached on what he is expected to accomplish and what it will cost. Having done this, each supervisor is responsible for planned performance. Budgeting then becomes a trained, disciplined approach to problems, which recognizes the need for standards of performance in order to achieve results.

An official of a Massachusetts company writes:

> The Company believes strongly in the principle that for budgeting to be effective it must be done at all levels by the people who are responsible for the operation of the Company. Consequently, each of the divisions of the Company prepares its own budget which, after review and approval by management, are consolidated to give the over-all Company budgets. . . . To ensure a reasonable degree of consistency, certain major premises on which the budget is built are agreed upon and issued to the divisions.

A good many firms, however, are in the position of one steel company which presently, and admittedly, prepares its budget from the top down. Upper management, coordinated by the controller, puts together estimates which are then broken down into schedules and functions for distribution to the appropriate lesser management people who are held responsible for the performance indicated. Plans are now being made, however, for reversing this procedure to build the budget from the bottom up, with each unit supervisor given the initiative and responsibility for projecting his own operations.

The difference between these two approaches can easily be exaggerated, however. A subordinate's budget must always be approved, and it is always set on the basis of sales and production estimates which are determined elsewhere; it is, moreover, often based on "predetermined costs." Thus the degree of actual control at this level may be quite slight. Indeed, in some companies which make a fetish of supervisory participation in budget planning, preliminary estimates are sometimes prepared by the accounting or budget or controller's department for "approval" or "suggested modification" by the supervisor. Nevertheless, there is considerable merit in providing each supervisor with an opportunity to be heard before his part of the budget is written into the whole. Such a hearing may convert what otherwise would be an imposed task into a personal commitment. Indeed, there are reasons, as will be noted subsequently, why this "principle of participation" has become not just a shibboleth of a self-conscious management but a significant development in the organizational structuring of large-scale business enterprise.

The 1958 Controllership Foundation survey of business budgeting practices reported [1] that "common patterns of participation could be identified in the cooperating companies."

> First, it was evident that many lower-level supervisors participate in planning by actively developing or reviewing plans for the area supervised. Second, a successive screening and coordinating of plans occurs at each higher level of management prior to final approval by top management. Third, generally one individual assumes responsibility for consolidation of all plans into a master plan of operations. Fourth, it was obvious that top management finally coordinates and approves the over-all planning program and formulates general planning objectives.

Budgeting Philosophy

In all budget planning there is an inescapably ambiguous element. The essence of such planning is an effort to control the firm's future. This implies that the budget sets goals which are expected to be achieved by the means which are spelled out in the document. The corollary is that every effort will be made to adhere to the plan as cast. At the same time, every person connected with the preparation or execution of the plan is aware that because it is impossible to control the firm's environment, changes in the underlying situation and the firm's consequent position

[1] Sord and Welsch, *Business Budgeting*, p. 93.

(improved or worsened) can be expected. There thus runs through the planning process an *expectation* of achievement of objective coupled with an *expectation* of economic change which will make the result something different from plan. These two expectations are necessarily inconsistent.

The same inconsistency underlies any planning process, in any sphere of activity. The future cannot be wholly controlled, but neither is it necessary that it be left wholly uncontrolled. The element of uncertainty is what creates risk. It also creates opportunity. The development of the budgeting procedure in business has necessitated the development of an accompanying philosophy, which is sometimes included and explicitly labeled as such in budget documents. That philosophy emphasizes three characteristics of good budgeting practice: (1) the posing of specific goals, (2) the planning of specific paths to those goals, and (3) continuing attention to changes in the underlying assumptions which may suggest the desirability of modifying both ends and means and alertness to seize unexpected opportunities which were not foreseen at the time of budget preparation.

However frequently changed, the comprehensive budget imposes on management the necessity of thinking through the effects of particular actions on all phases of the business. It helps to emphasize interdependence and interrelationships within the organization, the moving general equilibrium within the firm. In this sense budgets cannot be said to "freeze" initiative, although the charge is sometimes made. They simply state the expected conditions under which any changes would have to be introduced.

The controller of one company put the matter in this way. "While we operate under complete budgetary control, we at no time will allow budget estimates to interfere with progress. If an expenditure or program is worthwhile, it shows as a variance and is explainable. We use budgets as a guide and a tool to achieve a goal, but the goal is not limited to dollar amounts that may be provided for in a budget."

The secretary-treasurer of another company similarly comments: "We believe that budgets should be a tool to be used in achieving better operating results. We have found the preparation of plans for the coming year to be one of the most valuable contributions budgeting can make to our operations. We have no hesitancy in making decisions which will result in variances from the budget if circumstances warrant such an action. We have learned such special actions are on a better foundation because of the earlier planning process."

In later chapters we shall examine in some detail the major facets of this planning program. First, however, it may be helpful to gain an overview of the process, shorn of detail, as it works itself out in three companies. One is a food processing firm, another a publisher, and the third a public utility. They have been selected because the very dissimilarity in the nature of their operations underscores the basic similarity in the planning approach.

The Case of a Food Processing Company

First, let us take a look at the budgeting procedure followed by the H. J. Heinz Company.[2]

> Keeping in mind that the profit plan covers one fiscal year in great detail and is influenced by, as well as consistent with, the company's long-range objectives and goals, preliminary work begins about four months prior to the completion of the operating plan. . . .
>
> The starting point is an objectives review. . . . The company's previous history of sales, earnings, price-cost relationships, market penetration and share of market obtained, etc., is reviewed. Particular attention is paid to the current year's operations and results to date and an up-to-date profit projection to the end of the current year. Major perennial problems are re-examined in the light of current progress (or lack of it) toward their solution. New problems that have arisen since the last objectives review and anticipated problems are carefully considered and appraised in establishing the basic objectives toward which the next year's profit plan will be projected. Also considered in establishing these objectives are the forecasts of profit and growth programs projected for the next five years. After considering and weighing all these factors, an over-all profit percentage of sales or minimum dollar amount is selected as an objective for the coming year. It is one which appears to be reasonable and acceptable in view of the company's current operations, long-range growth objectives and current and expected operating and profit levels of competitors.
>
> After the profit objective has been selected for the year, a sales budget is developed by the Marketing Division. . . . This budget details physical unit sales for every product, by size of container. Current selling prices are reviewed—base carload prices as well as order size mark-ups and cash discounts. Generally the policy is to use the current carload base price for the next year's budget except where there are unusual circumstances involving a particular item or where there are very sound reasons for expecting a change and some indication of its direction and magnitude. . . .
>
> A budget is also prepared by the Sales Promotion Department in collaboration with the Product Managers for special allowance and campaign discounts that have been planned for the coming year. This is developed by product and by time period. Sales units are then priced out by these various factors and become the sales income plan for the profit budget. . . .

[2] *Management Planning and Control: The H. J. Heinz Approach* (New York: Controllership Foundation), pp. 62–69, 61.

The next step in the program is the development of the production schedule for the year. . . . This is based on probable inventory schedules at the beginning of the fiscal year plus items in the sales budget less desired inventory at the year end. As with sales projections, the production plan is developed in detail for each product by size of container. This is done by discussions and cooperative analyses made by staffs of the Distribution Division and the Manufacturing Division. The production agreed upon is then allocated to the various factories. Among variables taken into consideration in making these allocations and developing the factory production schedules are available facilities, their relative efficiency, location with reference to sources of major ingredients and with reference to regions of heaviest projected sales of the varieties, etc. The production plan and factory production schedules then become the basis for determining overhead expenditures and rates for each factory point and thus the standard for absorption of overhead throughout the year. The development of individual factory schedules has an important effect on decisions to contract acreage for major agricultural commodities which are chief raw materials required for many of the allocated or scheduled varieties. It also has important connotations on the total delivered costs of products due to the relationship of production site versus market location. . . .

New individual consolidated cost sheets for each [product] variety are prepared at each factory. . . . These are based on the respective factory—

1. Production schedules.
2. Revised manufacturing standards for costs and yields.
3. Direct labor requirements.
4. Overhead distribution. . . .

These are utilized to develop weighted average standard costs in arriving at variety profit projection. . . .

Standard ingredient and packaging material unit costs generally are established at current levels as of the date the budget is prepared. This policy corresponds with the use of finished goods selling prices that are in effect as of the same date, and assumes that a realistic job has been done to keep selling prices in line with unit costs. These unit costs are not changed during the budget period. As the individual variety consolidated cost sheets are completed at a factory they are sent to the Comptroller's Division. There they are consolidated on the basis of the total allocated factory production into a weighted average variable manufacturing cost and a weighted average fixed manufacturing cost per variety. This becomes the inventory value of the variety for the coming year and the value that is charged against sales. . . .

The next item that is budgeted is freight. This is outgoing freight on the finished products and is the cost of transportation to the various sales warehouses and direct customers. Each product is analyzed, based on production location, expected geographic distribution, weight, and freight rates. An average freight cost is established for each product for the coming year.

Every sales branch location is responsible for the development of its expense budget for the fiscal year (based on experience, expected sales volume, etc.). Expenses are classified into variable and fixed cost elements. Budgets are consolidated by regions and for the total U.S.A. The variable costs are allocated to the individual varieties at the Home Office and also become part of the variety profit projection. . . . A profit projection for gross return (dollar and rate on sales) is developed for each variety, the components consisting of sales income, variable manufacturing costs, freight, and variable branch house expense. Each division and department of the Home Office prepares a detailed expense budget of all its expenditures by months for the coming year. All major changes from previous experience are explained in detail by department heads.

The advertising budget is developed early in the profit planning period and is built within the broad outline of policy objectives established at the time of the profit plan objectives review. Within this general framework of control, the Advertising and Sales Promotion Departments develop their strategy for individual programs. These are well coordinated with sales plans, growth objectives for individual products, market penetrations, special sales campaigns, introduction of new products, etc. . . .

Miscellaneous Expense and Income include such items as interest on borrowed money, miscellaneous rental expense and income, purchasing cash discounts, company's management profit sharing plan, contributions, etc. These items are budgeted by months and most of this planning is done in the Comptroller's Division and is based on past experience and knowledge of the profit plans for the coming year.

The various budgets and plans when completed and approved are then condensed and coordinated into an over-all company income statement. . . .

A capital expenditure budget is developed in detail for each fiscal year, and major capital expenditure plans are an integral part of the long-range profit forecast. . . .

A cash budget is also developed to portray how the cash position of the company will be affected by the attainment of the objectives set forth in the various operating budgets. Though not in itself a primary element of planning or control since it is dependent on and derived from the more basic operating plans, when properly prepared it will clearly disclose whether or not the company's reserves are going to be adequate to finance the volume of activity planned either for the coming fiscal year or during the projected five-year program. This budget is also the basis for determining interest expense, and, in the case of the long-range forecast, whether or not these plans can be financed on a temporary basis, or will require external financing of a permanent nature. It enables management to consider well in advance the means of obtaining the funds required.

The primary purpose of the cash budget, therefore, short-term or long-term, is to eliminate the element of surprise in finance operations and it has been developed to achieve this end. In order to show the effect on the company's financial condition resulting from attainment of the objectives of the operating plans, all major items of the balance sheet are budgeted. . . .

The plan is completed about three weeks prior to the beginning of the new fiscal year. It is then presented to the Operating Committee [composed of the six vice presidents and the Comptroller] for review and revised in accordance with the Committee's suggestions and requirements. After approval by the Operating Committee the plan, together with the long-range forecast, is presented to the Board of Directors for their consideration and approval. . . .

Once the fiscal year plan has been reviewed, refined and approved by the Board of Directors, it is not changed during the year. It becomes a rather rigid measuring stick against which operating results are compared. Variances are computed with reference to it and causes of such variances are highlighted while, at the same time, their composite effect on planned profit is estimated.

The Case of a Publisher

Next, let us examine the planning approach followed by the Meredith Publishing Company of Des Moines, publishers of *Better Homes and Gardens, Successful Farming,* and a number of handbooks for the home. The procedure is recounted by the company's controller:[3]

> Our system of budgeting was begun in 1928. . . . We have a Budget Committee, which provides the over-all guidance of the budget program. This Budget Committee is composed of the vice president and general manager of the company; the vice president in charge of circulation; the vice president in charge of advertising sales; the director of manufacturing; the assistant to the president, and the treasurer and controller.
>
> This committee represents all the divisions of the company, giving it an over-all viewpoint of operations and responsibility, as it could not do if made up entirely of financial people. We do not have an operating committee at our company, and this committee does not function as one, although problems affecting expenditures and profits and budgets may be brought to it for discussion and recommendation. Since the members of this committee are division heads, they carry

[3] Kenneth W. Hill, "A Case History in Budgeting and Cost Control," in *Budgeting, Forecasting and Return on Investment,* Controllers Institute, papers presented at the 24th annual conference, 1955, extracted from pp. 10–16.

back to their division and departments the budget philosophy and thinking.

Within the Financial Control Division we have a Budgets and Standards Section, which does most of the budget work from an accounting point of view. . . .

Our fiscal year begins on July 1 and our budgets are made up for twelve months in advance.

We begin our budget planning as early as the month of April. During that period, our Advertising Sales Department is busy with what we call our Sales Review Sessions. Our home office people go to the branch offices and discuss with the branch manager and the individual salesmen the probable amount of advertising sales revenue that we will sell to each advertising customer that is in each man's territory. These figures are gone over very carefully with each salesman and the branch manager involved; as a result, each salesman is made to feel that he is a vital part of this over-all sales planning for the coming budget year.

These estimates of unit advertising sales are then brought back and summarized by our Research Production Department. Our Advertising Department is then able to estimate advertising sales for each magazine for each month of the coming fiscal year. These figures are carefully reviewed to see whether or not they seem reasonably possible of attainment, to assure us that they are the best estimate of our sales volume for the budget period. Necessarily, in the magazine business this is the very key to the workload for many of our departments. Not only is it tied with the amount of sales effort and promotion that will be required, but it also is the governing factor in determining the number of pages in the magazines.

During the same period, the sales analysis section of our Book Sales Division has been preparing the sales projection for each book; planning ahead as to how many copies of each book will be sold, and determining what sales and promotional efforts will be necessary to meet the desired sales volume. From these budgeted sales quantities we are able to project revenue and manufacturing costs for this division.

Our Circulation Department does its planning as to what sales effort it will have to make, and what mailings will have to be undertaken, in order to maintain the circulation figures at the desired level for each given month. It prepares detailed plan sheets of promotional mailings to be sent out—including production and mailing costs, anticipated revenue and returns—to make sure there will be the proper number of subs in the house at the proper time to maintain the desired level of circulation. It necessarily works closely with our newsstand distributor, the S-M News Company, to determine the estimated newsstand draw, estimated return and net sales, as well as what the costs will be for the year ahead.

From such figures obtained from the Advertising, Book and Circulation Divisions, we are able to determine accurately for each magazine the total budgeted revenue; the book sizes; the press run of each issue, and the manufacturing costs of the books to be sold. As soon as this estimated workload is determined, each department affected receives that information before it begins the preparation of its particular budget. . . .

We ask each department head to prepare his budget on the basis of the expected workload as previously furnished him. The Budgets and Standards Section of the Financial Control Division then takes this budget and completes it by filling in payroll and social security, and prepares it for review by the Budget Committee. . . .

In preparation for the budget review sessions, the Budgets and Standards Section summarizes all budgets and pulls them together on the basis on which they are submitted, in order to give the Budget Committee a picture of what the results would be if budgets as presented were met for the year ahead. This preview of the operating statements for the two magazines and book operations gives the Budget Committee a chance to evaluate the anticipated results, and to formulate plans and policies to curtail contemplated excessive expenditures, where necessary. . . .

From the preview that was given the Budget Committee of results as budgeted, it was easy to determine where our operations appeared to be strong and where they were weak, and what should be done in order to strengthen them. Then, we went into our Budget Review Session with each of the department heads, with the Budget Committee having received the Budgets & Standards Section summary of the department's budget along with explanatory comments, comparison with prior years and other pertinent information.

We regard this budget review session as the department head's "day in court" in which he is given an opportunity to detail his plans, state his problems and acquaint the Budget Committee with any new developments in his particular line of work. We feel that it accomplishes these things:

1. Better understanding of company objectives on the part of the department heads.

2. It serves as a means to up-date the Budget Committee on problems and operations of all departments.

3. It brings up the need for special studies on situations or problems that need checking and special attention.

After the various budgets are reviewed—and we have over 50 in all—we prepare the budgeted operating statements for each of the magazines and the Book Sales Division. We show expected earnings by product, by month and for the year. These final budgets are summarized for the Budget Committee. If tentatively approved, they are then reviewed with our president and general manager for final acceptance. We carry the process to the point of making up budgeted balance sheets and cash forecasts.

If it appears that budgeted profits, in the opinion of the Budget

Committee, are not adequate, then the division heads are asked to review their budgets with their department heads in order to cut back expenses and help provide an adequate profit. One year, our budgeted figures showed that departmental expense was increasing at a far more rapid rate than justified by our revenues. We went over the budgets again and were able to cut back on certain projects which, although desirable, were not essential to the efficient operation of the company. As a result, we were able to provide a more satisfactory operation.

The Case of a Utility

A third example of the budgeting process is drawn from the profit planning and budgeting guide of a major Middle Western public utility.

FIVE-YEAR LOAD AND REVENUE FORECAST

The basic planning instrument of the budget program is the Five-Year Load and Revenue Forecast. Income, expenses and capital expenditures are closely related to the trends of kilowatt hour sales and peak loads, thus the entire planning program depends upon the accuracy and validity of the Load and Revenue Forecast.

This forecast is prepared in the fall of each year and covers the succeeding five-year period. The first two years show data by months and the last three by annual totals. Principal components of the Load and Revenue Forecast are:

(1) Economic outlook of general business activity including such items as new plant and equipment expenditures, construction activity, inventories, government and consumer expenditures, housing starts, and industrial production.

(2) Customers, kilowatt hour sales and revenues by rate schedules.

(3) Steam heating sales and revenues.

(4) Fuel and purchased power.

(5) Plant heat rates.

(6) Peak loads.

(7) Generation statistics.

Preliminary estimates of kilowatt hours, peak loads and revenues are made in the Budget and Statistical Section. Representatives of the Finance, Marketing, Operations, Engineering, and General Services Groups participate in establishing the principal components of the forecast. The basic premises of the forecast are then reviewed by the Vice President—Finance and the Vice President—Marketing and approved by the Chairman of the Board and the President, before release of the data for general planning purposes.

After approval the data are incorporated in the Load and Revenue Forecast which becomes the basis for future planning, forecasting, and budgeting. Pertinent data relative to customer growth, industrial activity, kilowatt hour production, peak loads, price levels, and revenues are furnished to all departments to guide them in the preparation of their budgets. This ensures that individual departmental planning, both construction and operating, is based on the same set of assumptions regarding the future. . . .

OPERATING BUDGETS AND FORECASTS

(1) *Functional Budgets*

Immediately following the release of the approved premises for the Load and Revenue Forecast, each department manager should start the preparation of his Functional Budget for the subsequent year. Functional Budgets are normally prepared in October and comprise estimates for each month of the succeeding calendar year. Revisions may be made if developments occur which are significant enough to alter the basic premises used for Company planning.

Departmental plans and budgets should reflect the basic assumptions contained in the Load and Revenue Forecast and the Construction Work Schedule, as well as the individual needs and requirements of the element.

In planning for the future, careful consideration should be given to all areas of the element's operations. Some of these areas are:

Performance goals
Performance measures to be installed or improved
Procedures and methods changes
Training and development of employees
Organization planning
Safety goals
Operations Improvement
Workloads
Backlogs
Personnel requirements
    Replacement of key individuals
    Turn-over rates
Man-hours, wage rates, and labor costs
    Regular
    Overtime
    Operation and maintenance
    Property and plant
Other-than-labor expenditures
    Discretionary items such as petty and travel expense, training, maintenance, and special assignments
Staff activities

The results of the planning in terms of requirements for employees, regular and overtime hours, wage rates, and other-than-labor expenditures should be recorded by departmental supervisors on Functional Budget forms. . . . Budget estimates should be approved by the responsible Group Vice President and returned to the Budget and Statistical Section for incorporation in the Company Operating Budget.

Wage costs are computed in the Budget and Statistical Section, for each function. Summaries of employees, man-hours, wages, and other-than-labor expenditures are tabulated by Groups on a departmental basis. The Budget and Statistical Section furnishes each manager with a summary of these data for his department early in November.

(2) *Budget Planning Reports*

Functional Budgets should be supported by Budget Planning Reports which contain all pertinent information on the plans and proposals incorporated in the budget figures. A list of the primary areas covered in these reports is shown under "Functional Budgets." A Progress Section is also included in which comments should be made on progress towards the goals previously established in the budget for the current year.

Each Group must submit a Budget Planning Report comprising an over-all summary and individual reports from divisions and departments. These reports are due on the first of December. Copies are sent to the Chairman of the Board, President, and the Budget and Statistical Section.

(3) *Preliminary Income and Cash Forecasts*

Using the data contained in the Load and Revenue Forecast and the Functional Budgets, the Budget and Statistical Section prepares preliminary income and cash forecasts for each month of the budget period.

Major components of the income and cash forecasts also include taxes, depreciation, interest charges, credits to income for interest capitalized, and construction expenditures. All elements specializing in these areas are consulted in making these estimates. These forecasts are prepared during October and November.

(4) *Budget Presentation*

A review of the over-all financial outlook based on the Load and Revenue Forecasts, Functional Budgets and Preliminary Income and Cash Forecasts is prepared in the Budget and Statistical Section. A critical analysis of all phases of the budget program is made, including such items as earnings, rates of return, man-hours and dollars per customer, labor costs, taxes, depreciation, cash position and financing. The Budget and Statistical Section is charged with the responsibility of determining and reporting on favorable and unfavorable trends that may affect future operations.

The results of this review are presented to the Chairman of the

Board and the President about the first of December. This report provides top management with an analysis of the over-all financial effects of the functional planning of all elements in advance of consideration of individual budgets.

(5) *Approval of Functional Budgets*

Group Functional Budgets and Planning Reports are submitted to the Chairman of the Board and the President for review and approval on December 1. Individual meetings are scheduled with several Vice Presidents during December. Division and department heads may be invited to these meetings to discuss specific plans within their areas of responsibility. The Budget Planning Reports provide the basic information for discussion of each element's plans, goals, and requirements for labor and other costs.

Changes in plans affecting number of employees, man-hours, and other-than-labor expenditures resulting from these December meetings are incorporated by the departments in their Functional Budgets. The plans and associated expenses agreed to at these meetings constitute the approved program for each Group for the succeeding year.

(6) *Approved Income and Cash Forecasts*

Preliminary income and cash forecasts are then revised by the Budget and Statistical Section to reflect the approved functional budgets and any other changes in basic forecasts which have occurred during the budget review period. All budgets and forecasts for the calendar year are normally completed by January 1 of that year. . . .

(8) *Chronological Summary—Operating Budget*

The chronological sequence of the steps required in the preparation of the Operating Budget is summarized as follows:

1. Five-Year Load and Revenue Forecast is prepared and significant data released by the Budget and Statistical Section early in the fall.
2. Functional Budgets for the succeeding year are prepared in October by department supervisors using the basic premises of the Five-Year Load and Revenue Forecast as a guide.
3. Budget Planning Reports are written by department managers and Group Vice Presidents in support of their budget requests during October and November.
4. Preliminary Income and Cash Forecasts are assembled in the Budget and Statistical Section during October and November.
5. Review of the budget outlook is presented to the Chairman of the Board and the President about December 1.
6. Approval of Group Budgets is obtained at individually scheduled meetings with the Chairman of the Board and President.
7. Operating budgets including functional, income, and cash

budgets, are revised to reflect any changes resulting from the executive review and are released normally by January 1.

The Budgeting Sequence

Outlines of budgeting procedures, such as the three reproduced above, convey an impression of an orderly sequence of steps leading logically to an end result. Actually, information which is provided by any one of the steps frequently depends on information from other steps both prior and subsequent to it, or, more correctly, many estimates logically should be made simultaneously. Thus an estimate of sales revenues requires prior estimates of volume and prices projected, but to some extent the prices selected depend on the costs of production, which cannot be determined until volume is known, with volume in turn depending on prices. Costs of production depend on the production function (the combination of machines and men), which in turn is governed by capital investment, which is affected by the rate of return on investment (profit) both of single processes and of company performance as a whole, the latter in turn being partially determined by the costs of production. As a matter of practice, however, the process is simplified by expedient short cuts which do for the purpose. Most companies reach their budget results by a series of approximations, taking present rates as the point of departure.

In all three of these instances of the budgeting process, and quite typically, planning starts with a sales (revenue) forecast. From this are projected a production schedule and the cost of sales. This yields the gross profit margin. Supplementary schedules set out overhead expenses for selling, administration, engineering, and research, leaving the net profit margin. Capital expenditure budgets complete the allocations against revenues, except for payments to the owners. If sales revenues do not add up to an inflow sufficient to cover the projected outflow, other forms of financing must be provided for.

There is no reason to suppose, however, that the results reached on the first "trial run" will be viewed as satisfactory. Despite the reasonable assumption, mentioned in the Heinz statement, that "a realistic job has been done to keep selling prices in line with unit costs," there are a variety of reasons why projected inflows may not cover projected outflows at the level of operations which, given the anticipated circumstances, management considers both feasible and desirable and at the same time return a profit consonant with corporate objectives. When this is the case, adjustments in the proposed budget are called for in an effort to come closer to the mark. In some cases there may be as many as a dozen trials before a budget plan is put together the achievement of which would be considered satisfactory.

Managerial Manipulations

We shall examine this process in more detail later. It is enough for present purposes to realize that the job of budget making is more than simply putting a number of projections on paper to see where the company is likely to be, financially, twelve months hence. A *planning* process is at work, in which the numerous estimates must be cut to a pattern in order to achieve the fit which is wanted.

The cutting and fitting are not simply with respect to figures on a piece of paper, however. It is the next year's operations which are being tailored to accomplish a desired result. In this process management possesses a number of degrees of freedom, as we shall see. The introduction of new products or the modification of old ones may be accelerated or postponed. Prices may be moved up or down. Costs may be manipulated by varying the materials component, the production function, the design or quality of the product, the work flow, and so on. The amount of industrial research and capital investment may be modified.

All these are adjustments which can be *planned,* before the budget year begins. They are designed to enable management to come up with what may be called the *projected balance.* It is not simply a question of seeing to it that outflows are covered by inflows. It is not even primarily a question of balancing inflows against outflows in such a way as to achieve the desired profit objective, though that comes closer to the purpose. Even more basically, it is the attempt to plot inflows against outflows not only to achieve some profit target but also to accomplish this at a level of operations, and with the kind of operations, which hold together the organization whose many parts it is management's job to coordinate.

That coordination is not simply a technical matter of assuring that the right number of the various kinds of skills and functional contributions are present to provide the flow of products and services which the short-run and long-run plans call for. It is that, to be sure; but in order to effect such technical coordination it is necessary first to satisfy the demands or requirements of all those who are necessary to the technical result. This is a coordination of the bargains which all the participants are striving to make with the company—bargains which involve levels of remuneration, promises of advancement, and assurances that personal judgments on what is regarded as desirable business practice will be accepted. Since these demands, made by people of conflicting interests and points of view, cannot normally all be satisfied, it is necessary for management to manipulate the demands in such a way as to make them consistent and compatible not only with each other but also with the budget. Whatever additional costs are entailed in the meeting of certain demands (that wages be raised, that stock options be granted, that research funds be increased, that advertising for a new product be doubled, that office space be expanded, that severance pay be awarded, and so on) must be embodied in the budget, and in such a way that not only are they adequately covered by inflows (even if these must be gained through borrowing), but the meeting of such demands as are necessary to hold the organization together does not itself endanger the corporate objectives, either short-run or long-run.

In the next few chapters we shall be examining the principal budget items and the basis on which their values are projected for planning purposes. In these chapters one of the central points of interest is the flexibility permitted to management in deciding on the projection which also becomes the plan. The market forces and the technology within which management must operate are powerful determinants of what management is free to do, but they are not wholly determining. There remain areas and respects in which management is capable of deciding what, whether, how much, and when. It is this discretionary element which makes planning purposeful.

As time unfolds, the circumstances anticipated when the budget was drawn may not materialize. Economic forces and market pressures may prove to be different from what was expected, modifying actual performance from planned performance. Management's hopes may turn out to have been rosier or grayer than the facts, so that operations exceed or fall short of plans. In either event, some adjustment is called for. The *actual balance* which is being realized deviates from the projected balance. It may not be possible for management to take such effective action that, in the circumstances actually prevailing and now expected to prevail, it can achieve the original target. But by manipulation and adaptation it may be able to do better than it is currently doing, to come closer to the original target even if it cannot reach it. This calls for budget revision, for the substitution of a new plan for the old—now unrealizable—one. We may call this the *preferred balance*. In later chapters we shall examine the nature of such adjustments, which are designed to put the budget back in tune with a future which is realizable and can be planned for. For once budgets lose touch with the realizable, they cease to be a guide to action.

The Corporate Image

One other point is worth noting. The making of a budget necessarily involves the building of the image of the company, both to itself and to its public. Behind every estimate is some conception of the character of the company. In computing sales revenue, product and price are inescapably components, and together they reveal where the company chooses to put itself on the price-quality spectrum for the industry. Into costs go wage rate levels, revealing where the company prefers to locate itself on the community's wage escalator. Costs are also contributed by materials, with the amount depending on the quality of the ingredients which are built into the company's product. The nature of a company's investments indicates how management regards the operation—as one to be held together at minimum cost for maximum quick return, or as one which builds for growth and expansion over a long-run future. Every decision which finds its way as an estimate into the budget plan constitutes a line in the corporate portrait.

Chapter 7

THE PRINCIPAL SOURCE OF FUNDS: SALES

Sales as the Pivot of Planning

The principal source of funds in a business is sales. Production for sale is also the principal cause of outflows. Sales thus constitute the pivot on which profit-making activity swings. In a going business they are the focus of all planning. This is as true of long-term planning—with its projections of the likely sales resulting from and justifying new investment—as of short-range budgeting, which involves contracting for the materials and men needed to fulfill the sales about to be made. In the words of one corporation official:[1]

> On both a short- and a long-range basis, the sales forecast is an important element in our financial planning and control. It is used as a cornerstone for such things as budgeting capital equipment expenditures and projecting future cash flows and sources of funds. In production it is used for such things as equipment and facilities planning, raw material stockpiling, and purchasing plans. The sales forecast plays an equally important role in other company areas: It is used as a basis for our budgetary controls systems, for planning manpower requirements, and for setting sales quotas.

Particularly in those industries which have seasonal peaks, requiring prior production to meet peak demand, is sales planning essential if idle equipment and customer delays are to be avoided. "We must produce for inventory in the cement business, since our summer shipments far exceed our production capacity. We set our production schedules at the first of the year based upon sales forecasts."

[1] John E. Menz, vice-president and general sales manager, Kaiser Aluminum and Chemical Sales, Inc., "Coordinating the Marketing Plan with the Sales Forecast," in *Materials and Methods of Sales Forecasting*, A.M.A. Special Report 27, New York, 1957, p. 193.

An official of the Minnesota Mining and Manufacturing Company reports: [2]

> We have in our company case histories in which manufacturing costs have been reduced 10 percentage points in a three-year period. The prime mover has been sales forecasts, intelligently converted into manufacturing language, which sets the stage for constructive programs for cost reduction. Some of the results have been:
> —Unemployment costs reduced to the basic minimum.
> —Machine run time increased from 70 to 90 per cent of available time.
> —Operator performance attainment 20 per cent above normal.
> —Waste costs reduced.
> —Inventory investment controlled to approved limits.

And with respect to long-run forecasting, the head of market analysis of a rubber company wrote: [3]

> Decisions regarding capital expenditures and capital requirements invariably are based on estimates as to future prospects. The probable trend of demand for a specific product or for a class of products, or of demand in a specific area and of the probable profits are, in the final analysis, the foundation for any decision as to what we will make, how much capacity we will build, where we will build it, and how and where we will distribute what we do make.

Forecasting in Perspective

The same high estimate of the importance of the sales forecast and budget in business planning is a persistent theme in all discussions of the topic. Repeatedly phrases occur such as "Comprehensive budgeting begins with the sales budget," or "Business planning starts with the sales forecast."

Perhaps the greatest deterrent to the practice of formal budgeting is the double recognition (1) that sales forecasting is essential to it and (2) that sales forecasting is fraught with pitfalls. One company writes that it abandoned its efforts at budgeting when it found that they were largely a fruitless exercise in outguessing the market. Particularly in some lines of business is this feeling of helplessness found. The president of a hotel chain says that it has come to rely on day-to-day adjustments by local managers. "Our rooms are sold one day at a time and our restaurant sales are subject to the whims of a transient clientele. In addition, neither the use of our rooms on one day nor our food prepared for service at one meal

---

[2] Harold W. Rehfeld, "The Manufacturing Man's Viewpoint," in the same, p. 189.

[3] Quoted in Robert Eisner, *Determinants of Capital Expenditure* (Urbana: University of Illinois, 1956), p. 80.

can be returned to inventory and sold later. Since we have no contracts for the sale of our services, we cannot budget sales."

Some analysts, observing the frequent degree of error in business forecasts, have tended to cast doubt on the feasibility of business planning in general, at least in the sense of laying out a course of action stretching much beyond the point in time at which one stands.

Beyond the question of how accurate, in fact, the sales forecasts of a business firm are, however, is the further question of how important it is that they be accurate. That question may at first sound strange in view of the universal testimony of business managers that the sales estimate underlies all business planning.[4] Nevertheless, it is possible that a high degree of accuracy may not be as vital as at first appears, and that accuracy within as wide a margin as 5 or even 10 per cent in any one year may be sufficient for planning purposes, however desirable a higher degree of approximation may be. There are two reasons for this view.

For one thing, the very act of planning alerts an organization to contingencies, even if the basis on which plans are laid proves to be in error. While a correct plan is obviously preferable to an incorrect one, it may also be the case that an incorrect plan is better than none if it makes the parts of the firm more conscious of what may arise to upset their calculations. An example is provided by the controller of the A. B. Dick Company.[5]

> Suppose, for example, that you are a general sales manager. You are asked by the controller for a budget of sales volume and expense for the coming year—the first three months separately and the remainder of the year by quarters. This is a fairly common way to make a budget. You pinpoint the period immediately ahead but are not asked to be quite so accurate in timing the remainder of the year.
> You know from experience that you have to do a good job in pre-

[4] And this vivid description of the penalties of poor forecasting provided by John A. Blum, operations analysis manager, Lever Brothers Company, in "Expense Control in a Changing Business Environment," *Control of Non-manufacturing Costs,* A.M.A. Special Report 26, pp. 20–21: "Failure to be realistic in sales budgeting is bound to have a critically adverse effect on the entire organization. Impossibly high quotas are set for the field sales staff, whose spirit can be broken in the process. Manufacturing schedules, initially set in relation to budgeted sales, must be cut drastically as inventories mount and working capital is tied up. Advance contractual commitments —for insertion schedules, for example, or for broadcast properties for a number of months ahead—hang around the neck of the advertising manager. Plant layoffs and other reductions of manpower follow, with all their attendant costs and individual hardships. Work programs of one sort or another are similarly affected throughout the organization, and morale drops to an unproductively low level. This is certainly a pathological condition in business."

[5] James L. Pierce, "The Planning and Control Concept," *The Controller,* September, 1954, p. 4.

paring this plan—not because you will be fired if you do not meet it, but because the actions of so many other people are geared to your planning. You also know that there are going to be a lot of explanations to make if your actual performance is not according to plan. So you resolve to plan very carefully and insist that your subordinates do likewise with respect to their parts of the process.

But the first thing you stumble on is a new product shortly to be released by the research division. . . .

The difficulty is that the research director can give no firm date by which the new item will be available for distribution. It may be six months or it may be twelve. Unfortunately, this makes it impossible to plan effectively the advertising program with which the product must be introduced. It raises difficult questions about the hiring and training of additional sales personnel. It upsets any fine calculations as to the necessary lead time for the purchase of materials and the hiring of production personnel, the development of the necessary tools and the devising of appropriate factory layout. Yet until all these elements can be properly meshed together, it is impossible to determine whether the sales budget for the coming year will include revenues from the new product and what the production budget will include in the way of costs.

Even in this difficult situation planning is not wholly out of the question, however. Depending on the nature of the product development, it may prove feasible to pin down the research director to a more specific completion date, although this means that the imposed deadline holds out the danger of added pressure on and overtime work for the research staff. But even if such a date cannot be set, responsible officials in the organization have been made more conscious of the need for maintaining an alert to this probable development and for ensuring a proper coordination of their roles when it comes. At a minimum, it will be possible for the sales manager (and his colleagues in other departments) to work out a schedule indicating when it will be, after completion date for the new item, that he and they will feel the effects in their actual balances and to prepare in advance the operating adjustments which will then have to find their way into budget revisions.

There is, however, an even more telling reason why forecast accuracy is important only within limits.

In a previous chapter it was noted that business planners customarily budget to achieve some target. With a realization, however, of the penalties of gearing an organization to the achievement of an objective which proves, in the event, impossible of realization, there has developed over the years the principle of flexible or variable budgeting, which we shall examine more fully in a subsequent chapter. Briefly, this involves working out the appropriate budget relationships of all variable and semivariable expense items for any level of activity within a relevant range. As the firm moves into its budget period and actual performance can be laid alongside budgeted performance, any material variation of one from the other can be made the basis for prompt budget revision by substituting the cost figures appropriate to the actual level of activity for those in the original budget. Prompt action may thus forestall some of the more dire consequences of inaccurate forecasting pictured in footnote 4 above.

Flexible budgeting cannot, however, do much about fixed expenses, which may have been incurred in anticipation of the original budgeted sales level and which may again prove appropriate if present performance turns out to be temporary. It is with respect to fixed costs that accuracy in forecasts is most important. But for this purpose it is the long-run, rather than short-run, forecast that is most relevant—the trend rather than fluctuations around the trend. A 5 and even 10 per cent variation of actual sales from those budgeted, if viewed as temporary, will normally not be regarded as fatal or even serious to the financial health of the firm.

Under flexible budgeting, then, the operating plan sets out an objective which is viewed as feasible, but standby plans are held in readiness for changed circumstances. A high degree of initial accuracy is not necessary to make planning effective if one is prepared to modify plans as time unfolds. The projected balance is the objective sought in anticipation of what is to come, but as the actual balance departs from it, the firm's goal may realistically be altered and incorporated into a new, preferred balance (preferred, that is, over the actual, not necessarily over the original projected balance). The preferred balance and the budget which leads to it now become the new projected balance. Should the actual again deviate significantly from it, again a new preferred balance is struck through budget revision, becoming once again the projected balance and the new (revised) budget, and so on into the indefinite future.

A budget is thus always in the process of being approximated even though seldom realized. As helpful as it is to start out being close to one's mark, initial inaccuracy does not mean that the planning effort is pointless but only that adjustments must be made sooner or more frequently or more sweepingly than otherwise would be necessary. But the planning effort is helpful in revealing the adjustments which should be made more clearly and more quickly than otherwise would be the case.

The Time Scale for Sales Planning

Time is a continuum over which projected balances continually are at variance with the actual balance being realized and continually give way to new preferred balances, which continually become the new objectives and so the new projected balances. Discrete time intervals into which the continuum is divided are simply arbitrary stages for taking action. It is not really material whether the sales plan extends for a year, or whether revisions are made monthly or quarterly, or whether a long-range plan is for five or ten years. These are simply convenience points in time for planning the continuum as far as one can see (like birthdays or New Year's Days, in a person's life, when he normally takes stock of where he is and where he is going, even though he also does so at other less "formal" times in the year).

The nature of the business will dictate the intervals at which the convenience points for forecasting or reforecasting are set. One respondent, the treasurer of a publishing company, comments:

> The business of publishing syndicated newspaper supplements is a volatile one. Our primary source of revenue is advertising sales; and we have found that forecasting the sale of advertising for a full year's period is merely a mental exercise. What we do instead, and this has proved to be more practical, is to forecast one quarter ahead on a fairly firm basis and six months ahead on a tentative basis. . . . Direct costs are projected in the same way advertising sales and revenue is projected—by quarter and six-month periods.

The president of one Western railroad writes:

> We have found that an earnings forecast beyond a six months period is of little value because of the importance of agricultural products upon our freight revenues. A twelve months forecast would require much better advance weather information than we now have. In other words, it is almost impossible to forecast, for example, in the month of February the rail movement of a crop the seed for which has not been placed in the ground. Furthermore, marketing patterns have changed radically under Government loan programs,which has further complicated revenue forecasts. There might be a heavy rail haul in a poor crop year because of the movement out of storage of crops raised in prior years. The reverse can also be true. A major portion of the crop raised in a good year might be placed under Government loan and stored on farms and at other interior locations with only a minimum movement by rail.

Similarly, some retail operations or clothing lines operate with seasonal forecasts centering around a spring and a fall season. The important point, however, is that—like planning itself—some estimate, covering some time interval extending into the future, must inescapably be made as long as a business continues. Sales budgeting within the planning framework attempts to systematize the forecasting process, to identify all the variables likely to affect it (particularly those over which management itself has some control), and to relate actual performance to expected performance at frequent enough intervals to permit adjustment of the organization to changed circumstance.

Forecasting and Budgeting

One other point should be made before we explore how the process actually works out in American business. Sales budgeting, within the planning framework, is not identical with sales forecasting. It begins with the forecast, which purports to show the level of activity which might be realized under given conditions. But because planning is directed to a target, the forecast result is not always viewed as satisfactory. The planning aspect of the process enters when management seeks to modify the results originally viewed as probable to achieve results considered preferable. Promotion may be stepped up. The sales and distribution organization may be revised. Product design may be improved. A number of managerial decisions may be made intended to change the result from that forecast by modifying the underlying conditions on which the original forecast is based.

Forecasting Procedures: The Basic Assumptions

Although there are numerous variants of forecasting procedure in business, it is possible to identify what may be called the typical approach. First, there is a projection of general business and economic conditions for the country as a whole. These are sometimes referred to as the "basic assumptions" on which any company forecasts are presumed to rest. Second, there is an estimate of the likely level of activity in the relevant industry or industries. Finally, there is a forecast of company activity, usually distilled from three sources: the product managers (those responsible for a particular line or product group), the area or sales managers (often involving the participation of the field sales staff), and the home-office market research unit.

There is little point in elaborating business practice with respect to economy-wide projections. The largest corporations rely on their own staff economists for these estimates, but most businesses tend to adopt forecasts prepared by government economists, trade associations, private research groups such as the National Industrial Conference Board, or economics staffs of the larger banks. They may adopt estimates from some single source or effect some "compromise" among several estimates. They may undertake the latter themselves, or they may enlist the services of a consultant. In any event, there is no dearth of ready-made material. The problem is one of selection. By and large, this presents no major obstacles to most enterprises.

The first-stage procedure at the Westinghouse Electric Corporation has been described as follows: [6]

> All company forecasts are based on estimates of general business conditions prepared by the business projections committee. This group, which is made up of the treasurer (as chairman), the budget director, sales vice-president, purchasing vice-president and the manager of market planning (who reports to the sales vice-president), meets twice a year to forecast the pattern of general business conditions for the succeeding five years. This involves reviewing, revising, and extending year-by-year forecasts for about ten major business indexes. In doing so, the committee makes all important assumptions which may affect general business conditions and company sales—assumptions such as the rate of government spending, the international situation, etc.
>
> All members of this committee have company-wide interests and are in a position to be objective. While none is a professional economist, the members keep abreast of economic and business developments by extensive reading and by maintaining contacts with knowledgeable people in their respective fields. Also, the committee is free to retain consultants. The economic forecasts issued by this group form the framework for subsequent forecasting activity throughout the company and assure common thinking insofar as external business conditions enter into consideration.

Forecasting Industry Sales Levels

Forecasts of the level of activity for the industry or industries in which a company operates are generally made by simple or multiple correlation based upon some general economic series. Again, the Westinghouse experience is illustrative:

> The headquarters market planning (marketing research) group uses the basic forecasts of the business projections committee in developing estimates for about one hundred indexes that have proven valuable in forecasting the level of sales of electrical products. . . .
>
> These five-year forecasts are tabulated and charted in a booklet that is distributed to divisional and sales district market planning men. It is the latter's function to establish both the long-term (five-year) and short-term (one-year) estimates of total industry sales for their particular products. These are generally based upon statistical analyses of the historical relationship between their product lines and selected indexes from among those forecast by the headquarters market planning department.

Examples of simple correlations which are actually used in industry

[6] *Forecasting in Industry,* NICB Studies in Business Policy, no. 77, New York, 1956, p. 37. The quotation immediately following is from the same source, pp. 37–38.

forecasts are readily obtainable. In the ethical drug industry it is said that for every 10 per cent change in disposable personal income, there is a corresponding 5 per cent change in industry sales.[7] "Many years' experience has shown a strong correlation between disposable income and [soft floor-covering] volume. A normal year's industry volume equals 0.21 per cent of actual disposable income." [8] Other industries have relied on multiple correlation techniques. A spokesman for Republic Steel has described that company's approach: [9]

> We have found through multiple correlation techniques that five portions of the gross national product are particularly related to the demand for steel. They are: (1) consumer durable goods expenditures; (2) investment in producers' durable equipment; (3) new construction; (4) government expenditures, exclusive of construction expenditures and wages and salaries; and (5) changes in business inventories. The forecasts of these GNP components are combined in a mathematical formula to give us an estimate of the nation's over-all steel requirements.
>
> While the foregoing over-all steel demand forecast is being worked out, our market analysts are studying the activity and outlook for each of twenty-two major steel-consuming industries. Subsequently, these industry-by-industry forecasts are totaled to give another over-all forecast of steel consumption.
>
> The most elaborate of the industry analyses are those for the three largest users of steel: automobiles, construction, and machinery. Current and prospective trends in sales, orders, production, and inventories are studied for each industry. These trends are examined in the light of factors such as the outlook for capital expenditures, personal disposable income, scrappage or demolition rates, depreciation policies and many others, depending on the industry being reviewed. There is nothing unusual about our methods of statistical analysis, which include correlation studies, examination of the supply and demand situation, evaluation of current expert opinion, and interpretation of historical trends.
>
> The key forecast in the case of each industry is that for production. We estimate each industry's steel consumption on the basis of our forecast of its total production and data on the amount of steel required per unit of production. These latter data are based on records of past performance in various steel-consuming industries and, where available, on actual bills of material listing the items incorporated into a finished product. American Iron and Steel Institute statistics of shipments to steel-consuming industries are a source of information for this part of the forecast.

[7] The same, p. 24.
[8] *Materials and Methods of Sales Forecasting*, A.M.A., p. 83.
[9] W. P. Carlin, "Sales Forecasting Operations," in *Marketing Research in Action* (New York: National Industrial Conference Board, 1957), p. 28.

The two estimates of total steel demand, one derived by the over-all GNP approach, and the other by an analysis of the major steel-consuming industries, are then compared and integrated into a single final projection for the total industry. It is at this point that such factors as new product developments, industry sales promotions, and other "noneconomic" factors are considered. Such short-term factors as changes in interest rates, current unfilled orders and new orders rates, model changeover dates in the automotive industry, and many others are also reviewed in making our final adjustments.

An even more complicated approach is followed by one company in the office equipment industry.[10]

Burroughs is a member of the Office Equipment Manufacturers Institute, the industry's trade association, which collects data on industry-wide orders and distributes it among its membership. The company developed a mathematical formula relating new orders of the office equipment industry to relevant factors in the national economy such as gross national product, wage rates for office help, and changes in the number of records the average company keeps (income tax withholding, Social Security data, etc.). By means of this formula, the industry's orders are geared to the national economy to give an estimate of industry volume and trend in the forecast period.

The formula attempts to measure four things:

1. The "floor," or the stock of equipment currently in use. This, like other calculations, is expressed in dollars of equal purchasing power, to eliminate the effect of price changes. The stock of equipment in use is calculated by applying an estimated wear-out formula to actual past year-by-year sales. For example, if the wear-out rate for a particular type of office equipment is estimated at 10% per year of the original number of units sold in any one year, the total stock in current use is approximately the sum of 100% of current year sales, plus 90% of the previous year's sales, plus 80% of the units sold two years back, and so on down to 10% of the total number of units sold nine years ago. In this case, all of the units sold ten years ago, or more, have presumably been scrapped by this time.

2. The "ceiling," or maximum amount of office equipment that the market can be expected to absorb. This is based on the following factors: the size of the national population; the level of living standards as measured by the amount spent per capita on goods and services; and the economic advantage to using office equipment in preference to manual methods.

This last factor depends on three things. First, the spread between clerical wage rates and office equipment prices. The cheaper office equipment is relative to wage rates, the greater is the incentive to mechanize. Second, the company makes allowance for the trend to-

[10] *Forecasting in Industry,* NICB, pp. 54–55.

wards increased productivity of office equipment due to technological improvements. This factor provides an additional cost advantage both over clerical labor and obsolete office equipment still in use. Third, an allowance is made for the increasing load of paperwork in offices, which likewise acts to expand the market.

3. The potential market, which is the difference between the "ceiling" and "floor" figures, representing net growth in the general economy, potential sales to customers converting to office equipment, as well as replacement demand deriving from the retirement of worn-out equipment.

4. The forecast industry orders, or the portion of the potential market which will be converted into new orders in the coming year. According to the formula, this depends upon the level of forecast business activity as measured by gross national product. Under depressed conditions only a small part of the potential market will be converted to sales, whereas in boom times a very high percentage of the potential is realized.

In the rubber industry, economists of the Big Four and a number of smaller companies meet quarterly to compare and pool industry forecasts.

Forecasting Company Sales

Estimates of future levels of industry activity are useful only as a bench mark by which an individual company may judge or test forecasts of its own level of activity. Indeed, one common method of computing company sales consists simply of taking the accustomed or target percentage share of expected industry sales. It is seldom, however, that forecasts are based on any one method. More often the results obtained following one procedure are checked against those obtained by another route.

Perhaps the most prevalent practice is to calculate future company sales on the basis of past trends, making such allowances for seasonal, random, and cyclical disturbances as appear advisable. One survey of 389 companies indicated that 80 per cent followed this practice.[11] In the case of short-run operating budgets, however, the allowance for variation from trend may be the critical consideration. This method would seldom be used alone as a basis for estimating sales expected within the forthcoming year or a shorter period.

The same survey indicated that 45 per cent of the companies responding used what has become labeled "the jury of executive opinion." This is simply a pooling of the expectations of the company's top executives, with particularly heavy reliance on the vice-president in charge of sales or the sales manager. Agreements are hammered out in discussions, and the final com-

[11] Sord and Welsch, *Business Budgeting,* p. 138. Other figures on frequency of use of particular methods come from the same source.

promise results are written into the budget. The effectiveness of this technique depends on how well informed individual executives are and on the methods by which each arrives at his independent conclusions.

One method which has many supporters relies on the sales division, and in particular the field staff, for an informed estimate. "Our sales budget is a composite of all the territorial and customer budgets, produced from the viewpoint of 'hoped for' sales item by item, customer by customer. As a result, attainment of the budget is rather an optimum performance." "Budgets are prepared on an annual and quarterly basis. Sales predictions are prepared by salesmen, by customer. These are reviewed and adjusted by the Division Sales Managers." Another executive states: [12]

> Early each summer, the divisions send out to their salesmen what we call "customer account surveys." The salesman lists, for each product, the names of his customers and prospects, how much each one bought the previous year; expectations for the current year, based on orders to date; what he thinks he will sell next year; the customer's total purchases, including those from other suppliers; and, finally, the frequency of his sales calls. . . . These account surveys are reviewed by the district sales managers and then sent to headquarters, where they are summarized and interpreted by the sales manager and his staff.

The most common criticism of such sales force estimates, even by those employing this method, is that "salesmen, by nature, seem to be mercurial. They may be highly optimistic one day and overly pessimistic the next. It would not be wise to depend exclusively on their views." [13] It has also been suggested that salesmen tend to avoid paper work and time-consuming surveys by such short cuts as giving this year's figures as next year's expectations, sometimes slightly adjusted.

In the large multiproduct firms, this reluctance to rely exclusively on sales department estimates has led to the development of a second set of projections derived from the product managers. The product manager, as the name implies, is a specialist who coordinates all the functional activities relating to a particular product or product line or group. As such, his orientation is different from that of the sales department, which is generally organized on geographical lines to handle all or a number of the firm's products. By drawing on the specialized knowledge of the uses to which his product is being put, and the state of its markets, the budget director or controller can piece together from the product managers as a group a second sales forecast to be laid alongside that deriving from the sales force. In this way estimates based on area are checked against estimates based on product lines.

---

[12] M. Whitney Greene, assistant manager, market and economic research, Koppers Company, in *Materials and Methods of Sales Forecasting*, A.M.A., p. 141.

[13] The same, p. 140.

Where disparities emerge, they are resolved either by high-level discussions or by staff members of the budget office. In one steel company, it is said that in the reconciliation of district (area) sales estimates and product managers' estimates by industry for perhaps twenty-five different lines of products, there is some tendency to give preference to the latter. In part, it is admitted, this is due to the fact that the sales estimate, by product lines, is an integral part of the operating budget and as such must be justified to the product managers, whereas no area breakdown of the total sales forecast is included in the budget and hence no justification to the district sales managers is required. Indeed, even should the district estimates be ignored in favor of product estimates, the former, just as given by the district sales manager, are allowed to stand as the target against which the sales department measures each district's performance.

There is, however, one time when this company gives district sales estimates more serious consideration than those of the product managers. When an economic decline is expected, on the basis of general business and economic indicators, it has been found that sales offices are likely to produce more realistic estimates on the strength of their closer customer contacts.

There is another way of reconciling differences between sales and product forecasts. The market analysis of a research staff is frequently employed for this purpose. The forecasts of the two sets of company operating personnel may be checked for reliability against the conclusions of the research staff, or the believability of market analysis may be checked by the two sets of operating figures. In a company of any size (sales of $100 million or more) all three approaches to the deriving of a sales forecast are likely to be used. Examples of this interplay are cited below.

The Republic Steel Procedure

On a previous page an official of Republic Steel outlined the procedure by which his company derived its industry estimate. The same official goes on to describe the steps then leading to the company forecast.[14]

> Probably the most difficult step in the forecasting procedure, is to relate this over-all steel forecast, which has no product detail, to our own company operations. In the case of our company, this is by no means a straight-line relationship, i.e., we cannot assume that because the steel industry's production will change by a certain percentage our company's output will follow suit. There are a vast number of internal factors such as the company's product-mix, sales policies, market areas served, and similar influences that can cause our operations to vary from the industry pattern. Thus, the industry forecast is only a picture of the economic framework within which our own company is going

---

[14] *Marketing Research in Action*, NICB, pp. 28–29 and 30.

to operate. We must determine what differences, if any, there will be between our company operations and those of the industry.

In short, the forecast of total company shipments is derived from:

a) Past relationships of our company's operations to those of the industry.

b) Knowledge of special situations in markets, product-mix, etc., which would cause the company to deviate from the industry pattern.

c) Company policies that would influence performance and cause variation within the industry pattern.

This company forecast is first prepared on a tonnage basis for the total of all products. The next step is to break this down into the various product lines for which we wish estimates. This is done by examination of the past composition of the company's product-mix and the outlook in industries which consume our steel products.

The proper selection of products and product groups for analysis is important. If too much detail is attempted, the over-all task becomes too great to be well done, while if there is not enough detail, important facts and changes may be concealed. Product groups have, therefore, been selected on the basis of experience. They provide the minimum amount of detail that can be obtained without obscuring specific markets or products whose sales may vary from the over-all trend. Also, products are grouped so that forecasts can be made for each of the segments handled by our various product division managers. . . .

The problem of timing is most important, yet hardest to solve. Annual forecasts cover a calendar year, but the difficulty is that few economic factors perform exactly within the confines of a calendar year. Automobile model years, general business expansion programs, military programs and inventory cycles are examples of factors that do not start in January and end in December. Although the analyst may be quite accurate about the performance of any of these factors, a slight error of several months in timing can make his calendar year forecast look bad. For this reason we are careful to note in our forecast not only the factors influencing the outlook but also to comment about timing. . . .

Up to this point, the work has been carried on entirely in the commercial research division of the company. If a forecast is to be accepted and used it must have the concurrence of all those who will be using it or who will be affected by it. To achieve this end, our next step is to check the forecasts by quarters for the various product groups with the division sales managers. These sales managers, who are in close touch with the company situation in the markets for their products, are often aware of circumstances which may affect the company's sales yet not affect the industry's over-all performance. Their advice and counsel is particularly valuable on the short-term outlook. The experienced judgment which these men can apply to a purely statistical forecast is extremely important.

The next step following conferences with the sales managers is to present the revised forecast to general sales management. While this is done on an informal basis, it is nevertheless the point at which the forecast begins to be accepted both as a guide to actions to be taken and as a measurement of performance. The value of having worked in detail with the over-all business situation and the individual steel-consuming industries is now realized, because that background gives us answers to many questions top management may have regarding the forecast.

Once approved, the tonnage forecast is turned over to the accounting department, where an actual sales operating budget is prepared. Costs, estimated selling prices and estimates of gross profit are added to the forecast and this budget becomes a working tool throughout the company.

Forecasting at the Monsanto Chemical Company

Another example of forecasting techniques is provided by the Monsanto Chemical Company: [15]

> The Monsanto Chemical Company has experienced a gradual broadening of the forecasting function. The evolution of sales forecasting at our former Merrimac Division (which was absorbed at the time of Monsanto's over-all reorganization some three years ago) illustrates this trend. In this division—which manufactured chemicals used principally in the textile, shoe and paper industries—the sales manager and his assistant originally made all sales forecasts and budgets. At a later date the procedure was modified in that the salesmen were asked to make estimates of their next year's sales on the basis of "grass roots" contacts with their customers. After these estimates were consolidated, the final decision was made by the sales manager.
>
> Subsequently, with the development of a product-manager organization (with a group of products placed under the responsibility of each product manager), the sales forecasting job was transferred to the product managers. However, after one or two experiences in which sales estimates made by the product managers turned out to be rather far from actual sales, a new procedure was developed which combined separate sales estimates made by the sales department and the product managers with a forecast based on an over-all statistical analysis of general economic factors and historical relationships. . . .
>
> The approach we followed for our major product group (known as the "general products group") will illustrate the method we adopted.
>
> The general products group consisted of some thirty products having wide use in nonmetal industries. After experimenting with various national economic series, we found that sales of these products tended

[15] Shea Smith III, assistant to the president, Monsanto Chemical Company, "Forecasting Sales," in *Marketing Research in Action*, NICB, pp. 24–27.

to follow the trend of the Federal Reserve indexes of the physical volume of production of consumers' semidurable goods.

This determination was made after we constructed a number of scatter diagrams comparing the product group's sales history with that of various business indicators. Consumers' semidurable goods production was chosen because: (1) it was a logical choice, since it included many of the industries that were important consumers of our "general products"; and (2) analysis showed that the relationship between the semidurables production index and the product group's sales was more reliable than in the case of any of the other alternative series tested.

The company had a record of the annual dollar sales of the general products group going back to 1931. Our first step was to remove from this series the effect of changes in selling prices over the years. To do this, we constructed a price index for the product group, using value-per-pound-sold figures for major products, which comprised approximately 90% of total sales. The average price levels prevailing in the years 1947 and 1949 were used as par or 100%, and the price levels of all other years were expressed as a percentage of this base period. . . .

The annual dollar sales figures were then divided by this price index, thus converting the sales data from a dollar value basis to a physical volume basis. We next sought to determine the average relationship that existed during the years 1931 through 1952 between our sales volume and the volume of production of semidurable goods for the United States as a whole. The Federal Reserve Board does not publish data on semidurable products production *per se,* but the following industry components are reported and can be combined to form such an index: textiles, clothing, leather products, consumers' rubber and plastic goods, and stationery and magazines. We obtained data on this particular combination of semidurable goods by subscribing to the services of a private economic consulting firm. They were able to provide us with data tailor-made to meet our specific needs.

We drew a scatter diagram . . . , plotting our sales volume against the semidurables index our consultant had created. We noted that the relationship between the two series seemed to be linear, and proceeded to fit, by the statistical method of "least squares," the line which best represented that relationship. We felt the relationship shown was sufficiently reliable and constant for us to recommend that the basic trend of sales for the company's general products group be regularly forecast by this mathematical method.

But, in order to forecast sales, we first needed a forecast of the index of total semidurable goods production. We decided to rely on the forecasts of this index that were periodically provided by our economic consultant. Once we had these forecasts, it was a simple matter to read from [a chart] the implied level of our sales for the corresponding period. For example, if the index forecast was 100, expected division sales would be about $5.2 million at 1947, 1949 price levels.

The final step was to adjust these forecast sales for current price levels. Our approach was to relate the price index we had constructed for our products to the Bureau of Labor Statistics' index of wholesale prices, using the same correlation procedure we followed in the case of the production indexes. As a result, we could then obtain a forecast of our products' selling prices, based on our economic consultant's forecasts of the over-all wholesale price level. As a check, we determined whether the sales department contemplated making any changes in our quoted prices during the period being forecasted, and adjusted the economic forecast accordingly.

To arrive at a sales forecast in dollars, we multiplied the sales forecast, excluding the effect of price changes, by the forecast of our price index.

From this annual sales forecast, we obtained month-by-month forecasts by applying the seasonal pattern of our sales to the annual total. . . .

As previously indicated, the forecast was used mainly to check the reasonableness of the detailed product sales estimates of the sales force and of the product managers. The procedure was as follows:

Annually, the salesmen were asked to forecast their sales by products for the following year. This was done in the belief that the sales people's firsthand knowledge of their customers' needs might reveal situations that otherwise might be overlooked by the other forecasting methods. The salesmen's estimates were combined to give division-wide totals by products.

The totaled product sales estimates, together with available market background data, were tabulated on product data sheets, which also provided the sales record for the first and second halves of the current years, both in dollars and pounds. These product sheets were then sent to the appropriate product managers who, on the basis of what they knew about the market and the company's marketing plans, made their own sales estimates for the products they handled.

When all such estimates had been made, the total for each of the three estimates (salesmen's, product managers', and marketing research department's) as well as the supporting product data sheets, were sent to the members of the sales budget committee for final reconciliation.

The Case of Emery Industries

The director of market research for Emery Industries offers still another example of the use of market analysis as a check on figures compiled from the estimates of operating personnel.[16]

> Emery Industries produces a varied line of chemical products, of which fatty acids comprise an important segment. Fatty acids are chemicals derived from animal tallows and greases, vegetable and fish oils, and have many industrial applications. They are used in the manu-

[16] L. C. Church, "Sales Budgeting," in the same, pp. 16–19.

facture of such diverse products as rubber, soaps and cleaning compounds, paints and varnishes, cosmetics, textiles, plastic materials, etc.

Participation in the budgeting of Emery's sales of fatty acids is one of the principal responsibilities of the market research department.

We participate in the sales budgeting activity in four ways: (a) we compile and maintain a record of sales in a form which will aid our sales management in estimating sales in the next fiscal year; (b) we prepare independent estimates of sales for management's consideration; (c) we help incorporate the sales budget into the company's over-all planning; and (d) we provide periodic reviews of actual performance versus the budget.

The responsibility for establishing and approving our company's sales budgets for fatty acids rests with a committee consisting of the vice-president in charge of purchases and sales, the manager of the fatty acid sales department and his assistants, and myself. As a rule, this sales budget committee meets about two months prior to the beginning of the fiscal year to determine prospective sales volume during the coming twelve-month period.

We have found it convenient to base the final sales budget on two separate and distinct budgets. The first part is called the "key accounts" budget and consists of sales to large accounts taking 40,000 pounds or more of our products annually. Customers ordinarily purchasing such quantities of one or a combination of several chemical products account for a large percentage of our total pound sales of fatty acids. Yet they are not so many in number as to make a customer analysis of the group unwieldy. The second part of the over-all sales budget pertains to all of the remaining accounts and is referred to as "LCL accounts" budget. . . .

Territory budgets on sales to LCL accounts are established by our department. We base such estimates on the indicated trend of sales over the past three years. For example, if sales of a product to LCL accounts in a certain territory have been increasing at the rate of 10% per year, we will budget a 10% increase for the coming year unless we have specific information to the contrary.

Where no discernible trend has been apparent in sales, we rely mainly on the over-all outlook for our industry, based on our estimates for business in general. For example, if we expect a 5% increase in our industry's sales, we will apply a 5% increase to all LCL sales where we have no other criterion to go by.

The estimates for key accounts and LCL accounts are then tabulated and a preliminary summary obtained of budgeted sales, by product, for each sales territory and for the company as a whole.

As a check on the preliminary sales budgets, our department prepares two independent sales forecasts. One is based upon a forecast of total industry sales of fatty acids and our company's share of this market; the other is based upon an analysis of the end-uses for our products. . . .

We have found by means of correlation studies that over the past fifteen to twenty years a close relationship has existed between the consumption of fatty acids and the movement of selected components of the Federal Reserve's index of nondurable goods production. A similar situation exists for a few major groups of fatty acids for which consumption data are available from government or trade association sources. Our forecasts of the Federal Reserve index thus enable us to estimate demand for fatty acids in total, and by various types, with a fair degree of accuracy.

By analyzing the trend of our company's participation in these markets, we estimate the proportion of industry sales our company will obtain in the coming year with respect to all fatty acids and by separate groups of these products.

The second approach we use in estimating our company's sales in the coming year employs information on the end uses to which our products are put. All products appearing on our invoices are coded according to their end use. This information is transferred to punch cards and the sales then tabulated by product groups according to end uses.

We then correlate our end use sales data with appropriate measures of activity within the various consuming industries; and consuming industry activity is in turn related to one of the general business indicators for which we prepare forecasts.

For example, the drug and pharmaceutical industry is one market for our fatty acids. We have found that retail sales of selected drugs and pharmaceuticals which normally use our products are related to consumer expenditures for nondurable goods (a major component of GNP which we forecast regularly). We therefore can base our estimates of drug and pharmaceutical sales on our forecasts of consumer expenditures, and then estimate our fatty acids sales for this end use.

We combine the end use sales forecasts into a composite company total and compare this with the total derived from our industry-company forecast. Before settling upon a final forecast we review our projections of (a) industry sales, (b) company sales and (c) our company's share of the total market in the light of long-term studies we maintain on the markets for fatty acids and with the long-term objectives established for our company by our management.

The sales forecasts prepared by our department are submitted to the sales budget committee and other executives of the company to consider along with the preliminary territorial sales budgets. Indicated changes from the previous year's sales, both in total and by individual territories, are reviewed for consistency, and where conflicting patterns are apparent, budgeted sales by accounts and products may be checked for possible revision.

The sales budget, by products, as developed thus far is then referred to the production department, where it is checked against productive capacity and for product balance. It is not essential that the sales budget match capacity in every respect, but obviously neither the over-all aggregate nor the totals for products requiring specialized processing facilities can exceed capacity to produce. If such excesses are found, the sales budget is reduced correspondingly or action is taken to supplement our own manufacturing facilities.

Having been adjusted by the production department, the sales budget can then be finalized, taking on the form indicated below:

Product	Territory 1	Territory 2	Territory total	Unallocated	Financial budget
40	700	500	1,200	...	1,200
50	300	500	800	200	1,000
55	200	600	800	...	800
1,200	1,500	400	1,900	...	1,900
1,220	800	2,000	2,800	100	2,900
Total	3,500	4,000	7,500	300	7,800

Individual territory figures are then converted to quotas, which form the basis for our sales incentive program. The financial budget becomes the basis for all other planning of the company and constitutes the objective to which all activities of the company are committed.

The final budget being on an annual basis, it is the responsibility of market research to allocate the annual totals into month-by-month budgets. This we do on the basis of statistical studies of the seasonal pattern in our sales in past years.

Formula Approaches

A few companies have worked out complicated mathematical techniques, making use of computers, to derive their sales forecasts. At Timken Roller Bearing, for example, multiple correlation involving seven unknowns is attempted with IBM equipment.[17] Other companies have adopted similar "formula" approaches. For example: [18]

> General management, through the financial vice-president's office, issues to each division the official forecast of the economic climate anticipated during the future fiscal year. This forecast, in the case of Carrier Corporation, is in terms of the Federal Reserve Board Index for durable goods manufacturers and serves as the base for all budget thinking and planning. Thus, besides the overall ground rules and policies, the personnel responsible for budget preparation have avail-

[17] The procedure is described in *Materials and Methods of Sales Forecasting*, A.M.A., pp. 125–136.

[18] Worth Probst, controller, Bryant Division, Carrier Corporation, "The Budget as a Tool for Financial Planning and Coordination," *N.A.C.A. Bulletin*, September, 1956, sec. 3, pp. 125–126.

able an indication of the economic activity that they may expect to live in during the next fiscal year.

The budget director for each division converts the official forecasts into terms of the divisional sales dollar. This conversion is done by the application of a slide rule device called a "level sheet." This is the by-product of a statistical study in which the normal trend of growth for the division and the correlation between the divisional volume activity and the general business activity are developed. Since the "level sheet" is the basis for determining sales volume budgets, it has the tendency of eliminating over-enthusiasm and severe pessimism, ailments that often cause budgets to be in error. The "level sheet" sales volumes for the year to be budgeted are forwarded to the sales department and to the market research department where they are revised for:

1. New product lines to be incorporated during the future year.
2. New promotional programs to be utilized during the future year.
3. New market areas to be established in the future year.

Nonmanufacturing Applications

Most of the above descriptions of practice are drawn from manufacturing corporations, where use of budgeting is more common. The principle applies to other forms of business activity no less, however. The application to retailing and wholesaling operations is readily apparent. In other industries some adjustment for terminology may be necessary. In banking, for example, "sales" (the principal source of revenue) are the loans which a bank makes, supplemented by special services which it supplies for a fee, such as check cashing, trust services, provision for safe deposit.

In industries where forecasting entails particular difficulties of uncertainty, it is sometimes the practice to estimate a range of expected sales. This may be in the form of three separate forecasts—minimum, maximum, and likely ("reasonable expectancy"). The vice-president of one railroad writes: "It is not unusual for forecasts of traffic expectancy to be expressed in terms of ranges of probabilities. Expense plans and programs which are subject to management decision (those which are neither fixed nor related to volume) are usually based on the low-level revenue expectancy. Upward modifications may be made in these if actual revenues approach the high-level expectancy."

Forecasting the Product Mix

It is time now to correct any impression which the foregoing discussion may have created that it is enough to cast the sales budget in the form of the total volume expected to be sold during the period covered by the operating plan. In most companies this figure must be broken down by product or product line, by time segment, and sometimes also by geographical areas.

The necessity for budgeting the product mix is readily apparent on reflection. It can be illustrated by experience in the automobile industry, where each manufacturer offers a variety of body styles, options, and accessories. "The permutations and combinations are so enormous that it would be possible to turn out an entire year's production of over 1.5 million Ford cars and never duplicate any car previously built." [19]

First, forecasts of the mix of models and styles which will be wanted are important in order to make sales. "Forecasts of *total* volume are not too critical at the start of the model because all producers are engaged in 'filling the pipeline.' But it is highly desirable to forecast a correct *mix* of product sales. This is the only way to maximize volume in the early days of the model, when dealer stocks have not yet been built up to desired levels." ". . . Total production means almost nothing to our dealer or our supplier. The dealer has difficulty selling a station wagon to a customer who wants a convertible, and the supplier who makes station-wagon parts is not helped when the convertible business booms. In other words, totals alone are not enough. Our projections must be broken down in detail by mix, options, and accessories."

Second, mix is as important as volume when it comes to selective selling. It is rare when a company earns the same rate of profit on all product lines. By special promotion or selling emphasis on lines with the most profitable margins, the company's target rate of return may be more readily attained. As one company has set out in a proposed budgeting guide, "Sales plans must be built up by product line, group, or type. This is particularly necessary where there is a wide range of profitability from one line or group to another, i.e., where sales mix is a key determinant of company profit."

Third, product mix is important in scheduling production, supplies, and personnel, in so far as different facilities, different materials, and different skills are called for by one product or style in contrast to another.

Fourth, estimates of the mix are important to proper inventory planning. "At the end of the model run, an accurate forecast of both total production and mix is essential to avoid having leftover parts and materials running into many millions of dollars."

Fifth, forecasts of mix are important to investment planning. "For example, our new automatic transmission plant going up in Cincinnati is based not only upon estimates of total automotive volume but also on the proportions of those cars which will have automatic transmissions. Each year, our tooling expenditures run into hundreds of millions of dollars. . . .

[19] Edwin H. Sonnecken, programming manager, Ford Division, Ford Motor Company, "Sales Forecasting in the Automobile Industry," *Materials and Methods of Sales Forecasting*, A.M.A., p. 90. Other quotations dealing with the automobile industry's product mix come from the same article, pp. 91 and 95.

A forecast of automotive mix—i.e., the proportions of various body types to be built—is extremely important for tooling."

Similarly, forecasts of sales broken down by time intervals—quite commonly by months in a fiscal year—are necessary for scheduling production, materials, and personnel; for ensuring that goods which are seasonal (clothing is a good example) reach dealers as planned; and for programming cash needs.

The magnitude of the planning involved is easily illustrated.[20]

> Take the specific case of a manufacturer of light bulbs who wants a forecast of his sales for the coming year. He must have this before he can properly plan production, control inventories, determine sales quotas, plan advertising programs, forecast profits, and anticipate cash requirements. Forty years ago his problem would have been relatively simple. He would have then produced clear household bulbs in a narrow range of sizes and perhaps a few miniatures for automobiles and flashlights. Today he has several thousand items in his line. In household bulbs alone he markets a wide range of styles, sizes, and colors. . . . If he also produces fluorescent tubes his problems are multiplied. Beyond this, he probably manufactures industrial bulbs which may range in size from those as small as a pencil eraser to those as large as a basketball. Finally, he probably produces specialty items which have a seasonal demand, such as Christmas tree bulbs and bug-repellent bulbs.

This problem of seemingly impossible dimensions is made manageable, however, by classification.

> As in many cases where a broad line of products is concerned, the important volume may be generated by a relatively small percentage of the total number of items. In such instances it is not uncommon to find that up to 85 per cent of the volume comes from 25 per cent of the line. The accounting department can make such analysis from a tabulation of invoices. Once this relationship is determined, the marketing research department can concentrate its attention on this big piece of the market. If management can plan with confidence on 85 per cent of its volume, it will rarely go too far astray on the balance.

Nevertheless, the problem of making forecasts by product lines compatible with an over-all sales figure is not an easy one. A food manufacturer provides an illustration.[21]

[20] Gilman B. Allen, management consultant, Robert Heller & Associates, "What the Accountant Should Know about Market Research," *N.A.A. Bulletin*, August, 1958, sec. 3, pp. 6–7.

[21] *Forecasting in Industry*, NICB, p. 53.

Take, for example, a typical product manager making a forecast of the items under his wing. He will sit down with the list, some thirty or forty products in number, along with historical sales data for each. To start with, he may consider that normal growth should produce a sales increase of five or six per cent, so he keeps that in the back of his mind as he goes down the list.

He comes to item D. It is anticipated that this product will be more competitively priced in the coming year and in view of the fact that we currently enjoy only a very small share of the market, this should produce a sales increase of about 35%. That's logical. Item H? A new, attractive package in the works should add 15% to its volume. Sounds good! Then item J—we are boosting the ad budget for this product 50%, which should give us about 30% added volume. Reasonable! Then there are those two new products which will be introduced shortly after the first of the year—we should get about four and a half million out of them. Possible!

All of these estimates in themselves are entirely reasonable, but when we add them up and multiply by ten product managers, we have the American consumer spending half of his food dollar on our products. This is an exaggeration, of course, but it illustrates how far we might go astray if we were just to add up a number of individual forecasts without applying some over-all economic yardstick.

Other examples of the nature of product-mix forecasting come readily to hand. From a drug manufacturer: [22]

The Lederle Laboratories Division of the American Cyanamid Company is a producer of one of the broad-spectrum antibiotics in finished forms available for use by the medical profession and by the animal feed industry. It manufactures 78 products, in 142 package styles, based on this antibiotic for the medical profession alone. . . . A semi-annual statement of demands, broken down by month and by package style and label, shows anticipated gross sales for the next 12-month period.

From a beverage manufacturer:

The soft drink business is highly seasonal and it is an individual business in each of the major markets. In addition, weather, hot and cold, rainy and fair, plays an important part in the soft drink consumption habits of people. For these reasons, company planning is a composite of twenty different soft drink products or groups of products, two hundred individual markets in the United States, Canada and abroad, and the additional monthly budgets of sales and monthly programs of promotions. The twenty product groups times the two

[22] Jerome E. Plitt, manager, production planning and inventory control, Lederle Laboratories, in *Successful Production Planning and Control,* A.M.A. Special Report 5, New York, 1955, pp. 193–194.

hundred locations times the twelve months approximates fifty thousand separate budget units to make up the composite annual plan for the company.

From a paper products manufacturer:

Sales forecasts (we use the term Program) are prepared a year in advance, by months, in sufficient detail (several hundred items) to provide information necessary for master production schedules. . . . For practical operating purposes, revisions are made to the sales program periodically in order to control finished goods inventories and maintain proper product mix in line with actual trends.

From a television manufacturer: [23]

Planning for the immediate future starts at least eight months in advance of the period and begins with the commercial program planning. . . . At this stage, quantities are established by type of model, color, screen-size and by features and performance. To do this, it is necessary to put together on paper a complete line of merchandise. . . . The mix of models, i.e., the quantities of table models, open face consoles, door consoles by screen sizes, is determined from commercial trends, buyer surveys, present movement, and seasoned commercial judgment.

Eastman Kodak Practice

The practice at Eastman Kodak has been described by the company's chief statistician.[24]

It is not enough for sales forecasts to be made in broad totals. Sales of individual products and product lines must be forecast, and that means linking these individual product sales to external economic factors. Sometimes these may be particular external factors which are primarily related to the demand for a particular product. I think it is clear that an economist permanently employed by a business firm is better able to know what future economic changes are likely to affect future sales and how those changes will influence particular products.

Our procedure at Kodak is to prepare the economic assumptions twice each year. Beginning about August 1 (and also about February 1) we work out the economic forecast for the coming year and for a

[23] George K. Bryant, operations manager, R.C.A. Victor Television Division, "Equipping Management Controls with Power Steering and Power Brakes," *N.A.C.A. Bulletin*, November, 1956, sec. 1, p. 396.

[24] Edmund R. King, "Translating Economic Trends into Realistic Corporate Plans," paper presented at an American Management Association meeting, New York, June 4, 1957, pp. 6–10. (Mimeographed.)

total of five years into the future. The forecast is worked out in terms of Gross National Product, Disposable Personal Income, and several other economic indicators. These data are then submitted to top company management for review and approval. This presentation is usually made verbally to a management committee and includes a discussion of the factors and reasoning leading to the suggested general business assumptions.

After review and approval by top management the general business assumptions are presented verbally with visual aids to several groups of division and department managers. They are also circulated in written form within the company. A memorandum incorporating the figures and related discussion is sent to all who may be involved in the sales-estimating and budget-making procedure.

This complete review of the economic forecast twice each year is supplemented by a brief review of business conditions each month, as discussed later.

Once the five-year economic forecast has been prepared, approved, and circulated, the next step is preparation of the sales forecasts. Our sales forecasting techniques are diverse and vary considerably from product to product. In general, however, we have two methods of sales forecasting, a trend-cycle method and a multiple-correlation method.

In the trend-cycle method, we extrapolate the past trend of sales and then modify that trend projection by the economic forecast. This means examining the forecast of an economic indicator which, in the past, has moved in synchronism with product sales. Then the product sales forecast is changed from the trend value as suggested by past experience.

In the multiple-correlation method, we attempt to relate product sales in an exact mathematical way to what seem to be the important variables. These will include such factors as economic indicators, price ratios, demographic factors, and trend elements. In using this method, we insert into the mathematical equation the economic variables as assumed for the interval ahead and thereby obtain a forecast of the company product sales.

The starting sales forecast is thus a kind of statistical projection based on the economic forecast. The second step is to modify that statistical sales forecast by various factors such as expected changes in the competitive situation, the size of dealer inventories, any price or product changes, and special sales or advertising plans.

The starting or statistical sales estimates are worked out by representatives of the various statistical and planning groups in the company. These include the planning organization of the Kodak Distribution Center (the planning group in the central company warehouse), the statistical and/or production-control department from the plant producing the product under discussion, and the personnel from the Kodak Office Statistical Department, which has the twin responsibilities of preparing the economic assumptions and coordinating the sales forecasts. This is a cooperative project by these various statistical and planning groups.

The second step of applying the modifying factors is accomplished through a series of conferences with those executives who have the responsibility for company policy and for the production and sales of the individual products. In these review sessions, the responsible people are best able to help the planners make the best application of the modifying factors to starting statistical sales forecasts.

After the sales forecast for each of the products has been considered in one of several of these preliminary review meetings with the sales, production, and planning people, all of the forecasts are reviewed in detail by a Finished Products Committee. This committee gives final approval to the estimates.

The chairman of the Finished Products Committee is the Vice-President and General Manager of the company. There are six other vice-presidents who are also members of this committee. They are responsible for various aspects of sales, production, advertising, and general management considerations. Other members of the committee are the company Treasurer, the Comptroller, additional major sales executives, the Manager of the Distribution Center and two of his staff, representatives of the plant production and planning personnel, and the Chief Statistician of the company. In all, the Finished Products Committee has nineteen members at present.

The sales forecasts approved by the Finished Products Committee are, in effect, the "sales budgets." In our terminology, the one-year forecasts are the "original budget estimates" and the five-year forecasts are the "long-term estimates."

These estimates are prepared and considered by these committees in quantity terms. The annual quantity estimates for the year ahead are further refined by the planning groups in the Kodak Distribution Center. The product-group figures are broken down into data on each individual finished product, size, kind, package, etc. The annual data in each category are then allocated to each period (a four-week interval) on the basis of seasonal indexes. These quantity data are utilized by the various production planning departments to do in-process and related planning.

The estimates in quantity terms are converted to sales forecasts in dollar terms by the Kodak Office Statistical Department. Therefore, we try to have annual estimates in money for five years ahead almost continuously available for financial and cost-control planning purposes.

Sales Potentials and Sales Manipulations

In an earlier chapter it was pointed out that, logically, budgeting is not a series of sequential steps, each one following from the other. It involves the making of a number of decisions which are so interrelated that theoretically they should be made simultaneously. Revenues and costs are mutually influencing, for example. That principle is apparent in the process of sales budgeting. As already noted, sales forecasting is not the same thing as revenue planning. The sales which could be predicted on the basis of existing or foreseen circumstances may not satisfy the goals which management has set for the firm, so that cost-incurring actions will be undertaken with the objective of increasing revenues more than costs. The sales expected thus cannot be stated without a simultaneous decision on the expenses which will be incurred in promoting the product, on the price which will be charged for the product, on the channels of distribution for the product, and even on whether changes will be made in the product itself to increase its salability. How much will be allocated for such activities depends on past performance relative to profit goals and the net favorable effect anticipated from each increment of expense.

Moreover, expenditures designed to improve the revenue-producing qualities of a product are sometimes themselves alternatives, each possessing differential costs and producing differential returns. Thus price change and promotion are sometimes viewed as substitute routes to the desired objective. If promotion is increased, the price may be maintained. If the price is reduced, it takes the place of additional promotion. A price increase, however, would call for further promotional support.

In addition to (really, as a means of achieving) over-all corporate objectives, it is common practice for firms to set objectives by product lines, in terms of both volume of sales and resulting profit. These targets are often based on extensive surveys of a product's "potential," relying on estimates of its functional utility to classes or categories of customers (individuals, households, other businesses, institutions) and a time schedule of acceptance, taking into account increasing familiarity, price and income elasticity, the spread of complementary products or services, increasing substitutability for other products through improvements. This timetable is subsumed under the general term "rate of saturation."

The potential is not automatically realized, however. It must be achieved by design and plan. An official of one of the earliest of corporate budgeters, the Bausch & Lomb Optical Company of Rochester, New York, emphasized this point three decades ago.[25]

> Analysis of the potential market, the possibilities of exploiting these markets, and the incorporation of this factor as a definite part of the sales budget, represents the dynamic element in forecasting. It is the only element that yields a definite plan of lifting the Company's sales out of the rut of the past, and of directing the sales program effectively

[25] Elihu Hedges, "Profits through Controlled Distribution," *N.A.C.A. Bulletin,* Apr. 15, 1933, sec. 1, pp. 1165, 1173, 1171–1172.

towards sales progress. . . . It is desirable, therefore, . . . to appropriate the necessary selling expense to produce these sales in accordance with a predetermined program. . . . The budgeted selling and advertising expense represents the planned effort to produce sales in accordance with the sales budget.

One corporate controller has expressed the matter this way: [26]

The sales program and marketing costs are interrelated and interdependent. The objective is to secure the combination of elements of selling effort which will, in the long run, produce the most profit. Almost any sales volume can be secured if enough selling effort eventually reaches a point where the additional sales produced do not compensate for the additional effort. Conversely, the selling cost can be reduced to almost any point desired but with the ultimate effect that sales volume will be reduced so low that no profit will result. Somewhere between such extremes must be found the proper amount of sales effort to be used. This principle applies not only to sales volume as a whole, but also to individual classes of products, individual territories, and individual groups.

It is interesting that this corporate official regards as an "extreme" the case which economists have taken as typical—that selling effort (like production) will be pushed to the point where additional sales produce no profit. While the idea of "incremental costs" and "incremental returns" is prevalent in the business literature, the notion that their point of equality constitutes the preferred profit position is relatively much less common if not actually uncommon.[27] The only apparent explanation for the relative absence of this conception is (as in the case of the use of loan capital only if it returns a rate at least equal to that currently being earned) an underlying belief that the potentialities for profit exceed management's capacity to embrace, so that the marginal limit need never be reached, and indeed, an approach to that limit suggests misuse of limited skilled personnel, particularly managerial, as the strategic variable.

In later chapters attention will be given to the pricing problem, product planning, and to a lesser extent selling and distribution expenses. It is

[26] Roy L. Brittain, controller, the V. D. Anderson Company, "Sales Forecasting and Marketing Cost Control," *N.A.C.A. Bulletin,* November, 1953, sec. 1, p. 305.

[27] One curious maxim offered by an official of Sylvania Electric is this: "We have learned historically that it is unwise to assume that a ratio of sales expense to sales is necessarily a suitable or adequate tool for budgeting. One of our objectives is to budget in such a way that any incremental cost will at least be equaled, and probably exceeded, by the extra profit we expect to attain. An illustration of this would be expecting to add, as a result of our promotional activities, dealers who would create for us more profit through the volume added than the cost of such promotion." *Controlling Marketing Costs,* A.M.A. Marketing Series, no. 100, New York, 1957, p. 18.

enough for the present to note that lack of consideration of these elements in the present discussion of sales budgeting is not to be construed as implying their lack of relevance. It is simply that, despite the interaction of most of the budget categories, it is impossible to discuss them all at once. As relevant as pricing is to the sales plan, pricing itself cannot be discussed without consideration of production costs. We can now only note that the sales budget or sales plan incorporates a number of areas of managerial discretion which modify any original forecast. The original sales forecast is not generally taken as fixed or determined but is subject to manipulation by management in the pursuit of its objectives. One manager reports: [28]

> During the third quarter of our fiscal year, an annual forecast for the coming year is made of the total expected sales by product and size. . . . We then alter this preliminary forecast, taking into consideration the changes we know are going to occur. Many and varied, these changes will involve such factors as the effect of the introduction of new products on sales of present products; the original-distribution pipeline filling for a new product; price fluctuations (upward or downward) . . . , and the time such changes occur; anticipated seasonal influence changes; changes in promotional effort by products or sizes of products; changes in advertising emphasis by product or product lines; sales effectiveness with sold and unsold accounts; new market activity; growth of related items; and anticipated competitive activity. Therefore it is necessary that marketing plans for the future year be fairly well completed before the forecasts are made.

Disaggregating the Sales Budget: Sales Quotas

The final stage in sales budgeting for the operating period is in the assignment of specific sales quotas to the selling units in the organization. This is the process of disaggregating the budget by assigning its pieces to the units which, respectively, have the responsibility of fulfilling it.

In those companies which make use of their sales staffs in the estimation procedure, the assignment of quotas presents no difficulties. In one company [29]

> The target survey, which started out as a forecasting tool, now becomes the major instrument in the field for planning the district sales

[28] John C. Doub, manager—marketing and sales research, "Sales Projections," in "From Forecast to Reality at McCormick & Company," *Case Studies in Production Forecasting, Planning and Control,* A.M.A. Manufacturing Series, no. 223, New York, 1957, p. 38.

[29] Howard C. Holmes, assistant general sales manager, Kaiser Aluminum and Chemical Sales, "The Role of the Field Sales Force," in *Materials and Methods of Sales Forecasting,* A.M.A., pp. 206–207.

program and measuring its results. The district manager uses it in reducing his district quota to individual quotas by salesman, product, and account. Together, he and the salesman develop a sales program that involves establishing sales quotas, call quotas, and specific plans and techniques for accomplishing the desired objectives.

The marketing research director of the General Tire and Rubber Company has provided a description of how branch sales planning is tied in with corporate sales budgeting.[30]

> A forecast of total industry shipments by various products is basic to our procedure for setting sales quotas.
>
> Automotive equipment sales, such as ours, are of two types: those made to motor vehicle manufacturers (to be used as part of the original equipment), and those sold to car owners to replace worn-out equipment. In this case, we were concerned with replacement sales only.
>
> The statistical committee of the Rubber Manufacturers Association, of which we are members, prepares a forecast of industry shipments, by products, in terms of units, twelve months in advance. Every three months, a group of representative rubber companies submit their estimates of industry sales, by products, for the following year. These figures are averaged by the statistical committee, and at quarterly meetings they are discussed and a consensus is reached. (Incidentally, these forecasts of industry tire shipments are available only to participating companies.)
>
> Our own industry forecasts are based on the age distribution of registered vehicles and upon a study of various business indicators. We compare our forecast with the official industry forecasts, and arrive at a final revised set of forecasts for setting sales quotas and other uses.
>
> Our next step is to determine, product by product, the share of the industry shipments we can reasonably expect to capture in the coming year. This share is always slightly larger than the previous year. In doing this we rely not only on records of our past performance but also upon discussion with our various product sales managers. These talks provide us with field information on current and prospective sales conditions and familiarize us with the company's forthcoming marketing plans.
>
> The third step in our forecasting procedure is to estimate the average unit selling prices we expect to receive for our various products in the twelve months ahead. We take into consideration price changes that have occurred during the past year and any changes anticipated by the sales department for the coming year.
>
> With these estimates established, we can derive shipments forecasts for our various products in dollars, by multiplying the industry unit

[30] Henry H. McKee, Jr., "Setting Sales Quotas," in *Marketing Research in Action,* NICB, pp. 72–73.

forecasts by our anticipated per cent share of the industry, and applying our estimated unit sales prices. These dollar estimates become our company's product quotas for the ensuing year.

Now we compare these product quotas with our actual dollar sales in the current year. When actual sales for the entire current year are not yet available, we estimate the annual total on the basis of cumulative year-to-date sales, and project the remaining months' sales on the basis of our knowledge of the seasonal pattern of sales for each of our product lines. We then compute the percentage change between the current year's sales and next year's product quotas.

Next we compare our sales performance, by products, at the various branches with the amount of business available there. In our case, the number of passenger cars, trucks, or tractors registered (depending on the product involved) is a good measure of tire sales potentials. Data on total registrations, by states, are regularly published so that we can readily make these branch-office comparisons.

We figure our national and branch sales performance by dividing the current year's dollar sales of each product by the appropriate registration figure for that area, and call this performance "sales per vehicle." At this point, we have available the following data, product by product:

a) the company's national sales quota for the coming year, in dollars
b) the percentage change of the national quota from the current year's sales
c) the company's current annual dollar sales per vehicle registered
d) the branches' current annual dollar sales per vehicle registered.

With these figures in hand, we can now determine what the product sales quotas should be for each sales branch by first applying the following formula:

National Sales per Vehicle × Percentage Change of National Quota = Branch Sales per Vehicle × Percentage Change of Branch Quota

The first three components in this formula are known, enabling us to determine the percentage changes in dollar sales during the coming year required of our various branches.

The current year's sales at the branch are multiplied by this computed percentage change, and the result is added to the current year's sales. This becomes the branch's dollar sales quota for the product involved.

Let us illustrate this with a numerical example. Assume that the company's national sales performance for one of our products is $3.59 per vehicle and the national quota for this item shows a 14.5% increase over the current year's dollar sales. The branch sales per vehicle, let us say, is $3.89. By putting the known figures into their proper spots in the formula, we get:

$3.59 × 14.5% = $3.89 × percentage change of branch quota
Percentage change of branch quota = 13.4%

The 13.4% increase is then applied to the current year's actual sales. If these sales were, for example, $10,000, the branch quota for the coming year would be set at $11,340.

This formula is so designed that for those branches whose current sales performance is better than the company average, the percentage increase in sales required to reach quota will be less than the company-wide increase. On the other hand, branches with less-than-average sales performance must exceed the companywide increase in order to make quota. By this method, when all of the branch quotas for any item are added up, they automatically equal the national quota.

These quotas as they now stand represent average performance, after taking into consideration the various factors affecting the company's industry position in the coming year as well as any anticipated changes in our selling prices.

There is one problem which does intrude in the use of sales force esti-mates both as one basis for the corporate sales forecast and as a basis for assignment of quotas. It will be recalled that one criticism of sales depart-ment projections is that they tend to be overly optimistic and must often be scaled down to more realistic forecasts prepared by product managers and market researchers. At the same time, use of such reduced estimates in as-signing sales quotas to the selling units would act as a damper on enthusiasm and incentive. The solution which a number of companies have adopted is to work with two sets of estimates. "Realistic" scaled-down figures are built into the company budget and become the basis for financial planning. "Optimistic" figures submitted by sales force personnel are, however, re-turned to them as targets to shoot for. Branch sales managers who have sought to "look good on paper" or to "show the proper spirit and drive" are left with their own estimates as the basis for evaluating their efforts.

A few companies have reported the reverse problem: that sales force estimates are set intentionally low so that actual sales, which are expected to be higher, will make them "look good." This temptation is somewhat reduced, however, in those situations—quite common—when advertising and promotion allocations are based on forecasts, so that low estimates penalize a sales office by automatically curtailing its promotional budget.

Long-run Sales Planning

The sales forecasting we have so far examined relates only to a short-run period, a fiscal year or some segment of it. An increasing number of companies (with a high degree of correlation with size) have also been undertaking long-range sales forecasting and planning. The purpose is to chart directions and distances in which the company may most profitably move, so that actions necessary to achieve a plotted destination may be taken with adequate forethought and on schedule. This is particularly important when new plant investment is involved and plant location must be determined.

Some of the important considerations in such planning have been suggested by an official of the Kaiser Aluminum and Chemical Sales Company.[31]

> Kaiser Aluminum produces and sells eight basic types of mill products: (1) electrical conductor; (2) foil; (3) merchant; (4) rod, bar, and wire; (5) extrusion; (6) forging; (7) pig and ingot; and (8) sheet. . . .

> Long-range planning is an enlargement of our already existing sales programs. It is designed to insure not only a greater share of the market over a number of years, but also that our company will contribute fully to the growth of the market through research, product development, and sound marketing practices.

> We begin with the share of the market that each basic Kaiser mill product currently represents. Market Analysis provides these figures for each major industry. We then establish, as objectively as we can, with Market Analysis counsel, the reasons why we arrived at that particular share of the market. This involves a searching and objective analysis of all the competitive factors and of our own shortcomings which may have a bearing on the subject. These factors include: capacities, availabilities, profit margins, plant and geographic advantages, service and quality, development projects, advertising, critical sales relationships, and sales coverage.

> From this review, the product manager and market analysis manager determine, as best they can, what competitive advantages will continue or increase during the next five years, and which of our shortcomings we can reasonably plan on overcoming in this same period.

> We then agree upon a tentative share of each industry as a reasonable goal of attainment during the coming years (usually five years ahead). This is not a sales quota; rather, it is our best planning guess of exactly where we should be five years hence, as far as the sales of a particular product within a particular industry are concerned.

> All the foregoing is recorded by the product manager and his staff as the facts are developed, industry by industry, and subsequently refined and consolidated.

> From these consolidated data, we build up the following information:

> 1. Projected total sales by product for each year included in the plan.

> 2. Required capacities and availabilities, and their estimated capital expenditures.

> 3. Development and research projects' target dates.

[31] Raymond G. Boyd, assistant general sales manager, "The Development and Operation of Sales Plans," in *Materials and Methods of Sales Forecasting*, A.M.A., pp. 201, 203–204.

4. Levels of mill and distributor stocks, and their dates of build-up to meet the goals as forecast.

5. Objectives and projected budgets for advertising and sales promotion.

6. A projection of needed sales calls and probable increases of Field Sales personnel.

7. Product Office personnel requirements.

8. A course of action which must be followed by the districts on a scheduled basis, and the control forms developed to check on progress.

9. The need and tentative schedules for special field and general office training courses.

10. Required mill service performance and quality standards for the specific purposes defined in the plan.

11. Relative dependence of one product upon another. (Thus, we know, for example, that certain special extrusion alloys must be urgently developed, despite high cost and low sales volume, because they are integral to products demanding considerable quantities of sheet).

12. Obvious pricing inconsistencies are spotlighted, corrective studies undertaken, and the dates of changes projected.

13. Areas for further market analysis are indicated, and the surveys scheduled.

The long-range plan book is sent to the top executives in our company. In a joint meeting with production management, under the chairmanship of the executive vice president, each plan is reviewed, discussed, and refined, and action is specified. These reviews are scheduled every six months.

To summarize, our planning centers on our eight basic mill products. Coordinating the product activities of mill production and the direct field sales organization is the function of a product manager. One of the product manager's prime responsibilities is planning for the future. The keystone for that planning is obviously the most accurate market forecast possible.

The same Republic Steel official whose descriptions of industry and company fiscal-year forecasting were previously given has commented as follows on his firm's ten-year forecast: [32]

> First, in making the long-term forecast, we place more emphasis on the analysis of trends in the steel-using industries. Technological changes are accorded much greater importance, since these do not cause much change from one year to the next, but can cause substantial change over a period of several years. In the ten-year analysis we also look more closely at trends in such basic business factors as population,

[32] *Marketing Research in Action*, NICB, pp. 29–30.

income, productivity, consumer preference, and differences in rates of growth within various industries.

Second, because the company's long-term operation may be materially affected by changes in its productive facilities, more attention is given to changing trends in product-mix, prospective introduction of new products and changes in the nature of our markets than is the case in making our one-year forecasts.

Third, the long-term forecast must of necessity closely examine regional trends for consuming industries and the steel products involved. Trends, which over a one-year period may be of little significance, can have an important effect on our markets in a ten-year period. We compile figures on regional employment by type of industry (issued by the U.S. Bureau of Labor Statistics), Census data on manufacturing, and any other regional information that is available. We even find data on water usage and availability a guide in determining past patterns of regional industrial growth and seek, in these data, trends which may give clues as to future growth. . . .

While the long-range forecast is, in a way, an extension of the annual forecast (with added geographic detail), its findings go beyond a mere statement of the company's expected industry position at the end of the period. Rather, it sets forth goals for the company. Whether these goals are achieved (assuming the estimates for the industry are right) depends on the policies and actions management finds it possible to take during the forecast period.

Long-term forecasts help management formulate policy and make long-range plans with respect to plant expansion, product diversification, sales and market development, and other factors that affect the company's competitive position. At Republic, the ten-year forecast is distributed to about twenty of the company's top executives. Marked "company confidential" it often serves as the basis for more detailed studies of future developments in our industry.

In the same way that coming-year sales forecasts must be broken down by product line, so is it frequently necessary for long-run forecasts to project sales by broad product groups. An example of this procedure comes from the American Cyanamid Company.[33]

> Let us assume that we want to determine what the prospects for the next five years are for a group of organic chemicals, used in the vulcanization of rubber, which we want to call Rubber Chems "A".
>
> The end consumer analysis is simple in this case because the usage of these rubber chemicals is tied exclusively to the consumption of rubber. Therefore, our first step will be that we try to develop a long range projection for rubber consumption. This can be done by calculat-

[33] Henry K. Klopstock, budget accountant, American Cyanamid, "Long Range Planning," *Business Budgeting,* June, 1960, pp. 11–14.

ing a trendline or by establishing a correlation with an important economic index. . . .

There are a few factors which would indicate a sharper rise in rubber consumption, like an increase in the number of families who own two cars and stepped up consumption of rubber for industrial purposes, e.g. conveyor belts. However, a further investigation reveals that in some end usages rubber is being displaced by various plastics like polyurethane, and silicone.

In view of these offsetting factors it seems reasonable to assume that there will be no significant deviation from the past growth pattern and we can estimate that new rubber consumption in 1963 will amount to about 1,750,000 LT in accordance with the post-war trendline.

But we have to take into consideration that the growth does not take place in the form of a straight line as there are the ups and downs of the cyclical fluctuations. Therefore, the question comes up how large a deviation we can expect from the computed trendline value of 1,750,000 LT for 1963. This question is answered by computing the standard deviation which in this case amounts to +6.3%. This means that new rubber consumption in 1963 can be expected to be between 1,640,000 LT and 1,860,000 LT.

It is more realistic to indicate a range than to give a definite figure, because we do not know at what point of a business cycle we shall be 5 years from now.

The next step is to establish the correlation between rubber consumption and usage of rubber chemicals in the U.S. We have to take into consideration that synthetic rubber requires about 1.5 times as much Rubber Chems. as natural rubber. Therefore, we must try to project the share of natural and synthetic rubber in 1963. There has been a definite shift towards synthetic rubber as the following tabulation indicates:

Year	Natural rubber	Synthetic rubber
1947	50.1%	49.9%
1948	58.7	41.3
1949	58.1	41.9
1950	57.2	42.8
1951	37.4	62.6
1952	36.0	64.0
1953	41.3	58.7
1954	48.3	51.7
1955	41.5	58.7
1956	39.1	60.9
1957	36.8	63.2

As this trend is likely to continue we can assume that the ratio of synthetic to natural rubber will be about 70 to 30 in 1963.

In the following tabulation we are showing consumption of natural rubber in col. 1 and of synthetic rubber in col. 2. In col. 3 we have adjusted the synthetic rubber consumption by the above mentioned factor of 1.5 and in col. 4 natural rubber consumption and adjusted synthetic rubber are added up. In col. 5 US sales of Rubber Chems "A" are indicated and the last column shows the ratio of US sales of Rubber Chems "A" to the Adjusted Basis as in col. 4.

We can see that in the years 1954 through 1957 the ratio has remained pretty steady with an average of 22.1. In 1955 the ratio was somewhat higher. This is due to the fact that in a beginning boom there is a tendency on the part of dealers and consumers to increase their inventories while in a recession the opposite takes place. Therefore, it seems appropriate to use the average ratio for a number of years which constitute a full business cycle.

TABULATION

Year	1 Natural rubber cons. thous. LT	2 Synth. rubber cons. thous. LT	3 Synth. rubber cons. adjust.	4 Total adjust. basis	5 US sales of rub. chems "A" in mill. lbs.	6 Ratio col. 5 to col. 4
1954	596	637	956	1552	33,743 (Adj.)	21.7
1955	632	891	1337	1969	46,756	23.7
1956	563	876	1314	1877	10,748	21.7
1957	539	926	1389	1928	41,034	21.3
Estimated						
1963	525	1225	1838	2363	52,200	22.1

Source for US Rubber Consumption: *Survey of Current Business;* Source for Rubber Chemicals Sales: US Tariff Commission Report.

We have now progressed so far in our analysis that we can project the US sales of Rubber Chemicals "A" into 1963. We have computed the expected total new Rubber consumption for 1963 at 1,750,000 LT and we have seen that the anticipated ratio of synthetic to natural rubber is about 70 to 30. Therefore, we can calculate the adjusted basis of rubber consumption as follows:

525,000 LT of natural rubber plus 1,225,000 LT of synthetic rubber, the latter adjusted by a factor of 1.5 due to the higher requirements of rubber chemicals, result in a total adjusted basis of 2,363,000. As there are no indications of a technological change whereby the ratio of rubber consumption will change we can extend the Adjusted Basis of 2,363,000 by the above mentioned ratio of 22.1, resulting in a projection of 52,200,000 lbs. for US sales of this group of Rubber Chemicals in 1963. Here the standard deviation applies again, resulting in a range of 49.2 mill. to 55.5 mill. lbs.

We are now ready for the last two steps, determination of the market share of our Company and distribution of the total sales of the Product Group between the various types of these chemicals. For obvious reasons we can not go into any detail and show any figures but we can indicate the general procedure.

We have to calculate the ratio of Company sales to US sales of these Chemicals for a number of years. This will tell us if our market share is pretty constant or if there is any significant up or down trend. We have to discuss with our technical and sales personnel the reasons for such trends and in particular we have to try to evaluate how future events will influence our market share. Does our Sales Dept. plan a special advertising campaign in a certain area, or can we expect considerable improvements in the quality of some of our main products? However, our future market share is influenced not only by our own actions but also by the activity of our competitors. If our competitors are able to market new products which are more effective or substantially less expensive, then our market share may be impaired considerably. This is of course the most difficult part of the long range forecasting procedure as we usually do not know the plans of our competitors. However, sometimes we may be able to get a clue by studying the new patents of our competitors. For it usually takes several years for a product to move from the laboratory or draft board into commercial production.

Inventory Planning

It was previously noted that one of the purposes of sales budgeting is to enable the firm to schedule production more effectively. An aspect of business operation which relates to both the production and sales functions is inventory control. Raw-materials and goods-in-process inventories are more closely geared to production scheduling. Finished-goods inventories relate more directly to the sales planning process and are influenced by the sales budget more than by any other factor.

Collectively, inventories assume considerable financial importance. They represent almost one-third of the total assets of American industry, and the largest single current asset of many industrial firms. They therefore occupy a significant place in comprehensive budgeting.

Five distinct objectives of inventory planning have been recognized by most managements: (1) Adequate servicing of the firm's customers is the most obvious function of inventories. When an order is placed, prompt filling is often a condition of the sale and in any event is likely to affect future ordering. (2) Stabilization of employment is sought not simply or even primarily out of consideration for workers but because irregular employment leads to higher costs through the penalties of increased turnover, loss of morale, and start-up costs. (3) Procurement costs may be reduced through prior planning and proper scheduling of raw material or component purchases. (4) Economical lot-size production is made possible only by balancing inventory carrying costs against unit production costs, both of which are affected by lot size. (5) Since inventory constitutes investment, minimizing the inventory which will serve the previous four objectives increases the firm's return on investment.

Determination of the inventory policy which will most effectively achieve some balance of these multiple objectives usually requires collaboration of representatives of the sales, production, and financial departments. Otherwise the sales people are likely to call for inventories high enough to avoid any chance of "stock-outs" which lose them sales, the production people are likely to schedule runs in lot sizes that can be most readily accommodated in their working schedules, and the financial people are likely to prefer inventories at the lowest levels they can get away with in order to free working capital.

Extreme inventory policies carry their own penalties. The costs of inadequate inventories are the sum of lost profit from lost sales due to stock-outs, production losses attributable to idle facilities and underutilized labor at one time and overtime and overtaxed facilities and labor at another, and the premium prices which often attend rush purchases of materials. The costs of excessive inventories involve not only the added carrying costs but also the dangers of pilferage and obsolescence, both of which loom significant enough to be widespread causes of managerial concern.

Because of the special costs attaching to poor inventory policy, whether based on inadequate or excessive inventories, standards governing inventory policy have been established by most businesses which budget. Perhaps the two most commonly employed are the minimum-maximum levels and turnover.

The former sets a lower and an upper stock limit for all major inventory items, thus providing simultaneously a prescribed point at which production for stock is undertaken and a maximum lot size, but discretion and flexibility as to the production run within the two limits. In setting the upper and lower levels it is customary to take into account such factors as sales experience, the importance of prompt order filling, the ordering habits of customers, competitive sources of supply, dangers of obsolescence or perishability, availability of storage space, unit value of the item, manufacturing lead time required, and economies of varying lot-size production. The actual setting of the limits is usually a process of judgment and compromise among conflicting functional objectives.

The turnover standard is based on the ratio of inventory to sales or a supply of a specified number of days. Here, too, judgment and compromise are the bases on which turnover standards are set. Obviously, minimum and maximum levels must be established since it would be impossible to maintain stocks at some constant level, but the difference between the inventory-to-sales ratio and the previously mentioned minimum-maximum approach lies in the provision of a specific standard which limits discretion as to production runs and provides a basis for managerial evaluation of the appropriateness of inventory levels. Nevertheless, the two procedures are very similar.

In some companies which are subjected to fluctuating sales levels (particularly nonstyle hard goods industries), variable turnover rates have been set to avoid the problems which would be raised by permitting inventory fluctuations to accentuate the impact of sales irregularities on production scheduling. In these instances a "normal" volume of sales may be determined from experience. Fluctuation below that volume would result in a disproportionately smaller reduction in inventory, while sales peaks above that normal volume would call for a disproportionately smaller increase in inventory. Inventory thus becomes a buffer which shields production from the more erratic gyrations of sales and lends it greater stability.

As with sales budgeting, finished-goods inventory levels must be set not only on an over-all basis but by product or product line. In companies handling hundreds and even thousands of products this presents the same complications which were earlier discussed. As in the case of sales, however, it is generally true that relatively few product lines account for a high proportion of the total value of inventory. Concentration on effective management of those items is then the key to effective inventory control.[34]

[34] An example of one procedure designed with this objective is the so-called ABC method, which has been described as follows:

"*A Items.* It is not unusual to find that 10 per cent of the items used in manufacturing represent 75 per cent of the company's dollar inventory investment. These should be ordered, scheduled, and rescheduled for receipt on a weekly, daily, or even hourly basis. Their movement through the shop should have priority and represent the least possible time. The protective stock on such items should be kept to an absolute minimum, and both the vendor's and the manufacturing department's supervision should watch the flow carefully to be sure that no interruption is permitted.

"*B Items.* These items are of secondary importance. From a value standpoint, they do not require as detailed and close control as the *A* items, but they cannot be classified as *C* items because they do need some degree of control. Thus they represent an 'in-between' area. This class normally accounts for 20 to 25 per cent of the total number of items and about 20 per cent of the inventory investment.

"*C Items.* These are numerous inexpensive items that, together, make up a minor part—perhaps only 5 per cent—of the inventory dollar investment. However, it is not unusual to find that they represent 70 per cent of the total items, and production may be held up if any one of them is lacking. The method of control is the exact opposite of that prescribed for *A* items. These *C* items should be stocked economically to minimize the time and effort they require on the part of buyers, order clerks, record clerks, stockkeepers, engineers, cost accountants, and receiving clerks. The company can carry a large protective supply with a minimum investment and, at the same time, receive the benefits of decreased paperwork and handling."

Inventory control policy has also become a favorite field for the application of linear programming techniques.

Conclusion

This, then, is the way in which the American business firm of the type with which this study is concerned makes provision for its future. In planning for the time ahead, it examines the markets in which it is currently operating, to determine their short-run sales potential and to consider their long-run adequacy as a base for corporate continuity. Recognizing the hazard in attempting to foretell the future, it nevertheless cannot, for its own security, avoid making some judgment about the general state of the economy in the coming planning period—whether business firms as a class will be prospering or struggling. Within that general framework it considers the special factors which may accentuate or offset the impact on itself.

The future as seen need not, however, be taken as given. Even should the underlying circumstances develop approximately as expected, the firm's place in the broad economic spectrum is not wholly determined for it but is at least partially subject to its own control. Actions may be initiated which are designed to take advantage of favorable circumstances or to minimize the adverse. Planning such actions requires a survey of the competitive field and decisions on how the firm can most effectively improve its position—at a minimum, retain its standing—relative to the rest of the field.

The result of this effort to foretell and control the future is a calculation of the level of activity at which it expects to be operating. The importance of this calculation is that it enables management to gear its organization to that level, a process requiring time. But the expectation is not always borne out by the fact, and the anticipated level of activity may not materialize. Adjustment may be required. The more accurate the expectation, the less painful and costly the adjustment, but error in judgment is not fatal. The gearing of the organization to expected levels will have entailed certain costs which require time to modify, but the planning process itself will have developed a clearer understanding of the kinds of adjustment which can and will have to be made to move the firm, through budget revisions, from projected to actual to preferred balances, repeating the cycle over and over, month after month, quarter after quarter, as the need is indicated.

Herbert J. Richmond, "Control of Production and Supply Items on a Proportional Value Basis," *Successful Production Planning and Control*, A.M.A., pp. 57–58. While the above statement is geared to materials and work-in-process inventory, it is equally applicable to finished-goods inventory.

Chapter 8

THE PRINCIPAL USE OF FUNDS: COSTS OF PRODUCTION AND DISTRIBUTION

Production to Order and to Stock

Business firms may be classified in a variety of ways. One meaningful distinction is given by dividing them into the two categories of those which produce to order and those which produce in anticipation of orders. In the first category, production must wait until an order is placed, with its detailed specifications. In the second category, production may be planned without respect to specific orders, governed by the firm's own convenience and economy in such matters as leveling out production to permit the retention and efficient use of a stable work force, avoidance of tying up capital in excessive inventory, and effectiveness in completing sales to customers' needs.

One aspect of industrial progress in the last 150 years has been the transfer of the production of many items from the first category to the second, facilitating business planning. This has been made possible by such developments as standardization of styles and sizes (in products ranging from clothing to machine tools), improved interchangeability of parts, on the production front, and specialized distributive functions increasing the ready accessibility of merchandise when the customer wants it.

Job shops which produce only to order are still prevalent in certain industries; they include not only the small machine shop which can provide a specialized tool but also such major industrial activities as General Electric and Westinghouse (which build generators to order), Bethlehem Shipbuilding and Maryland Shipbuilding and Drydock, and large-scale industrial contractors. The list can be extended by the reader without difficulty. Even in these instances, however, the interchangeability of parts permits some production in advance of actual receipt of orders.

140

In moving from the sales budget to the production plan, a firm's actions are affected by whether it is producing to order or in anticipation of order. Firms producing to order tend to operate with shorter planning periods. With less possibility of using inventories as a buffer against production fluctuations, there is more tendency to ups and downs of output. With such variability of output, capital investments which lead to high overhead charges must be treated with caution. The same care must be exercised by other firms which, although operating in anticipation of orders, are producing goods whose life is limited by fashion.

If, in the subsequent discussion, there is some tendency to concentrate on operating plans of a year's duration, this is not intended to imply that production budgeting for such a duration is customary or usual. It depends, among other things, on how much production to order and production for fashion enter into the firm's product mix. Nevertheless, whether a firm is budgeting costs on a two-week or a one-year basis, or (as is perhaps most common) on a one-year basis with periodic revisions, the general intent remains the same—to permit management to manipulate and adjust its production schedules and methods in ways which facilitate achievement of its profit objective.

Production Planning

The point of departure for production planning and cost budgeting is the sales budget. "Our basic premise is the sales budget. The manufacturing people can begin to know the level of their activity only after the marketing end of the business has formulated its plans. The ability of a manufacturing unit to function is directly related to marketing program." [1]

The kind of sales budget needed for effective production planning, however, is not one which simply estimates total sales. Breakdowns by product lines and by time periods within the over-all budget period are needed. Preliminary production plans for perhaps three or four months into the future provide the basis for personnel hiring and materials procurement, but actual production plans are frequently not made final—the tickets issued and the work programmed—until one or two weeks in advance.

> Marketing research releases the detail sales estimates as soon as they are set. Special covering instructions include percentages of total units of each item to be delivered to the shipping room by specified dates.

---

[1] This and the statement in the following paragraph were responses by members of the National Association of Accountants to inquiries made about their production and inventory planning practices, contained in the research report, "Serving Sales through Planning of Production and Inventory," *N.A.A. Bulletin*, January, 1959, sec. 3. The foregoing quotation is found on p. 7 of that report, the succeeding quotation on p. 8.

These percentages are based on experience as to the ratio each line item bears to the total quantity in each style group, tempered by executive judgment as to the quantitative influence of assortment selling, style trends, promotions, etc. We add a safety margin in the beginning-of-the-season percentages.

The developing sales picture is watched by the marketing research unit. As early as possible after the start of the season and as soon as we detect any unusual deviation, we instruct the various production and procurement departments to adjust to the new unit sales goals. This is accomplished by issuing a revised unit sales estimate. If an unusual order is involved, we alert the affected departments immediately.

Other practices are reported:

The market research and analysis section and the sales-production-inventory planning section cooperatively prepare annual and four-month sales forecasts.

The company's policy is to adjust the sales forecast within the year only if the actual cumulative sales deviate from the forecast by more than one month's forward sales. If this condition should prevail for two consecutive months, a re-appraisal of the sales outlook is made and the forecast for the balance of the year is adjusted accordingly.

From the annual sales estimate on each product, an average monthly run is worked out, considering each of the following points.—
1. Average monthly sales
2. Steady employment of workers
3. Minimum economical run
4. Coordination of machines
5. [Coordination of product] lines on same machines
6. [Coordination of] equipment on different machines.

Production planning must also be integrated with inventory control. Expected sales rather than actual sales tend to motivate production planning, but actual sales do intrude into the production schedule via their impact on inventory. As sales draw down the stocks of particular items, the reaching of the predetermined minimum level or stock turnover rate may trigger an order for production of that item, to recover its inventory position, regardless of sales forecast. "The result is that production intended to serve sales and maintain inventory is frequently planned to proceed under the dual authority of the over-all plan and the [inventory] correctives programmed into it." [2]

One food processing company summarized the process: "When our inventories and commitments have been established, the Scheduling Depart-

[2] All the foregoing quotations are from the same, pp. 9, 10, 16, and 11.

ment picks up the ball. Its function is to put together actual sales to date, sales projections, inventories, and commitments, plus data on production facilities, and come up with answers that will guide the month-to-month production operation of our company." [3]

Just as the sales budget must be broken down to product mix, however, so must the production schedule be broken down to work center. The schedule not only indicates the number of finished pieces of particular items which are wanted within a specified time period but identifies the processes which are necessary to achieve the desired output. It is a detailed statement of what work each center will be engaged in processing throughout the time period being programmed. This detail is needed not only to assure that personnel with the appropriate skill requirements are on hand. It is also required to avoid the unexpected emergence of bottlenecks, which might be occasioned by the confluence of several products, all calling for the same processing step, on the same work center, though that center might have been quite capable of handling them seriatim. Or a bottleneck might be caused by a concentration of sales and production in particular seasons beyond the capacity of one or more stages in the production process to handle within the given period, suggesting the advisability of prior production for inventory. Or the emergence of a bottleneck beyond the powers of a production planner to remove by rescheduling the plant's own facilities will signal the necessity for subcontracting some component, or possibly the desirability of capital expansion.

Manpower and Materials Scheduling

With production mapped out tentatively over a period of from several months to a year, and firmly for a period of from one week to several months, it is possible to review the manning table to ensure that workers with appropriate skills are available in the numbers needed, for work weeks which do not require excessive overtime. New hiring or layoffs may follow from this review, which is an integral part of the production planning process. "Our sales projections, interpreted in terms of basic work centers, permit monthly calculations of the direct labor requirements. . . . We relate direct labor to the machines on which it will be used, calculate the manning by machine line, and finally get a total by work center on a monthly basis. Our plant-wide totals, in turn, are the sum of the work-center requirements." [4] Similarly, from a schedule of the product mix which is wanted

[3] Howard C. Wolf, assistant director of purchases, McCormick & Company, in *Case Studies in Production Forecasting, Planning, and Control,* A.M.A. Manufacturing Series, no. 223, New York, 1957, p. 42.

[4] Jack D. Englar, production manager, McCormick & Company, in the same, p. 45.

within the specified production period, the purchasing department can make firm the delivery orders for needed materials and components which may have been tentatively placed some time earlier.[5]

The Multiple Aspects of Costs

The end objective in this scheduling of production, manpower, and materials is the fulfillment of the sales budget with a degree of efficiency that permits achievement of the profit target. It is a low "cost of sales" which is sought. Accomplishment of this objective depends on a variety of factors, among them a high rate of productivity (itself affected by technology and capital investment, supervisory talent, efficiency of labor, low scrap rates, and rate of utilization of capacity) on the one hand, and the prices of materials, the rates of labor, and the cost of capital on the other hand.

As we pursue this subject, we shall encounter diverse uses of the term "cost," and it will be necessary to define that term as we use it. We may initially note two uses which are sometimes confused: economic cost and accounting cost.

By economic cost we mean opportunity cost—the return or value which has been given up by making this product instead of another, and now instead of some other time. The cost of producing A is the profit we could have earned if we had produced B or invested our capital in company C or deposited it at interest in bank D—whichever one of these and other such opportunities is most rewarding. A great many companies think of

[5] "Good purchasing decisions depend upon good forecasting. If we know within reasonable limits the anticipated sales [production] requirements, at least nine purchasing benefits will follow:

1. The amount of materials needed for production to standard specifications can be estimated. . . .

2. Orders can be grouped much better for purchasing in quantity. . . .

3. The amount of cash required to buy what is needed can be estimated accurately. . . .

4. The danger of ordering materials too far in advance of their need can be minimized. . . .

5. The purchaser has sufficient time to line up reliable suppliers and dependable vendors. . . .

6. The manufacturer has time to visit vendors' plants to see whether they are capable of meeting his requirements for quality of work and ability to produce on schedule. . . .

7. The purchasing manager can move quickly to cut back purchasing schedules when sales forecasts indicate a dropoff in expected business. . . .

8. Better vendor relationships can be established by focusing an accurate eye on the future. . . .

9. 'Hurry-up' negotiating of purchasing orders is eliminated. . . ."

David S. Gibson, vice-president—purchasing, Worthington Corporation, in *Aspects of Modern Marketing*, A.M.A. Management Report 15, New York, 1958, pp. 46–47.

economic cost, at least in a limited sense, when they consider how they can invest retained earnings most profitably—though a great many companies limit their field of alternatives to those which their company's own operations present and would not dream of investing earnings in another company even if it brought a higher return. They also make use of the concept of economic cost when they consider whether to put their efforts into one product line rather than another.

By accounting cost we shall mean the cost figures which a company enters on its books, however they may be derived. For some items, such as labor and materials, accounting costs are market costs and do not differ from economic costs. For other items, however, there may be no standard or measure other than convention; depreciation costs fall into this category. The thing which they are designed to measure is understandable enough— the proportion of the remaining value of capital goods which has been used up by producing—but there is no measure of depreciation which can be said accurately to reflect that use. There are several conventions, any one of which is acceptable to other accountants, to other managements, to investors, to internal revenue authorities, though they give different answers; there is no basis for saying that one method is more correct than another, though it may be more beneficial to a company. Thus a surprising number of accounting costs contain an arbitrary element.

The total (accounting) costs of operating a firm over a period of time may be disaggregated—broken down into the pieces which compose the whole. The process of disaggregating costs (as distinguished from allocating costs) does not add any further arbitrary element to what was already present in the aggregate sum. While the method of disaggregation varies from company to company (and even within a company several breakdowns may be obtained for various purposes), one customary breakdown distinguishes between variable costs and period (overhead) costs. Variable costs are so called because they vary with volume. When any change in volume is accompanied by a change in costs, the variable costs are known as direct costs. This applies to the materials and labor which go into a unit of product. The size of a product run cannot be increased, even by one, without using more of both, nor can it be decreased without using less of both. Except in the case of such direct costs, however, other costs remain fixed over some range of output or (what amounts to the same thing) some period of time. Some costs (such as the interest on a bond issue) remain fixed regardless of the level of output; whether the company temporarily ceased production altogether or produced at maximum capacity would have no effect on such payments. These costs are known simply as fixed costs.

Many costs, however, fall somewhere between direct costs and fixed costs. They would remain fixed at any volume between, say, 70,000 and 80,000 units. Below 70,000 units some of these costs could be cut; above

80,000 units additional costs would be incurred. This might be true of the costs of supervision or maintenance, for example. Or the number of salesmen may bear no direct relation to the amount of sales; total sales might fall off or increase by perhaps 25 per cent without any sales personnel being laid off or hired. It is apparent that there is some element of variability along with some element of fixity in such costs. They remain fixed over a range of output or time, but beyond certain limits they vary with output or sales. These have sometimes been labeled semivariable or semifixed costs. They have also been collectively referred to as "period" costs, since they are incurred not on a per piece basis (as is true of direct costs) but for a period of time (range of output). Since the same can be said for fixed costs, it is possible to lump all nondirect costs into a single category called period costs. Thus we may divide all the costs of operating a firm into direct costs and period costs, recognizing that the latter combines some which have a "stepped" relationship to changes in volume (variable period costs) and others which do not fluctuate with volume (fixed period costs).

In disaggregating total costs, we may further divide them into functional categories corresponding to the way they were actually incurred. Thus we would have:

The costs of manufacturing (which would be composed of direct labor and material costs and the period costs of manufacturing)

The costs of selling and distribution (which are considered to be period costs, since the direct relationship of cost to sales is insignificant; the same costs would have been incurred even if a given sale had not been made—the cost of losing a sale may be as great as the cost of making one)

The costs of research and engineering (not always separately identified; these too are period costs)

The general costs of administration (these are not specifically identified with the functions of making or selling but relate to the general management of the company and are period costs)

The financial costs (primarily the cost of capital, a period cost)

Except for the labor and material component of goods produced, then, all other costs are considered as costs relating to a period of time or a range of output. Most of them have a degree of variability along with a degree of fixity, and this variability can sometimes be measured (power costs may be a minimum of $2,000 a month plus $200 for each additional 1,000 units of production over 10,000).

In addition to disaggregating total costs into categories which represent the ways in which expenses were actually incurred, aggregate accounting costs may also be *allocated*—broken down, for control or evaluation purposes, into categories which do not represent ways in which expenses were actually incurred but which are in someone's judgment the portion of some total cost that may fairly be charged to some activity or operation. The two principal ways in which costs may be allocated are by administrative or subordinate units and by product lines.

In the administrative case, total costs of a company may be apportioned among the Dallas sales branch, the engineering division, the Wichita factory, the personnel office, and so on. This requires arbitrarily assessing these administrative units some share in the cost of general administrative and financial period costs.

In the case of allocation by product line, the total costs of running an automobile company are divided among the four-door eight-cylinder sedans, the two-door six-cylinder models, and the station wagons and convertibles and compact cars and all the other models which the company makes. This again requires the arbitrary apportionment of certain general costs of running the company.

In the case of both the administrative-unit and product-line breakdowns, it is the allocation of joint or common costs which contributes the judgmental or arbitrary element. There is no generally accepted standard by which one can logically maintain that common costs should be allocated. We shall not be concerned with the allocation of accounting costs until considerably later in this chapter.

Standard Costs

One other set of cost definitions should be added to our list—expected or budget costs, actual costs, and standard costs. The first two of these are self-explanatory. Expected or budget costs are management's estimates of the costs which it anticipates will be incurred in producing the volume called for by the sales budget. It would be a surprising phenomenon, however, if management's estimates turned out to be exactly right. One can count on there being some deviation of actual costs from those set out in the budget. Hence actual costs are calculated for comparison with estimated costs to see how much of a variance there has been, and why.

There is nothing in either such expected or actual costs, however, that reveals whether they represent an efficient performance, whether either the expectation or the actual is the result of good or bad practice, whether the expenses which were expected to emerge or which did emerge were due to built-in inefficiencies or chance strokes of luck that distorted prior cost experience, on which expectation was based, or to the present level of performance, which gives rise to the actual costs. Cost estimates or collected cost figures do not in themselves constitute bench marks or yardsticks by which to judge whether—if actual cost varies from budget—the cause is due to poor estimates or poor production or something of both.

Standard costs are intended to provide such a guide. They constitute measures of the cost of producing goods under efficient conditions. They are thus useful for controlling production standards as well as for making financial estimates. As an early statement explained the purpose, "The procedure is based on the theory that under normal efficient operating conditions the product can be made for a stated sum, which can be readily calculated from known conditions, and that any expenses incurred in excess of this sum are unnecessary—an economic loss, which it is the duty of management to eliminate." [6]

The earliest recorded account of standard costing goes back to 1908, when an article in the *Journal of Accountancy* gave a tentative statement of its use in a shoe factory. Coming at approximately the time of the rapid spread of cost accounting (stimulated first by World War I and later by NRA regulations) and scientific management (with its methods for determining efficiency in operations), and soon followed by the spread of budgeting in business, standard-cost procedures have become common in many industries, though they are still absent from others. One survey of 388 companies found that some 57 per cent were using standard-cost methods. [7]

The same approach sometimes goes by the name of predetermined costs, since the intent is to establish in advance of production the cost standards which should govern production. The standards which predetermine expected costs vary with company philosophy. In some firms they represent the best possible performance, an ideal or "perfection" standard, one capable of being realized but not often attained, a goal to motivate workers to high-level achievement. Other companies, probably a majority of those using standard costing, pitch their production standards at a level which requires sustained but attainable good performance. There is some allowance for waste and lost time, but the standard is one which, if it is realized on a continuing rather than a spasmodic basis, represents satisfactory efficiency. Occasionally a company is satisfied to write into its standards the average of past performance, without respect to whether that performance has been less efficient than could reasonably be expected.

The philosophy generally encountered among budget officials is that standards which are set so high that they are seldom reached embody unrealistic targets, while standards set so low that they can be reached without effort constitute no standard of efficiency at all. The prevailing preference is for standards which represent a performance which can be reasonably and continuingly realized by a conscientious worker. "If standards are tighter than performance currently attainable, the lower cost will not necessarily follow unless the cost reduction program has first shown a

[6] George Rea, *An Introduction to Predetermined Costs,* National Association of Cost Accountants Official Publications, vol. 5, no. 7, Dec. 15, 1923, p. 4.

[7] Sord and Welsch, *Business Budgeting,* p. 162.

practical method whereby the tighter standard can be attained. On the other hand, a standard which is so loose that it can be met by poor performance buries the very inefficiencies that standard costs are intended to disclose." [8]

Procedures which are designed to accomplish this function of controlling costs by conforming them to predetermined standards are concerned with total, not unit, costs. They provide an instrument for calculating the costs associated with producing what the sales budget calls for, so that profit levels may be projected. They also constitute a tool for controlling actual costs as the budget year unfolds. Costs which exceed standards can be analyzed to discover why, and action can be the more intelligently taken to bring them into line with standard. When the over-all comprehensive budget is broken down into budgets for each administrative unit, not only is each subordinate budget—when based on standard costs—composed of controllable costs, but the standards by which the adequacy of its cost control will be judged are built right into the budget.

For these two objectives of planning and estimating total costs and seeking to control actual costs by reference to standards, fixed costs do not apply. They are, of course, part (sometimes a major part) of the budget, but there are no standards by which they are controlled or reviewed. By their nature they are *in fact* predetermined. Unresponsive to fluctuations in output, they require no special care to ensure that they conform to a level which represents efficient performance for the actual volume which materializes, whatever the budget projection may have been.

Standard-cost procedures for purposes of budgeting costs thus have two characteristics: (1) they are concerned with aggregate (total) costs; (2) they are concerned with variable (controllable) costs.

In some plants, particularly those which produce to order, by job lot, standard cost is computed for each order, as is the variance from standard cost. This requires adding the standard costs of all the operations which have been involved to determine the standard (variable) cost of the product, which is then multiplied by the number of units run. In companies engaged in "process" work, where there are customarily longer runs and larger inventories (production for stock rather than to order), it is more customary to compute the standard costs which are to be "credited" to a work center over a period of time (a day, a week, a month), and it is against this total figure (which represents work on a number of products and orders) that actual costs are debited to determine variances. The work center "collects" the standard costs for each type of product on which

[8] *How Standard Costs Are Being Used* (New York: National Association of Cost Accountants, undated, but bringing together materials originally published in the *N.A.C.A. Bulletin* during 1948), p. 9.

it works times the number of units of that product which it has run, and it is "charged" the actual costs which it has incurred in all the processing it has done.

Budgeting Direct Costs

Keeping in mind the above distinctions between economic and accounting costs, direct and period costs, variable and fixed period costs, actual and standard costs, let us examine the way that costs enter the budget. As we noted earlier, the point of departure is the sales forecast leading to the production schedule. This is the bill of goods for which costs must be computed. The first step is to compute the direct labor and material costs.[9] These are, as we know, the amount of labor and materials associated with any change in volume of output. Since not even one additional unit of product can be produced without some cost in labor and materials, direct costs are often thought of as unit costs. They are often computed as such— the amount of labor or materials per unit of output. This is true even for *standard* direct costs, despite the previous assertion that standard costs for budgetary purposes are aggregate costs. The unit method of calculation is usually employed as the most convenient method of deriving aggregate direct costs, since these vary with any variation in output.

In smaller plants or those which follow less systematized procedures, direct labor costs are usually estimated by each foreman for the particular operations for which he has responsibility, for that quantity of output for which the production schedule calls. These cost estimates may be simple informed judgments, based on last year's or last month's costs adjusted for volume, and reviewed by his superior and perhaps the controller's office for consistency and accuracy. Sometimes the foreman converts by formula the number of units of product into hours of labor, of various types, which are required. Alternatively, he may first convert units of product into the machine running time which is needed to produce them, and from these machine hours the number of labor hours may be computed. Labor costs are then derived by multiplying man-hours by the relevant wage rate. This may be an average of rates or specific rates for specific skills.[10]

[9] The definition of "direct labor" has created problems in some companies where technological change—automation in particular—raises questions about which production operations are "direct" and which "indirect." This is bound to be the case where, as in one company, direct labor is defined with respect to the process or product—labor which changes the size, shape, or appearance. For control purposes, however, financial variability is the only relevant consideration—whether the cost of a particular labor contribution changes directly with each unit of product.

[10] A complicating problem is presented in years when collective agreements fall open for negotiation. To budget labor costs on prevailing rates, when it is expected

Materials estimates follow the same general pattern. Either from knowledge based on experience or from a table of allowances, the foreman calculates the materials required for the projected output, making due provision for scrap and wastage. Frequently the purchasing department will have compiled a catalogue of materials prices, in some instances using current prices and in other cases forecasting price changes, on the basis of which total materials costs for the unit, for the period, for the volume, and for the product mix, can be calculated.

In companies which have adopted standard costing procedures (and even in some which do not follow the standard costing system in its entirety), direct costs are usually computed somewhat more systematically, by any or all of three methods—industrial engineering, historical, or statistical analysis. The best known of these is probably the industrial engineering approach, often subsumed under the rubric of scientific management. One controller describes it briefly:

> We have material quantity standards for each component that we make. It is, therefore, a simple matter to determine the quantity of each kind of material we should have used for the parts which were actually produced in the primary operation. . . . For example, if we are making a part out of steel tubing on an 8-spindle automatic machine and the part is ⅞" long, and the width of the cut-off tool is ⅛", each one of those parts will require 1" of material. If the tube is 10′ long or 120" and the butt end is 4", this would leave 116" of tubing which should provide 116 parts. If fewer parts are produced, then extra material beyond the standard allowance was used, which would represent excessive waste. . . .
>
> Now a word about productive labor standards. The part we are using in our illustration is produced on an 8-spindle automatic machine. Let us assume the basic machine time to complete the operation is 30 seconds. This means that every 30 seconds we will produce one

---

that a new rate will be bargained, introduces distortion into the figures. To use an estimate of what the new rate will be, however, tips management's hand if the information gets out, as it might easily do if foremen are involved in the budgeting process. Practice varies on this point. "It is the policy of the company to prepare the original budget each year without consideration of the wage increase that may be granted in the renewal of the union agreement. The original budget is revised after the union agreement has been signed and the new labor cost has been estimated." A steel company reports that it budgets on the ostensible basis of existing rates, but disguised allowances for probable wage increases can be built into the figures by the use of unspecified contingency reserves, disregarding offsetting productivity increases, or by assuming that subsequent price increases will offset wage increases. Another company reports that it figures on the basis of "our guess as to the amount of the annual wage increase," and another writes in its administrative manual, "No attempt should be made to predict and include in Plans the inflationary or deflationary movements in general wage or price levels. However, expected increases or decreases in labor rates, costs of materials, etc. for the budget year should be recognized."

part, which is two per minute, 120 per hour. This is the maximum output per machine hour. However, we know it would not be practical to use this as a standard, as the operator must be allowed time to load his tubing, check his work, adjust his tools and for personal needs. Let us assume these allowances will reduce the maximum output by 20 per cent. This means the practical output per machine hour is 80 per cent of 120 or 96 pieces. If an operator runs two machines, then the practical output per man hour is 2×96 or 192 pieces. This is converted into standard man time per 1,000 pieces by dividing 192 into 1,000 which is 5.201 hours, slightly more than 5 hours per 1,000 pieces.[11]

When "engineered" standards are not used, as may be true in small firms, standard direct costs can be computed by studying past experience to derive figures which, judgmentally, appear to represent desired standards of efficiency. Statistical systematization of this historical approach is sometimes attempted by the least-squares method.

In companies producing a variety of products, it is necessary to compute the labor and material costs per unit of each product. This schedule of the direct costs of each product multiplied by the expected volume of sales of each product when summed gives the budget item of total direct costs. Since the processing of a product is usually carried on by more than one shop or department, however, and since each subordinate unit has its own budget (the appropriate segment of the over-all comprehensive budget), estimates are customarily made of the direct labor and material costs which are incurred in processing a given product by a particular departmental unit. Just as in the case of the over-all company budget, so in the case of the shop or departmental budget can total direct costs be computed by taking the labor and material (in this case per operation) times the expected volume of each product and summing these.

[11] Nicholas St. Peter, divisional controller, New Departure Division, General Motors, "New Concepts of Information for Management Decisions—in Production," *N.A.A. Bulletin*, August, 1959, pp. 7–8, with slight transposition.

Mr. St. Peter continues: "We have productive labor standards for every component that we make, which makes it possible for us to determine by burden center the standard hours represented by actual production, by simply multiplying the standard time per 1,000 pieces for each part of the number of actual pieces produced. If we divide the actual hours required to produce these parts into the standard hours earned, we will arrive at the per cent of efficiency. We issue an efficiency report each week to each plant manager and each foreman, showing for the week and the month to date by burden center total standard hours earned, total actual hours and per cent of efficiency. The report is a good barometer of performance, as wasted man hours mean also wasted machine time and floor space. Many of these operators are using expensive machine tools. For example, an efficiency of 80 per cent would mean that, not only labor cost but also the fixed capital for floor space and facilities was higher than it should be by 25 per cent."

Variable Period Costs

We turn now to the variable period costs of manufacturing, which are sometimes referred to as overhead, burden, factory expense, or indirect costs of manufacturing.

Actually, of course, all expenses are variable beyond certain volume ranges and over time periods, as economists have recognized with their conception of "long run" as a period within which all costs become variable. Thus depreciation, generally regarded as a fixed cost, based on past investments, is variable over a period when management must decide whether to add to investment and thereby increase the depreciation charges. General administrative salaries are commonly regarded as part of fixed costs, yet members of management who have lived through periods of business downturns or prolonged strikes can testify that their salaries have at times been subject to downward revision.

Nevertheless, for periods as short as the operating year and over the foreseeable range within which output will fall, certain costs can be regarded as fixed and others as varying with volume in some degree which requires determination. Included in the latter category would be such items as supervision, repairs and maintenance, supplies not included in direct material costs, telephone, fuel, and utilities.

There are several ways of computing budget figures for this classification. One method frequently followed in smaller businesses is simply to base projected indirect manufacturing expenses on past experience, modified by anticipated changes in cost or level of activity. Records of the expenses incurred in previous years may be supplied by the controller's office to staff or operating personnel, providing them with a basis for computing various expense categories at the expected levels of production. In establishments large enough to make use of specialized staff assistance, the industrial engineer may estimate schedules for indirect labor, the plant engineer the expense for maintenance and repair, the power engineer the costs of providing power, heat, and light. Such adjustment of current costs on the base of budgeted changes in volume provides a reasonable measure of the bill of indirect expenses for the coming budget period.

The difficulty with all measures of variable period costs is that they are based on some estimate of likely volume (deriving from the sales forecast and budget and the production schedule), and it would be purely coincidence if the budget estimates should turn out to be right. Particularly is this the case when it is recalled that such estimates are based on a presumed product mix and a presumed rate of sales and production by time period, in all cases broken down by administrative units. The chances

for actual performance departing from projected performance are too great
to be ignored. This probability of variance from budget raises problems of
how the budget can be adequately used to control standards of performance. If cost estimates are based on some presumed volume and the
volume does not materialize, the firm operates with a high and inefficient
variable overhead. If volume exceeds prediction, the firm operates with
a low and probably inefficient variable overhead.

The problem does not, of course, arise in the case of direct labor and
materials, since these costs vary by unit, and unit standards have been
provided. But in the case of variable period costs, there is no similarly
simple way of telling that the indirect expenses associated with the actual
level of production are justifiable. The fact that the budgeted expense rate
may have been carefully calculated on the basis of a volume which did
not materialize provides no reassurance that the actual expense rate is
geared with equal justification to the actual level of output. The budget
does not necessarily constitute a standard when the volume basis on which
it was calculated has shifted. This is because some portion of variable
period costs is, by its nature, fixed, just as some portion is variable, and
whether the budget figures remain appropriate even after output levels have
risen or fallen depends on the fixed and variable mix of each of the expense
categories.

Flexible Budgets

To meet this need the flexible budget has been devised. It complements
the engineered work and material measurements in the direct-cost category
as part of the standard-cost procedure, though flexible budgets may also
be used by firms which do not practice standard costing.

The intent behind flexible budgeting is to determine the amount of all
variable period expenses which are appropriate for whatever level of production actually materializes. The planning budget, based on some anticipated sales and production level, in effect constitutes a first approximation,
on the basis of which financial needs may be estimated, personnel may be
hired, materials ordered, and the plant, in general, "tooled up." But if the
actual level of production deviates materially from what was planned, it
is helpful if a new budget is readily available to substitute for the original
one. This the flexible budget provides. It can be used both for the company
as a whole and for a subunit.

In some instances, there is a predetermined variable period expense
budget prepared for several identified ranges of activity. If capacity is
figured at 93,600 units of output or man-hours of direct labor, for example,
a budget of all indirect costs associated with that level of production can
be prepared in advance. Similarly a budget can be prepared for 90 per cent

of capacity or 84,240 units or hours, for 80 per cent of capacity of 74,880, for 70 per cent of capacity or 65,520 units or hours, and so on (Exhibit 1). More frequently and understandably, flexible budgets provide for expenses associated with some range of output (say the range from 80 to 85 per cent of capacity). Under flexible budgeting, whatever output level develops, there is a predetermined budget available to indicate what the appropriate associated expense level is. That becomes the *standard* governing the variable period cost.

Some companies work with larger ranges and fewer substitutable expense budgets. At Burroughs Corporation, for example,[12]

> In order to establish a relationship between individual overhead expenses and direct labor hour volume in each department, three levels of volume are established in each. While more than three levels of volume may be desirable statistically, experience has shown that three estimates receive the optimum of conscientious effort on the part of the department managers. The department manager estimates, for each level of volume, the individual accounts over which he exercises control. . . . Number of direct employees is used instead of quantity of direct labor hours. This figure can be more readily comprehended by the department manager and can be easily translated to hours in the development of the variable budget. . . . The B level represents the average number of direct employees forecast for the coming year and is referred to as the 100 per cent budget. The A level was established at approximately 75 per cent of the B level and the C level at 125 per cent. Wherever possible, one of the levels is made to coincide with the average for the past year.

Rate-of-activity Approaches to Variable Period Costs

Another procedure for providing flexible measures of the indirect costs which should be regarded as "standard" for any given level of output makes use of a rate relationship. Statistical relationships are developed between each of the various indirect expense categories and some measure of the level of activity, perhaps most frequently the direct hours of labor required for the given volume.

One example of how a company segregates and budgets its fixed and variable period expenses, using a rate-of-activity approach to the latter, is given by its controller:

> Non-variable Expenses—We consider this group as those expenses associated with productive facilities, management payrolls and the administration of the business which are kept in readiness without regard

---

[12] Harry J. Schmieg, "Control of Overhead with a Variable Budget in a Research Operation," *N.A.A. Bulletin,* August, 1959, sec. 1, pp. 48, 50.

Exhibit 1
Budget of Period Costs for X Company

	56,160 units (60% capacity)	65,520 units (70% capacity)	74,880 units (80% capacity)	84,240 units (90% capacity)	93,600 units (100% capacity)
Fixed costs (uncontrollable)					
Depreciation	24,000	24,000	24,000	24,000	24,000
Supervision	29,000	29,000	29,000	29,000	29,000
Rent	10,720	10,720	10,720	10,720	10,720
Insurance	4,400	4,400	4,400	4,400	4,400
Taxes	6,760	6,760	6,760	6,760	6,760
Total	74,880	74,880	74,880	74,880	74,880
Variable costs (controllable)					
Indirect labor	25,000	27,200	30,000	33,000	36,000
Supplies	3,300	3,740	4,200	4,700	5,200
Small tools	4,000	4,600	5,200	5,800	6,400
Power	3,700	4,300	4,480	5,040	5,600
Maintenance	3,200	3,600	4,040	4,500	4,920
Payroll taxes	3,000	3,500	4,000	4,500	5,000
Payroll insurance	1,440	1,680	1,920	2,160	2,400
Total	43,640	48,620	53,840	59,700	65,520
Total period costs	118,520	123,500	128,720	134,580	140,400

to actual volume of production or sales. These expenses are more or less rigid in nature; they accrue with time and fluctuate little, if at all, with volume or activity. This group of Expenses is controlled by management decisions through departmental statement. The budget is a fixed dollar amount monthly representing one-twelfth of the annual budget.

Variable Expenses—The remaining expense classification within a department are those variable with volume or activity and management's day to day decisions. These expenses fluctuate dollar-wise with activity, but remain rather constant with the rate or percentage developed for the activity. Control of this group is through individual departmental statements. The monthly budget is determined by applying the fixed budget rate to the actual variable that actuates the budget [such as sales]. This gives us a sliding budget that adjusts itself to the actual level of activity.

Another example has been given by the budget director of the Allen B. DuMont Laboratories of how the indirect labor cost in a departmental operation is analyzed to identify the rate which is "actuated" by some variable (in this instance direct labor) associated with fluctuating production, to derive the appropriate expense item.[13]

The method instituted at DuMont is the direct analysis method wherein each indirect employee and each expense account of any significance is analyzed and the fixed and variable costs determined in direct consultation with the various department heads. The method is direct, simple, and easily understood by the people whose operations are being controlled.

The first step is to determine the level of activity for which the estimates will be made. This should be a recently experienced level, the results of which are fresh in mind, rather than some hypothetical level which is difficult for the operating people to visualize. For this example let us assume that we are setting up a variable budget for the material control department of the Automotive Products Division which manufactures the electronic engine analyzer. Let us assume that recent experience is based on the manufacture of 300 EnginScopes per week so this will be the level of activity used for determining the fixed and variable costs. Any deviation from this 300 per week level can be compensated for by application of the fixed and variable formula to the actual volume level. Direct labor is the budget base to be used in this example. Let us assume further that the amount of direct labor for this level comes to a payroll of $87,000 per week.

We are now concerned with the determination of how much indirect labor is needed in order to service a productive level of 300 Engin-

[13] Thomas S. Dudick, "The Variable Budget: A Modern Tool for Overhead Control," *Business Budgeting*, June, 1958, pp. 22–23.

Scopes weekly. The material control dept. will be used as a basis of illustration.

In discussing the personnel requirements with the department head, we find that after elimination of 2 extra people who were needed on a temporary basis, his estimate of requirements for the 300 per week level is as follows:

Job classification	Number of employees	Total weekly payroll
Section head	1	$140
Secretary	1	80
Planners	5	450
Material handlers	8	600
Storekeepers	5	400
Total	20	$1,670

Now that we know how much indirect labor is needed to service a production level of $87,000 in direct labor, the next step is to break the cost down into the fixed and variable portions.

First, it should be emphasized that fixed costs used for budgeting should be those costs which remain constant within the normal range of operations rather than minimum or standby costs at zero activity. With this as a background let us assume that the department head lists the following personnel as being fixed within the normal range:

Job classification	Number of employees	Total weekly payroll
Section head	1	$140
Secretary	1	80
Planners	2	230
Material handlers	1	80
Storekeepers	1	96
Total	6	$626

Now that the total payroll for Material Control and the fixed portion are known, we can arrive at the variable by simply subtracting the fixed from the total, with the following result:

Job classification	Number of employees	Total weekly payroll
Planners	3	$220
Material handlers	7	520
Storekeepers	4	304
Total	14	$1,044

At this point we know that the fixed portion of the material control department will be budgeted at $626 per week. Our problem is to find a basis for budgeting the variable portion. Since the variable costs will fluctuate with production activity, it would seem logical to relate the variable cost as a percentage of direct labor. Dividing $1,044 by $87,000 gives us a variable percentage of 1.2% of direct labor cost.

On the strength of such analysis, it is possible for a budget director, in preparing his statement for the coming year, to reach such a conclusion as: "From previous experience, supported by historical records, the Budget Department ascertains that $50.00 per month should be budgeted as non-variable in the stationery and office supply account. Present experience indicates that the variable cost in this account has been $.0023 per dollar of direct labor, and the economic trend indicates that an additional $.0003 should be provided for in the budget during the next budget year." [14]

Variants on the Rate-of-activity Approach

Instead of tying each indirect expense category by some rate to the actual level of activity, some companies develop an over-all rate for all variable period expenses. An example of this is provided by one company which adds to direct costs an overhead allowance for each machine-hour of production: [15]

> We utilize individual machine hour rates, or, if several of the same type of machines are in use, the group may be specified as a cost center, and a rate applied for the group. These rates are composed of two elements—the direct labor rate for the productive personnel involved, and an amount of factory burden applicable to the machine or cost center. To illustrate, let us say that an engine lathe carries a machine-hour rate of $6.20 per hour. The machinist operating the engine lathe receives an hourly rate of $2.45. The difference, or $3.75, represents the burden absorption rate for the machine center. Therefore, each productive hour will absorb $3.75 of the total manufacturing expense. If our operation generates 70,000 direct labor hours, total expense absorption would be $262,500, assuming the same center rate and direct labor rate referred to above. Manufacturing expense is, therefore, injected into prime cost through the use of the machine-hour or cost-center rate.

[14] Travis H. Cramb, staff analyst, Sundstrand Machine Tool Co., "Outline for the Development of a Flexible Direct Labor and Manufacturing Expense Budget," *Business Budgeting*, June, 1958, p. 12.
[15] Henry C. Doofe, "The Profit Path as Seen through the Budgetary Control Program," *N.A.A. Bulletin*, November, 1959, sec. 1, p. 51.

A variant on this general approach first estimates the costs which are associated with a particular operation over a period of time. This combines variable direct and variable period costs to arrive at the total (standard) variable costs for that operation. This figure is divided by the standard labor hours which were used (deducting for wastage and rejects) to yield a figure of the standard variable costs per standard productive labor hour. This becomes the unit of measurement. In estimating standard manufacturing costs for the budgeted sales or production volume or for any operation (any subunit, any length of run), the number of productive standard hours required are multiplied by the standard cost per productive standard hour to give total standard variable costs for that operation.[16]

Variable Period Costs as Direct Costs

All variable expenses in period costs are necessarily of the kind which combine an element of fixity with an element of variability, since if they were entirely variable they would then be defined as direct costs (and if entirely fixed they would cease to be variable). For this reason objection has sometimes been raised to the use of a straight percentage of activity (whether the activity is expressed in units of sales, output, direct labor) as a basis for calculating expenses. This argument is justified where individual expense categories are so calculated, since they are thereby converted into direct costs, which they are not. The argument is still pertinent though less valid if applied to a rate which derives overhead expenses collectively. One corporate budget official defends this practice in his own company: [17]

> There are those who will argue that expense with relation to volume does not take the form of a straight line when charted but, rather, rises and falls in steps. This may be true with a single expense classification but, where a number are involved, the steps in each classification will invariably occur at different times, thus tending to offset each other. As a result, in practice, the line of expense with relation to volume takes on a surprisingly smooth and uniform appearance.

It is not, of course, inevitably the case that step variations smooth themselves out in such a way as to validate a single rate of variable expense. In some cases, the step variations may be superimposed on each other to emphasize discontinuities in expense. Nevertheless, the likelihood

---

[16] This is the procedure recommended by Stanley B. Henrici, an industrial engineer, in *Standard Costs for Manufacturing,* 3d ed. (New York: McGraw-Hill, 1960), pp. 49–55.

[17] Henry C. Doofe, *N.A.A. Bulletin,* November, 1959, sec. 1, p. 53.

is in the direction pictured by the above statement. To the extent that period variable costs as well as direct costs vary with volume in a straight-line relationship, there results, of course, the constant unit variable costs which some economists have maintained prevail "over the relevant range" (which is to say the range for which the above phenomenon holds true). The rising marginal costs which have more commonly been assumed in economic theory are deferred by the fact that, as one or another component cost of production steps up to a new plateau, further production improves rather than diminishes factor proportionality, at the same time that for other costs which are near the limits of their existing plateaus, the same increase in production pushes them up to a new level where factor proportionality is inferior. The two effects—at least in some instances—offset each other to preserve some uniformity of variable unit costs.

Controllable and Uncontrollable Expenses

A further distinction which is sometimes made is between controllable and uncontrollable expenses. These are not the same as variable and fixed expenses. They refer, rather, to the location of responsibility for the control of expense, and we shall encounter the concept more immediately in connection with the attempted correction of variances from budget. From the point of view of the company as a whole, fixed expenses may be regarded as noncontrollable during the budget year. From the point of view of an operating segment or administrative unit within the company, however, expenses which are variable for the company as a whole may be non-controllable to it, the unit. Heat, for example, is a variable expense to the firm, but the individual foreman or department head may have little or no control over the expenditures for heat in his own shop.

In breaking down the comprehensive budget into component parts which provide a financial plan and control to each subordinate administrative unit, one principle which receives nearly unanimous approval is that the partial budget should include only those items which are controllable by the unit. These are the only expenses for which the unit can reasonably be held responsible.

Placement of responsibility for expense sometimes is a dual affair. For example, the foreman of a shop may have control over the amount of power which his shop uses, so that he may be properly charged with its cost. But the company's power plant engineer, who provides the power, is responsible for the cost of the power which the foreman actually uses. In this instance, the budgets of each—foreman and engineer—would include controllable costs which together would determine (or help to determine) the total power costs for the company.

Standard Cost of Subcontracted Parts

In addition to computing standard costs on their own manufacturing operations, some large firms which do extensive subcontracting also compute with care the costs which should be standard for their suppliers. At Ford, for example, a cost department estimates a reasonable cost for what it conceives to be the most efficient method of manufacturing a part which is to be bought from another company, without respect to the manufacturing process actually being used by the supplier. This becomes the basis for negotiating the price which will be paid for the component. The same practice is followed by R.C.A.[18]

[18] George K. Bryant, operations manager, R.C.A. Victor Television Division, writes as follows in the *N.A.C.A. Bulletin,* November, 1956, sec. 1, pp. 398–399: "In the Television Division, the cost of purchased material is by far the greatest element of total plant cost. For this reason, we use our standard cost system to control both purchased material costs and plant manufacturing costs. Our standard costs are based on engineered standards which remain in effect for a twelve-month period. For them we establish certain fundamental cost data. First, all raw material standards are based on a survey and study of mill prices of basic materials in all their forms and shapes. Second, a survey is conducted once a year to determine direct labor wage rates by occupation in certain geographical areas. Third, we determine, by survey, overhead liquidation rates by machine center prevailing at our outside suppliers in the same geographical areas. With this basic data at our command, it is possible to engineer our standard costs.

"Normally, a standard cost is issued the same day the blueprints are released. The part or sub-assembly is processed, assuming minimum runs of 10,000 pieces on modern machinery and employment of efficient tools. Material is calculated allowing for efficient utilization and minimum waste. The direct labor is processed by laying out the sequence of operations and then applying synthetic time values, or 'pre-rates' as they are sometimes called. The standard wage rates and overhead liquidation rates are applied to arrive at an efficiency standard cost. This is the cost we would expect our own plants to achieve if the item were to be manufactured by them. We then add a factor for administrative and sales expenses and profit to arrive at the purchased standard cost. Standard costs are engineered for most but not all purchased parts. Exceptions are hardware shelf items which can be procured on the open competitive market at essentially the same price from all suppliers. Also excepted are electronic tubes and highly specialized items, such as ground lenses. These few items have standard costs based on current market prices.

"Our purchased standard costs are used as control tools in many ways. For example, a copy is forwarded to the purchasing department where it is routed to the buyer responsible for the particular type of part. The standard is filed in the office of the buyer long before he receives requisitions to purchase the part. The buyer is, therefore, better equipped to evaluate quotations when received and to negotiate with suppliers when prices seem high. Through discussion of the material content and cost, the sequence of operations, the direct labor value, plus overhead value, set-up allowances, and administrative and profit figures, suppliers are usually convinced that we know what these costs should be and their quoted price usually falls in line. Millions of dollars have been saved in our company by proper use of this control tool."

The costs of subcontracted parts or components is a direct cost to the purchasing company, but the standards which companies like Ford and R.C.A. apply to their purchase price involve both the direct and variable period costs of production in the supplier company. These are based on standards which the purchasing company believes comport with the standards of efficiency which it expects from its own operations.

Completing the Cost Budget

We have now examined, even though cursorily, the budgeting of direct and variable period costs. For companies using the standard-cost approach, these are the only two categories of cost which are relevant to budgetary control, since they are the only costs which are controllable within the budget period. The combination of standard labor and material costs (directly or statistically measured) and of standard variable period cost (as derived from a flexible budget) together yield the standard cost of an operation for a given volume or period of time.

To complete the company's comprehensive budget, however, some additional cost figures must be added to the direct and variable period costs of manufacturing. First, the variable period costs for the nonmanufacturing end of the business must be added in. (It will be recalled that for all practical purposes all such costs may be treated as period rather than direct.) In nonmanufacturing operations there is less employment of a standard-cost approach. A few companies have attempted to apply the flexible budget approach, but in these instances it has been more a matter of managerial judgment about how much expense should be permitted at a given level of operations rather than how much expense is required.

The reason for this discrepant treatment of manufacturing and nonmanufacturing costs lies primarily in the fact that work measurement is most meaningful in the case of repetitive operations, such as characterize production. Where a work hour is filled with a continually changing assortment of tasks, most of which differ from even the previous performance of the same or similar task in some—perhaps minor—respect, the applicability of time and motion measurement is materially weakened. Nevertheless, in some types of clerical operations, as in banks and insurance companies, where large numbers of clerks perform relatively routine functions over some period of time, work standards have been developed. Somewhat more simply, one company which employs a large number of white-collar personnel reports that "based on studies, we have established the optimum workloads for numerous key operating and clerical positions. By relating the actual activity to these 'standards' we endeavor to keep a high percentage of our payroll cost 'variable' rather than 'fixed.' "

In the distribution end of business activity, order filling has shown it-self to be more amenable to the development of work standards in such operations as warehousing and shipping, which can be scheduled in ad-vance, than order getting, in which results are dependent on factors which preclude scheduling. The efforts which have been made to work out the standard cost of calling on a sales prospect, of typing a letter, of entering an invoice item, of posting a remittance, or of making a window collection are related less to the engineering measurement of what time should be allowed for any such operation than to the statistical measurement of what level of efficiency or cost may reasonably be expected in the future for a "period" of such operations (when the length of letters and the difficulties of making a sale or the peculiarities of remittance posting, and so on, are given time to average out). Such statistical measures constitute a standard which can be used to control excessive costs by analyzing the reasons for variance from them, but the control is less direct and precise.

One last set of figures must now be added in to complete the cost budget. These are the fixed period expenses—depreciation, general management, property taxes, insurance. Any control over these sums must have been exercised at the time they were incurred, in a period preceding the budget period. "Standards" are not relevant to these items for budgetary pur-poses.[19]

---

[19] This statement involves some exaggeration, in so far as changes in fixed costs may sometimes be negotiated, and in so far as their amount is based on accounting practices which may be changed by management. This is seen from the report of one "practice session" on the subject of budgeting maintenance expenses during the 1956 conference of the N.A.C.A.:

"A member in the chemical industry revealed that capital investment is the base used to calculate a reasonable budget figure for maintenance charges. The budget for the company as a whole, as well as for individual departments, bears a percent-age relationship to the respective capital investment. It was stated that this company has trade sources which can provide industry-wide data on what other firms are spending for repair and maintenance in relation to capital investment. The reason-ableness of the figures can thus be verified against those of competitors. . . .

"The use of an allowance per ton factor was described by a participant. Depart-mental foremen are given an amount each month based on forecast production and each is held responsible for living within his budget. The rate per ton is based on experience over a five year period. . . .

"Sales form the basis of another company's maintenance budgeting procedure, which was described to the group. Inasmuch as everything (costs, expenses, profits, etc.) must come out of the sales dollar, it is considered desirable that the over-all repair budget be in proportion to the sales in the year. . . ."

From "Control of Maintenance Costs," *N.A.C.A. Bulletin,* September, 1956, sec. 3, p. 157.

It is clear that where maintenance charges are based on capital investment, they constitute a nonfluctuating, fixed expense for the budget period. Where based on tonnage or sales, they are treated as a variable cost. It would be stretching a point,

The total of direct costs and period costs gives a measure of the outflows which can be expected to result from the year's level of operations, based on the sales budget. They can be matched against the sales revenues to give an initial rough idea of the profit which can be anticipated if the sales budget is made good. The sales revenues minus the direct and period costs of manufacturing yield the gross profit for the firm. From this must be deducted all other period costs to determine the net profit. An alternative way of arriving at the same result is to deduct projected direct costs from the anticipated sales revenues, giving what is sometimes labeled the "contribution margin," out of which must come all period costs and whatever profit is to be earned.

To summarize, budgeted costs include direct material and labor costs, the cost of any subcontracted parts or components, and variable and fixed period costs. The standard costs which are used as a guide to budgeting aggregate cost levels on the strength of predetermined standards of efficiency are direct costs (based on engineered or statistical measurement of unit costs) and variable period costs (incorporated in flexible budgets for output ranges or as a rate of some variable associated with volume).

Standard Product Costs

The standard-cost procedures which have been described above apply to processes or operations. They are concerned with predetermining the *total* costs of producing a given output. For this purpose, as has already been noted, fixed costs are not relevant, since they do not fluctuate with levels of output. For cost-planning purposes, standard variable costs (direct and period) are all that are needed.

Standard costs may also be used, however, to analyze the costs associated with turning out a particular product or product line, and for this purpose the *totals* of *variable* costs are inadequate. It is generally considered necessary to determine the *full unit* cost of the product or product line. Among other things, this necessitates inclusion of fixed costs in the standard-cost procedure.

The uses which managements make of standard product costs are several. Such costs are clues to the products which should be included in the product line, the sales emphasis which should be applied to each, and the prices which should be sought for them. The relative profitability of one product group may be ascertained relative to other product groups already in the company's line, relative to proposed new product groups, relative to the same group's past performance, and relative to some profit objective. The importance which is attached to such analysis is indicated by one

---

however, to say that in the first instance they are beyond the possibility of control or manipulation by management during the budget period.

survey which disclosed that fifty-nine out of seventy companies interviewed had developed such information.[20]

> It has long been the practice of my company to bring to management's attention, and particularly to our sales people, "all in" costs and to compare these "all in" costs with selling prices. Our schedules display the income both before and after taxes for each and every product we manufacture. We have always found this information not only a valuable guide in pricing, but also in the selection of products for intensified sales effort, for investment viewpoints, and a useful tool to factory management in specific cost studies.

> One company stated that the first time it determined the profit margins being realized on individual products, it found that certain items were highly profitable, but that sales volume for these items was small, presumably because little sales promotion work had been done on them. When these products were stressed more heavily in advertising and selling, a substantial increase in volume was obtained with a beneficial effect on over-all profits of the company.

> A company in the retailing field emphasized the value of knowing the cost of each service which was added to the merchandise. Here it was stated that management was in a better position to decide when such services as gift wrapping, demonstrations and advice to help customers select and use merchandise, delivery, etc. were desirable.

Another report states: [21]

> A full cost allocation and a resulting net profit by products gives [the company] evidence of the extent to which each product they are merchandising is contributing to [an] adequate return. Since they are presumably in business for the long pull, they are interested beyond the point of whether the products they are merchandising cover the related direct expenses. They want and should have knowledge as to whether these products are covering, not only the direct expenses, but also those general expenses necessary to carry on the business from year to year. If these latter expenses are not covered properly, obviously the company will not earn its proper profit return on an over-all basis.

This type of information and analysis is not directly related to budgeting, since it requires an allocation of costs along lines which do not conform to any administrative responsibility. The unit-cost figures which are developed are accounting abstractions, having no counterpart in reality, en-

[20] *Analysis of Non-manufacturing Costs for Managerial Decisions* (New York: National Association of Cost Accountants, undated), p. 42. The next three quotations are from the same publication, pp. 62 and 63.

[21] Arthur H. Smith, assistant controller, General Mills, Inc., "Distribution Cost Analysis Points the Way to More Profitable Business," *New Frontiers for the Industrial Accountant* (1950 Conference Proceedings, N.A.C.A.), pp. 89–90.

joying no conceptual relationship to real life by which their reliability may be tested. Several alternative answers can be plausibly developed to the question, What is the cost of producing Product A? and there is no way by which it can be demonstrated that one is right and the others wrong.

The problem comes in allocating among several or many products or product groups costs which are common to them all. Costs which vary with different levels of output of a particular product can be measured and attributed directly to it, but costs which, whether variable or fixed, cannot be attributed directly to any product because incurred on behalf of them all can only be allocated on some kind of arbitrary basis. "Fundamentally, overhead is a product cost impossible or impractical to charge directly with accuracy. If this is so, how can it be charged accurately by allocation?" [22]

"Reasonable" Allocation

The general principles which tend to guide cost accountants in allocating common or joint costs attest to the element of judgment (arbitrariness) in their decisions. "Fairness" and "reasonableness" are most often invoked. "Bases of cost allocation must be fair and equitable." ". . . the ideal selling price should reflect all costs allocated as equitably as possible among all products." "Allocation bases are chosen for reasonableness of the underlying assumptions because it cannot be demonstrated that any one basis is correct to the exclusion of others." [23]

The only costs which escape arbitrary allocations for product costing purposes are directly variable costs incurred in producing a single product —the actual changes in the amount of materials and labor when output of a given product changes. All other costs (those which we have here referred to, collectively, as period costs, as well as the direct costs of jointly produced products) require allocation—if allocation is attempted—on a judgmental basis which may be defended as "reasonable" or "equitable" but not as "necessary" or "valid."

Period costs, as has been noted previously, may be classified as variable and fixed. The variable period costs differ from direct costs in that they do not vary by units but in steps or ranges. They contain some element of fixed cost along with an element of variability and are hence often referred to as semivariable or semifixed. Because they contain an element of fixity, like period costs which are wholly fixed in nature they require arbitrary

---

[22] Marion H. Simpsen, corporate controller, R. G. LeTourneau, Inc., "The Fallacies and Postulates of Accounting," *N.A.A. Bulletin*, February, 1958, p. 41.

[23] The first two quotations are from *Analysis of Non-manufacturing Costs for Managerial Decisions*, N.A.C.A., pp. 20, 25–26, and the third is from *Costing Joint Products* (New York: N.A.C.A., 1957), p. 30.

allocation. But because they also contain an element of variability which can sometimes be attributed on a small-run or short-period if not a per-unit basis, the degree of arbitrariness in their allocation is not so great as in the case of costs which are wholly fixed.

The judgmental nature of the cost allocation problem is especially evident in the case of what may be termed "dependent products" (those which, like by-products, are derivatives of other "major" products, whose output fluctuates directly with the parent product and inversely with alternative by-products which might be made in their stead). In these instances the customary accounting practice is to impute all costs of production to the major product up to the point at which the dependent product is separated off, and to deduct from those costs any net revenue from the sale of the dependent product. The "credit" to which the by-product gives rise is in effect the portion of the joint costs which have been allocated to it, since total costs have been reduced by that amount. For example: [24]

> A meat packer finds it important to know profit or loss promptly on each lot of animals purchased in order that management may know when action should be taken. Byproducts are not always sold immediately. Moreover, it is not practical to measure the actual yield of byproducts from each lot of animals. Through numerous tests the company has developed standard yields for the byproducts from each kind and grade of animals. Standard prices (which are current market prices less costs of disposal) are applied to standard yields and the resulting standard values determine the amount of the byproduct credit for each lot of animals processed.

In other companies, however, the cost of by-products is considered to be only those processing, distribution, and administrative costs which occur from the point of separation from the major product: [25]

> Through research, uses were developed for a byproduct which was previously a waste difficult to dispose of. The byproduct is now transferred at no value to the plant which uses it because management feels that the development of the byproduct did not reduce costs of the major product and that the profit arises from utilization of material formerly wasted.

The place of "reasonableness" in making such determinations is further demonstrated when a by-product which once was viewed as only a means of reducing costs of the major product assumes increasing importance, even to the point of being upgraded to the status of a major product in its own

[24] *Costing Joint Products,* N.A.C.A., p. 15.
[25] The same, p. 19.

right. Under such circumstances, the accounting procedure too is likely to undergo change: [26]

> An integrated steel company determined the cost of coke by charging coke with all costs of producing the coke and the accompanying byproducts. Sales value of the byproducts was credited to the coking operation to obtain a net cost of coke produced. With growth in demand for some of the coke byproducts as raw materials in chemical manufacturing, they had become substantially more valuable. As a result, management of this company concluded that customary byproduct accounting procedure understated the cost of coke and also understated the cost of steel produced. It decided that items classified as byproducts had now become co-products. Byproduct accounting procedures were therefore discontinued and methods instituted for determining a separate cost for each product.

The above cost allocation practices relate to dependent products derived from the manufacture of major products. In the case of independent products—a case which is more frequently found in a company's product line—the basis for cost imputation would appear to be more substantial. The sale and production of one product may increase without concomitant effect on the output of other products. Direct variable costs will of course increase, and if the increase in volume carries past the limit of the range for which variable period costs are adequate, then variable period costs will also increase. If the output of no other product has simultaneously changed, it would in this instance be possible to ascertain the incremental cost of the added output. Even where the volume of other products changes, and these products share in the services represented by the variable period costs, it would seem theoretically feasible by multiple correlation analysis to untangle the change in costs which might be attributed to the one product.

For certain types of decisions (such as whether the company should accept new sales at a concession price) such incremental costs may indeed be computed, but this is not the information about which we are now talking. Identification of the incremental costs involved in a change of output does not disclose the per-unit cost of producing that product at all. And this is the problem with which cost accountants wrestle when they attempt to derive a *standard* cost of a product. Thus, even in the case of "independent" products, the imputation of common variable costs to any

[26] R. Weaver Self, "Developing Better Byproduct Costs for Pricing," *N.A.C.A. Bulletin,* September, 1956, cited in *Costing Joint Products,* N.A.C.A., p. 23. The latter report is based on field investigation of accounting practices of forty companies. "The field study disclosed a few instances where extreme increases in price of a byproduct had caused the byproduct credit to exceed the entire cost of the main product."

one product necessarily calls for the use of judgment and reason, not subject to proof or disproof of validity, hence arbitrary in this sense.

Allocating Period Costs among Products

The allocation of period costs (whether variable or fixed) on a unit-of-product basis really involves two quite distinct questions: (1) In a multi-product line, how may costs be distributed among the several or numerous products to arrive at a cost per product? (2) In attempting to determine the cost per unit of product, over what volume should overhead be distributed? This second question would be pertinent even in companies producing a single homogeneous product. Let us consider these two problems in the above order.

Probably the most generally followed procedure for allocating costs among a clutch of products is to select, for the particular cost to be allocated, some common factor or denominator by which the sum may be divided. For example, in allocating the costs of warehousing products, their relative cubic content may be the basis. Administrative costs may be allocated in another way: [27]

> A company which desired to allocate expenses of a divisional administrative office defined the functions of this office as planning, developing, and operating the division to obtain the best possible return on capital invested in it. The company then reasoned that expenses of carrying out these functions were related to the capital invested in the division and that divisional administrative expenses could be properly allocated to sub-units of the division on the basis of relative amount of capital invested in each.

In the search for "reasonable" and "equitable" bases on which to assign costs, two broad principles seem to have been favored most frequently. These are that the factor or denominator used should apportion costs in line with the "benefit" which each product can be presumed to receive from the common cost item or that it should be in line with the "ability" of the product to carry the cost load.

The allocation of divisional administrative costs on the basis of invested capital, referred to above, is an example of apportionment on the basis of presumed benefit. Most frequently the basis for allocation by benefit is some physical component—raw materials by weight or volume, for example. "A chemical process splits a raw material into three co-products in essentially fixed proportions. Joint costs are allocated to the products on the basis of pounds of each product produced." "In the production of

---

[27] *Analysis of Non-manufacturing Costs for Managerial Decisions*, N.A.C.A., p. 21.

natural gas, both gas and liquid petroleum condensate are jointly produced from gas wells. One company allocates producing costs between the
two products on the basis of energy content measured in British Thermal
Units." [28]

This benefit basis for apportionment encounters difficulty, however,
when the relative sales value of the end products differs markedly from
the relative amounts of the common element incorporated in them. For
example: [29]

> . . . at a given time, a bushel of soybeans could be converted into
> approximately 47 pounds of meal and 11 pounds of oil at a cost of
> $2.32 for materials and processing expense. At the same time, market
> prices were $0.025 per pound for meal and $0.12 for oil. By allocating
> costs on a poundage basis, a cost of $0.04 per pound would be as-
> signed to each product. The resulting product costs are compared with
> market values in the table below.

| Product | Output | Cost allocated on poundage basis | | Market values | | Profit or (loss) on production |
		Per lb.	Totals	Per lb.	Totals	
Meal ...	47 lbs.	$.04	$1.88	.025	$1.175	($0.705)
Oil	11 lbs.	.04	0.44	.120	1.320	0.880
Totals			$2.32		$2.495	$0.175

> It is seen that the resulting cost of meal is in excess of market value
> of the inventory and management would likely question reasonableness
> of product profit or loss figures in a situation like this. Moreover, it is
> difficult to see how these product costs would be helpful in managerial
> decisions with respect to the products since both must be produced
> together in practically fixed proportions.

In such a case, it is likely that the benefit basis would be abandoned
in favor of the ability-to-carry-the-load basis of cost allocation. Under this
approach, the several products share the common cost load in proportion
to the prices which the market sets on them or permits to them. An example of that practice is as follows.[30]

> A company which processes soybeans and other similar materials
> determines cost of co-products for inventory purposes in the following
> manner. For purposes of illustration, it is assumed that one bushel of
> soybeans yields 47.50 lbs. of meal and 10.95 lbs. of oil, with 1.55 lbs.
> loss.

[28] Both examples come from *Costing Joint Products*, N.A.C.A., p. 31.
[29] The same, p. 32.
[30] The same, p. 33.

Basic Data

a. Current market price of soybeans—per bushel	$2.42½	
b. Add crushing expense and margin	.22	
c. Total replacement cost of products at market ..	$2.64½	

Market Ratio of Oil and Meal

d. 47.50 lbs. meal at market price of $50.00 per ton	$1.18¾	48.3%
e. 10.95 lbs. oil at market price of 11.61¢ per lb. .	1.27	51.7
f. Total market value—58.45 lbs. product	$2.45¾	100.0%

Product Cost Determination

g. Cost of meal—48.3% of $2.64½	$1.27¾
h. Cost of oil—51.7% of $2.64½	1.36¾
i. Total market replacement cost	$2.64½

Here again, however, difficulties may be encountered, in this case due to product "costs" which fluctuate with disproportionate movements in product prices, even though nothing in the production process has changed and raw-material components have remained stable:

> Some companies participating in the field study reported that they had found such fluctuations in product costs and profits were confusing to management and that the figures had sometimes led to undesirable shifts in sales emphasis or selling prices. It was also suggested that the method might mislead management if it created the impression that all products were equally profitable because they show the same margin per dollar of allocated joint cost. One writer has commented that "This is really not so much a method of allocating costs as it is a device for allocating profit or loss according to sales value." [31]

An example illustrates the dangers which attend the use of a price- or sales-value figure as a basis for apportioning costs: [32]

> One company which allocated a considerable amount of cost to products on the basis of sales dollars raised prices on certain specialty lines. At the end of the year it found that low priced products on which the prices had not been advanced showed higher profits despite the fact that unit volume and total costs for these products were very close to the same figures for the previous year. Management questioned the product profit figures because bonuses were being paid to product sales managers on the basis of net profit. Study of the situation disclosed that an increase in dollar volume of sales resulting from increased selling prices on some products had reduced the ratio between sales

[31] The same, p. 34. During 1960, when the home appliance market was experiencing a considerable slump, at least one company which produces both an automobile and an appliance line eased the charges on its appliance division by shifting a somewhat higher fixed-cost allocation to its automotive line.

[32] *Analysis of Non-manufacturing Costs for Managerial Decisions,* N.A.C.A., p. 23.

and costs allocated on a sales dollar basis. Since the same ratio was used in costing all products, the low priced products were not charged with as much cost as before.

When the objective of product costing is to obtain some measure of profit by product, a method by which costs are dependent on sales offers little guidance. When product costs arrived at in this matter are made the basis for pricing, the misuse is compounded and can only lead to circular reasoning, with costs which are based on prices being made the basis for price determination.

Thus, despite the effort to apportion a common cost item on some reasonable and equitable basis, using whatever factor seems most appropriate to a particular expense item, the judgmental element cannot be escaped—the element which is arbitrary in the sense that another basis might also rationally be justified. In one survey of ways in which companies allocated non-manufacturing costs, the following results emerged: [33]

Basis of allocating advertising costs among products	*Number of companies*
Dollar sales volume (actual)	9
Dollar sales volume (projected)	3
Projected sales in physical units	1
Cost of goods sold	3
Other	2
	18

Basis of allocating general administrative expenses	*Number of companies*
Sales volume:	
Budgeted dollar volume	3
Actual dollar volume	9
Actual physical units	3
	15
Cost of goods sold:	
Budgeted cost	6
Actual cost	14
	20
Estimated division of executives' time	2
Gross profit	1
Total of other costs	1
Other	3
	42

This diversity of practice provides ample reason for questioning the significance of the cost figure for producing a unit of a given product in a multiproduct line, after all costs have been absorbed.

[33] The same, pp. 53. 59–60.

Perhaps in part because of this uncertain and arbitrary element in the cost apportionment problem, some companies have adopted a simplified procedure, akin to that for determining standard variable period costs by operation or process, described earlier. The total of all costs, other than direct costs, is estimated as for a budget. This includes factory burden, selling costs, and expenses of general administration—all the costs, in fact, except direct labor and material costs. This total of all overhead (period) costs is then divided by the budgeted number of direct labor hours required over the period or for a given volume to obtain an overhead rate (termed an "application rate"), which becomes the general measure of overhead costs. The cost of any unit of product may then be determined by multiplying the number of direct labor hours involved in its production (as estimated from engineering, historical, or statistical analysis) by the application rate, and adding this to its direct cost.

The rationale behind this simplified procedure is that the reasonable or equitable share of any product in overhead costs is in proportion to the amount of direct labor incorporated in it. This is the benefit theory again, here applied to period costs collectively. As we already know, however, this presumption is not always justified. The following example makes the point.[34]

> In costing a packaging operation a company applied indirect costs of the packaging department on the basis of direct labor hours. Hourly burden [application] rates were high because expensive equipment was used but unit costs were low because volume was large. The sales department then designed a new display package which it wished to test for effectiveness before buying special purpose packaging machinery to handle the new design. Some of the operations were done by hand. While the unit labor cost of these operations was reasonable, addition of departmental burden to this labor made the cost of the package exceedingly high. The sales department contended that this was not a correct cost and that it would discourage improvements in packaging which might be beneficial to profits by increasing sales. This contention seems to be justified because introduction of the new package caused little, if any, increase in the total amount of indirect costs to be allocated in the packaging department.

Allocating Period Costs over Volume of Output

We have been discussing product costing where apportionment must be made among costs which are common to a number of products. In the search for a figure representing the unit cost of a product, management also encounters a second problem—the volume of output over which fixed costs are to be apportioned.

[34] The same, p. 24.

As with cost allocation to products, this is an accounting rather than a control problem. As volume varies, there is nothing that a foreman or the president can do about modifying costs that are fixed. The interest in allocating fixed costs over some volume of output lies chiefly in the attempt to determine the "full" unit cost of a product, which requires a determination of how much of period costs can be said to be incorporated in each unit. The two procedures for doing this which are most widely practiced are absorption costing and the use of standard volume.

Under absorption costing the fixed costs for a period are divided by the actual output for that period, so that total costs are always wholly "absorbed" in the cost-per-unit figure. This can be done either on an ex ante basis for purposes of predetermining unit costs by making use of the output estimates in the budget, or on an ex post basis by using actual figures. The difficulty with this procedure lies in the fact that the resulting unit costs fluctuate from year to year as output fluctuates. This makes cost comparisons quite meaningless. Moreover, where unit cost figures are the basis for pricing policy, or even one consideration in pricing policy, unit costs determined by the absorption method become actually mischievous, since they would seem to dictate raising prices when volume (demand) was low and lowering prices when volume (demand) was high.

Unit-cost figures based on wholly absorbed overhead costs likewise contribute difficulties to income accounting. While all fixed costs may have been "absorbed," for accounting purposes, into the products produced, how much they are credited with contributing to current income, by a return of costs, depends on sales rather than production. The overhead element in costs is impounded in inventory (affecting assets), from which it is later released to affect income. For the current income period, the extent to which overhead is covered, in an accounting sense, depends not only on the amount of sales out of inventory but also on the year in which they were produced and in which they incurred their overhead charge. Thus, under absorption costing, we have the peculiar result that fixed and variable costs are the reverse, on a unit basis, of what they are on an aggregate basis: on a per-unit basis, fixed costs become variable and directly variable costs are fixed.

Standard Volume

Because of these disadvantages associated with absorption costing, an alternative method of allocating fixed costs to derive full unit costs has been devised. This is the standard volume (sometimes called normal volume) approach.

Standard volume is a predetermined output on the basis of which overhead is allocated, but unlike absorption accounting—which sets volume equal to the sales forecast—standard volume is presumed to be the "average" or "normal" volume over a period of years, usually construed as a "cycle." It may, however, also take trend into account in the same way, that is, by setting output at a level which is expected to average out over, say, a three- or five-year period.

Where a single product is produced, standard volume can be stated in terms of so many units of that product. In the case of a multiproduct company, standard volume is often stated in terms of "capacity," and fixed costs are divided by the number of direct labor hours associated with the percentage of capacity which has been selected as "normal." This yields standard fixed costs per productive labor hour. Since standard *direct* labor costs per unit of product have already been calculated for budgetary purposes in companies following standard-cost procedures, it is then possible to apportion overhead per unit of each product in the product line on this basis. United States Steel is said to use 80 per cent of capacity as its standard volume, the Aluminum Company 70 per cent, General Motors 80 per cent, International Harvester 70 per cent (at least in one division of the company), the Linde Division of Union Carbide 90 per cent.[35]

When actual volume exceeds standard volume, so that total overhead credits are greater than costs, overhead is said to be "overabsorbed." When actual volume falls short of standard volume, overhead is said to be "underabsorbed." The difference does not usually enter into inventory valuations, however, but is charged off directly to the profit-and-loss account. The distinction from absorption costing in this respect is expressed in the statement of one financial manager that "unabsorbed costs are costs and they

---

[35] These figures are taken from A. D. H. Kaplan, J. B. Dirlam, and R. F. Lanzillotti, *Pricing in Big Business* (Washington: The Brookings Institution, 1958), pp. 15, 26, 50, 71, and 123.

Albert Bradley, former General Motors chairman, explained that company's standard volume concept to a Senate committee as follows:

> "We endeavor in planning for capacity to—we take the number of days there are in the year, and then take out the Sundays and holidays, and then we take out the minimum number of days . . . to turn around—I mean to bring out new models.
>
> "From this we find there are 225, taking out all the Sundays, holidays, and Saturdays, and 15 full days, or 30 half days, for turning around, giving 225 days, which we would like to run the plants year in and year out.
>
> "But we don't use 225, we use 80 per cent of that as a standard volume, because ours is a business that you might call cyclical. . . . So, to allow for that cyclical factor and other conditions beyond our control, we take 80 per cent of that 225 days. . . . So that gives us 180 days. And that, multiplied by our daily capacity, gives us a standard volume, which we work up by divisions, and which we hope to average."

From *Administered Prices: Automobiles, Report of the Subcommittee on Antitrust and Monopoly, Committee on the Judiciary,* 85th Cong. 2d Sess., November, 1958, p. 106.

belong in the profit and loss statement but not in the cost of manufacturing the products we are fortunate enough to be still making." [36]

We have been talking here about fixed period costs. It will be recalled that variable period costs likewise have a fixed as well as a variable element. This introduces a complicating problem. It is not consistent to allocate variable period costs (in so far as they contain a fixed-cost element) to an actual output different from standard volume, when standard volume is the basis for distributing fixed costs. At the same time it is not consistent to allocate variable period costs on a standard-volume basis to the extent that they fluctuate with actual output like direct costs. For this reason there is considerable pressure on and by cost accountants to redistribute all variable period expense items to either the fixed- or direct-cost category.[37]

Where this can be accomplished, the standard-volume concept achieves the purpose of establishing *unit* product costs which are fixed rather than variable, in distinction to absorption costing. If variable period costs cannot, however, be assigned to the direct- or fixed-cost categories, management is faced with the choice of one or the other of the inconsistent policies mentioned above—allocating variable period costs on an actual-volume basis or on a standard-volume basis.

Uses of Product-unit Costs

What should be emphasized in all full-cost unit estimates is that such figures, however useful they may be for other purposes, have no use for control purposes. The allocation of common overhead costs over some arbitrary volume to derive a figure which may be labeled "full unit cost" constitutes no aid in cost control, since it is based on an arbitrary assumption which could be replaced with another assumption having equal rationale, and since it applies to nothing about which any administrative unit can do anything. As noted previously, as long as period costs are involved (and

---

[36] Processing Costs," discussion at the 1954 Conference, *N.A.C.A. Bulletin,* September, 1954, p. 143.

[37] The cost accountant's ideal, indeed, is to view all costs "as ultimately clinging to definite items of goods sold or service rendered. If this conception could be effectively realized in practice, the net accomplishment of the enterprise could be measured in terms of units of output rather than of intervals of time." (W. A. Paton and A. C. Littleton, *An Introduction to Corporate Accounting Standards* (American Accounting Association, 1940), chap. 2. Again, "It seems certain that period accounting is less impressive to the cost accountant than product accounting." (Donald M. Russell, "Applications of Generally Accepted Accounting Principles to Cost Accounting," *N.A.C.A. Bulletin,* Aug. 15, 1948, sec. 1, p. 1542.) The continuity of enterprise makes the achievement of this ideal impractical, but the cost accountant is prepared to settle for "next best"—a two-category division of costs into directly variable and fixed, as is the basis for break-even analysis.

they cannot be escaped), aggregate costs are the only costs which are relevant for control purposes.

This does not mean that aggregate costs may not be disaggregated to achieve meaningful budgets for subordinate units; this procedure involves no distortion, since it involves only breaking totals down into the same pieces from which the totals were constructed in the first place. It is the process of allocation (assignment, apportionment), requiring the use of judgment on an arbitrary basis, which makes unit-cost figures useless for control purpose, however helpful they may be in product-line or profit planning by top management.

The predetermination of fixed overhead application rates is thus distinguishable from the predetermination of variable application rates. The latter are usable for control purposes, providing a standard (imperfect as it is) by which to measure performance. The former are of accounting interest only, constituting no operational standard but only an estimate of dubious value as a guide.[38] Standard process costing (employing measured direct costs plus flexible budgets) is a useful tool for constructing budgets. Standard product costing may be useful for policy planning but not for budget planning.[39]

Indeed, considerable doubt may be raised over the usefulness of full-cost allocations for most policy questions, such as pricing. It is arguable that fixed costs are sunk costs and should not affect the prices of products. Economists would contend that as long as a product brings some return

---

[38] The N.A.C.A. research study, *The Analysis of Manufacturing Cost Variances* (New York, 1952), which was based on a survey of practice in twenty-seven companies using standard costs, comments: "The field study seems to indicate that assignment of responsibility for control of service costs is often not distinguished from allocation of these costs for costing products. In general, accounting allocations are unsatisfactory for fixing responsibility for costs. As stated by the representative of one company in describing his company's experience, the practice 'results in a chronic argument about fairness of the charges.' The reason is that bases of allocation which are 'equitable' for cost finding purposes are often not directly related to short period fluctuations in controllable costs."

[39] As is the case with most flat assertions, there are exceptions to this proposition in practice. The example of one company is illustrative of a budget procedure which makes use of product costs. In this company standard volume is construed as the number of standard labor hours in a month, on a two-shift five-day week. In the example below this amounts to 14,500 hours for the particular unit. Normal volume (in labor hours) multiplied by the variable rate per labor hour plus fixed costs yields total overhead costs for normal volume. Divided by normal volume, this gives an overhead rate per production hour. As scheduled output changes, the new budget allowance is based on this overhead rate. In this instance, then, monthly budget allowances are based on projected volume times a unit rate which includes a predetermined overhead rate based on normal volume. It is not readily apparent, however, how this procedure provides cost control as effective as the use of flexible budgets for the projected actual volume plus fixed costs.

above variable costs, its sale is warranted (assuming no adverse reaction on other sales). Businessmen themselves tell tales in their literature of how their firm, or one of which they know, turned down business which was not paying its "fair share" of costs, only to find profits suffering as a consequence.[40]

(Footnote 39, continued)

Overhead Rate

Normal volume (in std. hrs.)		Variable rate per 100 std. hrs.	Variable dollars	Constant dollars	Total dollars	Overhead rate
14,500	Direct lab. losses	4.440	644	—	644	
"	Oper. ind. labor	36.700	5,322	—	5,322	
"	Hrly. shift & O.T. premium	—	—	737	737	
"	Base salaries	—	—	2,039	2,039	
"	Sal. shift & O.T.	—	—	52	52	
"	Supplies	5.300	769	—	769	
"	Tool expense	58.200	8,435	—	8,435	
"	Repairs & maint.	53.000	7,689	800	8,489	
"	Deptl. expense	2.170	314	—	314	
"	Util. & rent	2.710	393	400	793	
"	Other costs	26.000	3,771	194	3,965	
"	Dep., ins. & taxes	—	—	5,188	5,188	
"	General expense	—	—	—	—	
14,500		189.000	27,337	9,410	36,747	2.53

The overhead rate is computed by dividing the fixed budget at the normal volume ($36,747) by the standard hours at the normal volume (14,500).

[40] "One company related that . . . it attempted to improve an unsatisfactory profit by discontinuing production and sale of products which showed a net loss after allocating to them what was considered an appropriate share of all costs of operating the company. Despite vigorous attempts to sell more of the profitable items, over-all volume and profits declined. Since the company's products were sold principally by truck delivery routes which brought a full assortment of items to the customers daily, the decision to reduce product variety had little effect on costs of operating the trucks or wages paid to driver-salesmen. Once this situation became clear it was seen that an error had been made in reasoning from cost data which included an arbitrary allocation of joint costs which were not reduced by the actions taken. Had the analysis of costs been limited to those costs which were actually affected by the decision made, or had the over-all absorption of overhead and its effect on company net profit been considered, it would have been apparent that the discontinued products made a substantial contribution to the remaining joint costs and net profit. When management of this company realized that a mistake had been made, it took steps to build up sales volume again by increasing the variety of goods offered for sale even though the added items could not carry a full share of allocated distribution costs and still show a profit. Following this change the company's profits improved." *Analysis of Non-manufacturing Costs for Managerial Decisions,* N.A.C.A., p. 14.

Despite these strictures, reasonable though they are, many if not most managements continue to find full product costing a useful tool. It may be true that sunk costs are not relevant to present and future decisions in a perfectly competitive market. In markets where a company has some discretion in pricing its product, due to some uniqueness of position which it enjoys, full-cost allocations on a reasonable even if arbitrary basis may be a useful guide to judgment. We shall explore that question a little more fully in the next chapter. The important conclusion now, however, is the lack of relevance of product costing to the budgetary planning of costs.

Direct Costing

For this reason some accountants in recent years have advocated abandoning the allocation of fixed costs altogether, even for accounting purposes. They have proposed as a substitute a practice which goes by the name of direct costing. The basic idea behind this procedure is that fixed costs of operation should not be incorporated into unit product values and carried to inventory, as is the case under both full-absorption and standard-volume cost accounting. Instead, they are written off for the period in which incurred, as a cost simply of doing business during that period, regardless of the volume of output. Product costs, which are carried to inventory, reflect only direct costs. The income statement for the period is thus not distorted by "producing for inventory," that is, increasing income by production in excess of sales, as would be the case under the systems which allocate fixed costs to products. (Under those systems, production in excess of sales would increase inventory assets over the direct costing approach by the amount of fixed costs impounded in the product and thus would decrease charges against current income, whereas sales in excess of production would, in contrast to direct costing, draw down inventory assets by the amount of fixed costs released and thus increase charges —"cost of sales"—against current income.)

Instead of balancing discrepancies between actual volume and standard volume by an item for underabsorbed and overabsorbed overhead, the total fixed costs for the period are charged directly to the period, and their recovery is sought by whatever means management considers most feasible. Managerial decisions (on pricing, on concessions) are not misled by any feeling of compulsion to secure some margin over "full cost." Instead, management is enabled more clearly to see variable costs—the direct out-of-pocket expenses—as something which must be recovered in every sale, but the return of fixed costs must be sought solely by the most effective possible manipulation of price policy and marketing practice, unfettered by any cost formula which has only an accounting and not an economic rationale.

In summary, the advantages claimed for direct costing are that it frees management from the uncertainties of calculating what constitutes "normal" performance and from the belief that "normal" full costs should somehow control, that it encourages management to follow pricing practices which produce greater profit, and that it avoids the illusion of wealth that comes from producing for inventory when inventory is made to absorb period costs.

This is no place to evaluate the relative merits of fixed-cost allocations versus direct costing. The fact is that there are merit and disadvantage in both methods. Whether or not it is used for costing or pricing purposes, managements cannot escape some version of "standard volume" if only for investment purposes and capacity planning; but it is also true that standard full costs have a limited relevance to pricing policy except in situations where the firm exercises a degree of market control that many if not most do not enjoy. Absorption costing (whether based on full cost or standard volume) may mislead managements into refusing concessions or rejecting sales which would add to profit; but it is also true that excessive attention to marginal cost for pricing purposes in the short run can lead to disregard of the need to plan for return of fixed costs in the not-so-long run. Both approaches suffer in their treatment of variable period costs, laboring under a compulsion to treat these either as directly variable or fixed for the period. As economists have long realized, there *is* no satisfactory way of imputing unit product costs where there are costs which are common to a family of products or costs which are chargeable to the continuity of the enterprise.

Nevertheless, it seems clear that—whether or not employed as a system of cost accounting—information on the incremental costs of producing additional units of product is useful to managements. Where all costs can be divided into direct and fixed, or where variable period costs are virtually converted into direct costs because, while each may be fixed for a range and move up and down on a step basis, collectively their steps are so arranged as to give a smooth cost curve, each unit of product which sells above direct costs contributes some margin to apply to fixed costs or to profit.

Where costs are not so readily divisible into direct and fixed categories, the "contribution margin" approach can be employed only for larger increments than single units—increments of output, for example, over which at least certain variable period costs (indirect expenses or factory burden) remain relatively fixed. On the same basis, the contribution margins of certain administrative units (sales offices or territories, for example) may be computed. At this point, however, it is evident that we are moving back from product-unit costs toward administrative-unit "aggregate" costs (and aggregated in ways that do not involve accounting allocations of common costs). The contribution-margin approach in this sense may represent a workable blending of standard costing for budgetary purposes (measured direct costs plus flexible budgets for variable period costs) and the direct costing approach.

Budgetary Cost Control

Most managements are cost-conscious. They are made so by the pressures of competition and by efforts to achieve profit objectives. The control of costs has become a major area of strategic and tactical planning.

Budgeting and standard-cost procedures provide the firm with one set of instruments for controlling costs. The instruments are not automatic—there is nothing in the budget or in the measured or estimated "efficient" costs per unit or per period which is self-applying. They are nevertheless effective instruments since they are quick to reveal departures from what had been planned or expected, permitting prompt inquiry and—where possible—correction of conditions giving rise to poor performance. Such an inquiry is known as "analysis of variance"—variance from standard cost or variance from the budget. We shall examine the whole field of budget variances later, but it is perhaps worthwhile to take note of their relation to cost control at this point.

There are three principal categories of cost variances which may arise: (1) materials variances, (2) labor variances, and (3) overhead variances. We shall not be much concerned here with the techniques of analysis which have been developed, but it will be instructive to suggest the general pattern which they follow.

In the case of materials, variation from budget allowances may be due to a difference in the quantity of materials bought (usually arising from a difference in actual output over planned), to a difference in the cost of the materials over what had been expected, and to a difference in the yield of product from the materials over what had been calculated as standard performance. Assume, for example, that the materials allowance for a department had been set at $1,000 for the month of February, based on an expected purchase of 1,000 units of material at $1 per unit, with each unit of material expected to yield one unit of product. The month's performance shows 900 units of output with materials costs of $1,045. Actual expenditures for materials have thus been $45 more than budget. To what may this be attributed?

The variance which was due to quantity of output is evidently $100 (100 fewer units at the planned material price of $1 per unit). The variance due to use of more material per unit of product (yield) than is called for by standard is +$50 (50 units of material at a standard or budgeted price of $1 per unit). The variance due to a higher cost of material is +$95 (the

950 units of material actually purchased, at $0.10 more per unit). The net variance from original budget is thus an overage of $45; from a flexible budget (based on standard costs), $145. It is clear that purely from a cost point of view, the controllable items giving rise to that variance are the price of materials (can other sources of supply be found at the former price?) and yield (are the circumstances producing less output per unit of material something which can be corrected?).

	Production	Total material in units	Unit price	Cost of material
Budget (standard) .	1,000	1,000	1.00	1,000
Actual materials at				
standard price ..	900	950	1.00	950
Actual	900	950	1.10	1,045

Labor variances are similarly calculated to trace their cause either to an expenditure of more labor time for the actual output than standard allowances would call for or to labor time paid at higher rates than those on which the allowance was based. This last variation may be attributable not only to an increase in rates but also to the labor mix—the use of higher-rated workers than standard performance of the operation calls for.

Overhead variances arise from two principal causes: a smaller volume than budgeted or considered "normal" ("volume" or "capacity" variance) and less efficient performance than is considered standard ("efficiency" or "productivity" variance). If the volume which is actually budgeted or the volume which is considered "normal" (either standard is used, according to company practice) is not achieved, or is exceeded, the difference in volume times the overhead per budgeted unit gives the volume variance. Thus if planned production on a 24-inch steel mill had been 22,212 tons, but actual production amounted to 22,176 tons, the difference of 36 tons times planned monthly fixed costs of $1,000 per ton would give a budget variance attributable to volume deficiency of $36,000.

Overhead is sometimes allocated on a basis of labor hours, with volume variance traceable to a difference in the number of labor hours actually employed in production for the budget period. If the standard direct hours of labor were budgeted for the period at 2,000, with overhead allocated on a basis of $0.50 per standard hour, but the number of direct hours actually paid for amounted to 2,200, then volume variance would show a credit of $100 (unless allowances were adjusted under a flexible budget).

Volume variance is less controllable than yield or labor time, at least from a production point of view, since it is generally due to a change in production schedules based on a change in orders or sales, and the latter are commonly the result of market or economic circumstances beyond the production department's control. At times, however, volume variance may be attributable to production problems, which are thereby pinpointed.

Overhead variances are also traceable to deviations in efficiency or productivity. These are related to labor-time variations; along with the actual direct labor component of production there goes an indirect expense or factory burden or period cost, as we know. If more or fewer hours of direct labor time are consumed in turning out a given volume, these indirect (overhead) expenses will vary in the same direction. This is not the same thing as volume variance (since volume may actually be what was budgeted or what is considered "normal"); it is an expense variation ancillary to direct labor-time variances.

Improvement of Production Standards

Variance analysis revealing adverse conditions does not, of course, carry with it any necessary implications about the proper correctives. In some cases it may be the budget or standard which is at fault, not the performance. Nevertheless, it has become a major business tool for highlighting costs which are out of line. Nothing about variance analysis, however, contributes to cost improvement over standard. If actual performance should equal budget, cost performance would be considered satisfactory. And yet the pressures for cost reduction would remain—not felt quite so ineluctably as if adverse variances had appeared, perhaps, but still inescapable in so far as the forces of competition and the motivation of profit objective drive managements toward continued improvement of performance. Variance analysis is thus inadequate by itself as a cost control instrument. It is one facet of the strategy and tactics of cost reduction, but it does not represent the whole campaign.

Cost control proceeds by three main routes: forced draft, opportunism, and institutionalized procedures. Every company employs the first two, but only companies engaged in systematic planning usually employ the third.

The forced-draft approach is used under pressure. In the face of a poor profit position, all budgets may be slashed by some arbitrary percentage, leaving it to the heads of departments and divisions to determine where best to make the cuts. Most managements look with disfavor upon such a blunt approach, but many argue that periodically it serves to eliminate useless expenditures which have a way of creeping into the budget. That there is always some place where cost reductions can be effected is a principle given wide credence in managerial circles and borne out by experience.

In times when cost compression is sought, some managements have resorted to the dubious practice of setting expected sales figures, on which administrative units base their budgets, at an arbitrarily low figure, thereby securing a reduction in controllable period costs in the budgets of the affected units. If sales volume is greater, as is anticipated, every effort is made to hold the administrative units to their original budgets.

Such arbitrary attempts at cost reduction may proceed even when a company is not experiencing the harsh driving force of adversity. In one session of the annual meetings of the National Association of Accountants,[41] "a member explained that maintenance costs had been reduced in his company by (more or less arbitrarily) cutting the maintenance department crew."

> On an experimental basis, one maintenance employee was dropped. Results were observed carefully and it was noted that down-time did not rise and that the general plant remained in good repair. Several months later another member of the crew was let go. Over the past four years, approximately five employees have been removed from the maintenance department in this manner without any observable bad results. It was this company's feeling that this procedure has automatically picked-up those people who were not performing a full day's work and has eliminated (at least partially) the practice of sending excessive crews to do a job. As yet this company has not reached the point at which rising down-time, poor plant conditions or overtime indicate that maintenance service is suffering.

The opportunistic approach to cost reduction consists simply in a readiness and alertness to profit from any beneficial changes which might be called to management's attention from any source. Chance reading of business literature, attendance at executive training or trade association sessions, and conversations with other businessmen are some of the ways in which usable suggestions may filter into a company. The employee suggestion system, that butt of many a bitter joke, is another such device.

In the companies which are systematizing their procedures and which are engaging in formal planning, however, cost reduction has increasingly become institutionalized. The procedures and practices vary, but all rely on a systematic study and examination of administration, organization, production, marketing, and finance in a conscious effort to lay bare sources of inefficiency or potentials for reduced cost. In general, these efforts tend to rely on a group of professionals who have become identified as methods engineers or industrial engineers. In some companies the industrial engineering department has become a very sizable undertaking. In other firms industrial engineering departments are built into each operating division.

Their function is continuously to review the use of materials and the use of production methods to discover economies which may be effected. Beyond this, they are sometimes concerned with redesigning products, plant layouts, inventory procedures, transportation arrangements—all with the

---

[41] "Control of Maintenance Costs," *N.A.C.A. Bulletin,* September, 1956, sec. 3, p. 158.

objective of maximum economy. Particular attention is paid in some firms to the use of engineers at the time when new models or new products are being introduced.[42]

As an example of one company's organization of its engineering functions, the Bigelow-Sanford Carpet Company reports that it maintains three research groups: [43]

> *Product Research and Development,* which is constantly at work developing new products, new styles, and new textures and searching out new materials.
> *Industrial Engineering,* which is constantly devising new plant layouts, plans for work simplification, productivity improvements, etc.
> *Manufacturing Engineering,* which is constantly investigating new equipment offered in the market, as well as developing improved machinery for arriving at a desired end point.

An instance of the continuous "searching out" process at work is provided by one who participated in it.[44]

> To show you how important and how involved getting some of these cost items can be, another example—again from my experience at Ford —may be to the point. We were machining the drive pinion for the Ford car on lathes of a well-known make. They were very good machine tools, so nothing I am saying here is in criticism. We used about twenty of those machine tools and we machined those parts at about 150 to 175 surface feet a minute. However, we found by experimentation, that a few of the forgings came through which could be machined at four or five hundred surface feet a minute, perhaps ten per cent of them. We had a cost man make a study as to what the benefits would be if we could get all of the forgings to machine freely and allow us to machine at that rate. His findings were such that we went ahead with a very serious investigation.
> We found that by coupling a salt bath furnace with an upsetting

---

[42] Kaplan, Dirlam, and Lanzillotti, writing of General Motors in *Pricing in Big Business,* p. 52, remark: "Coincidentally with the evolution of a new model, the engineering, manufacturing, and procurement departments are continually called into consultation in an effort to find out what can be anticipated in the way of unit cost for the suggested style and other alterations. Pressure is on these departments to devise methods of cutting costs on both new and old constituents of the model, to provide leeway for introduction of new features."

[43] Elliott I. Peterson, vice-president for manufacturing, Bigelow-Sanford Carpet Company, "The Competitive-demand System of Capital Budget Preparation," in *Tested Approaches to Capital Equipment Replacement,* A.M.A. Special Report 1, New York, 1954, p. 55. Product redesign is of course an important contributor to cost saving.

[44] Roy T. Hurley, president, Curtiss-Wright Corporation, "What We Need in Cost Reports—For General Management," in *New Frontiers for the Industrial Accountant* (1950 Conference Proceedings, N.A.C.A.), p. 103.

machine, we could get 100 per cent of our forgings so they could be machined at 1,000 surface feet a minute. We then established a cost on that basis, a synthetic cost before the fact—and that gave us enough encouragement, so we went to the machine tool people and said, "We want designed and built a machine tool to machine these pieces at 1,000 surface feet a minute." . . . Three of them took the place of the twenty old machine tools. The approach which brought this about was possible only by getting the processing engineer and the cost man together early in the game.

Such institutionalized cost-reducing operations are not confined to the manufacturing end of the business. A petroleum company reports: "Within our general office sales organization, we have a sales operating department whose specific responsibility is the continuous analysis of all sales department operations and costs for the purpose of increasing efficiency and reducing costs." An electrical appliance manufacturer similarly comments: "Our organization for handling distribution includes in its staff groups of specially trained engineers who make continuing studies of merchandising and office methods. From the results of these studies the company develops new procedures or improves those in use." [45]

These specialized staff activities make possible one further source of improved practice and new developments. To an outsider it is surprising the extent to which companies are willing to reveal to their sharpest competitors technological and operational advances which they have made. As long as these do not convey to the product some unique quality which gives it greater salability (a style or design characteristic, an improvement which can be capitalized on in merchandising the product), most companies are willing to reveal all. In a survey conducted by the *Harvard Business Review* and based upon 1,558 completed questionnaires, almost 69 per cent of the respondents said that if their company wished to enter a new field in which a competitor was strong, and their company lacked know-how, they would "forthrightly ask their competitor" for needed information. More than 61 per cent similarly replied that they would ask "forthrightly" if their company was considered a leader in the industry but another company had done some valuable research which they did not have. To a considerable extent, this type of informational exchange takes place among expert staffs who constitute the focus of cost-reduction efforts.

The use of such staffs, with a license, charter, and directive to determine where costs may be cut throughout the company's operations, builds cost reduction into the company's organizational system. They are driven to achieve results by the pressures on them to justify their organizational existence. This sometimes leads to excesses of misplaced ingenuity, but there

[45] *Keys to Efficient Selling and Lower Marketing Costs,* NICB Studies in Business Policy, no. 71, New York, 1956, p. 6.

can be no doubt that, over-all, the effect is favorable enough to bolster the belief that the strategy of cost control is important in the reaching of a planned profit objective.

Summary

In budgeting the cost components of the operating plan, management starts with the sales budget—the bundle of goods, by product line, which it expects to sell, by time segments, over the planning period. From this are constructed the production schedules, the manning tables, and the purchasing timetable.

The costs with which management is concerned are divisible into direct and period costs. The former vary with any and every change in output, unit by unit. The latter are further divisible into variable period and fixed period costs. Variable period costs change with output, but not on a unit-by-unit basis. They remain fixed for some period of time or range of output, but vary beyond these limits. The fixed costs remain fixed throughout the planning period.

For purposes of budget planning, it is the costs which vary with output, and therefore are controllable, which are relevant. The variable elements are naturally different for a one-month plan than for a one-year plan; similarly, certain costs which are fixed in a one-year operating plan are variable over a five-year planning period. Whatever the duration, however, it is the costs which are controllable and manipulable within that period which are the most relevant to planning.

The process of budgeting creates one set of standards with which actual performance can be compared, but there is nothing about budget estimates in themselves which gives assurance that they describe a superior, or a good, performance rather than a mediocre showing (to which past practice has perhaps given the color of acceptability). To meet this deficiency, *standard-cost* procedures have been devised; they attempt to measure (by engineering or statistical methods) the performance which can be reasonably expected of workers and the yield of product which can be expected from materials of specified quality. Actual performance can then be compared to these standards.

This measurement of the standard *direct-cost* components of production is supplemented by standard budgets of *variable period costs* for any level of output (so-called flexible budgets). Because variable period costs are semi-fixed as well as semivariable, each of these budgets usually is considered to relate to an output range, within which these costs remain fixed but outside of which they vary. Some companies, however, tend to treat total variable period costs as a direct cost on the ground that they are composed of a number of separate cost elements, each one of which may be fixed over some range, moving up and down with output on a step rather than a unit basis, but since these steps do not coincide with each other but are experienced successively, the result is to give a close approximation of a smooth cost curve. In these instances an "application rate" is developed, covering all variable period expenses, so that these expenses are regarded as a rate of direct labor costs.

To the direct and variable period costs of manufacturing must then be added the fixed manufacturing costs and all nonmanufacturing costs. The latter are largely period costs (variable and fixed) and for the most part are reflections of managerial judgments about efficiency and value rather than of either engineered standards or necessary outlays.

Standard costing has also been extended to obtain unit product costs. For purposes of setting prices or determining relative product profitability, managements have usually sought unit "full costs." This requires allocating to each product some portion of the costs which are common to a number of products and determining over what volume of output fixed costs will be allocated. These decisions are matters of arbitrary judgment—arbitrary in the sense that any one of a number of possible allocations might be justified or rationalized. Business managers and accountants talk in terms of allocations which are reasonable and equitable. In the case of apportionment among products these terms have generally been taken to mean allocations based either on the "benefit" which a particular product is supposed to have received or on its "ability" to carry its share of the common cost. In the case of costing units of a total volume, there has been some tendency to regard a "normal" or "standard" volume as a reasonable and equitable basis for apportionment—a volume which presumes to average out the ups and downs of a period of years.

These full-cost estimates may be useful for certain policy questions, such as pricing, which obviously have their effect on budgeting and planning. But they are no more relevant than market data, the hunches of business experience, the practices of competitors, and other such information. Full-cost accounting has no special place of importance in the budgeting or planning process, and the "standard-cost" concepts associated with it are not to be confused with standard costing as a basis for estimating and controlling budgetary costs.

For these purposes—estimates and controls—it is the total costs of a process, not unit costs, which are most relevant, and variable costs, not full costs.

While standard costs seek to establish measures of efficiency with which actual performance may be compared, standard-cost procedure does not by itself lead to cost reduction via improved methods and technology. To a considerable extent it is competitive pressures which drive managements to new and improved production processes and administrative procedures in an effort to preserve profits by cutting costs. Two methods of cost reduction which every company resorts to are forced-draft methods (arbitrary methods instituted under the spur of declining profits, such as across-the-board budget reductions) and opportunism (the acceptance of useful ideas which come by chance from employee suggestion systems, salesmen of supplier companies, other businessmen, trade associations). Increasingly, however, more progressive companies are institutionalizing the search for ways of reducing costs, and the search goes on continuously, not simply in times when adversity presses. Some companies have instituted whole departments of methods engineers and industrial engineers whose primary function is to attack systematically the problem of how costs may be reduced.

The important consideration is that "costs" are not some stable and rather immutable function of sales and output, like taxes. In the planning process, the category of costs embraces a number of elements which are subject to managerial control and manipulation. In management's effort to achieve its profit objective, costs become not simply a burden but also a tool; they are not just a drain on income but also a variable which management may manipulate to preserve income; they are not an outflow which, like a spigot, is turned off and on by the volume of production but an outflow which can be budgeted by management as by a housewife.

Chapter 9

THE USE OF PRICE IN PLANNING

Price Policy in Relation to Profit Targets

The price of a company's product is a tool which (along with other tools like product design and the marketing organization) helps to create a volume of sales. Price is thus a peculiarly strategic variable in the firm's budgeting and planning operations.

As such, price policy must necessarily be closely related to the firm's efforts to achieve its objectives. For firms which plan, one frequently sought objective is some specified rate of return on investment. If, instead or in addition, the objective is a rate of return on sales, this can be related to investment by the number of times capital turns over, so that one objective is translatable into the other. (With a capital turnover of three times a year, for example, a 5 per cent return on sales is equivalent to a 15 per cent return on investment.) In general, then, price policy is designed to set the general level of company prices at a sufficient margin over costs, at an assumed volume of sales, to yield that profit which the target calls for. "The controller, in making his decision as to which [overhead application] rate to use, found that the particular product under review was earning a profit on sales of 9 per cent which was considered to be satisfactory. Anything over this amount would invite competition. As a result, the mark-up factor in pricing was frozen at a point which would realize 9 per cent profit on sales, with a volume of sales set at a level which would result in a return on investment of 25 per cent." [1]

[1] Thomas S. Dudick, "How an Electronics Manufacturer Sharpened Cost Responsibilities," *The Controller,* February, 1960, p. 60. Dudick was budget director for Allen B. DuMont Laboratories at the time of writing this article, and although the figures cited related to an hypothetical example, they represented the kind of budgeting approach which had been instituted at DuMont and were based on general levels of expectation in the electronics industry. The overhead application rates in the example were taken as a percentage of direct labor costs (variable period costs as a constant 70 per cent of direct labor, fixed period costs of $1,850,000 as a variable

The posing of such a profit objective, and the determination of a general price policy designed to assist in achieving it, implies a degree of managerial discretion, an area within which management can freely move around to decide how price can best be manipulated to gain its goal. The posing of a profit objective does not, of course, itself provide discretion in pricing. It constitutes a challenge to management to move within the market forces which bound its discretion, the competitive elements which constrict its judgment, with as much ingenuity and skill as it can muster, to come as close to the target as it can. At times and places the market and competitive forces may be sufficiently controlling that managerial efforts are unavailing. At other times and places there is considerable latitude for judgment. A pricing policy does not, therefore, imply some formula which can consistently be enforced against the market, but serves as a guide to pricing decisions which is rested on an appraisal of underlying market forces.[2]

---

percentage of direct labor costs, declining with increasing volume). Direct labor costs were assumed to be 10 per cent of sales. Dudick adds: "The determination of the necessary sales volume [to achieve the returns mentioned in the text above] is simply a matter of mathematics, since 25 per cent [the target rate of return on investment] divided by 9 per cent equals 2.8. This means that the investment of $15 million must be turned 2.8 times per year, requiring a sales volume of $42 million."

[2] In one of the earliest, most forceful, and most frequently cited statements on the relation between pricing and business financial policy, Donaldson Brown, as vice-president for finance of General Motors, commented: "Ordinarily prices cannot be fixed according to mathematical rule, or at figures calculated to yield a predetermined rate of return upon capital employed. Competitive conditions and other practical considerations are more apt to determine the prices which should be established, with the result that actual prices will rarely coincide exactly with the theoretical prices in accordance with an expressed pricing policy. This fact, however, does not mean that the expression of policy loses its significance; on the contrary, it makes clear the importance of interpreting the conditions which lead to apparent departure from the expressed policy, with a view to determining whether a modification of the policy is required, or whether the conditions are of temporary import. . . .

"While competitive conditions and other practical considerations ordinarily are the chief determinants of the price which shall be charged for a product, nevertheless comprehensive financial policies are necessary in business organizations which employ large amounts of capital. The pronouncement of a basic pricing policy, in terms of the economic return attainable, should be understandable as a policy, and should not be misapplied as a dictation of specific price. In other words, the impracticability of frequent adjustment of prices must be recognized, necessitating the maintenance of prices which at times may be above, and at other times below the base price [formula-determined] equivalent. With due allowance for deviations of this nature, the method of price analysis affords a means not only of interpreting actual or proposed prices in relation to the established policy, but at the same time affords a practical demonstration as to whether the policy itself is sound. If the prevailing price of product is found to be at variance with the base price equivalent, other than to the extent due to temporary causes, it must follow that prices should be adjusted;

If actual prices deviate from target prices to the extent that they fail to realize the profit objective not only occasionally, but regularly, the alternative is not necessarily to adjust to "reality." The profit objective may be held to, but actions other than those in the field of price may be undertaken to realize it—a new promotional program, redesign of the product, substitution of one product line for another, pressures for radical cost reduction. At times a target rate of return may be set which cannot possibly be achieved at going prices, not in any expectation that price levels can be altered, but to spur the organization to greater efficiency. In these instances the continuing failure of price levels to yield target rates of return cannot be construed as a failure of price policy. The intent is for the organization to become efficient enough to realize the rate sought at the prices prevailing.

Price Policy and Price Actions

In view of the importance of pricing policy in a company's planning processes, one might expect that interest in pricing practices would be both intense and widespread among a company's top management. The distinction between general price policy and specific price actions, however, rules this out. A Brookings Institution study reported: "It was evident that most of the executives with whom the interviews were conducted did not ordinarily concern themselves with pricing details; instances appeared in which they were not intimately aware of how their products were priced. Even officers who were quite familiar with company policy in the pricing area were among those who could not illustrate the policy by a detailed follow-through of particular price decisions." "In a compilation of pricing methods employed in various du Pont divisions, the company brought to light the indifference that evidently had attended the pricing of many products. While subordinates were familiar with the basis for pricing products they sold, it appeared unnecessary for top management to review the pricing of items that were profitably produced and presented no problems to the sales force." [3]

In part, too, this seeming indifference of top management to a factor of such strategic importance is attributable to a general tendency toward price stability (the widespread policy of not changing prices more than once a

---

or else, in the event of conditions being such that prices cannot be brought into line with the base price equivalent, the conclusion is necessarily drawn that the terms of the expressed policy must be modified."

Extracted from "Pricing Policy in Relation to Financial Control," *Management and Administration*, vol. 7, 1924, the full statement appearing in February (pp. 195–198), March (pp. 283–286), and April (pp. 417–422).

[3] Kaplan, Dirlam, and Lanzillotti, *Pricing in Big Business*, pp. 5 and 150.

year) and to a policy of making adjustments in prevailing prices—at times when changes are made—rather than of reviewing prices from scratch. Under these circumstances price, while retaining its importance in corporate operations, requires relatively little attention from top management.

The placement of price-setting authority within a company varies with the nature of the decision and the nature of the business. In companies whose revenues are chiefly derived from a few major products, not only is price policy set by top corporate officials and usually reviewed by the company's directors, but corporate officers often enter into more specific price decisions within the policy framework. In the automobile industry, annual prices are typically set by recommendation of the top division management responsible for a make of car (say the Plymouth line in the Chrysler Company or the Pontiac line in General Motors) and reviewed and approved by a small committee of top corporate management. In smaller businesses it is also more common for the chief executive and his principal officers to become involved in questions both of price policy and of general price-level changes. Typically, the sales manager is one of the most influential in committee actions or informal group discussions.

In multiproduct companies in which no single product line produces a dominant proportion of corporate income, it is common for specific pricing authority to rest with the divisional management, subject to general corporate pricing policy. Price changes may require approval, but this is generally forthcoming. Product diversification thus tends to a dispersion of authority just as product concentration tends to centralize pricing authority.

Indeed, in some companies whose product "line" may consist of thousands of product varieties (as in steel, where production is frequently to specification, and in parts-producing companies or chain store operations), the setting of actual product prices may be pushed down the line to clerks (a specialized "pricing division" which works from a catalogue of prices), sometimes to individual salesmen, or to store managers. In these instances the price set is likely to be derived from formula, requiring little discretion, or to be suggested (though not necessarily dictated) by a list of recommended prices. Basic price policies (usually the question of general up or down revisions) are reserved to top corporate management, however.

In the case of major new products, it is top corporate management which customarily acts on the basis of recommendation from a sales or divisional manager.

Cost-plus Pricing

Unless a firm simply reacts opportunistically to market forces, obtaining as much for its product over marginal cost as existing circumstances permit, it is bound to have some kind of policy. In this sense one may think of a firm's basic pricing policy as one which abstracts from market and competitive pressures, which applies to all its products indiscriminately, without respect to their relative competitive positions, and which embodies some elements of a philosophy. The policy which seems to characterize more managements than does any other policy is that prices should bear some "equitable" relation to costs. Indeed, the same notion of fairness and equity which we observed governing the allocation of common costs among products is present in the belief that the "fairest" form of pricing involves a common markup over costs. "The perfect sales price is the sum of all costs plus the profit which will yield the goal return on capital employed." [4] Public utility rate regulation is usually premised on a recovery of costs plus a fair return on investment. "Fair trade" pricing is based on a philosophy that sales at less than cost plus a fair profit are injurious to "honest" merchants. "The laborer is worthy of his hire, and a sale without a profit is a sale without honor, and an indictment of the American people." [5]

While it is recognized (as in Donaldson Brown's statement, note 2 above) that circumstances will force modification of such a cost-plus policy, this at least represents the point of departure. It represents what management would like to be able to do, in the absence of pressures which force it to do something else. It constitutes—not least of all—a policy which management believes it can justify to others.

Cost-plus pricing takes a number of forms, but the principal ones involve a markup which is related to direct costs (gross-margin pricing), a markup which is related to total allocated costs either actual or at standard volume (full-cost pricing), a markup related to allocated investment (rate-of-return pricing), and finally a variable markup (flexible pricing). The first three proceed by formula and make no concessions to external influences. Flexible pricing represents management's adjustments to the results obtained by formula as it attempts to manipulate the price variable to achieve its profit target in the budgetary plan.

Gross-margin Pricing

Gross-margin pricing is probably most commonly found in retail and wholesale operations, though it is not confined to those sectors. It consists in applying a standard markup either to the cost of goods which have been purchased for resale or to the total of direct costs involved in producing a good or service. In either case, the markup is set at a level which, for

[4] Keller, *Management Accounting for Profit Control*, p. 387.

[5] W. W. Wachtel, president of the Calvert Distillers Corporation, in *Temporary National Economic Committee Hearings*, 1939, part 6, p. 2558, cited in A. R. Oxenfeldt, *Industrial Pricing and Market Practices* (Englewood Cliffs, N.J.: Prentice-Hall, 1951), p. 164.

the firm's total volume of sales, is expected to cover all period costs plus the target profit.[6]

In job machine shops at one time it was fairly standard to apply a markup of 100 per cent of direct labor to all orders for this purpose. An official of one steel warehouse (which sells at less than carload lots to producers whose operations are too small to purchase directly from the mills) remarked: "We shoot for around a 30 per cent markup." Sometimes a markup becomes standard practice in an industry, as one means of coordinating industry price changes with prevalent changes in labor or materials costs.

This type of price policy is most suited to a firm with a relatively homogeneous product line with rough price comparability. In situations without these characteristics gross-margin pricing inherits all the problems attributable to the allocation of total overhead costs on the basis of direct costs which were noted in the previous chapter.[7]

Full-cost Pricing

Efforts on the part of business planners to secure a sounder measure of a product's full cost have led to other methods of apportioning common costs. We have already examined some of these. One is the allocation of

[6] Professor Richard Heflebower is, I believe, responsible for naming this form of cost-plus pricing "gross-margin pricing." It is his contention that the markup over direct costs is not so logically related to the remaining period costs as to warrant designating it a method of recovering full costs, even though that result is assumed. National Bureau of Economic Research, *Business Concentration and Price Policy* (Princeton University Press, 1955), p. 367.

[7] One authority has said, with respect to merchandising operations, that "a profit evaluation on the basis of initial markup assumes that all items handled within a department or merchandise classification incur the same costs—and that all costs have a direct relationship to selling price. This, of course, is basically not true for several reasons. First, many costs are not influenced by the selling price of an item. For example, I believe we will all agree that the delivery cost in dollars and cents will probably be the same for a $200 or $400 refrigerator. . . . The second reason . . . is that the physical characteristics of the merchandise . . . can influence the amount of costs incurred. For example, a table lamp may incur twice the amount of delivery cost if the shade is packed in a separate box. The third reason . . . is that the merchandising policies and practices of the supplier can be an important factor . . . —this may influence the amount of repair and merchandising adjustment cost as well as the cost of merchandise returns." Harvey E. Kapnick, partner, Arthur Andersen & Company, "Merchandise Management Accounting," in Frank M. Bass (ed.), *The Frontiers of Marketing Thought and Science* (Chicago: American Marketing Association, 1958), p. 121.

Similarly in manufacturing, "one product might require six dollars worth of labor and one dollar worth of depreciation, while another may require one dollar worth of labor and six dollars worth of depreciation, with the result that prices which are based on variable costs only might lead to a shift of sales to the product which gave rise to the most fixed cost without absorbing its proportional share of it." "Direct Costing," in 1954 Conference Proceedings, *N.A.C.A. Bulletin*, September, 1954, sec. 3, p. 164.

period expenses, at some standard volume, to each product or product group, using some direct-cost element such as labor hours or machine hours as the basis of apportionment. Instead of a standard markup covering both period expenses and profit margin, there is a differential allocation of period expenses coupled with a standard markup. Such full-cost pricing is widely employed in conjunction with standard unit product costs.[8]

While this effort at more precise apportionment of period costs eliminates some of the rule-of-thumb characteristics of gross-margin pricing, it does not remove them all. Particularly is it usually true that on this kind of formula approach prices are set proportionate to total costs which have been derived without respect to (or at least without full allowance for) the differential capital investment component of costs, by product or product group. For companies which link their profit objectives to return on investment this is a serious limitation. To overcome it, some firms have adopted an approach which attempts to relate markup more directly to investment.

Return-on-investment Pricing

The general formula is provided by the case of a single-product company, or one whose products are sufficiently homogeneous to be treated in like manner. Standard costs for a standard volume are first computed. The ratio of aggregate standard-volume costs to total investment (sometimes called the investment ratio, other times capital turnover) times the target rate of return gives the markup on standard costs which must be applied to the product or (on the average) to the firm's several products.

$$\frac{\text{Capital investment}}{\text{Standard cost at standard volume}} \times \frac{\text{budgeted profit}}{\text{capital investment}} = \frac{\text{budgeted profit}}{\text{standard cost}}$$

or

Capital turnover $\times$ target rate of return = markup on standard cost

In applying this general formula to a multiproduct line, where the amount of invested capital varies relative to each product's costs, total investment must be allocated by product lines. This is normally done by the same apportionment methods that are used to allocate common costs. Investment is first allocated to cost centers (also labeled burden centers, production groups, or responsibility centers, though there are shades of meaning

[8] As noted in the previous chapter, sometimes individual itemized period expenses are allocated to each product on the basis not simply of one common denominator such as direct labor but of a common denominator appropriate to the particular expense (square feet of space, perhaps, or the dollar value of equipment and tools). In instances in which the joint processing of a number of products complicates this procedure, a company may fall back on the direct-labor or machine hours embodied in each product as the basis for allocating manufacturing expenses but apportion individual nonmanufacturing expenses by applying different denominators appropriate to the common cost. Where this is not feasible or appears to yield no advantage, nonmanufacturing expenses are often allocated on the basis of unit manufacturing costs.

to these terms), each of which commonly performs certain processes on a number of different products. On the basis of the target rate of return, the profit expected from each such center can be computed. This profit itself is then "unitized" by dividing it by the number of direct labor hours or machine hours in the center (whatever the factor for apportionment may be). Standard product unit price is then derived by adding direct unit costs, period expenses on the basis of the number of units of the factor of apportionment contained in the product, profit on the same basis, and selling and administrative costs allocated in whatever way is considered equitable.[9]

The Flexible Markup

Under gross-margin, full-cost, and rate-of-return pricing, a formula leads to an arithmetic result without respect to competitive or market conditions or any other considerations which may be relevant to a particular product. Although in some instances (as in the catalogue pricing of a large number of parts) prices might actually be set on this basis, this is not often the case. Managements quite generally, even when they have sought to make their formula approach more precise though more complicated, recognize that the results are only a first approximation. "Total unit cost plus profit to yield the desired return on capital employed should be developed for each item in the line to serve as a guide to pricing, to cost reduction where margins are inadequate, to marketing emphasis, and to product-line revision. These 'target prices' must then be modified by management judgment to meet competitive conditions or to capitalize on unusual market opportunities." [10]

This adjustment of a formula-determined price is what is known as the "flexible markup." Employed in conjunction with an initial full-cost markup, it is probably the most widely used single pricing approach for firms of the type we have been discussing.

There are a number of factors which might influence managerial decisions on how formula prices should be adjusted. Cost advantages or disadvantages over competitors, the strength of the desire to expand market share in a given product line, competitive prices, estimates of consumer response, the possibility of segmenting markets for "preferential" or "discriminatory" pricing—all these elements can be given their place in a calculated manipulation of formula prices up or down. Some companies set floors (seldom ceilings) to such manipulation, as in the case of H. J. Heinz Co., which has adopted a formal statement of policy that "While the gross profit margin will vary between varieties, we should maintain a sufficient margin on each variety to cover its share of allocated cost." [11]

[9] See the appendix to this chapter.

[10] Keller, *Management Accounting for Profit Control*, p. 387.

[11] *Management Planning and Control: The H. J. Heinz Approach*, Controllership Foundation, p. 95.

One finance officer has suggested a parallel between a company's family of products and a typical household, on the premise that individual products "cannot be judged entirely by the contribution they make during any single year. It may be as unreasonable to expect all products to pay a like share of this year's cost as it is to expect the baby, young sister, older brother, and grandparent to contribute alike toward the household expenses. Some are relics of the past still worth preserving, some are the sustenance of the present, while others are the hope of the future." [12]

Because of such price adjustments, many of them in response to competitive influences, a number of economists have discounted the importance of formula pricing. If the full-cost and rate-of-return markups are computed only to be abandoned in the face of market forces, why, they ask, should not the economist ignore such formalistic approaches, whatever the businessman chooses to do about them? Such criticism misses the purpose of business pricing procedure, however.

As has been noted, few businessmen have contended that they use one of the formula approaches as an instrument for setting actual product prices. Their descriptions of practice are almost always qualified by the reminder that, after all, the "market" or "competition" has more to do with actual prices than does the formula or any general policy. But they go on to assert that the formula results constitute a useful guide. The usefulness of such a guide can be appreciated only if one concedes the importance in modern business operation of planned rates of return. A target rate of return, whether used in the form of a markup over standard full costs or employed in conjunction with allocated investment, constitutes a first approximation of the over-all results which management would like to attain. The individual prices are not "ideal" in any sense, although managements have sometimes used that term. There is no special significance in the particular allocations—whether of common costs or common investments—by which the initial and tentative results have been reached. As long as managements recognize that any apportionments based on "equity" or "reasonableness" or "ability to carry the load" are purely arbitrary, and at best suggestive, they are in no danger of misleading themselves.

The significance to the formula approach lies only in that it is a convenient method of arriving at some initial set of numbers which is bound to bear some relationship to prices prevailing in the market. These can then be adjusted downward however much may be necessary to meet competition, and upward as much as competition permits. But the critical consideration in all such adjustments is that their net effect should be to leave the original return on investment untouched. All downward adjustments should find their compensation in upward adjustments elsewhere, unless there is some possibility of offsetting the otherwise adverse effect through cost reductions or improved or increased promotion to augment sales. The

[12] E. Stewart Freeman, "Pricing the Product," N.A.C.A. Year Book, 1939, p. 31.

really critical consideration, then, is that in so far as management operates with a realistic target in mind, prices—which have originally been set to realize the profit objective—must be adjusted in such a way as to continue to permit the achievement of the profit goal. Whatever prices are finally set, times the volume which it is anticipated can be realized at those prices, should yield a sales revenue which, minus the costs of the output thus calculated, gives the profit which has been set as goal. At the stage of the budgeting process at which we have currently arrived in our analysis, (where sales revenues and costs have been computed in a kind of first-draft or tentative effort), that result is seldom achieved. But it is the purpose behind formula pricing approaches which gives point to the practice.

If the result which is sought—the planned profit, on the basis of realistically adjusted prices of the product line—cannot be achieved even on paper in the budgeting process, over a period of time, then this is the signal to management either that it has set its sights too high or that it had best take steps of a cost-reducing or product-redesigning or innovating or promotional nature to modify the underlying situation which precludes its goal realization.[13]

Price Policy over the Life of a Product

Among the considerations prompting a company to adjust its price from an original formula calculation "consumer response" was mentioned. This is the familiar price elasticity of demand or price-volume relationship. In general, however, most businesses take this relationship into consideration during the planning process only when some product is moving into a new phase in its life cycle. On the "established" line of products—that is, products which are not new nor passing from the scene nor expanding greatly nor particularly declining—there is little in the way of a continuing review

---

[13] Where price-setting authority is decentralized, as typically in a department store, where departmental buyers frequently are empowered to determine product prices (although top management looks over their shoulders, noting, for example, whether they are following a markup policy which is considered "normal" or "traditional" for the particular line of goods), the process of manipulating prices can lead to friction and byplay between the buyer, who is often judging merchandise costs and sales prices on an item-by-item basis (relative to competitors or past performance) and his superiors, who are thinking in terms of the over-all departmental performance which results from the individual actions. As Prof. Stanley Hollander of Michigan State University commented in *Relationship of Prices to Economic Stability and Growth, Hearings before the Joint Economic Committee*, 85th Cong., 2d Sess., 1958, p. 319, the "pricing process in a department store has been described as an interesting conflict between the buyer who is interested in particular bits of merchandise, who makes particular judgments with regard to specific items, and his superiors and the controller who are thinking in terms of the statistical averages for the department as a whole."

to ascertain whether a change in price with a consequent change in volume would produce a more favorable profit showing. As long as these products seem to elicit about the expected response, and that response is "satisfactory" in terms of over-all profit planning, price changes come chiefly in response to cost changes or to cyclically changing consumer incomes (when they are more related to income elasticity than price elasticity).

The life cycle of a product begins with its introduction by the particular firm. If the product is one which is directly competitive with other products, it tends to be priced like other products—that is, a markup over costs designed to realize the profit target and adjusted as necessary in the light of competitors' prices. If the product has no direct substitutes, however, a producer has broader discretion. If it is one which is faddish—meeting with a quick acceptance but promising to wear out its popularity quickly —standard procedure is to price high and make a quick return.[14]

In the case of new products which are expected to have a long life, such as new household appliances, it is also usual practice to start off with a high price, though in this instance the markup is likely to have a closer relationship to cost than in the case of the fad: early costs, including the costs of experimentation and promotion, simply lead to high prices because they are high themselves. Since high prices are not associated with high profits, however, they do not in themselves induce competitors to enter the field. It is only an expectation on the part of rivals, no less than the innovating company, that the market may ultimately expand and become a profitable one that encourages others to challenge a new line. In the meantime, however, the innovating company is obliged to win acceptance for its product.

In the case of a major new item (the dishwasher and garbage disposal unit are frequently cited examples) acceptance is not likely to be a function of price. The product itself is unknown and uncertain, and until it has been tested in households and found satisfactory, and the word has spread from user to prospective buyer, price is not decisive in decisions whether or not to take a chance. It is more frequently the desire of upper status groups to distinguish themselves by being "first" in trying the new product, or of upper income groups to take a chance on what promises to be a major convenience or to provide special enjoyment. In early experimentation with the price of its dishwasher, for example, General Electric is reported to

---

[14] It is interesting that despite the business morality which underlies the practice of pricing by a reasonable markup over cost and views price cutting and gouging both as immoral, the policy of "get all you can while the getting's good" is commonly regarded as perfectly compatible with business ethics in this special case. The rationale appears to be that no value standards need apply to the unique product with a short life. Under the circumstances it is only good business sense—in keeping with the business objective of profit making—to make as much of a profit as one can as long as no one is thereby "harmed."

have concluded that a 20 per cent reduction resulted in only a 5 per cent increase in sales.

It is after the product has gained initial acceptance, and interest in acquiring it has begun to spread more generally among households, that price becomes the key to a widening market. If the costs of research and experimentation, promotion, and small-scale output all contribute to the setting of relatively high prices in the first ("introduction") stage, it is a calculation of the ultimate size of the market and the share which the innovating firm hopes to preserve to itself which is likely to determine price in this second ("widening of the market") stage.

An example of the kind of calculation which a firm is likely to make at this stage was provided by Albert Bradley when he was still assistant treasurer of General Motors, in a paper published in the National Association of Cost Accountants *Bulletin* in 1927. The problem he posed for firms in the then expanding automobile industry was how much of an increase in sales would be required to make good the profit lost on existing volume if prices were dropped by 5 per cent. From such computations the organization, drawing on its sales force and its research staff for supporting opinion, would then decide whether growing acceptance of the product would be sufficiently accelerated by a 5 per cent price decline to produce the additional sales needed within a tolerably short period of time.[15] Simi-

[15] The calculation which Bradley made for this problem ran as follows:

	Total (a)	Per unit (b)
1. *Volume Basis*	66,400	
2. Sales at Present Prices	$50,080,098	$754.22
3. Sales after 5% Reduction in Price	47,576,093	716.51
4. Net Profit at Present Prices	5,100,467	76.81
5. Net Profit after 5% Reduction, Present Volume	2,596,462	39.10
6. Difference Representing Additional Net Profit through Added Volume (Item 4–Item 5)	2,504,005	

Calculation of Additional Net Profit Resulting from Added Volume

7. Fixed Manufacturing Expense	$2,599,500	$ 39.15
8. Fixed Commercial Expense	2,108,033	31.75
9. Net Profit after 5% Reduction in (list) Price (Item 5)	2,596,462	39.10
10. Additional Profit Resulting from Each Car of Added Volume		110.00
11. Additional Volume Required to Offset Price Reduction (Item 6 ÷ Item 10)	22,764 cars	
12. Additional Volume as Percent of Present Volume (Item 1)	34.28%	

(From "Financial Control Policies of General Motors Corporation and their Relationship to Cost Accounting," *N.A.C.A. Bulletin*, Jan. 1, 1927, sec. 1, pp. 430–431.)

lar calculations might have been made for price changes of varying amounts. The decision would rest not on which price-volume combination produced maximum profit in the next year, but on which would be conducive to maximum profit over some longer time span. A time sequence of price reductions might figure in such planning.

At some point, however, market saturation can be foreseen. At that point price reductions cease to have the effect of expanding sales. The consequence is to shift industry's attention from selling to new users to repeating sales to present users. To achieve the latter, style changes and quality changes are more effective than price. The product line fans out into a variety of differentiated models falling into price classes ranging from economy to luxury. The price of each class tends to be relatively stable, but the product itself changes and improves over the years.[16]

Price Stability

The reasons for this tendency toward price stability with respect to "mature" products are several, but it is not important for purposes of the present analysis to do more than mention the most influential. One is the development of a quasi agreement among the major producers—an understanding derived from experience rather than collusion—about the limits of price changes which may be made without inviting retaliation. Minor price reductions not disturbing relative competitive positions may be made, within these limits, without provoking offsetting price adjustments from rivals, but any price cuts outside these limits will meet with retaliatory price

[16] Note the following testimony of the director of business research of the Chrysler Corporation in *Administered Prices, Hearings before the Subcommittee on Antitrust and Monopoly,* U.S. Senate, 85th Cong., 2d Sess., part 6, 1958, p. 2782:

"It is important to note that the growth of the industry has manifested a development of what we refer to as several price classes of cars reflecting the demands of various types of buyers and the capacities of various income groups to purchase these cars.

"Within any one of these price classes from the very beginning there has been intense competition to supply the maximum amount of product value.

"Cost has necessarily to be a limiting factor because of the limitations in the market place in available income. So the similarity within a price class through the years in the character of the product is a phenomenon of the market place and does not represent any attempt of one manufacturer to ape another."

Donald M. Russell, partner of Lybrand, Ross Bros. & Montgomery, remarks in "The Function of Costs in Pricing" (1949 Conference Proceedings, N.A.C.A.), p. 52: "In the automobile business and in most industries which produce an engineered product, the most important competition between members of the industry takes place in the engineering and cost accounting departments, which, given a budgeted number of dollars to design and produce a product, then apply every known means of science, technology, and planning to build into the product the maximum of utility for the customer.

actions, leaving none of the producers as well off as formerly.[17] Under the circumstances a standpat pricing approach makes good sense. Another reason for price stability with market saturation has been antitrust legislation, which has limited the eagerness of the dominant firm to seize a preponderant share of the market. Under the circumstances, that firm has good inducement to leave product prices high enough to shelter less competitive firms which it could easily undersell but in doing so might drive to the wall, exposing itself to monopoly charges.

Still another reason is that price reductions, if they do not succeed in winning a larger share of the market either because they are met or because, despite them, other differentiated products retain the loyalty of their consumers, cannot so readily be reversed; if price competition is thus ineffective, its only result is a loss in profit. Finally, there is a prevalent business morality which—once a market has been "stabilized"—regards price cutting which is not a consequence of cost reductions as an act which is unethical, unless indeed there is a kind of industry consensus about its desirability. We shall explore this aspect of the matter more fully in a later chapter.

Controlling Costs to Predetermined Prices

The development of price classes for a wide variety of products which have passed through their stage of most rapid growth in acceptance has led to the phenomenon of tailoring the cost of a product to a predetermined price. This is often true of new models of familiar products (such as automobiles and men's clothing) and also frequently true of new products competitive with familiar products (long-playing records versus short-playing, for example).

This procedure is a natural response to the business philosophy of preserving stable price relationships with rivals (for the reasons given above —an objective which is usually described as "meeting competition"), and competing on the basis of product. In automobiles, a president of Chrysler commented: "We start with clearly defined cost targets and we make cost estimates at each step. We revise design or engineered specifications as necessary to make sure that a particular model can be mass produced at costs suitable for the price class for which it is intended." [18] In an ac-

---

[17] The most effective exposition of this phenomenon has been supplied by William Fellner in *Competition among the Few* (New York: Knopf, 1949).

[18] *Administered Prices*, part 6, p. 2777. Kaplan, Dirlam, and Lanzillotti have provided a good description of the process in the automobile industry by which the product, its cost, and its price are planned concurrently, starting with the initial design (thirty months prior to the final price setting). Recognizing the "convention" of price classes, design is developed with careful restriction of costs. *Pricing in Big Business*, pp. 48–54. Two officials of a motor company similarly remarked in interview

countants' "practices" session, the representative of a manufacturer of golf equipment remarked: "Before setting selling prices, competitive selling prices must be considered and, if we are out of line, adjustments must be made. Once the selling price is set we try to keep our costs within percentage limits of our selling price in order to attain the profit objectives envisioned in our established price." Another member of the same session "indicated that he turns his selling price objective over to his cost and engineering department to develop his product processes to meet the target price profitably." [19] An official of R.C.A. advises: [20]

> Do not be misled into believing that list prices are determined solely on the basis of cost and standard gross margin. In our highly competitive business, suggested list prices are primarily established by competition. Obviously, if the basic price level in the industry for a television table model is $199, we could not arbitrarily elect to create a sales program around an RCA Victor table model television line beginning at $259. Although competition is the major factor in establishing price ranges, our standard cost system does provide the necessary tool in further developing and refining our sales program to fit into the price requirements as established by competitive pricing.

In this process of controlling costs to provide the target profit at a predetermined price, the degree of pressure which management puts on its engineering and production personnel depends in part on the standard volume which is used for pricing purposes. A standard volume set at 60 per cent of capacity obviously imposes a harsher task of cost tailoring than one set at 80 per cent. A realistic limit to the pressure thus applied is provided, however, by the necessity of coming up with a product which is competitive on style and quality standards. One of the subjects of endless debate prior to the freezing of design, cost, and price of a new model is the extent to which some "feature" warrants the added cost (often minute, on a unit basis), involving speculation on whether the change will have its effect primarily on price, volume, or profit.

Business Practice and Economic Theory

All the considerations which have been mentioned in this chapter as affecting the pricing process take place in the stages of planning and budget-

---

that their company starts with the price of the car—where it fits "appropriately" into the price spectrum of the industry—and works back to costs. Not a great deal of adjustment is possible, they reported, since the company feels itself "frozen" into a particular status position in the industry.

[19] *N.A.C.A. Bulletin,* September, 1956, sec. 3, p. 153.

[20] G. K. Bryant, "Standard Costs in Control and Planning," *N.A.C.A. Bulletin,* May, 1954, sec. 1, p. 1113.

ing, in the ex ante calculation of what costs will give rise to what revenues to yield what profit. The calculations may not, of course, be borne out by performance. Market and competitive pressures may be more intense than had been expected, so that the premises on which the original budget was based may prove to be erroneous. Actions, including price actions, may have to be initiated in an effort to remedy a deteriorating situation and to achieve as much of the target profit as possible; the budget will be revised.

Under such influences price decisions may be remade along lines which represent a departure from original plan to accommodate external pressures too strong to be resisted. We shall explore the possibility and nature of such price revisions in a later section. The fact that external influences require the remaking of decisions does not, however, deny the validity of internal planning. The plans of others are often the external influences which we encounter. The pricing policies which business firms make are as important to the economist as the market forces which sometimes unmake them. The area of discretion is as interesting to explore as the area of induced reaction.

Whatever the end result may be (the plan, with such a priori modifications as market pressures may suggest), how does the businessman's approach to pricing compare with the economist's conception? How can we summarize the pricing decisions which enter into budget planning?

First, we must recognize that pricing policy falls into a number of classes.

1. Firms which market a large number of products tend to rely on a markup over full allocated costs at some standard volume to meet a target return on investment, as a first approximation, adjusting the resulting figures for varying competitive and market pressures but still seeking, after such adjustments have been made, to achieve the target return.

2. Firms producing to order are more inclined to rely on target markup over full costs as a definite pricing policy. In soft markets some price concessions may be contemplated and budgeted for, however.

3. Pricing policy varies with the life cycle of a product. New products, for which no adequate substitute exists, may be given high prices either to skim the market quickly or to recover developmental costs while waiting for a market consciousness of the product to build up. Where a product is expected to have only a limited market, price is likely to remain high (that is, above standard markup, offsetting products which can take only a below standard markup) since the total profit potential is not inviting enough to require a price set low to ward off competitors. When a product is expected to have a large market potential, a declining price policy is likely to be followed in part to expand the market and in part to make the field somewhat less attractive to possible rivals.

4. In the case of "mature" products or products which, while new, have

close substitutes, price is likely to be predetermined by custom. Price ranges and quality differentials develop from which a firm cannot easily deviate. In these instances products are produced to a cost ceiling which is calculated to yield, at the customary price, the target rate of return.

5. In industries operating with low fixed costs and a high material-cost component, there is relatively little room for pricing discretion. The number of producers (with easy entry) is too great to effect any price pattern, and prices will be largely determined by fluctuating materials costs.

In all the above cases except the last, management tends to rely on a markup over full allocated costs at some standard volume as the basis for its pricing policy rather than to attempt to set its price equal to marginal cost at the volume where marginal cost equals marginal revenue. Indeed, there is some reason for questioning whether the latter is very often feasible. If marginal cost is constant over some significant range (the "relevant range" frequently alluded to in the literature), a price set equal to marginal cost, at any volume within that range, would not permit recovery of fixed period expenses. One cannot realistically conceive of businessmen setting prices on such a basis. If one relaxes the assumption and permits marginal cost to rise modestly, the volume at which a price set equal to it would permit some recovery of fixed costs might be too uncertain ("abnormal" rather than "normal") to make it a reasonable basis for planning.[21]

There is nothing definitive, conclusive, or even persuasive about the cost allocations which lead to the figure on which a markup is based. Nor is there anything controlling about the rate of return on investment or sales which management has set as its target and on the basis of which it has calculated a standard markup. These are simply useful instruments in its objective of making a profit which, while not a theoretical maximum, represents as good a performance as management can expect in its effort to secure certain rather specific primary and anterior goals.

If market forces require adjustments which drive it in the direction of marginal-cost pricing, it is unlikely that "in the direction of" will translate into "all the way." Moreover, steps may be taken of a promotional or product-design nature which will arrest or reverse the movement, and it is further possible that offsetting price actions on less-pressured products will provide budgetary compensation. We shall explore these possibilities in a later chapter.

[21] An interesting empirical examination of one industry of which this appears to be true has been provided by T. Kempner, "Costs and Prices in Launderettes," *The Journal of Industrial Economics,* vol. 8, June, 1960, pp. 216–229. I have discussed the feasibility of marginal-cost pricing further in *A General Theory of Economic Process,* pp. 247–250.

Appendix to Chapter 9

PRICING FOR A RATE OF RETURN

A variety of formulas for rate-of-return pricing have been devised, and while there is no particular point in surveying the field, examples of some of their salient characteristics may be instructive.

In some instances investment in fixed plant is distinguished from current investment (accounts receivable, inventories), on the ground that "since capital employed has a portion which varies with sales dollars, for example, accounts receivable, the price will in part determine the amount of capital employed, and capital employed will determine the profit and the sales price. This presents the problem of two interrelated variables. It can be solved by using the following equation to calculate sales prices: *

$$\text{Net unit price} = \frac{(C + RF)/V}{1 - RW}$$

The symbols indicate the following:

C Total of factory cost, selling, and administrative expense.

R Percentage return desired on capital employed.

F Fixed portion of capital employed, e.g., property, plant, and equipment.

W Variable capital employed expressed as a percentage of sales volume.

V Annual sales volume in units.

If this formula is used, the period expenses need not be unitized. The total dollars allocated to the product are used in the formula. The use of the formula is illustrated . . .

Assuming that $C = \$100,000$, $R = 15\%$, $F = \$20,000$, $W = 30\%$, and $V = 200,000$, the sales price would be

$$\frac{(\$100,000 + 0.15 \times \$20,000)/200,000}{1 - 0.15 \times 0.30} = \frac{0.515}{0.955} = 0.539267$$

This is proved as follows:

Sales 200,000 @ 0.539267	$107,853.40
Cost	100,000.00
Profit	$ 7,853.40

Capital employed:

Variable, 30% of $107,853.40	$ 32,356
Fixed	20,000
Total	$ 52,356
15% return on capital employed	$ 7,853.40

* From Keller, *Management Accounting for Profit Control*, pp. 396–397.

Whereas Keller's approach is through current investment as a percentage of sales volume, and aggregate rather than unitized costs, another approach illustrated by Harvey O. Edson, of Haskin & Sells, Management Advisory Services, in "The Application of Return on Investment to Product Pricing," *The Controller,* October, 1959, pp. 464ff., differentiates current investment from fixed investment, relates it to cost rather than sales, and unitizes it. Summarizing his statement:

Given for Product A:

1. Sales terms—Net 30 days.
2. Company policy to maintain 20 days cash requirements at all times.
3. Finished Goods inventories to be maintained on three-months turnover basis.
4. In-Process and Raw Material inventories to be maintained on a one-month turn-over basis.
5. Cost Factors Product A:

	Per 1000	%
Factory Cost	$252.00	80%
Selling and Administration	68.00	20%
Total Costs	$340.00	100%
Less depreciation	34.00	10%
Total Cash Costs	$306.00	90%

6. Desired ROI [return on investment] = 25%.

Since return on investment ratios are always expressed at annual rates, all time factors must be expressed as a percentage of the year for conversion into a common ratio to total costs thus:

Current investment element	Period required	% of 1 yr.	Cost factor	Ratio to total cost	Conversion to annual investment factors (expressed as a ratio to total costs)
Cash	20 days	5.5% ×	Cash Cost	90% =	4.95
Accounts Receivable	1 month	8.33 ×	Selling Price	125%* =	10.41
Finished Goods	3 months	25.00 ×	Factory Cost	80% =	20.00
In Process and Raw Materials	1 month	8.33 ×	Factory Cost	80% =	6.66
		Current Investment Requirement		=	42.02
		(expressed as a ratio to total cost)		Use	42%

* The 25% mark-up used here is a knowledgeable approximation. The precise calculation of this mark-up can be determined by algebraic computation. In most applications such estimates will suffice, occasioning but little distortion of the final result.

The factor of 42% expresses the relationship between the unit cost and the current investment requirements, i.e., for each dollar of unit cost, a current investment of 42¢, on the average, will be needed. It follows that the pricing additive needed will be the product of the current investment requirement (42%) times the desired rate of return (25%) times the unit cost of the product ($340.00 per M) thus:

$$.42 \times .25 \times \$340 = \$35.70 \text{ (per M)}.$$

The $35.70 (per M) is the pricing additive needed to provide a 25% return on the current (variable) investment employed. . . .

TRANSLATING THE FIXED INVESTMENT TO PRODUCT COST . . .

The analysis and allocation of fixed assets is intended to assign in a logical manner all fixed investment to the direct productive equipment by cost center and to the administrative and sales divisions. In effect, the fixed investment is "boiled down" to a few group totals which can be converted into the loading factors to be applied on machine hours (or other suitable base) in the pricing formula to provide a predetermined rate of return on the fixed investment.

Assume, for purposes of illustration, that the total fixed investment of $1 million of the company producing our hypothetical product A, has been allocated to four direct production machines and to the administration and sales divisions as follows:

$$
\begin{array}{lr}
\text{Machine \#1---\$} & 132,000 \\
2\text{---} & 330,000 \\
3\text{---} & 198,000 \\
4\text{---} & 247,500 \\
\text{Administrative} & 42,500 \\
\text{Selling} & 50,000 \\
\hline
\$1,000,000
\end{array}
$$

THE FIXED INVESTMENT IN PRODUCTIVE EQUIPMENT

To correlate the fixed productive investment to product lines (in this example to product A) factors for the operating level and the production rates of the machines (capacity factors) on a product line basis are required.

For product line A the following are given factors:

1. Product A is produced on machines #1 and #2, the product being first processed on machine #1 and completed on machine #2.

2. The unit capacity of machine #1 is 2000 per hour. Excess capacity of this machine cannot be utilized on other products.

3. Unit capacity of machine #2 is 1000 per hour.

4. Unit sales are estimated at 3300M for the year.

5. Desired ROI = 25%.

Translating the fixed investment into a factor per M units of product A would follow thus:

	Total fixed investment		Annual machine hours oper- ating level		Investment per machine hour		Product machine output per hour		Fixed in- vestment per M units
Machine #1	$132,000	÷	1,650	=	$ 80.00	÷	2,000	=	$ 40.00
Machine #2	330,000	÷	3,300	=	100.00	÷	1,000	=	100.00
									$140.00

The factor of $140.00 represents the fixed investment per M units of product A. It follows that the pricing additive needed per M units will be the product of this fixed investment factor per M units ($140.00) times the desired rate of return (25%) thus:

$$\$140.00 \times .25 = \$35.00 \text{ (per M)}$$

The $35.00 per M units factor is the pricing additive needed to provide a 25% return on the fixed productive investment employed. . . .

THE FIXED INVESTMENT IN SELLING AND ADMINISTRATIVE EQUIPMENT

In our example, the fixed assets assigned to the selling and administrative functions total $42,500 and $50,000 respectively (4.25% and 5% of the total fixed investment). . . .

In order to apply the S & A fixed investment to unit costs, a correlation between the S & A cost and investment factors must be established. For the purpose of our example, it is further given that S & A expenses for all products total $462.500. By relating the value assigned to the S & A fixed investment ($92,500) to total S & A expense ($462,500) a ratio of 20% is computed. This factor of 20% expresses the relationship of the total S & A fixed investment to each dollar of S & A cost. The S & A pricing additive needed will be the product of fixed investment factor (20%) times the desired rate of return (25%) times the S & A costs identified to the product ($68.00 per M) thus:

$$.20 \times .25 \times \$68.00 = \$3.40 \text{ per M}$$

The $3.40 per M factor is the pricing additive needed to provide a 25% return on the fixed S & A investment.

DETERMINING THE TARGET PRICE ON PRODUCT LINE A

Using the three factors which have been developed to this point, the product target price to yield a 25% return on investment would be computed as follows:

Total Product A Costs and ROI Factors Computed For:	(Per M) $340.00
(a) Current (variable) investment	35.70
(b) Fixed (productive) investment	35.00
(c) Fixed (S & A) investment	3.40
Target Price—(25% ROI)	$414.10

By projecting product A's unit price, cost and investment factors at the budgeted level of 3,300 M units for the year the 25% return on investment is demonstrated, thus:

Sales at $414.10 per M	=	$1,366,530	100.0%
Costs at $340.00 per M	=	1,122,000	81.1
Operating Profit, before taxes	=	$ 244,530	17.9%
Investment Employed:			
Current (variable) at 42% of total costs	=	$ 471,240	
Fixed-Productive Equipment	=	462,000	
Fixed—S & A (allocated as 20% of S & A expense)	=	44,880	
Total Investment Employed		$ 978,120	
25% on Investment Employed		$ 244,530	

In all rate-of-return pricing formulas, the important consideration is that the markup varies with the amount of investment (either fixed or current) allocated to the product line.

Chapter 10

PRODUCT AND SERVICE PLANNING

Importance of the Product-line Review

Having a product or service line to sell is obviously a precondition of doing business at all. As related to the planning process it is something more than that, however. It is generally something to be continuingly reviewed as an instrument for achieving target.

The size of the problem is apparent from the fact that typically in a moderately large corporation the product line runs to several hundred major products—and to a total of several thousand (sometimes even several hundred thousand) products if separately marketed replacement parts are included. Service-dispensing organizations seldom have so varied a line of activity, but if one contemplates the range of salable services offered by the modern bank, insurance company, or travel agency, he quickly appreciates that they are not far behind manufacturing businesses in the diversity of their offerings. To review so complex a line of activity becomes an enormous task.

It is not, however, a task which can be neglected. In a world where improvement in communications and transportation has made competitors of firms a continent or an ocean apart, the firm which lags in coming up with an improved product or service is in danger of being put out of the race by those which do. The drive to make obsolete a good or a service which one has only lately been advertising as the ultimate in perfection has become a commonplace observation. What the research and development arm of one's own firm does not outdate will be taken care of by one's competitors.

The process of reviewing the line is intended to reveal weaknesses and strengths among its components. In the light of the information uncovered, management may then plan its next moves—to shore up a faltering product or service, abandon it altogether, substitute a new offering which has reached the point of marketability, spur a particular research program, concentrate sales attention on certain items, and so on. Out of such a review come market strategies, in the broadest and most fundamental sense, determining the product mix for the immediate and long-run futures; identifying the focus of marketing and developmental activities; affecting sales efforts and sales budgets; having an impact on costs in terms of not only the level of operations but the production processes which must be introduced and relied on, plant and equipment to be purchased, personnel to be recruited and trained, inventories to be maintained and pruned; and disclosing as a result of all of these the cash needs of the organization.

Despite its fundamental importance, the product-line review is fraught with traps for even the most sophisticated. Comparisons of product revenues and costs, comparisons of profit by product line with the company's target rate of profit, and comparisons among products cannot be made, at least for the long run, without some form of common-cost allocation, if only of rough orders of magnitude, and we are aware of the judgmental character of such allocations. But businesses cannot be run without the use of judgment, and the fact that certain accounting procedures are less precise than their use of numbers would suggest does not mean that they cannot be useful—indeed, almost indispensable—despite considerable margins of error for which allowance must be made.

The two most basic questions which management must answer in reviewing the existing product line are: By how much is each of our products contributing more to earnings than to costs? And which of our products are increasing and which declining in volume of sales? The second question is a relatively simple statistical exercise, but the first question raises thorny problems.

The Opportunity Cost of a Product

In terms of economic (opportunity) costs rather than accounting costs, a product's cost of production is only its variable cost—providing there is no substitute product which might have been made in its place. But if there are substitute products which might have been made, using the same fixed resources, then the economic cost is not only the variable cost but also any greater return which has been forgone by making the original product rather than the substitute. Whether a product costs a firm more than its variable cost of production depends on whether the firm could have used its fixed facilities to greater advantage by making some other product.

Companies which calculate product costs on the basis of a full allocation of all costs, for purposes of measuring their contribution, operate on the implicit assumption that there are possible substitutes for every product in the line. Companies which calculate product costs on a direct-cost basis operate on the implicit assumption that there are no substitutes for any product in the line. In either case, however, the implicit assumption may be rebutted.

Full-cost allocation is obviously more appropriate for the long run, and indeed even necessary in the long run if the purposes of a product-line review are to be served. If some product is not producing a very adequate return on the portion of fixed assets which are employed in its making (however judgmental and imprecise that calculation may be), a management which gears its organization to a target return must look for alternative ways of using its fixed investment to achieve it. This may take time, during which the product is retained in the line as long as it makes some contribution to fixed expenses: [1]

> When a product . . . does not yield a satisfactory net profit, it is not summarily eliminated, but at the same time management takes steps toward making this product yield a more satisfactory margin or toward finding something else to replace it which will absorb its share of allocated fixed costs and show an adequate net profit. This is apt to be a gradual process in the course of which a number of proposed courses of action are evaluated by special studies to determine the effect they may be expected to have on profit. . . .

The direct-cost method is clearly more suited to the immediate present as a basis for determining whether a product should be dropped or not. Nevertheless it would still look to the long run as a time in which products yielding a greater contribution margin might be substituted for weaker performers in the existing line.

Both methods of product costing therefore tend to the same result. Some firms (perhaps most) employ absorption costing to allocate all costs, as a means of pinpointing problem products, but rely on direct costing to determine whether to retain the problem products in their line until replacement with more profitable items is feasible. Moreover, at times special studies may uncover reasons why even products which seem unprofitable should be retained—not only for the familiar reason of rounding out a "full line" for customer satisfaction but because further analysis reveals that the presumed unprofitability stems from a common-cost allocation procedure which in this case is unwarranted. (For example, "Many companies concentrate their promotional efforts upon relatively few items, yet promotional expenses are frequently charged to the entire range of products, thereby completely distorting the relative profit contribution of each item." [2])

---

[1] *Analysis of Non-manufacturing Costs for Managerial Decisions*, N.A.C.A., p. 27.
[2] John O. Tomb, McKinsey & Company, "Production Control and the Controller," *N.A.C.A. Bulletin*, April, 1952, sec. 1, p. 942. The reverse may equally be true. Non-

Profit Analysis by Product or Product Group

To reduce the danger of such errors companies often compute profit by broad product lines or groups rather than by individual products: [3]

> Determination of separate product net profit figures is limited to comparatively broad segments which are largely self-contained units of the business. For example, one company preparing net profits by product lines has a separate plant for each line and manufacturing costs are accumulated by keeping a complete set of accounts at each plant. Advertising and selling costs are also largely direct charges to product lines. Assessments to cover general company administration expenses and institutional advertising are made, but the proportion of such costs is small relative to the total of all costs. Product line income statements are prepared monthly by this company and are used by management in evaluating performance of the various lines. On the other hand, determination of costs of individual items within product lines is limited to manufacturing cost and no allocation of non-manufacturing costs is made.

The same field study giving rise to the preceding observation revealed that fifty-six of seventy companies interviewed prepared periodic reports of product profit margins, most of them on a monthly basis: [4]

> In 45 companies these product margin reports carry assignment of nonmanufacturing costs to the point where net profit by product line is ascertained. The remaining 11 companies do not report net profit by product classification, but do determine other margins. In 5 of these companies, no nonmanufacturing costs are assigned to products and the information with respect to product profitability is limited to gross margin after manufacturing cost. The other 6 companies assign some but not all nonmanufacturing costs to products.

Examples of company practice in costing products for measuring relative profitability indicate some of the patterns which are followed:

> (1) This company has six operating divisions, each of which produces a separate type of product. Each division prepares a monthly profit and loss statement covering its operations. The divisions in turn have a number of product lines which are composed of numerous items and varieties. A monthly statement of profit or loss is prepared

---

allocation of period selling expenses may erroneously suggest by a high gross-profit margin an equally high "full-cost" margin. The above-average margin may simply reflect above-average selling and marketing costs.

[3] *Analysis of Non-manufacturing Costs for Managerial Decisions*, N.A.C.A., p. 29.

[4] The same, p. 45. The examples which follow are drawn from the same report, pp. 47–48.

for each product line and gross profit is determined for individual products within the lines. . . .

(2) The great number of individual products, most of which represent a very small fraction of total sales volume, makes it impractical to calculate costs for all products at frequent intervals. For those individual products which comprise the major portion of the volume, costs are determined annually; for the other products, costs are determined when the information is wanted. Product line costs are determined annually. . . .

(3) A monthly statement is prepared showing [1] sales, [2] manufacturing cost, [3] gross margin, [4] costs of order filling and transportation, and [5] margin after deducting the latter costs from gross margin. Statements give the above information for product lines and for products within each line, but not for individual product sizes, colors, and other varieties. This company does not make a routine monthly allocation of selling, advertising, and administrative costs to products.

(4) Actual profit or loss for each individual product is determined by annual study in which all costs are assigned. At the same time budgeted profit by products is determined for the coming year.

From analyses like these the management of a company either can test each product or product line by some fixed standard (such as return on allocated investment) or can derive some notion of "average" product profit performance, taking steps to improve the showing of or eliminate altogether the below-average items and to push the sales of those above average.

Direction of Change

Such tests are inadequate by themselves, however. They must be coupled with an examination of whether sales of a product (both in absolute terms and as a share of the market) have been marking time, rising, or falling. A product which still returns a good net profit but which is slipping in its market position promises trouble for management in the future if action is not taken now. For example: [5]

> Take the case of the solenoid. Marketing manager Joseph Gauss [of the general purpose control department of General Electric] and product planner John Lewis reported in December, 1952, to William F. Oswalt, general manager of GPC, that solenoid sales were going up steadily, but that GE's share of the total market was dropping. Lewis' survey group had found that the old solenoid was not adaptable to a number of new machines coming on the market. The competition was moving into these new fields and the sales force could do nothing about

[5] From *Business Week,* Sept. 4, 1954, p. 149.

it. Oswalt had to make a decision. He had three choices: (1) He could continue in a highly competitive field with a product that had some drawbacks but a lot of satisfied users; (2) he could drop the line entirely and concentrate on some other product where the competition was less aggressive, or (3) he could redesign the old product and aim at leadership. Oswalt chose the last.

In some few instances the pressures on a company to do something about its product line are intense and immediate, as in the case of an aircraft manufacturer or shipbuilding company engaged in a governmental program which is abruptly terminated. The Fairchild Engine and Airplane Corporation reported: [6]

> The Corporation successfully designed and flew the Goose missile. The anticipated high volume production of this weapons system was cancelled by the US Air Force as a result of changing military strategy concepts. . . . The resulting excess capacity must be filled with products in new fields. An entry has been made into the field of radar antenna reflectors and other areas are being explored by your management and by outside consultants. However, the volume of business which must be generated in new product lines is very large and takes time to develop. The problem is further complicated by the fact that other aircraft manufacturers also have excess plant capacity and are competitively exploring the same fields.

More commonly, however, product-line review and new or revised product planning proceeds under less pressure and can be incorporated as a normal part of budget planning, both operating and long-term budgets, where it enters in terms of new products on which sales volume must be figured, sales and cost budgets for continuing product lines which reveal estimates of their relative profitability and market position, and budgeted research and developmental expenses.[7]

---

[6] 1959 Annual Report, pp. 3–4.

[7] "We prepare a detailed five-year program for each of our major product lines. This program shows the estimated sales and profit by year for each of the current products in the line, the planned model replacements, and the new products we hope to introduce, all based on market data, statistical data, economic trends and forecasts, and anticipated development progress. This program is submitted to management for preliminary consideration. Meanwhile, it is used by research and development supervision, the comptroller's department and the production organization in making tentative plans for the coming year. After any necessary adjustments and management approval, it becomes the formal program for the division.

"From this five-year program, we determine the projects to be worked on during the budget year. We re-examine projects currently under way and we appraise the new projects to be undertaken. Each of these projects is submitted to a detailed analysis, in which we predict:

"1. Total estimated development cost.

Product Styling

Product planning thus becomes an integral part of business planning and budgeting. "Product planning is expected to integrate the planning, the timing, and the pricing required to add the new, eliminate the undesired, and improve the existing products." [8] How essential a part of normal business planning and budgeting product review and development are will be appreciated by recalling, from the preceding chapter, that for products in the "maturity" of their life cycle styling rather than price is viewed as the basis of competition. "We learned that specialty salesmen need demonstrable differences. These differences were engineered into the product deliberately, to give our salesmen an edge over competition." [9] Moreover, the costs of style changes are rather firmly controlled by the necessity that such a product fit within its normal price class. Under these circumstances product development is treated as a variable at least as important as cost and price for purposes of business policy and budget planning.

Many companies rely on their sales forces to recommend style changes which have been suggested by customers or competition, thus linking the product-line decisions more closely to the marketing program. A company official writes: [10]

"2. Development cost for forthcoming budget year.
"3. Percentage of completion by the end of a budget year.
"4. Target date for releasing the design to production.
"5. Target date for delivery of the product to stock.
"6. Estimated manufacturing cost.
"7. Estimated tool cost.
"8. Estimated selling price.
"9. Estimated 3-year sales in units and dollars.
"10. Percentage relation of development cost to 3-year sales.
"Estimating development costs and establishing development schedules can be a discouraging task because of the difficulty of trying to schedule invention. . . .
"With approximately 150 different projects under development at one time, both the department management and the division management need frequent reports which reveal the status of each project."
Howard P. Allen, "Bird's-eye View of Operations-integrated Research and Development," *N.A.A. Bulletin,* December, 1957, sec. 1, pp. 15–16.

[8] Roy W. Johnson, as executive vice-president of General Electric's appliance and electronic group, quoted in *Business Week,* Apr. 18, 1953, p. 142.

[9] Robert M. Oliver, vice-president—marketing, Thomas A. Edison Industries, Mc-Graw-Edison Company, "The Marketing Concept in Developing Products for Profit," in *Control of Non-manufacturing Costs,* A.M.A. Special Report 26, pp. 85–86.

[10] George W. McCarty, vice-president—research and development, The Black & Decker Mfg. Co., "Establishing Product Objectives," in *Organizing for Product Development,* A.M.A. Management Report 31, New York, 1959, pp. 33–34.

At our regular meetings for regional and district sales managers, product planning is included on the agenda. Information and ideas gleaned at these meetings are considered, along with a great deal of other information, in our efforts to establish product objectives. We are currently involved in the complete redesign of an entire product area. Prior to the inauguration of the program, the product manager called in the key district sales managers for a review of the product in question. They were asked what they believed to be lacking in the existing product, what changes they considered necessary to correct these deficiencies, and what effect they expected competition to have in this area in the future.

Product Innovation

In newer industries, however, and with respect to products having short life cycles, new styling is not a sufficient product-line defense. Product innovation is necessary. The former is sometimes labeled "defensive research," the latter "aggressive research." [11] The executive vice-president of an electronics and control instrumentation company comments, "Because of the high rate of technological advancement in our chosen fields, we must base our planning on partial or complete obsolescence of our products on a cycle of approximately four to five years." [12] This company plans for the release of four major products a year, a "major product" being defined as one with the potential of generating a million dollars in sales within four years after release. The manner in which a new product is fitted into production and marketing schedules, involving the cooperative planning of all aspects of the business, is indicated in one case described by an official of Merck & Company in Appendix A to this chapter.

[11] "Despite an industry average of 11 years for the development of a product, we have been fortunate enough not to have to wait that long for many of our major products. We control our research efforts very strictly. As soon as a project gets beyond the fundamental-research stage and into the applied-research stage, it is given a code number. From this time on, the project's progress is followed closely on a cost-accounting basis. All information can then be consolidated on an IBM machine and entered on an 'R & D balance sheet,' which places all research efforts in two categories—'defensive' and 'aggressive.' By 'defensive' research we mean customer service, modification of current products and processes, and so forth; 'aggressive' research is concerned with the development of new products." Remarks of E. T. Collinsworth, Jr., chairman of the board of Velsicol International Corporation, in "Keeping in Phase with Changing Business Conditions" (a discussion), *The Dynamics of Management*, A.M.A. Management Report 14, pp. 15–16.

[12] Hugh F. Colvin, Consolidated Engineering Corporation, "Controls for Research and Development," *Controls and Techniques for Better Management*, A.M.A. General Management Series, 176, New York, 1955, p. 25.

Product Diversification

One difficulty with attempting to plan major new products is that research programs, on which such developments are based, cannot always be confined within predetermined channels. Even the effort to remain within the boundaries of an "industry" (that shadowy abstraction) may prove difficult: [13]

> Long-range product plans must be oriented to the *function* involved rather than to the particular products offered by the company to perform that function. If we [in the Whirlpool Corporation] think of ourselves as manufacturers of appliances which will wash clothes, prepare and preserve food, and clean dishes, we must, in the same breath, be interested in the kinds of clothes that have to be washed, the kinds of foods that have to be preserved and prepared, and the kinds of dishes that have to be cleaned. . . . A large segment of the engineering effort should be dissociated from the present product line, so that the company can continue to obsolete its own products instead of waiting for its competitors to do the job. . . . One may venture to suggest that, if the railroad companies had thought of themselves as being in the transportation business rather than merely in the railroad business, they might, over the past few years, have found some means of avoiding their present plight, or certainly of alleviating it.

An ambitious and imaginative management may therefore attempt to free itself of any industry orientation. Even if it plans new products as additions to some line which it considers its basic field, it may stand ready to follow the results of its research program into whatever fields they may lead.

> A company which is determined to remain in a single industry may well find, as a result of its breadth and depth of engineering, certain products outside its basic product concept which seem to have good commercial possibilities and to justify the investment of company funds to exploit them. To deal with such eventualities, long-range product planning is best kept sufficiently flexible that, so long as the basic product concept is not significantly weakened, management is not blinded to the real possibilities which appear as by-products of the major engineering effort. . . . Certainly, if the engineering effort justifies its existence, it will do so in part by the discoveries it makes which are not particularly germane to the company's present product line at the time the engineering effort was started.

[13] Mason Smith, vice-president and treasurer, Whirlpool Corporation, "How to Initiate Effective Long-range Planning," *The Dynamics of Management,* A.M.A. Management Report 14, pp. 71–72. The subsequent quotation is from the same source, p. 71.

With such a flexible orientation may come, however, a dispersion of management attention over a range of activities with which it has a decreasing familiarity. Without intentionally joining in any quixotic quest for diversification, a company may find itself extended in ways which rob its production, marketing, and managerial activities of a carefully contrived rationalization. Along with flexibility and imagination in the exploitation of new product lines, the most successfully managed companies have also found it necessary to stress discipline and foresight in determining the direction of their product innovations.[14]

Costs of Research and Development

The cost of developing and introducing a new product varies with the nature of the product and the market, but by any standard it is substantial. It has been estimated that the successful launching of a new bar of soap would cost $20 million in just the first year,[15] while the expense of putting the Ford Company's ill-fated Edsel on the market is reported to have amounted to $250 million. With investments of this magnitude it is understandable that managements should endeavor to systematize their decisions

[14] This danger of spreading a company thin probably accounts, at least in part, for what otherwise appears to be—and sometimes actually is—a shortsighted fixation on a particular field. "Oil men" tend to think in terms of oil, for example, and despite new areas of potential development which their own research activities may suggest, some of them promising attractive rates of return, they are likely to prefer investment (even at lower probable returns) in oil than outside it. But the danger of such a fixation is noted in this comment by Andrew Heiskell, publisher of *Life:* "Some companies have been ruined by the speed of changes in the market place. I have the impression that many business heads, in candor, will freely admit their very great uncertainty on where to lead their companies.

"I know one large company that has almost been totally liquidated and is now searching for a place to invest the stockholders' money. I know another with sales in the billions which is asking itself what it should do with the business. I know a third, also a great name on the American business scene and with sales in the hundreds of millions, which seems to be up against an inevitable downward trend, and which is searching frantically for ways to maintain its competitive position. I see ads regularly in the Wall Street Journal—companies (some desperately) seeking other means of diversification for working themselves out of a box.

"I know a so-called 'business raider' who says the failure of companies to evaluate their markets and to know when to change is what has made him rich. He says the stockholder is entitled to a management which will invest company funds in whatever way will save and make productive the stockholders' investment. Frequently radical action is called for. Certainly it must be preceded by knowledge of markets and careful research."

The Role of Marketing Research, Marketing and Transportation Paper no. 1, Bureau of Business and Economic Research, Michigan State University, 1958, pp. 7–8.

[15] Gilman B. Allen, Robert Heller & Associates, "What the Accountants Should Know about Market Research," *N.A.A. Bulletin,* August, 1958, sec. 3, p. 11.

on whether the corporation's future would be safer down one product avenue rather than another.

The most desirable basis for decision is the one we have consistently encountered—return on investment. The difficulty in applying it, however, lies in the virtual impossibility of measuring return, since consumer response to a new product, whose very characteristics are uncertain when research begins, can only be a guess, and since such a return should be measured over the life of the product, which can only be an arbitrary assumption, with even the possibility on any long-range project that intermediate events may make it obsolete before it so much as reaches the marketing stage.[16] In addition, the size of the investment is uncertain at the research stage, and indeed, what research costs are attributable to it are usually in doubt even after a product has debouched from the process. The succinct comment which that delightful Peruvian architect-writer Hector Velarde once made on his countrymen's character applies with equal force to the activities of industrial laboratories: "You never know for sure when a project begins, when it ends, what it will cost, or what it will be."

Intuitive and Flexible Judgments

These problems of estimation are considerably reduced when a project passes from the research to the development stage. If research is written off as a period expense up to the point at which it eventuates in a project to develop a specific product, the characteristics of which are now more

---

[16] One example of this has been given by Charles B. Thornton, as president of Litton Industries, in *The Dynamics of Management,* A.M.A. Management Report 14, p. 17: "Sometimes a company finds itself so far behind another company working on the same project that it must abandon its own effort. At one time, for instance, we were trying to develop a high-speed printing machine. We had spent a large sum of money on the project, and we had a fairly large engineering team ready to meet the requirement. I happened, however, to have lunch with the president of a company that had finished developmental work on a similar machine, which was going to be made available at an early date. We subsequently decided to cut our project off and devote our know-how to something else, even though our scientists and engineers said, 'Give us six months and a few hundred thousand dollars more and we can develop one just as good.' Two men even quit because we would not let them go on, regarding our action as an affront to their professional pride. We were satisfied, however, that we were saving time and money by giving up the project."

This case is strikingly parallel to the one described so vividly by C. P. Snow in his novel *The New Men,* based on the race for the atomic bomb between British and American scientists. In the instance cited by Thornton, note the "error" which would have been made in calculating a return on investment at the start of the project—an error to which any research project is subject, and which is increased by the length of the period over which research must be conducted before bearing fruit.

discernible, both subsequent investment and return are more calculable, providing a firmer base for computing a rate of return. Nevertheless, the estimation problem remains hazardous even at this stage. It is probably safe to assert that few decisions in the managerial repertoire rely more on intuitive judgment than those associated with product innovation. Under the circumstances, return on investment, while still the most logical basis for decision, is a speculative guide at best.

As a consequence the appropriation for research and development which finds its way into the operating budget is typically more an act of faith than a precise calculation. It is often set as a percentage of sales, a rule of thumb whose only real rationale is that it is a convenient way of arriving at a figure while avoiding meaningless debates over the value of one project relative to another. Such choices must of course be made, but they are removed from the budgeting process (to which they cannot contribute anything) to special committees charged with allocating the appropriation among competing projects. (Appendix B to this chapter provides examples of such committees.) The size of the research and development item in the operating budget is thus a function of managerial judgment, adjustable up and down as the expected profit figure may dictate, sometimes almost— like profit—a balancing item.

Most managements are convinced that some expenditure in this area is essential to a firm's survival, but the amount of the expenditure appears to bear no functional relationship to a firm's profitability. This year's appropriation may be cut—if there is need for economy in order to balance the budget at a level of inflows and outflows that promises the closer realization of the profit goal—without any sense that the firm's future is thereby endangered. Perhaps the amount will be made up later. Perhaps the sum which is lopped off would have borne no fruit in any event. Perhaps the temporary retrenchment will release the less able researchers and developers, who will be replaced later by more brilliant young men. Such actions cannot be taken year after year, it is true, without creating the danger which these rationalizations minimize, but the widely followed practice of hitching appropriations to a per cent of sales is itself indicative that some fluctuating level of research expenditures is to be expected.

Some industries and some managements are particularly research-oriented. The pace of competitive innovation is such as to increase their consciousness of the need for invoking change as a weapon against rivals. They are more loath to cut "R & D" budgets and at times will even move to increase them at a time when profits are being squeezed—almost as a dramatic assertion of faith, since even in these instances there is no discernible functional tie between research appropriations and profitability; a tie may exist, but it has not been established. The greater magnitude of the research appropriations in these instances—whether on an absolute or a percentage basis—is a reflection of a strange combination of an insurance and a gambling outlook. The larger the sum, the greater the probability (the better the gamble?) that some project will result which will pay off handsomely; the larger the sum, the greater the assurance that present investment will be protected.

With all its uncertainties and ambiguities, however, it remains true that research and development, at some level of budgeted activity, are essential ingredients of product planning, in both the short run and the long run, and that product planning is an inescapable aspect—indeed, from some points of view perhaps the single most vital aspect—of business planning. In the form of product innovations it is usually the basis for a firm's survival and growth, its long-run realization of its profit objectives. In the form of differentiated (styled) products, it is the basis for its short-run profitability. Product-line decisions enter into its sales budgets, its production budgets, its inventory and advertising budgets, its purchasing schedules and manning tables, its research and development budgets, its capital investment. They constitute perhaps the most risk-taking substantive decisions which managements are called upon to make.

Appendix A to Chapter 10

THE DEVELOPMENT OF A NEW PRODUCT *

Let us follow a particular new product, which we shall term "Vitamin X," beyond the Pilot Plant to determine—

1. How it is integrated into present production schedules and how it affects other items in the production area.

2. What allowances are made in the forecast for the integration of the new product.

3. How and why a priority may be given to such a new product and under what circumstances.

INITIAL APPEARANCE

On the memorable day when Vitamin X makes its appearance in the Pilot Plant, many people in numerous divisions of the company have been made aware of its progress through our system of encouraging simple and direct communication through and across the line organization with the varied staff groups acting as added eyes, ears, minds, and catalysts for coordinating the product's progress.

The following information should have been developed for Vitamin X and should now be available:

1. Operating procedures.

* By A. R. Fiore, production control manager, Merck & Co., from *Successful Production Planning and Control*, A.M.A. Special Report 5, New York, 1955, pp. 127–132.

2. Bill of materials.
3. Raw material specifications.
4. Product specifications.
5. Unit costs.
6. Engineering design.
7. Corrosion studies.
8. Safety studies.
9. Packaging data.

At this point, also, either of two situations can exist with regard to Vitamin X: (1) It will fill a gap in an existing field or actually replace a similar product; or (2) it will open up a new territory. Since production control is more difficult under the first set of circumstances, and Situation 2 involves only some of the problems encountered, we shall assume for the purposes of this discussion that Situation 2 prevails.

COOPERATIVE STUDIES

During the transition of Vitamin X from the Research Laboratories to the Pilot Plant, and during its development in the Pilot Plant, its progress is carefully watched by a product coordinator in the Marketing Division. He in turn acts as an informational center and keeps the various interested areas of the company informed. It is at this point that the Market Analysis and Production Control units enter the picture.

Let us suppose that Vitamin X is fairly well recognized at this time as a close relative of Vitamin Y; and, furthermore, all indications point to its increased therapeutic efficiency and lower toxicity levels. Animal tests in the Merck Institute for Therapeutic Research and evaluation of clinical data from various control points all suggest the possibility that Vitamin X may either completely replace Vitamin Y or at least reduce its consumption. The critical evaluation of this balance becomes a close collaborative study by the product coordinators and Market Analysis, making full use of the reports from the field sales force, the advice of merchandising specialists and of advertising and promotion personnel, panel surveys, and the other tools of the various divisions.

During this period many wheels are set in motion. Studies are made of price projections and cost requirements; trade channels; potential uses; selling methods; advertising and promotion; the required production center, including available facilities and engineering estimates; label and package insert wordings, package component design, and printing; and such problems as production scheduling, production interference, and raw material supply. These inquiries are undertaken simultaneously by many company groups: Production, Production Control, Chemical Control, Purchasing, Research, Medical, Engineering, and Marketing.

AUTHORIZATION PROCEDURE

Assuming now that the product coordinator has obtained the necessary information and justification and that formal management approval has been obtained, two developments take place:

1. The product coordinator issues an addition-to-the-line notice for Vitamin X.

This provides Production Control with the following information:

a. An estimate of the initial stocks desired.

b. An authorization to commit company funds to this project which may take the form of any or all of the following actions:

    (1) Requisitioning chemical raw materials and package components.

    (2) Requisitioning items to be purchased from other suppliers for resale.

    (3) Ordering manufactured bulk at the manufacturing level.

    (4) Ordering formulation, subdivision, and finishing of either manufactured bulk or purchased items.

2. The Market Analysis unit issues a sales estimate revision for Vitamin Y, usually for a year by quarters. This takes into consideration the effect of Vitamin X on the field and is the result of the thinking of many groups, including merchandising specialists, field salesmen, panel survey experts, and the Medical and Research Divisions.

MAKEREADY

. . . It will readily be seen that a vast number of groups and individuals are involved. At this point, however, responsibility for executing the program rests with the Production Division, of which Production Control is a staff member. Armed with most of the information listed [previously] Production Control begins its work of liaison and communication.

Manufacturing Facilities. First, it must make certain that the manufacturing areas are completely ready for their part in the project. This involves:

1. Insuring that Manufacturing has an approved process and the necessary facilities and staff available.

2. Confirming with the Chemical Control Division that product and raw material specifications exist.

3. Determining whether production of Vitamin X in the quantities requested will interfere with any other production schedule in the manufacturing area. Interference, of course, can be due to shortages of equipment or manpower, or both. These problems are studied jointly by Manufacturing and Production Control. Several courses of action are possible:

a. Having prior knowledge that the new product is being added to the line, we can temporarily increase production on the interference items, thereby exceeding our maximum inventory standard on a short-term basis. We can then stop production of these items when the time comes to produce Vitamin X. This is already routine procedure in our company on many items that use common equipment or a set manpower pool.

b. We can install additional equipment to break the bottleneck or common equipment point.

c. Additional personnel can be hired.

d. If a final allocation must be made—that is, if "we can produce all the Vitamin X required but none of the interference item," or "we can produce some of each in whatever ratio is desired"—the problem is presented to a Sales Control unit in the Marketing Division, whose answer is usually decisive.

Raw Materials. Second, the availability of raw materials is investigated. The

Production Control unit, working with a raw material inventory policy in mind, submits immediate and annual requirements to the Purchasing Division. Any problems are jointly discussed by Purchasing, Production Control, and Manufacturing. Purchasing submits availabilities, economic ordering units, alternate supply sources, and so on. A raw material requisition is prepared by Production Control and issued to the Purchasing Division.

Containers. Third, bulk container availability is checked. This usually presents no immediate difficulty unless the item is to be delivered as a finished package from the manufacturing unit. This is always cleared with a Package Development group in the company since, if the item happens to require manufacturing prefinishing or delivery to the Packaging Division within the company for smaller subdivisions, container components are often a very important factor.

The label wording usually has been set up by the Chemical Control Division upon the request of the product coordinator. This wording must be checked by various interested areas of the company, including Sales, Medical, and Research. After approval—in some cases, by the Food and Drug Administration as well—it is submitted to Package Development to be set up in the proper form for the label and such other necessary components as folding boxes, and preprinted corrugated or metal containers. Production Control requests from Package Development an estimated date for the availability of copy, and asks Purchasing and Printing to determine when the final components will be available. Again, it may be necessary at this point to invoke an allocation or priority to obtain label wording, insert wording, component design, or label printing.

THE PRODUCTION ORDER

The foregoing steps fall generally into the category of liaison and communication. More specifically, they might be called "the three C's"—Communication, Coordination, and Control. These investigations ultimately lead to the issuance of a production order triggering the actual commitment of men, materials, and machines to the production of an approved item according to an approved process.

In due course, then, the first lot of our Vitamin X is delivered by the manufacturing unit to the Packaging Division. Here it is subdivided according to a previously established schedule (coordinated between the Packaging and Factory Production Control groups) and shipped out to our sales branches in quantities as requested for initial stocks by the Marketing Division.

EFFECT ON PRODUCT Y

In the meantime, our old Vitamin Y has not been neglected. As stated previously, Market Analysis has reduced the quarterly and annual sales estimate on this item. We now have the simple problem of examining inventories and reducing production schedules in accordance with a well-defined plan covering—

1. Target quantities desired in inventory.
2. Production schedule reduction in relation to manpower dislocations.
3. Actual progress of the Vitamin X plan.

PROTECTING THE SUPPLY SITUATION

It is, of course, the third factor that causes the most difficulty. As with the best-laid plans, many things can go wrong. Procurement of raw materials may not develop according to schedule; new factors, such as competitive problems causing price revisions and cost evaluations, may arise; new specifications called for by customer preference may crop up; changes or troubles in process may occur; requirements may increase or decrease depending on market conditions; and, last but not least, problems in label wording, component design, and printing may take longer than anticipated. Any and all of these factors can throw the plan out of gear.

To protect the supply situation, inventories of our Vitamin Y are checked frequently. Revised schedules for Vitamin X arranged with new developments in mind are weighed against the inventory position throughout all sales branches and the replenishment center. It may even be necessary to increase production schedules of Vitamin Y temporarily to provide adequate coverage until sufficient supplies of Vitamin X are available. In any case, production of Vitamin Y will continue for some time as regulated by revised sales estimates. This is a circumstance that frequently occurs in the displacement of one item by another.

Appendix B to Chapter 10

THE ORGANIZATION OF RESEARCH AND DEVELOPMENT COMMITTEES

Company practice varies considerably in the way it organizes to invite and review suggestions for research and product development, to allocate funds among competing projects, to exercise control over expenditures, and to coordinate the network of activities in order to see a project through to the marketing stage. The following examples are not necessarily typical, but they are instructive.

At the Black & Decker Manufacturing Co. (makers of a line of portable electric tools), "we use a committee approach."

> This Product Development Committee, over which the executive vice president presides, meets for a full morning every other week, and sometimes more frequently. The Sales, Engineering, and Manufacturing Departments are represented, and the vice president of marketing brings those of his product managers whom the agenda for that meeting indicates he will need.
>
> Our product managers have been relieved of supervisory responsibility for outside (line) selling and are now full-time staff men. Each product manager is responsible for the profitability of his product line, and maintains a list of product ideas currently being considered for assignment to Engineering. If a product proposal is approved, it is sent to Engineering for detailed appraisal of development costs, design feasibility, patentability, and other considerations. After Engineering has developed detailed technical objectives, the product proposal is

again reviewed by the Product Development Committee; if it is approved, it is placed on the development schedule. The committee subsequently hears oral progress reports on development, reviews designs or patents for sale, budgets and reviews development costs, and provides for future product planning. (We now plan two and a half years ahead, but we would like to plan five years ahead.) Thus, the functions of our Product Development Committee include communication, coordination, decision making, and assignment dispensing. Nearly all decisions are unanimous, but when they are not the chairman has the final voice.—*George W. McCarty,* vice-president—research and development, in *Organizing for Product Development,* A.M.A. Management Report 31, pp. 34–35.

In Crane Co. . . . our Product Planning Committee . . . is composed of the vice presidents for sales, purchasing, engineering, and manufacturing; the controller, the assistant to the president for administrative planning; and the president himself. This group meets several times a month to consider definite agenda designed to stimulate action leading to broad policies or major decisions affecting our product lines and/or manufacturing operations.

The Product Planning Committee has three subcommittees composed of the managers of the same corporate functions represented on the parent committee. Each subcommittee is concerned with one of Crane Co.'s three main product lines—plumbing, air conditioning, and valves and fittings—and meets during the second week of every month to review, conclude, or initiate projects for the modification of existing products or the creation of new ones. These subcommittees determine project priorities; authorize the development of new products, the modification of existing products, or the elimination of products no longer deemed worthy of the company's attention; and establish schedules for engineering, manufacturing, and sales, particularly with regard to the development of new products. Each member serving on one of these subcommittees has the authority to make appropriate decisions and commit his division to the necessary schedules.—*Maurice Nelles,* vice-president for engineering, in *Organizing for Product Development,* A.M.A., p. 41.

From the very beginning, [American Can Company] regarded commercial development as a top management responsibility and an overall company activity, which therefore could not be delegated to a group subordinate to any of the company's operating departments. As a result, the function was organized as a corporate department headed by a vice president who is responsible only to the Executive Department of the corporation. Other companies, we are aware, have taken a different approach to commercial development, locating the function within their sales or research departments.

We have tried to include in the Commercial Development Department's responsibilities all functions which have a bearing upon the company's growth, the maintenance of its competitive position, and the determination of the direction in which it is headed. Among these functions, for example, are the planning and coordination of all efforts directed toward innovation, diversification, and expansion. Prior to the formation of the Commercial Development Department, these activities were dispersed among a number of operating departments as adjuncts to their primary responsibilities. The result was that they received secondary consideration, and performance was perfunctory. As the technological revolution began to make itself felt in our operations, however, the lack of adequate coordination became quite evident.

Among the responsibilities assigned to the Commercial Development Department, the following are worthy of note:

1. Analysis of long-range trends in consumer items for which the company's products are utilized.
2. Market investigation:
    a. Consumer preference.
    b. Potential volume.
    c. Probable price levels.
    d. Sizes and styles.
    e. Geographical and chronological demand.
    f. Distribution methods.
3. Contact with markets to determine needed modifications of currently produced products:
    a. From the user's standpoint.
    b. From the consumer's standpoint.
4. Coordination of efforts in the development and introduction of new products.
5. Coordination of efforts to translate successful research results into company practice.
6. Market testing.
7. Sale of pilot-plant production.

    —*F. B. Newcomb,* vice-president and general manager, commercial development department, in *Organizing for Product Development,* A.M.A., pp. 106–107.

Of the several product planning committees on which I serve, Zenith Radio Corporation's is, I believe, the most efficient. It consists of the vice president in charge of engineering, the heads of the mechanical, radio, and television engineering sections, the vice president in charge of sales, the sales manager, the merchandising manager, an industrial designer, a cost accountant, and other specialists as required. (One of the most valuable committee members is the cost accountant: He can provide cost information almost as soon as it is needed, and can prepare estimates quickly.) Minutes of the meetings are distributed to about 50 persons. Meetings are held every week, and approximately 100 products are processed in the course of a year. One-fifth of the time of two vice presidents, plus all the effort and time expended by the other committee members, adds up to a big bill, it is true; but Zenith's business increases while the industry declines, and its earnings record is excellent.—*J. O. Reinecke,* Reinecke and Associates, in *The Dynamics of Management,* A.M.A. Management Report 14, p. 102.

The Worthington Corporation manufactures a wide variety of industrial machinery and equipment. . . .

Product development is decentralized and handled on a plant basis because of the specialized nature of many of the company's products, and the wide range of industrial machinery produced.

A plant development committee at each plant coordinates all development activities for the entire plant. [It] consists of the divisional sales vice-president, the plant manager and the plant engineering head.

Reporting to a plant development committee are product teams consisting of the product sales manager, the production manager in charge of the product group (or a designated member of his staff), and the head of engineering for the product group. Under this arrangement the sales department actively participates in all phases of new product selection and development.

The product team, which may meet monthly or semimonthly, is organized on a permanent basis. It has full responsibility for keeping its particular product line competitive and profitable. In addition to initiating new-product developments, the product team considers all matters relating to sales, production, changes in product design, manufacturing techniques, and raw materials. . . . A new product must be approved successively by the product team, the plant development committee, and by the various top officers of the corporation before it can be produced and sold commercially.—*New Product Development: III. Marketing New Products,* NICB Studies in Business Policy, no. 69, New York, 1954, p. 38.

[Consolidated Engineering Corporation] is engaged primarily in electronics, analytical and control instrumentation, data-processing, and high-vacuum fields. These fields, as is well known, have been characterized by great and rapid technological advances and by rapid growth on the part of the many small and large companies engaged therein. . . . Research and development programming, therefore, is probably the most important single element in our long-range progress. . . .

We therefore feel that by far the most important continuing long-range problem of our entire company is *deciding in which fields we should work*—or, if you will—on which projects we should place our research and development bets. . . . A second most important consideration directly related to the first one is *controlling the projects from the standpoint of time.* . . . A third point of obvious importance is the *interrelationship of research and development with manufacturing and marketing operations and with the financial planning of the company.* . . . A fourth general problem . . . is that of *recognition of the several different phases of research and development and the amounts of time which must be devoted thereto.* . . . A fifth problem of management concern is that of *creating an atmosphere which insures freedom for a maximum number of new and creative ideas while yet retaining some control over the expenditure of research and development time and dollars.* . . .

The basic elements of control which we have developed to handle the foregoing and other related problems may be summarized as follows:

1. *Budgets.* Research and development activities operate with over-all budgets for expenditures, personnel, and capital acquisitions. These budgets are approved by the Board of Directors as of the first of each year, but are subject to revision where deemed advisable. Expenditures for research and development are normally set at 10 to 12 per cent of our predicted sales for the coming year. Research and development personnel normally account for 20 per cent of our total employees [1,450 in 1955]. Monthly comparisons of actual and budget figures are provided.

2. *Research Committee.* This committee is composed of approximately 12 people, including company officers plus four or five of our top scientists and engineers, and meets twice a year. It endeavors to obtain agreement on a rough outline of a three-year program of major projects, with consideration given to each project from the aspects of roughly estimated project costs, generalized market potential, field of application, and the company's plan of product lines. Rough priorities are set on these major projects. Projects previously approved are reviewed to determine whether they should be continued, abandoned, or accelerated. Exploratory projects involving expenditures of less than $2,500 are not reviewed by the committee. They are supervised entirely by the Research Department within its over-all budget limitations. In general, we try not to assign more than 65 per cent of the total budget to specific major projects.

3. *Development Committee.* This is the key committee and the principal organizational control of the company's entire development activities. It is comprised of approximately 15 company officers and top technical people and meets monthly, usually for a six- to eight-hour session. Perhaps the primary function of the Development Committee is to act as a traffic regulator for all the projects into and through the development and design stages. It also may assign projects to the research people where this seems appropriate. The principal ways in which this control is achieved are as follows:

    a. The committee endeavors to maintain at all times a rough outline of a three-year development program and schedule.

    b. A detailed schedule for one year in advance is maintained with carefully budgeted times and project costs. Our current objective is to assure the releases of four major products per year to manufacturing, these releases being properly spaced so as to prevent congestion at the manufacturing level. We arbitrarily define a "major" product as one which has the potential to produce $1 million in sales revenue within four years after release to manufacturing. In general, we feel that major products as a group should never be planned to take up more than 50 per cent of the development budget.

c. The committee has the responsibility for specifically defining objectives and assigning responsibilities and priorities for the various approved projects. Various check points are established, and approval may be given through one or more of these check points as follows:

(1) Study or investigation only.

(2) "Breadboard" (crude working model).

(3) Elaborate "breadboard" or "cakeboard" (refined working model).

(4) Engineering prototype.

(5) Manufacturing release.

The point to which a particular project is authorized depends on many factors, including, of course, an estimate of the degree of technical accomplishment possible. Budget appropriations are made for each project expected to cost more than $2,500.

d. The committee reviews performance and progress on previously approved projects and makes revisions of schedules and budgetary allotments where necessary. In general, the major projects have automatic priority over all other activities, and primary attention is focused on them.

e. Projects in the last stages prior to manufacturing release are given special attention. It is extremely important to adhere as closely as possible to established schedules on these projects because of the intimate correlation required with tooling, manufacturing planning, sales promotion, advertising, and other marketing functions. The committee may request additional personnel, overtime, or reassignment of departmental personnel in order to accomplish the desired schedule. Here calendar time becomes of the utmost importance, and extra effort is almost always justified if the project gives evidence of falling behind.

4. *Product Survey Committee.* This is a committee of people below the top executive level but representing all major phases of the company's operations. It is called upon as needed by the Development Committee. Its primary function is to assist the Development Committee in obtaining more complete information on new ideas or suggestions for new projects, including detailed information on potential markets, facility requirements, and so on. The committee is useful particularly on outside ideas which do not fall within the established pattern of the company's operations or the direct knowledge of the company's executive group.

5. *Product Planning Coordinator.* For historical reasons, this office is associated with the Technical Services Department of the Marketing Division. The function of this office is to maintain files for new ideas and projects prior to their consideration by the Research or Development Committee. It is responsible for presenting these ideas to the appropriate committee and for getting a definite decision for each idea submitted—"yes," "no," or "hold for further evaluation." This office is also responsible for market research and market potential surveys, which are frequently necessary in connection with project evaluation.

6. *Design Committee.* This is a hard-working committee with representatives from the several operating divisions of the company. It meets on call—usually twice a month. Its job is to prepare the official product specifications for all company products, including those in development. Its objectives are:

a. To contribute to the profit potential of the company by carefully integrating into the specifications the elements of marketing requirements, manufacturing skills and facilities, development skills, and costs.

b. To formulate specifications which define clearly and concisely the physical details, characteristics, features, performance, environment, and contemplated applications of products.

c. To maintain lines of products which are consistent with respect to performance, appearance, quality, and system compatibility.

When and if the situation arises where the specifications of the Design Committee and the facts arising in the development process cannot be reconciled, the project is referred back to the Development Committee for a specific decision. The product specification is the company's specific and authoritative definition for a product; and development, production, and all published information must be correlated with it. The specification in itself, however, does not authorize anyone to proceed with development, production, or selling operations. These activities are authorized and coordinated by the appropriate executives.

7. *Patent Committee.* The general manager, the two top technical executives, and the company's patent counsel serve as a Patent Committee, meeting once a month to review invention reports and patent problems.

8. *Operating Committee.* The seven principal executives of the company hold operating meetings twice a week to review current developments and make a variety of operating decisions not otherwise provided for. Both the vice president in charge of research and the vice president in charge of engineering are represented in these meetings, and their problems may be quickly considered where necessary.

9. *Management Meetings.* Approximately 35 of the top executive and supervisory personnel attend a monthly meeting where company policies, plans, and operating problems are reviewed and discussed. Research and development activities are major considerations, and

technical personnel are invited to the meetings to discuss individual projects and products. These discussions are held primarily for exchanging information and not for making decisions.—*Hugh F. Colvin,* executive vice-president, in *Controls and Techniques for Better Management,* A.M.A. General Management Series, no. 176, pp. 25–29 *passim,* and 30–33.

Chapter 11

FITTING THE PIECES TOGETHER: THE PROJECTED OPERATING STATEMENT

The Controller's Function

The process of business planning, whether for the coming year or a longer time span, relates each part of the organization to the total operation and often involves the active participation of everyone who has responsibility for the rate of inflow or outflow of funds. The amount of information which must be digested into the budget is enormous, and the summary figures which are ultimately submitted to top management for approval fail to disclose the base of detailed computations on which they rest.

Behind the gross sales figure lies discussion of the product line to which it relates (now and in the future), the prices of products, their profit contributions, the assignment of emphasis among products in the product mix, the structure of the marketing organization, the setting of sales quotas, the general nature and magnitude of the advertising program on which sales partially rest, the rate of sales over the time period, and finished inventory calculations.

Behind the production costs lie determinations of the standard costs of the labor component by product or product line; translation of total volume of output into manpower needs, both of these broken down by time intervals within the planning period; specification of the quality of the end product and the material components; calculation of standard material costs by product or product line and of the level of all variable period expenses associated with the projected levels of output; allocation of common costs for review of relative product profitability; scheduling of production to ascertain bottlenecks for purposes of computing overtime

needed; and estimation of subcontracting costs. Similarly detailed computations are required in connection with general administrative, selling,
and research and development costs.

The job of fitting together the enormous number of estimates and
schedules generated by the preparation of a comprehensive budget typically falls to the controller or a budget director. In effect, the controller
is not simply charged with the arithmetical exercise of making sense out
of the numbers with which various parts of the organization have provided
him; he must use the numbers as symbols for operations which are expected to be performed during the planning period and must relate these
operations to each other in what amounts to a detailed simulation of all
activities of the firm which have a bearing on its profit position. This is a
rationalization of the planned performance of each unit in the light of the
expected performance, over the same period and on the same general
assumptions, of every other unit in the organization.

While the corporate officials responsible for sales, production, research
or engineering, and general administration will have inspected each subunit's estimates before incorporating them in their own projected budgets,
the controller is in a uniquely favorable position for reviewing these from
a variety of points of view—their comparability with the past, their conformity to some standard of "good" performance, their compatibility with
the over-all company profit target—and for suggesting strategic areas or
the most likely spots for modifying planned operations to secure a superior
over-all performance.

When the production costs of a unit indicate an expected variance from
standard, or when they vary markedly from the projected costs of another
unit or another plant performing similar operations, or when they show
a deviation (up or down) from costs of a year ago not accountable for by
changes in labor rates or material costs, the controller's office can request
an explanation. Standard operating ratios (such as projected inventory
in relation to sales) may also be employed as yardsticks to measure the
reasonability of either subtotals or totals.[1] The danger here, however, is

[1] For example, a former General Motors official, Donaldson Brown, counseled
(making reference to some balance sheet as well as operating ratios): "Generally
speaking, except that there may be seasonal fluctuations, the amount of capital tied
up in working capital items should be directly proportionate to the volume of business. For example, the raw materials on hand should be in direct proportion to the
manufacturing requirements, . . . depending upon the condition and location of
sources of supply, transportation conditions, etc. Work in process should be in direct
proportion to the requirements of finished production, being dependent upon the
length of time required for the material to pass from the raw to the finished state,
and the amount of labor and other charges absorbed in the process. Finished product
should be in direct proportion to sales requirements. Accounts receivable should be
in direct proportion to sales, being dependent upon terms of payment and efficiency of

that such ratios or formulas are necessarily based on a past performance, reflecting historical relationships, whereas the logic of operations may dictate change. Nevertheless, they may be used to spotlight changing relationships which may then be examined on their own merits.

In reviewing the detailed schedules and in fitting the pieces together into a tentative comprehensive budget, the controller is, then, concerned with two aspects of performance. One is the acceptability of the planned operations of each subunit, in the light of its functional contribution. Here is where the comparisons with past, standard, other units' performance, or subunit goal enter. The second is the acceptability of the over-all results of the total operation in terms of the company's profit objective. Each of the subordinate operations might appear to be satisfactory, but the profit showing of the company as a whole might be unacceptable, suggesting the need for improving the performance of the operating units over what had originally appeared to be satisfactory. Or, on the contrary, the over-all profit showing might be quite acceptable in the light of corporate objectives, but individual units may appear to be falling below "standard" in their planned performance, suggesting a tightening of operations which, if successful, will lead to a corporate profit result superior to what had originally been thought satisfactory.

First Try

In consolidating the detailed schedules to ascertain the projected operating result, two general approaches may be followed: consolidation of functional breakdowns and consolidation of breakdowns by product lines. The consolidation by functional units involves summing gross sales revenues as computed from the sales department's estimates of what volume of what mix of products it believes it can market at what prices, and deducting from this the projected manufacturing costs of this bill of goods (direct and period both) as derived from all the manufacturing divisions, and deducting also the period costs of selling, engineering (research), and general administration, to arrive at profit before taxes. The profit figure may then be converted to a return on investment or a return on sales, to lay alongside the company's target return.

---

collections. Capital tied up in plant and other fixed assets is, of course, fixed investment, and should be considered in its relationship to factory cost of production.

"Standards of capital requirement should be established, representative of a normal average operating condition, in terms of their respective ratio to annual sales or annual factory cost of production according to whichever is the more direct relationship."

From "Pricing Policy in Relation to Financial Control," *Management and Administration,* vol. 7, 1924.

The consolidation by product involves computing a return on sales or investment for each line. This is done by deducting from its gross sales its direct costs of production plus the share of all period costs (manufacturing, selling, administrative) attributable to it, yielding the profit to which that product group gives rise. This figure may then be used with the product's net sales, or with the share of total investment (capital and current) allocated to the product, to arrive at its rate of return. The individual returns of product lines may then be compared with the over-all corporate return, which is derived simply by summing the profit by products and relating this to total sales or investment.

The consequences of a review by either or both of these approaches is an indication of how closely the company's target profit has been approached by the first fitting together of the pieces. The results are usually reported to a budget committee (on which sit high-level representatives of the company's functional or divisional units) by the controller, who is customarily himself a member of the committee. The controller may comment on or evaluate this first and still very tentative projected operating statement, suggesting respects in which it appears to satisfy or fall short. He himself, however, as a staff person, holds no authority to compel modification of any of the submitted figures, even along lines which appear to him to be plainly required or for reasons which seem to him compelling. Only the budget committee, directly responsible to the executive department and acting on its behalf, is capable of doing that.

Try Again?

Whether a projected operating statement is considered sufficiently acceptable for the budget committee to recommend its adoption to the president is not an easy decision to make. A comparison with the target rate of return is informative but not conclusive. In the first place, the validity of the profit objective is itself always being subjected to the test of experience. A target which is never realized or always exceeded ceases to have much significance. In the second place, a target rate of return is always a long-run matter, in any realistic sense only an "average" of profit realizations over a period of years. In some years even the most efficient possible performance will yield a below-target return, perhaps even a loss, while in other years the target rate can be surpassed without effort. These variations are not necessarily attributable to internal efficiency but more likely to external circumstance.

Sales budgets are usually related to expected levels of GNP, and cost budgets are usually related to projected levels of output and sales—all of which presumptively helps to establish an appropriate relationship between estimated profit and external circumstance. There remain, however, the highly judgmental factors of how much better a performance can be expected next year over previous years, after abstracting from general economic movements, or whether in the light of expected external conditions revised courses of action would lead to preferable results, or whether longer-run social trends suggest the need for more drastic longer-run programs even if the profit figure for the coming year is considered the best possible under the conditions foreseen, and other equally weighty considerations to which there are usually no firm or conclusive answers.

Despite the variety of determinations which a budget review committee might make with respect to the acceptability of the projected operating statement, one reaction is almost predictable. If the profit showing falls below the target rate of return, and even if it is evident that the target cannot possibly be achieved, the first tentative consolidation will be rejected and revision will be requested. A below-target projection will almost automatically be taken as a signal that "something must be done" to improve the planned performance. That "something" falls into one of two categories: either measures will be urged to improve the revenue from sales or steps will be taken to reduce costs. Usually both avenues are explored.

Emphasis on Sales Volume

The effect of an unacceptable projected operating statement in stimulating a renewed planning for expanded sales revenue is largely a recent phenomenon. To the extent that an increasing proportion of the firm's budget is taken up with overheads which are more or less fixed, it is a phenomenon whose importance is likely to increase in the future.[2] While automation may be one factor in increasing uncontrollable fixed costs relative to the more controllable variable costs, other influences are also at work. The proportion of skilled workers to unskilled is rising, and of white-collar professionals on an annual salary relative to hourly paid and weekly paid employees. The understandable desire of companies to retain skilled and professional employees makes the adjustment of the size of the work force to fit levels of output a less acceptable device than it once was, solely from a profit point of view. A spreading belief in the efficacy of research and development as a guarantee of a firm's future is steadily moving a number of companies in the direction of detaching their expenditures for that purpose from a present illogical tie to sales, as a percentage of them, and of establishing their laboratory and engineering efforts on a firmer continuing basis. In some firms even advertising appropriations, which have for long been viewed as something which "naturally" followed

[2] Comment to this effect appeared in *Fortune,* September, 1960, p. 66.

sales up and down, are being given an independence which endows them with greater stability than fluctuating sales.

For all these reasons the proportion of overhead expenses which are fixed, or at least sluggish, has increased and is likely to increase further. The effect is to limit the amount of cost cutting in which a firm can indulge and to increase the appeal of programs to stimulate sales as a means of more closely approaching the target rate of return in a poor year. Or to put the matter in another way, the emphasis is likely to shift from attempts to bring costs into line with revenues to efforts to plan sales that bear an appropriate relationship to the level of continuing costs which the firm has consciously chosen to carry year in and year out. Volume of sales rather than cost control may preoccupy managerial attention.

Break-even Analysis

One instrument which has been found useful to business for analyzing the effect of volume changes has been the break-even analysis. In its simplest form this consists of a diagrammatic representation of the volume at which a firm would cover all costs (would "break even") and of the impact on profit of volume changes above and below that point. All costs are first divided into fixed and variable costs. From the price per unit of product is subtracted the variable cost per unit, leaving the marginal contribution. Out of this must come any recovery of fixed costs and profit. By dividing fixed costs by the marginal contribution one can determine the break-even volume. At sales levels above this point all marginal contribution goes to profits, so that profits build up rapidly with increasing sales. Below the break-even point is the area of loss, and losses (in the form of failure to recover fixed expenses) mount rapidly with declining sales.

The usefulness of break-even analysis lies in facilitating the treatment of volume as a variable for purposes of profit planning. In the preparation of budget estimates, the sales budget is typically based on the expected realization of a given volume of sales. Cost figures are prepared on this basis. If the consolidation of all the detailed estimates and schedules into a projected operating statement indicates an unacceptable profit performance, data are not always in a form which can be readily manipulated to determine the effect on profit of a different volume of sales. Break-even analysis permits the reading off of such results from a prepared graph.

From such manipulation of the volume of sales the business planning team can determine whether a closer approach to the target profit is likely to be reached through efforts to improve the sales position or to curtail costs. They can readily compute the sales volume which would be needed to earn the target return on investment (fixed costs plus target return divided by marginal contribution per unit). They can ascertain by how much costs (whether fixed or variable) would have to be reduced, at the projected sales level, in order to earn the target rate of return. They can incorporate into their manipulations the additional costs (in the form of a price cut or an increase in advertising appropriation) which would be required to increase the volume of sales to the point at which the profit objective could be realized. With the advice of the sales department, they might experiment with the effect of a price increase coupled with a larger advertising budget.

Use of this kind of break-even analysis has been stimulated in firms which employ the direct costing procedure, where the separation of all costs into fixed and variable has already been made for accounting purposes. In such situations the contribution margin of each product has already been computed so that, weighted by the appropriate product mix, it can be divided into the already determined fixed costs to ascertain the break-even point.

There are, however, decided limitations in the applicability of the analysis in this simplified form. It rests on certain severely restrictive assumptions. Among the most important of these is that the product mix remains constant as volume varies, and that product price (or the composite product price) remains firm regardless of fluctuations in sales. It assumes that all costs can be readily divided into fixed and variable, and that the former remains constant over the relevant range while the latter varies with strict proportionality to volume. More complicated forms of graphical analysis can indeed dispense with or modify the severity of these assumptions, but as soon as one moves into these more sophisticated approaches to cost-volume-profit relationships the kinds of cost schedules which are developed in flexible budgets are frequently more useful. These, it will be recalled, identify fixed period costs, variable period costs, and direct costs for specified ranges of output.

Nevertheless, it will also be recalled that in some situations the volume ranges appropriate to the several variable period expenses are staggered rather than superimposed on each other. In these cases the effect may be to transform variable period expenses which, individually, are fixed within a given range into aggregate variable period expenses which approach the shape of a smooth cost curve. The division of all expenses into fixed and directly variable, such as is called for in the break-even analysis, then more closely conforms to the fact, and break-even charts may be useful even if only for test results.

One implication of break-even analysis warrants note. It is based on the premise that the more sales, the greater the profit.[3] The contribution

<hr/>

[3] This implication may be partially responsible for, but is not identical with, the drive for sales volume which has prompted some managements (more frequently in the past than now) to seek volume as an end in itself. Such volume-mindedness was often

margin remains constant over the "relevant range." This premise, it will be recalled, is one which rules out the economist's traditional maximizing formula of setting price equal to marginal cost at the volume where it is also equal to marginal revenue, since marginal costs, marginal revenue, and price are all constant or nearly so.[4]

Other Ways of Increasing Sales Revenues

An effort to improve the projected profit position by increasing sales revenues can be achieved by other devices than simply increasing unit volume of sales. In most companies' product lines there are items which carry considerably higher profit margins than is true of other items. It will be recalled from our examination of the pricing process that in the flexible markup approach there is frequently an initial determination of "full cost" (with allocation of fixed costs) which is then adjusted up or down as competitive or market conditions or long-run pricing strategy warrant. If a firm can stress the sale of products whose margins have been adjusted upward, perhaps diverting selling effort from those products whose margins have had to be adjusted downward, the consequence on total profit might be favorable. Differential selling emphasis is thus one other approach which firms often employ when spurred to reexamine their marketing program by the prospect of a below-target rate of return.

The same stimulus may lead to a review of all product prices to determine whether there may not be some which can be increased with advantage. The president of one company is reported as saying, "If the profit margins reflected in the sales budget are too low, I point out to the sales

---

at the expense of profits (through special price inducements or extra selling costs), whereas the break-even analysis clearly implies an increase in profit with sales, at constant prices and costs (fixed costs on an aggregate basis, variable costs on a unit basis).

[4] In the attempted manipulation of volume to achieve a superior profit showing, one cost increase which is incurred in the process, and which may be overlooked, is the additional cost of working capital needed to support the expanded volume. Increases in accounts receivable and probably in inventory are scarcely avoidable. These are additional costs which are incurred not in order to increase sales (such as is true of price cuts and promotional expenses) but as a consequence of increasing sales; however, they are no less relevant in determining the desirability of alternative courses of action.

Break-even analysis has sometimes led managements to stress the desirability of enlarging the contribution margin by undertaking long-run programs to reduce fixed costs. With products subject to wide fluctuation in sales volume this may be a reasonable effort. At the same time it would be poor strategy if substantial cost reductions could be achieved through the introduction of more capital-intensive processes (such as automation implies). There is no goodness inherent in low overhead as such, or we would still be in the handicraft stage.

people that profit margins are too thin. This allows the sales department to review pricing policies. This procedure generally brings about actions which result in satisfactory profit." The financial vice-president of another company similarly remarked: "If the executive committee decides that forecasted profit is not satisfactory, the committee requests two actions. First, the accounting department is asked to review carefully all cost figures, and second, the sales department is asked to investigate the possibility of more satisfactory profit margins. We are convinced that this procedure has given the company better profit margins in the last several years." [5]

One further effect which a poor profit showing may have on sales effort is to promote longer-run planning for the introduction of new products or the upgrading of existing ones, the reorganization of the marketing structure, or an increase in the size of the sales force. In one company a two-year experimentation in one market area with a sales force expanded to 250 per cent of its previous size indicated that the greater selling coverage added more to revenues than to costs. These measures will do nothing to brighten the operating picture for the coming year (they may even darken it further by adding somewhat to costs), but they look to future benefit.

Manipulating Costs

In addition to improving the projected operating results by stressing sales activity, most companies also explore the possibility of reducing costs. In a previous chapter we examined some of the methods by which this may be achieved. To the extent that a firm is engaged in continuous cost-reduction programs, however, the possibility of *engineering* a lower cost performance to meet the immediate problem of a below-target projection is made slimmer. Nevertheless, there are other ways of achieving a cut in costs. While most managements eschew the "meat-ax" approach of arbitrarily cutting all budgets by some percentage, they admit there are times when this must be done, and some will even suggest, a little apologetically, that it is a useful device, from time to time, to cut out the "fat" that the years tend to add.

One controller commented—echoing a familiar management line—that "you can always cut costs somewhere." He went on to say (paraphrased slightly): "There are always places where economies can be effected, even if only on a short-run basis: training and maintenance, for example. In 1958, when we had an unfavorable year, the budget review committee sent the proposed budget back with a directive to reduce costs to improve the projected profit. Most divisions were able to come up with savings amounting to 15 or 20 per cent."

[5] The two quotations are from Sord and Welsch, *Business Budgeting*, pp. 156, 157.

The process of trying to improve the projected operating statement is one of trial and error. A change effected in one schedule necessitates changes in related items in other schedules. A first try at cost reduction on an "economy requested" basis may meet with a cooperative response from certain subunits and irritated threats to "take the matter higher" from other units. The same sales department which only a few weeks earlier was arguing that the sales budget was too conservative and that it could really sell 10 per cent more than the budget called for will now, on a revision with intent to improve the profit performance, balk at taking responsibility for a 5 per cent increase in sales volume unless they are given more men and a substantial increase in the advertising appropriation.

The Budget as a Product of Bargains

The extent to which such problems and difficulties are faced depends on the seriousness with which the budget committee pursues the profit target. In some companies there is a disposition to take schedules as submitted, beyond a perfunctory inquiry of departments or divisions whether they cannot do better, whenever the projected profit falls short of the target, and an executive exhortation to economy in the coming year. In other companies the cutting and fitting become a painstaking and nerve-wracking experience: [6]

> Before the new program is finally launched, anywhere from 30 to 100 revised plans will have been issued. Most of these revisions are brought about by changes in model mix and selling prices. Often Plan No. 1 projected profit is unsatisfactory and much work is required to adjust the program (to everyone's satisfaction) to yield a satisfactory profit. For example, sometimes a specific model shows an unsatisfactory profit. When that happens, the engineering department may be informed that the design content is too high. At that point, the chief engineer usually can prove that, based on the sales specifications, the design is very economical. Then the sales department is asked to raise the price or shorten the discount on this model. The general sales manager quickly informs you that he is already $30 higher than competition and has the shortest discount in the industry. Somehow these problems are solved, although it takes a bit of doing.

The above statement suggests what is in fact the case—that in many companies the projected operating statement is a matter for bargaining and negotiation among the interested parties. It involves the resolution of numerous internal disputes of interest.

There are differences of outlook arising out of differences in responsi-

[6] George K. Bryant, operations manager, R.C.A. Victor Television Division, *N.A.C.A. Bulletin*, November, 1956, sec. 1, p. 397.

bility. The chief executive's office (the president or chairman of the company, to only a somewhat lesser extent the head of each profit center) views his first concern as achievement of a profit objective. Those under him with functional responsibilities, however, are more likely to be concerned with proper performance of their function than with the resulting contribution to profit. (The overengineered product is one familiar example. The desire of a sales department to trim price—and profit—in order to meet competition is another.)

Differences *among* functional responsibilities likewise lead to conflicts of interest. Sales and production may both argue for budgeting more inventory, the former as insurance of prompt deliveries and the latter as a means of stabilizing production schedules and the work force, whereas finance may maintain that too much capital is already tied up in unproductive investment in idle stocks of goods, some of which are going obsolete to add to the cost.

Conflicts at budget time can also arise over questions of equity. A foreman complains that the standard costs on which his budget for the year is based are too tight; the industrial engineers responsible have set up impossible production targets per standard labor hour which his men cannot possibly meet. A departmental supervisor maintains that the space, heat, and power charges allocated to him by the accounting office are unfair in that they have failed to take into consideration that a good 20 per cent of those costs are incurred on behalf of another department, and the adjustment promised last year has not been made. A product manager expresses his pique that his product is charged with the proportion of the advertising appropriation that its gross sales bear to total sales, but the advertising program has rarely so much as mentioned the product. A division manager is bitter because his operation is expected to "turn itself inside out" to realize a 20 per cent return on investment, while another division is permitted to "loaf along" as long as it returns 12 per cent. One department fails to understand why, in the process of tailoring costs to some predetermined budgetary limit, it is asked to slash more than another or by the same amount as another when it was more cost-conscious to begin with.

Finally, status differences may create their own budgetary problems. In one company the staff man in the budget director's office feels that he is not in a position of authority to question the expense budgets submitted to him by the heads of the executive, sales, and engineering departments, even though he knows they are inflated. At the same time, the expense budgets for manufacturing are prepared by another member of the budget director's office working directly with the departmental managers (roughly equivalent to general foremen), and here the relative status positions permit him to use his knowledge of operations to keep budgets down to what is defensible. But because of the inflated estimates for administration, selling, and engineering, when the cost figures (based on standard labor and materials, taking into account any productivity changes) are laid alongside gross sales (taking account of any possible price adjustments), the resulting profit figure is likely to be unacceptably short of the target. Since the administrative, selling, and engineering figures cannot be cut, the budget office tends to compensate for their inflation by arbitrarily reducing manufacturing estimates by that amount. Total costs thus approach realism, and the resulting profit figure is acceptable. The control value of manufacturing budgets is not adversely affected, since the plant manager holds the individual department managers responsible for the performance standards worked out with the budget representative. This is an extreme case which most managements would not tolerate, but it is interesting to note the frequency with which subterfuges are resorted to even in the best-managed companies to "beat" the budget, on the one hand, or to overcome efforts of high-ranking officials to minimize the control which the budget exerts over them, on the other hand.

If such conflicts do not have their perfect resolution, it is because the budget—in the present context, the projected operating statement—is inescapably a political document as well as a financial one, a product of bargains effected on the strength of relative power positions no less than a product of accountants and industrial engineers, a compromise and a consensus (in the sense of a willingness, however begrudging, to attempt to live under it) more than any "objective" statement of what is believed feasible.

Indeed, the building of a budget may be looked on as an integration of the variety of diffuse and sometimes diverse interests of which the organization is composed behind a program which all have agreed upon as workable. Looking at it from this point of view, one can more readily understand why so many companies increasingly stress the importance of subunit participation in budget planning. In the act of participating the subunit imposes on itself a commitment. Every such commitment rationalizes the total plan.

Chapter 12

THE CAPITAL BUDGET

The planning process which increasingly characterizes the medium- to large-size corporation today is summarized and systematized in three financial statements: the projected operating statement, the projected balance sheet, and the projected flow-of-funds statement. Each of these may be constructed for several time periods—a short run which includes time segments of up to one year, the intermediate span which may range from one to five years, and the long run which looks into horizons more distant than five years. The precision of each statement usually varies inversely with the nearness of time, with detailed statements correlated with short runs and vice versa.

Many firms are not equally systematized in all phases of the planning process. Some may put together detailed schedules relating to production, and not much more. Companies in the service and trade industries may limit themselves to manpower budgets, and, depending on the industry, the advertising appropriation may be spelled out in detail. Similarly, some firms which are thorough in budgeting their operations may treat capital expenditures on an *ad hoc* basis. Less common but nevertheless a statistical category are firms which leave operational planning to subordinate units, where it is practiced with varying degrees of sophistication, but which view capital budgeting as something to be subjected to more painstaking planning at upper corporate levels.

The planning process which we have traced so far, eventuating in the projected operating statement, differs among firms, but it probably is more representative of "general" practice and more nearly constitutes "typical" procedure than is the case of the capital budgeting techniques about to be described, which—along with dividend policy—are the principal determinants of the projected balance sheet. (Current capital plans, relating chiefly to inventory and accounts receivable and payable, are of course important, but are themselves largely a function of sales budgets.)

The Theory of Capital Budgeting: Two Measures of Return

The essence of capital budgeting lies in determining how much will be spent on depreciable assets and on what assets these funds will be spent. The general economic principle is that funds should be committed to any investment which promises to return more than its cost. The applications of this principle which have been advocated most frequently go by the name of (1) the discounted cash-flow approach and (2) the present-value approach, both of which are intended to value the returns from an investment, which then may be laid alongside its cost to determine its advisability. The names are unfortunate since they do not identify any distinction between the two. Each method involves discounting the expected stream of returns to its present value. It would be preferable if they were regarded as (1) the internal rate-of-return approach and (2) the external rate-of-return approach.

The discounted cash-flow or internal rate-of-return method involves, first, identifying all the streams of payments and returns to which an investment gives rise. If the only cost over its lifetime is the original price, then this is taken as the total outlay. If repairs and extraordinary maintenance are required to maintain its effectiveness over the period for which returns are calculated, these too must be added to the outlays. The objective, then, is to find (by a trial-and-error process, making use of discount tables) the interest rate which *equates* both of these streams of payment—the inflows and outflows, discounting the value of future flows to their present worth. The interest rate of which this is true is the internal rate of return. It is an "internal" rate because it makes no reference to the cost of capital or the interest rate structure prevailing in the market. It is comparable to the Keynesian concept of "the marginal efficiency of capital."

The present-value or external rate-of-return approach explicitly depends upon the market costs of capital. It discounts the same outflows and inflows to which an investment gives rise, but it does so by applying to them the firm's cost of capital. The result is the yield per dollar of investment. The discount rate is not *found* by *equating* outlays and returns; it is the *unequal* sums of outlays and returns (discounted by market rates for capital funds, which are *given*) which establish the yield.

By either method, the results when found can be ranked in order of preferability. By either method such rankings establish investment priorities, but the ranking of a given roster of investments by the two methods does not necessarily yield identical results. Moreover, given the amounts of the inflows and outflows projected, the discounted cash-flow approach will always yield the same internal rate of return, and hence the priorities of a given roster of investments will remain fixed. Given the same magnitudes of inflows and outflows, the present-value method may vary the priority rankings of a list of possible investments with changing market costs of capital.

It is the time pattern of an investment, coupled with the (changing) market cost of capital, which leads to these discrepant results. At low rates of interest, projects whose returns are more deferred to the future will have higher present values than they would with high rates of interest. (Their future income streams will be less discounted.) At higher discount rates, projects with more immediate payoffs will be preferred (since future streams will be subject to heavier discounts). Thus the preferability of a given investment project relative to other projects varies, under the present-value method, with a change in the market cost of capital. A drop in the discount rate will increase the worthwhileness of a project whose returns start low but build up in the future, and vice versa. Similarly, it would be possible for two investments having identical internal rates of return, and therefore presumably equally worthwhile under the discounted cash-flow approach, to have different present-value rankings depending on the time pattern of their flows.[1]

Problems of Comparing Unequal Time Patterns

Differences in the duration of investment projects also introduce problems of comparing the relative value of alternatives. While internal rates of return and present values can be ascertained for, say, each of two competing investments, one of which runs for five years and the other for ten, direct comparison of the rates would be misleading. Such a comparison involves an implicit assumption as to the returns which would be obtained from the reinvestment of the capital sum of the shorter-term project when it was repaid at the end of five years. The only valid comparison between the two competing investments would be between the internal rate of return or present value (whichever method is employed) of the ten-year project, on the one hand, and, on the other hand, the relevant rate of the five-year project plus whatever return is expected from its reinvestment over the second five years (when the alternative investment would still be running).

If the rate of return from reinvestment was less than from the original five-year project, then a direct comparison of the two investments of unequal duration would have overvalued the shorter one. When no rate of return on reinvestment is specified, there is an implicit assumption under

---

[1] Professor Armen Alchian, in an illuminating article ("The Rate of Interest, Fisher's Rate of Return over Cost, and Keynes's Internal Rate of Return," *American Economic Review*, December, 1955), has suggested the relevance of Irving Fisher's concept of "rate of return over cost" to the present-value approach and its distinction from the Keynesian marginal efficiency of capital, which is parent to the discounted cash-flow approach.

the discounted cash-flow approach that reinvestment would be at the same rate as the original investment, and under the present-value approach that it would be at the presently prevailing market cost of capital.[2] In some instances, however, these implicit assumptions would be found unacceptable if made explicit.

Minimizing Conceptual Differences

Institutional factors greatly reduce the significance of the difference between the discounted cash-flow and present-value approaches to capital budgeting, as we shall shortly observe. The significance would be greater if businessmen operated with expectations that prevailing rates of interest would continue unchanged over protracted periods of time; under such a circumstance, use of the present-value method would lead to a different pattern of investments if interest rates were low and were expected to remain low than if they were high and were expected to remain high. Because businessmen do not normally operate on such assumptions of long-term continuity, however, and because, as the literature of both economics and business has indicated now for a number of years, the interest rate is not normally controlling of investment decisions, the variability of investment ranking under the present-value approach is not as great as its theory would suggest.

Moreover, the heavy reliance by business firms on internal financing strengthens the operating rationale (even though not the economic logic) of using the internal rate of return as a criterion for choice among alternative investments. In consequence, it would appear that the contest between these two approaches is more illusory than real, and the more interesting conflict lies between the economists' insistence on some form of present-worth comparisons of future flows of funds and business reliance on less rigorous procedures.

The Cutoff Point: Market Cost of Capital

To continue with the theory of capital budgeting, however, regardless of whether the discounted cash-flow or present-value method is adopted, either application simply reveals the returns to be expected from given invest-

[2] A lucid exposition of this point has been provided by Prof. Ezra Solomon in "The Arithmetic of Capital Budgeting Decisions," *Journal of Business,* April, 1956. If I am right in interpreting his remarks to imply that when such assumptions are made explicit, they provide the means for reconciling discrepant results of the internal-rate and external-rate approaches, I fail to see how this would follow. It would remain true that the ranking of projects under the discounted cash-flow approach would be fixed, regardless of changes in the market cost of capital, whereas rankings under the present-value approach would, or could, vary with changes in capital costs.

ments. In order to determine the acceptability of a project, however (whether it is competing against other projects or not), it is necessary to lay alongside the projected return the estimated cost. Another way of expressing this is to say that once investment projects have been ranked in the order of their preferability (based on their returns), it is necessary to determine how far down the list the firm will go before it draws the line and says "no more." This is a more complex decision than is the relative-worth ranking. No attempt will be made here to explore the matter in any detail, but the broad outline of the problem will be suggested.

Economists have provided two main categories of solutions to the problem of the cutoff point. As in the case of project ranking, however, businessmen have provided other solutions of their own, as we shall soon see. The two economic methods of determining the cutoff rely on either market cost or opportunity cost.

The market cost (sometimes referred to as the "borrowing rate") sounds clear enough. It is the interest rate (plus any associated expenses incurred in effecting the loan) which must be paid for the use of money. The general prescription is that investments are to be undertaken as long as their returns are equal to their market costs. This would mean, under the discounted cash-flow approach, that a firm would be willing to move down its priority list of projects to the point at which the internal rate of return is equal to the market cost of capital. It would mean, under the present-value approach, that a firm would undertake investments as long as the sum of the expected returns, discounted to present value at the market cost of capital, was equal to the present cost of the investment. The difficulty with using this simple concept is, first, that money is provided on a number of different bases, and its cost varies with the basis, and, second, that most companies use money obtained on more than one basis. What, then, is the market cost?

Short-term loans carry different rates than longer-term loans; loans which have prior security carry higher rates than loans with lesser security (a Grade A bond over a second mortgage, for example); "loans" which involve equity rights (preferred or common stocks) carry different rates between themselves and also relative to other nonequity claims, and so on. When a company is trying to establish where it will draw the cutoff line on its roster of prospective investments, which of these market rates does it use?

A first-impression solution would be to obtain funds from whichever source provided them most cheaply and then to invest in projects up to the point where the expected rate of return equaled whatever this lowest-cost-obtainable rate might be. Since most companies find it necessary to finance their operations from a variety of capital sources, however, their cost of money depends to a significant degree on the particular "balance" of liabilities which they have created over the past and on how this affects their present credit position. A company might thus find that the lowest-cost funds available at the moment are in the form of twenty-year bonds, but it could not go on issuing bonds and increasing the amount of long-term indebtedness relative to equity financing without affecting the rate it would have to pay. The price at which it could market an additional common-stock issue would depend not only on its earnings but also on the amount of indebtedness it showed on its balance sheet. Most companies are therefore careful to keep their sources of funds—their liabilities—in some "proper" relationship to each other, some "appropriate" balance, not only because this means a cheaper average cost of money over time, but because it is necessary in order to preserve access to the money market at all: some companies which have embarked on ill-advised financing have found in time that funds were not available to them on any basis. Maintaining the proper relationship between the items in a firm's capital structure is one purpose of ratio analysis.

The "market rate" which might be used, then, under the discounted cash-flow approach to establish the cutoff point and under the present-value approach as the rate by which to discount future flows down to the point at which the return equals the investment, is an average cost of capital—a weighted average, with the weights depending on the kind of balance among sources of funds which the firm intends to maintain.

To put it another way, the firm would select investments from its priority list down to the point where the internal rate of return equaled its *average* cost of capital (discounted cash-flow method) or would use this *average* cost of capital to discount the future flows expected from an investment (present-value method).[3]

Opportunity Cost of Capital

More business investment is financed by retained earnings and depreciation allowances than by borrowing in the market or by floating securities, however. While a "market rate" for such internal funds may be simulated on the premise that they are supplied by the shareholders, it is more realistic in this case to make use of opportunity cost rather than market cost.

[3] A second-impression solution—that the firm would select investments down to the specific rate which was carried by the particular form of financing necessary at the moment to retain or reestablish the preferred balance—would not be acceptable since that would make the acceptability of a project vary with the balancing needs of the moment, leading to low-yield investment in those years when the proportioning of liabilities led to low-cost capital and shutting off higher-return projects when a similar consideration increased the short-run cost of capital. An average long-term cost of capital would provide a more consistent and defensible basis for establishing the cutoff point.

On this approach, one compares the company's own roster of prospective investments with other possible investments outside the firm. Appropriate allowances may be made for degrees of risk involved. The fact that the company has created its own source of funds does not mean that these are costless in any economic sense. Their cost is the opportunity forgone by using them for one purpose rather than another.

When funds are obtained from outside the firm, it can be assumed (with approximate correctness) that the market rate measures the opportunity cost, since if yields much in excess of that rate existed and were accessible to (opportunities for) others, the demand for funds would bid the rate up to that level. Any divergence between market cost and opportunity cost would thus be closed by profit-minded investors. But with internal funds there is no market cost and hence no "ready-made" or assumed-equivalent opportunity cost. A firm would have to ascertain for itself the existence of alternative outlets for its capital in order to avoid making investments in its own operations that carry the promise of a considerably lower return than could be had on investments in other companies, or to avoid making investments which offered the same return as, but with much greater risk than, outside alternatives. It would, for example, be pointless to put the company's funds into a new product which, as nearly as could be estimated, promised only a 2½ per cent return if risk-free government securities yielded the same amount. Nor would it seem wise to put capital into a new piece of equipment which yielded a 5 per cent saving when the same funds, used to purchase shares in a real estate syndicate, would carry equal assurance of 10 per cent.

In the theoretical development of capital budgeting, then, the worthwhileness of possible investments is established by ranking them on the basis of the present worth of the inflows and outflows to which they give rise (by either the discounted cash-flow or the present-value approach), after having taken account of differences in duration of competing projects by assuming reinvestment rates of return. The cutoff point, establishing how far down the priority list the company will go during the time period being budgeted, is determined by the average cost of capital when funds are being obtained from the market and by opportunity cost when funds are provided internally.

Let us turn now to observe how closely this normative theory describes business practice.

Capital Budgeting in Practice: Reserving Decision

Since capital expenditures include the building and equipping of new plants, often with new processes and sometimes for the production of new products, some degree of forward planning is inescapable. In companies which program their capital outlays systematically, however, planning embraces all capital expenditures and typically for time horizons of up to five years. Although there is no illusion that long-run forecasts of capital needs will prove accurate, some notion of the general magnitude and scheduling of major outlays facilitates cash planning. A bond or equity issue takes time to prepare, or if internal funds are to be made the basis for a major expenditure program, this will require a series of short-term investments with maturities coinciding with financing needs.

Because the desirability of an intended investment can change overnight, however, due to shifts in demand, product or technological innovations, or intentions newly revealed by competitors, most managements prefer to adopt the strategy of avoiding capital commitment until plans which originally looked good can be reviewed, perhaps a number of times but in any event as close as possible to the point in time when they require being made firm, if they are to be acted on at all. This strategy is effected by two mechanisms. One is a "continuous" capital budget, which is approximated by a sequence of budgets for varying durations, and the other is the appropriation-authorization procedure.

Under the continuous or sequential budget system, investment programs involving major expansions may first enter the capital-planning pipeline as long as twenty-five years before contemplated fruition. This is especially true of public utility systems, whose rates of growth are somewhat more predictable than is the case with producers of less basic goods, but even some manufacturing companies have taken to looking as far ahead. These plans are reviewed from time to time to see if they have remained valid; they are modified as seems desirable in the light of developments. A few long-term commitments may be made, primarily the purchase of available land for new construction, if this seems warranted. Even so, however, discretion and flexibility may be preserved by purchasing more than one site, on the premise that it will be easier to dispose of unneeded land at a later date—perhaps indeed at a profit—than to acquire a tract of the size needed in a desirable location when the time comes to build.

With the passage of time, the modification of plans as needed, and a few tentative commitments, the project eventually moves into the five-year budget. At this point it may be given a thorough airing, and if it still seems desirable, plans begin to be firmed. Specifications are drawn, architectural and engineering drafts prepared, mock-ups may be made, revenue and cost estimates are elaborated. Additional commitments may be made at this point, but still without the ultimate commitment to proceed with the project as a whole. At this stage, however, each passing period makes the place of the project in the budget more or less firm. "We normally make up the capital investment program as much as two, three, or four years ahead and schedule it accordingly." "Semiannually [units] concerned with major construction expenditures are requested by the Budget and Statistical Section to forecast projects which will be started during the next five years together with the approximate dates of construction for each project. Proposed projects are then incorporated in the five-year capital forecasts which are used for long-range planning in such areas as financing, rates, income and cash requirements." "Class A projects may extend over more than one budget year, and it is necessary that the annual capital budget schedules indicate the estimated cost applicable to each year as well as the estimated total cost."

The final budgeting stage is usually when the project moves into a one-year capital budget, which in some instances may be continuous. "Each month all organizational [units] should review their capital requirements for the succeeding twelve months. Contemplated additions or retirements during this period are included in the Capital Expenditures Forecast. . . . Inclusion of an item in the Forecast does not constitute approval for the work. The Forecast is used for general information purposes only; that is, to indicate the size and scope of the construction program for which approval will probably be requested during the next year." It usually is at this stage, when projects are competing for inclusion in the proposed capital budget, that their relative merits must be considered along with their absolute advantages.

The second device for ensuring that proposed capital expenditures are both soundly conceived and relatively advantageous is the requirement of specific project approval or authorization, even after funds have been earmarked for it in the appropriation. The appropriation is in the nature of a forecast for budgetary purposes; authorization is a control over actual outlays. "All expenditures for additions to or retirements from property and plant must have the approval of the Board of Directors before work is started or commitments are made. Proposed expenditures are submitted to the Board of Directors in the form of Budget Projects." Commonly such board (or executive committee) approval is required only for expenditures above some specified amount (say a minimum of $50,000 to $250,000). Smaller allocations are approvable by lesser authorities, usually down to departmental approval for amounts of up to, say, $250, out of a general appropriation for that purpose.

Thus capital planning may be viewed as a process extending over considerable periods of time (in the lumber and paper industries, with their tree-planting schedules, the horizon may be as long as half a century), with specific plans either dropping out altogether or becoming firmer as the horizon shortens, until at a closer point in time it has become fixed enough to compete with other projects for a place in an over-all appropriation, and at some time within a budget year to drop out or be deferred or to win final commitment. A particular firm may choose to confine its capital budgeting procedures to any portion of this time span (working back from the present), and a particular project may break into the firm's planning horizon at any point prior to the appropriation which includes it. Some projects which arise suddenly, from unforeseen circumstances, or are of lesser magnitude may be fed into the pipeline later and with less previous consideration than is true of the long-premeditated and major expansions.

Review Procedure of One Company

The procedures by which a company collects and collates the requests for capital allotments which arise throughout the organization are varied, but there tends to be an underlying element of similarity in that usually there is provision for project submission from units down to the level of the basic operating unit, a committee to review and rank the submitted proposals, and a decision on the size of the capital budget which may have been reached prior to, or is reached during the course of, an evaluation of the earning prospects. One such procedure has been described by a representative of the A. O. Smith Corporation.[4] Although it cannot be considered typical, it is instructive about the general nature of the process usually followed.

> The chief process engineer and the cost reduction engineer are a team of two to review, classify and evaluate all proposals for new equipment. Each capital proposal which passes their scrutiny is recorded on a Capital Project Request Control Card in duplicate.
>
> Under our present plan, capital expenditure requests are classified into five categories:
>
>   1. . . . Normal replacements.
>   2. . . . New products.
>   3. . . . Expansion of plant capacity.
>   4. . . . Cost reduction.
>   5. . . . Plant improvement.
>
> A key feature of our plan is that capital planning within a division will begin at least one year prior to the fiscal year in which the expenditure will be made. To accomplish this, a system is established in each division by which periodic reviews are made of capital expenditures which might be required or desirable in the succeeding fiscal year.
>
> The division completes its proposed capital budget for the succeeding fiscal year in the first part of the third fiscal quarter. Priority numbers are assigned to each project. The highest priority number is assigned to proposals which the division believes will yield the greatest advantage or highest return on investment. This annual evaluation

---

[4] Richard P. Connelly, management specialist in the management controls and operations analysis department, A. O. Smith Corporation, "The Judgment Factor in Capital Planning," *N.A.A. Bulletin,* June, 1960, sec. 1, pp. 46, 49, 52–54.

is performed in January by a divisional equipment review board composed of division manager, plant engineer, shop superintendent, and the aforementioned chief process engineer and cost reduction engineer. Others may be added. . . .

The next key feature to our plan is the establishment of a capital budget review committee composed of the vice president of manufacturing, corporation controller and the chief engineer. This committee visits each division during the third fiscal quarter and reviews each project as sequenced on the capital project control card.

This review occasionally causes the elimination of certain less desirable projects and frequently causes a change in the priority sequence. Sometimes, substitutions from a surplus equipment pool are proposed. When the study is completed, the committee makes certain that all changes are recorded on both copies of the capital project control cards, and returns to the general office with one set of the cards. No commitments have been given to the division, but a tally of the cards indicates the total dollars desired. When all visits are completed, the committee knows the maximum total desired by all units. It proposes then, in total, a preliminary corporate capital budget for the coming fiscal year. Since this is done before the development of formal shipment and profit planning, it is necessary to apply judgment to the determination of the profit picture. Basically, the planning follows these lines:

Net profit after taxes		$10,000,000
Less—Dividends	$3,000,000	
Loan payments	1,000,000	4,000,000
		$6,000,000
Plus—Depreciation		6,000,000
Maximum available		$12,000,000

The $12,000,000 could be increased by borrowing money or even by floating stock or bond issues if the incentive is great enough. In actual practice we hesitate to use the whole amount because if we do and profits drop we are squeezed in to a borrowing situation. Perhaps the limit recommended will be $10,000,000 or $11,000,000. Invariably, it will be in excess of the amount to be provided by depreciation.

Whatever the limit, it probably will be less than the total of the requirements of all divisions. The next step is to allocate it to the twelve divisions requesting funds. Since we are not only reinvesting the earned depreciation but also investing a portion of the profits retained in the business, it is vital that the dollars produce a return which will not only equal current yields but also achieve the increased return anticipated in our forward planning. With this in mind, as well as the return or advantage expressed on the individual control cards, the committee removes cards until the divisional requirements equal the agreed total. A proposal for total and divisional budgets is submitted to the executive vice president for approval.

Assuming the budgets are approved, the executive vice president gives the data and the control cards to the management controls and operations analysis department. This department promptly informs the division managers of the approved totals, along with advice that the amounts are approved in principle only and that the divisions are authorized merely to submit capital projects for final consideration. The divisions may also use the approved amounts for their formal forward plan for the coming year. This plan is due in the fourth fiscal quarter.

From this point on, the management controls and operations analysis department is the focal point for control of projects, appropriations and actual expenditures. This department is a part of the staff of the controller and serves the executive vice president as a center of information and control of the various areas of budget, forecasts, forward plans and actual results concerned with shipments, profits and capital programs.

Upon receipt of the approved totals, and coincident with the submission of the formal forward plan, the division managers may start to submit specific capital project requests for approval.

Size of the Capital Budget

The basis for deciding the total amount which will be included in the capital budget appears to be, in general, almost as casual as the above statement implies. Looking at the matter broadly, "the overall amount of the budget is generally determined in one of two ways." [5]

> Under one method a maximum amount available for capital expenditures is decided at the executive level. The various review and coordinating groups then take steps to see that the budget presented for approval is in substantial agreement with the figure. A second method used in establishing budget limitations is to summarize expenditure proposals and come up with a budget amount. The latter approach has the advantage of presenting to management all possible projects. Proposed savings, etc., on some projects may be so attractive that additional funds may be sought in order to accommodate them.

Except for the early life of a business or during periods of rapid expansion, it tends to avoid resorting to the capital markets for investment money. (In the aggregate, external financing in the form of net new stock and bond issues, other long-term debt, and short-term bank loans has amounted in recent years to only from one-fourth to one-third of net new investment in physical assets, inclusive of plant, equipment, and inventories.) In general, as a company matures and grows, there is a tendency for it to finance more

---

[5] "The Capital Expenditure Control Program," N.A.A. Accounting Practice Report 7, *N.A.A. Bulletin,* March, 1959, sec. 3, p. 10.

and more of its capital additions first through retained earnings, which are volatile, and then increasingly through depreciation allocations, which show greater stability. (In the aggregate, depreciation reserves constitute the single largest source of new capital expenditures, amounting in 1960 to about two-thirds of total expenditures for plant and equipment.)

In the period of corporate gestation and succeeding periods of rapid expansion, then, the size of the capital budget is determined by level of sales, and there is substantial reliance on external sources of funds. In the extended periods of steady growth, interrupted by occasional setbacks due to circumstances either peculiar to the company or general in the economy, the size of the capital budget is largely determined by a company's level of profits and liquidity (cash availability), and there is almost complete reliance on internal financing. "Capital outlays depend primarily on depreciation but the level of profits also has an important influence." "Capital spending is the largest and most controllable item in our cash forecast. Consequently, where our estimated cash position dictates a change, such a change is usually made in the level or timing of capital expenditures. In some cases, we may *even* decide to borrow funds to carry out our capital expenditure program." [6]

[6] The first statement comes from an official of a major manufacturing company principally oriented to the automobile industry; the second (with the italics supplied), from the controller of one of the major oil companies.

Professor Kent Healy has pointed out how the attitude or mental set of top corporate management also affects the level and timing of capital expenditures. Speaking primarily of railroads but with a relevance to other industries as well, he has commented: "Another variable in the decision-making process, probably more important than this complex of financial studies and statements, is the attitude of the top officers toward capital expenditures, their character, magnitude, and timing. Some officers have a keen interest in all the available improvements, and throughout the organization there is a feeling that capital expenditures get a sympathetic reception and that proposals for expenditures are to be actively developed and passed on up for decision. Other top officers seem more interested in squeezing everything possible out of existing plant; it almost appears that they have to be bludgeoned into making a capital expenditure by competition, group pressure, or a preponderant example of prior advantageous use of facilities by others. A different range of attitudes is evident when it comes to timing. Some of the key group go all out during good times because it is easy to find the needed money or because it is in the air. A few seriously plan for capital expenditure over a long enough period so that the possibility of getting things at lower prices during a contraction may have an appeal and so that even in the trough of business fluctuation there may still appear a reason for improving or expanding facilities in terms of future higher levels of traffic. It would be possible to go on almost indefinitely enumerating various attitudes and providing contrasts. But the key point is that there is this variation and that it provides explanations for some aspects of total industry behavior."

"Regularization of Capital Investment in Railroads," in National Bureau of Economic Research, *Regularization of Business Investment* (Princeton University Press. 1954), pp. 151–152.

The correlation of the size of the capital budget with liquidity and profit means that in periods of prosperity (whether corporate or general) managements may be under actual pressure to come up with reasonable investments to take off the cash flow being generated. Sums which are hopefully allocated to the capital budget schedule of the projected balance sheet may lie partially unused at the end of the fiscal year.

On the supply side, however, the increasing importance of depreciation reserves as a source of financing has provided a firmer floor under capital expenditures, regardless of shifts in the ceiling. As long as the noncash costs of depreciation assignments are covered by revenues, there is an internal source on which to draw for new investment, and one of significant magnitude.

Allocating the Capital Kitty

Along with the size of the capital budget the firm must determine its apportionment. This involves, as in theory, the two-stage process of first ranking projects on the basis of some criterion and then establishing the cutoff point (which may be given simply by stretching the predetermined total as far as it will go).

Two standards quite clearly dominate managerial appraisal of the worthwhileness of a project—its rate of return and the degree of risk attaching to it. Both of these are applied as tests in "grading" an investment —sometimes impressionistically and sometimes systematically. It is rare that one is used to the exclusion of the other. Here are several examples of the procedures employed. The first is a description by the vice-president for finance of the Continental Oil Company of "the steps normally involved in the measurement of returns on new capital investments." [7]

> 1. Estimate sales volumes, prices, costs of materials, operating expenses, transportation costs, capital investment requirements, strength and nature of competition, rates of obsolescence or depletion, and other economic and business factors.
> 2. Summarize basic estimates of annual income, life of project, and capital investment in convenient form for appraisal purposes. Commonly used yardsticks include: (a) years to pay out and (b) return on investment.
> 3. Exercise managerial judgment in determining whether or not: (a) the anticipated return is large enough to warrant the business risks involved, (b) the investment opportunity is attractive in view of the various alternative opportunities for capital spending which are available and (c) the timing of the investment is right, relative to anticipated developments in the near future.

[7] John G. McLean, "Measuring the Return on Capital: Relating Calculations to Uses," *N.A.A. Bulletin,* September, 1960, sec. 3, pp. 31-32.

In one steel company the capital budget is composed of three parts:

1. The carry-over from previous budget years in the form of projects begun but not yet completed. These constitute a first charge against the available funds and in some years may consume half the total capital budget.

2. An array of proposals which are reviewed by a planning and research committee supplemented by three top officers and representatives of the manufacturing division. The proposals generally originate at least half a year earlier with plant superintendents and are examined and given cost and revenue estimates by the engineering and sales divisions. (The latter, indeed, can frequently exercise a veto power over projects, depending on their assessment of customer wants.) The projects which have survived to this stage are ranked by the accounting department in terms of estimated earnings and payout period.

3. A lump sum is budgeted for minor expenditures and unforeseen needs and is allocated to the divisions to spend at their discretion.

Of these three categories, only projects in the second must compete against each other and be subject to elimination by falling below the cutoff point.

The Sylvania Evaluation Procedure

A somewhat fuller description of its evaluation procedure was reported a few years ago by the controller of the Sylvania Electric Products Company: [8]

> *New Plants Proposals.* In considering an investment in a new plant, we include the following factors in arriving at the total cost of the project:
>
> 1. The total cost of the building and the complete plant.
>
> 2. The cost of equipping the new plant for operation.
>
> 3. The estimated average value of raw, in-process, and finished goods inventories resulting from operations. As a guide in determining these values, the same ratio is applied that exists in other, similar plants.
>
> 4. The estimated amount by which accounts receivable will be increased through the additional sales created by the new plant. Here again, the existing ratio of accounts receivable to production is used in determining the new accounts receivable figure.
>
> 5. The additional cash reserves necessary to meet payrolls, accounts payable, etc.
>
> 6. Any deferred or special expense items. Particular attention is directed to starting-up expenses.
>
> The total of these items shows the investment of funds relative to

[8] L. C. Guest, Jr., "An Over-all System of Capital Controls," in *Tested Approaches to Capital Equipment Replacement* (New York: American Management Association, 1954), pp. 28–31.

the new plant, and this figure is compared with the total investment already existing in the same product line.

In addition to computing the investment in the new plant, we analyze its effect on our profit and loss position, paying particular attention to the factor of overhead. Broad proposals are supported by careful analysis of costs, usually in the form of projections of fixed and variable budgets. We want to be sure that any anticipated increases in overhead will be sufficiently offset by decreased direct costs and that the operation will have a net advantage. Though only common sense, this simple relationship between costs might be overlooked if instructions were not specific.

Other profit and loss items are treated as follows:

1. Sales. The increased volume of sales to be realized as a result of the new plant's output is determined. In this connection, we make a thorough market analysis to insure that the products involved can be sold at a price which will realize our desired profit.

2. Cost of sales. In determining the cost of sales, we consider any improved manufacturing efficiencies incorporated in the new plant. Depreciation on the new plant and equipment is included in all cases.

3. Distribution and expenses. The cost of obtaining the additional business produced by the new plant is computed. It is entirely possible that disposition of the new products will require extra sales effort and that distribution costs may rise. Furthermore, we must make certain that warehousing and other distribution facilities exist to handle the increased volume. If this is not the case, the cost of obtaining these additional facilities is taken into account.

4. Other expenses. Divisional and central expenses are allocated on our regular basis prior to determining the amount of profit, before taxes, to be realized from the new operation. In general, we want to be sure that all possible expenses are included in the profitability calculation.

The ratio of the "additional profit to be realized" to "additional investment required" yields the percentage return on investment. When the new plant is to manufacture a product we are already marketing, we evaluate the new return in relation to the old. With entirely new products, we weigh the anticipated return against the return that we are getting in other lines and against alternative possibilities—always, of course, in conjunction with qualitative factors.

Major Additions of New Equipment. In submitting proposals for the addition of new equipment in an existing plant, the same general principles are applied as have been outlined in connection with proposals on new plants. Specifically, the following factors are covered:

1. The additional productive capacity which will be obtained from the new equipment.

2. The amount by which the investment will increase as a result of the new equipment, with consideration given to all items already listed in connection with the acquisition of a new plant.

3. The effect on the profit and loss position. We also determine whether a market exists for the increased production and whether the company's distribution facilities can handle the increased sales. Special expenses related to the investment are stated.

Major Replacements of Old Equipment. In supporting permanent property programs for replacing old equipment, information is presented which reflects the effect on investment and profit of changing or remodeling old equipment as opposed to purchasing new equipment. Specific factors considered include:

1. The possibility of changing or remodeling the old equipment to make it acceptable from a manufacturing standpoint, and the costs and results that might be expected under such a program.

2. The maintenance costs of the old equipment as compared with an investment in new machines.

3. The comparative speeds of the old and new equipment.

4. The effect on quality and shrinkage of the replacement program.

Supplementing the return-on-investment measurement used in appraising program proposals, Sylvania's system requires that the cash payout period be entered on permanent property requisitions for actual expenditure approvals. This has a very practical significance in relation to requests for specific items of plant and equipment.

The cash payout period is calculated by dividing the annual added profit into the total cost. To keep requisition on a strictly cash basis, added profit is determined after taxes but before depreciation.

QUALITATIVE ANALYSIS

The qualitative criteria which we use in selecting capital programs and establishing priorities are measures of *"urgency."* They are applied in *the following order:*

1. Expansion to cover completion of projects to which we already are substantially committed. Ordinarily, these are carry-overs from the prior year's program.

2. Safety requirements and similar necessities. These, of course, rank very high, regardless of profitability factors.

3. Expansion of improvement necessary to retain our position. Like most companies, we are constantly comparing our position with that of the industry on all major products. Maintenance of industry position plays no small part in determining the projects in which we invest.

4. Replacement of worn-out or obsolete equipment.

5. Cost-saving items requiring no more than two years for repayment.

6. An expansion program from which a relatively good return can be expected.

7. An expansion program to provide complements to an existing line of products.

8. An expansion program from which a fair return can be expected.

9. Cost-saving items requiring more than two years for repayment.

10. Others.

Measures of Return

The specific measures of return which are most commonly found in use are the length of time required to pay back the capital investment, the rate of yield on the book value of the investment, and some form of time-discounted flows. In one survey of 127 companies (selected as being "well managed"), 116 reported using some measure of return, 66 made use of payback formula, 59 computed return on the book value of the original investment, and 38 employed some variant of discounted cash flows.[9]

The popularity of the payback method stems not only from its simplicity but also from its emphasis on the liquidity of the investment. Managements are noticeably biased in favor of projects which can be reconverted to cash in short order. "Payout figures are nearly always useful in investment analyses as measures of exposure to risk. With the passage of time, there are increasing possibilities of obsolescence in product design or equipment, of deviations from the original estimates of income and operating costs, and of changes in competitive conditions. Payout figures are useful measures of risk because they show the length of time for which the original capital investment is exposed to these hazards." [10]

Payback estimates are normally used in conjunction with other measures of return. "In one case a two-year pay-off was described as an automatic qualification, in another case three years; but more generally, passing of such a hurdle would merely qualify a proposed expenditure for consideration at the appropriate higher management level." [11] The supplementary rate-of-return measure which is most frequently used along with payback is what is referred to as the book-value or financial-statement or accountant's method, since it is based on the ratio of the income accruing from the investment (which shows up in the income statement) to the amount of the investment (which is reflected in the balance sheet). General Foods uses the following approach.[12]

> The [return on investment] computation is sometimes prepared on an annual basis, and sometimes on the estimated effective life of the proposed project. The approach used by General Foods, for example,

[9] James H. Miller, "A Glimpse at Practice in Calculating and Using Return on Investment," *N.A.A. Bulletin,* June, 1960, sec. 1, p. 73.

[10] McLean, *N.A.A. Bulletin,* September, 1960, sec. 3, p. 35.

[11] Eisner, *Determinants of Capital Expenditures,* p. 30.

[12] Leon E. Hay, "Planning for Profits: How Some Executives Are Doing It," *Accounting Review,* April, 1960, p. 237. (Italics are in the original.) General Foods also employs a payout formula.

is to relate the *average annual profit* before taxes in the first five years, and the first ten years, of a project's life to the *average funds employed* in the respective periods. The "average annual profits" in the General Foods computation includes all items of income and expense usually included in a division's income statement, including portions of existing overhead.

Another company in its capital expenditures procedure defines return on investment as "the annualized operating profit or net operating savings divided by investment." A research committee of the Philadelphia Society of Business Budgeting reported: "The Average Book Method was the name given to a system, used by many of the larger companies and employing forecasts of what the books will show during the life of the project. The general principle, common to all such systems, was the relating of average annual profit to the average book investment in plant." [13]

Because the payback method makes no allowance for differential earnings beyond the payback period, in comparing projects, and because the book-value method does not take into account the differential time pattern of returns from alternative projects, a number of firms have adopted the economists' preferred valuation approach and now discount future flows down to their present value. A procedure cited by one management official ran as follows: [14]

> 1. A minimum acceptable rate of return is chosen for each particular class of projects. This rate is based on the company's cost of capital, the rate of growth desired by its management and the degree of risk inherent in the given type of project. It is determined at relatively infrequent intervals and its determination generally would not enter into a specific investment evaluation.
>
> 2. Estimates of cash income and outlays are prepared in the same manner as for the discounted-cash-flow method.
>
> 3. All future income and outlays are discounted to their net present worth at the minimum acceptable rate of return. A ratio is then computed by dividing the present worth of net cash flow by the amount of the initial investment.

These are the more systematic approaches to the ranking of investment projects by their worthwhileness. Although there appears to be increasing

[13] Horace Hill, "A New Method of Computing Rate of Return on Capital Expenditures," quoted in Ezra Solomon (ed.), *The Management of Corporate Capital* (Glencoe, Ill.: Free Press, 1959), pp. 35–36.

[14] McLean, *N.A.A. Bulletin*, September, 1960, p. 50. The writer of this paper, who before joining the Continental Oil Company as vice-president had taught at the Harvard Graduate School of Business Administration, adds a fourth point: "4. The profitability index [a name which he gives to the result of this computation] is equal to the above ratio minus one. The purpose of this step is to make the index positive for acceptable projects and negative for submarginal projects."

managerial interest in discounting future returns by some internally or externally derived rate, by and large the procedures resorted to are simpler and allow more room for judgment. As for the establishment of a cutoff point, most firms simply extend the amount of financing made available from sources within the firm (depreciation and retained earnings) as far as these will go over the array. Where any other test is provided to establish the eligibility of a project for financing, it is usually to require that the investment return the company's present rate of earnings or its target rate.

In the case of the previously cited steel company, for example, the minimum return which the company exacts is one equal to present earnings on investment (at this time about 8 or 9 per cent) and the maximum payout period is five years. Capital expenditures would normally be financed out of internal sources, and even the availability of investment projects promising more than the minimum required return would not necessarily prompt resort to external financing. Even at bargain rates of interest, the company would be unlikely to borrow to finance capital projects which were expected to pay less than current earnings though more than the cost of funds.

This policy is based on a belief that it is unwise to "mortgage your good business to go after poorer business," a belief which appears to have a multiple origin in some notion that maintaining the higher *rate* of profit, even though it means a smaller absolute amount, preserves the company's credit standing, in the expectation that borrowing for low-return projects now would use up credit which might later finance better-paying investments, and also in the security consideration that going after low-margin business leaves little "protective margin" if conditions should change. These considerations seem to be related to some not clearly identifiable mixture of both the market cost and opportunity cost principles, though the tenuousness or fuzziness of the relation is indicated by one official's speculation that he "supposed" the company might lower its sights a bit and accept a return something less than it was then earning if it had "funds to invest" and not enough projects promising the "minimum" yield to employ all the available funds, though he emphasized that the question and answer were purely hypothetical since there was then no shortage of projects paying above the minimum required return.

The allocation procedure is sometimes much more informal than the practices which have been described. "The Committee found that a surprising number of companies had no system of evaluating or justifying a capital expenditure, but depended entirely on the judgment of their executives." [15] In some companies the replacement of old equipment is made

[15] Hill, in Solomon, *The Management of Corporate Capital*, p. 36. This survey by the Philadelphia Society for Business Budgeting was made in 1953.

more or less automatically, as though the continuity of the company's operations depended on it and a calculation of the return to be expected from it was not relevant.

When a company has been experiencing a period of prosperity, there may be a tendency to "accommodate" most of the capital projects submitted by divisional managers or functional vice-presidents. With swollen streams of internal funds the question may no longer be whether an investment should be undertaken, and only to a minor degree may it even be what projects shall be undertaken; the embarrassing question (but an embarrassment to which every management would welcome being subjected) may be, How can we spend the money? One outlet always available is, of course, an increase in dividends. In the next chapter, however, it will become evident that this is an alternative which management accepts only reluctantly. Under these circumstances (admittedly not of a continuous nature) an evaluation procedure is given little regard. If a case cannot be made on an earnings basis, there are alternative means of justifying it.

Nonmeasurable Returns

There are types of capital outlays which produce no measurable returns and which must therefore be accepted or rejected on qualitative judgment. As one company's manual reads, "Although as many projects as possible should be justified on the basis of return on investment, there will be cases which do not readily fit this pattern. Examples are projects to satisfy legal, safety, health or employee relations requirements, to achieve general plant improvement, or to implement long-range research and development." Sometimes an effort is made to give such projects a simulated rating.

"In lieu of a return on investment calculation, such projects should receive the following ratings:

1—Equal in importance to projects returning 40% or more.
2—Equal in importance to projects returning 30–40%.
3—Equal in importance to projects returning less than 30%."

Such simulated ratings cannot disguise the subjective character of the evaluation, however. Nevertheless, there is one important check on careless evaluation of projects, even in times when internal sources make money plentiful for investment. The availability of funds cannot be made the basis for slipshod accommodation of questionable ventures in the capital budget without jeopardizing a company's over-all measure of performance and its attempt to reach a target rate of return, since all such investments, by increasing the assets, add to the denominator of the over-all earnings ratio. Failure to review projects carefully carries the danger that future performance may decline.

Reconciling Theory and Practice

There are a number of reasons why economic analysis and business practice fail to coincide more closely. If economists have sometimes been critical of business rules of thumb as ignoring important considerations (the payback formula, for example, which has been roundly attacked for failing to consider returns beyond the payback period), and if business practitioners have continued to follow such short cuts despite economic criticism, it is possible that a clearer understanding of "reasons why" will help to reconcile the two positions.

1. The economists' preferred approach to capital budgeting—an evaluation of alternative investments on the basis of the discounted streams of income to which they give rise—is not more widely used in business not because there is disagreement with its premises but because there is skepticism about its practicability. The primary difficulty is that estimation of income receipts beyond a three- to five-year period strikes most managers as too problematical to be meaningful. Whether competing products will have ruled this one off the market, whether technological advances will have stripped this process of its present advantages, whether consumer tastes will sustain the present price structure, whether intensified competition will have shaved profit margins, whether a geographical shift in markets will undermine a present intrenched position—these and other unknowns make the procedure of giving specific values to such considerations not only speculative but a little foolish to many managements. It is not that they fail to take account of such considerations; there is little doubt that most of these potentials filter through their minds in the course of making a judgment. But many managers would be stumped to quantify the end results, whereas they would find it feasible to give their "feel" of the situation or express their "hunch" about the probable outcome.

Some firms have welcomed the increased attention to investment rationalizations which economists have forced on them by discussions in the professional and business journals, and some of their financial officers have joined in the controversy with skill and persuasiveness. The number of companies which now give explicit consideration to time-discounted income flows arising out of investments has increased considerably in recent years, and all evidence suggests their number will continue to grow. Even among the most enthusiastic business supporters of this approach, however, there is an insistence that, in the final analysis, it is the judgmental factor which controls. What the economists' formulas have done is to make explicit and more defensible considerations which previously were often implicit and rejectable.

One company representative has commented on the relative usefulness and limitations of a "formula approach" to investment, in this instance referring specifically to one of the most widely used methods of determining whether a machine should be replaced, that sponsored by the Machinery and Allied Products Institute and commonly dubbed the M.A.P.I. replacement formula.[16]

> Since factors other than the results of a formula computation enter into the picture, it would be well to explain the attitude of many of our staff and operating personnel toward the use of formulas in machinery and equipment replacement.
>
> To those in the shops, it seems so simple that equipment has to be replaced before it falls apart. They have known it for many years. They knew it before the Machinery and Allied Products Institute. They knew it before Univac. But, since it was so simple, they failed to consider that to the top management the need for replacement was not nearly so obvious. The shop foreman waved his arms and talked in terms of loose gibs, backlash in screws, chatter in spindles, and the accountant talked in terms of conservation of working capital, retirement of indebtedness, return on investment. They could hear each other all right but they were not communicating. Besides, they were a little suspicious of each other.
>
> We have seen in the M.A.P.I. replacement formula and in the many adaptations which have developed from it a new tool with a number of very important advantages. These formulas are effective because:
>
> 1. They take factors which the shop can understand, such as the cost of overhauling, price of the new equipment and the increased number of pieces per hour, and translate them into accounting terminology, which can be used to sell the need for the equipment. (We strongly feel that the forms and formulas should be kept simple, and in shop terms.)
>
> 2. By demanding an orderly and systematic consideration of all factors which have a bearing on whether or not a tool should be replaced, they make sure that nothing is overlooked in arriving at a decision.
>
> 3. The final document has a certain air about it. It appears to have been (and has been) worked out by experts; and it is a well-known truth at the shop level of the manufacturing business that whatever is contrived by an expert (ordinary man away from home) is ever so much more acceptable than data produced by the regular staff, even though it is the same information, paraphrased into longer words and artfully bound in hog leather. This approach helps *sell* the request.
>
> There are also a number of shortcomings which we have encountered, and these are worth mentioning. None of the replacement formulas which I have seen gives any consideration to the company's

[16] Connelly, *N.A.A. Bulletin,* June, 1960, sec. 1, pp. 49–52.

cash position. This factor is usually dismissed as another matter altogether. Unfortunately, it is not another matter.

Consider the situation in which the top management personnel of a large firm became so infatuated with the M.A.P.I. replacement policy that they looked at it as the answer to all problems. Just feed in the information for all pieces of equipment and then start buying in the order of greatest advantage. They painstakingly analyzed several thousand pieces of equipment and concluded that they "could not afford not to" buy $12,000,000 worth of equipment. However, to actually do so would have been disastrous. They settled for $2,300,000, and ended up with very satisfactory progress.

The selection of the particular piece of equipment to be replaced is not as simple as it sounds. You cannot merely select the one which shows the greatest "paper" advantage. For instance, our management believes that a well-equipped tool room is essential to the manufacturing business, not only for the service it performs but because it is a training institution for mechanical skills and future supervision. Yet it is difficult, under most replacement formulas, to make a good case for a tool room machine, for reasons which are entirely obvious to those who have ever tried to fill in the replacement formulas. . . .

Another area of considerable legitimate difference of opinion lies in the trends of the business. It is one thing to carefully work out an analysis based on a known work volume which is considered to be fixed and predictable but, in a diversified business, such as ours, we have to be flexible. Often, we cannot predict our future business in terms of exact numerical values, and the machine selection must be made on the basis of guessing where the expenditure will do the most good. Call it business sense, intuition, feel of the market or anything else you like, the fact is that the prosperous business is one whose management guesses right oftener than it guesses wrong.

Of all capital expenditure appropriations we issue, not over 40 per cent are supported by replacement analysis. We use it only if we can get reasonably factual data to back up the figures. We would rather use the device where it will work and we can defend its mechanics. Where the data is largely intangible, we prefer to say so. . . .

The answers yielded by use of replacement formulas are only as good as the data put into them. Our experience is that the input can, within limits of a reasonable degree of sincerity, be juggled to produce a wide range of answers. Trying to assign numerical values to such unknowns as the expected future maintenance of new types of equipment or trying to anticipate the degree of market participation which a new product will enjoy is, at best, guesswork. . . . A solid knowledge of past performance is more reliable here than hazy guesses on the future.

Even one of the most enthusiastic of "cash-flow discounters," Prof. Joel Dean, whose advocacy of this approach is one reason for its increasing acceptance in industry, has recognized the validity of these limitations. He has commented: [17]

> In the automobile industry, where demand is growing, where product improvements and innovations dominate capital outlays, and where competitors' innovations continually peril a company's market position, neat rate-of-return rationing of capital is not common. . . . Executives do not think of a decision to develop a new engine as a rate-of-return problem. Instead, it is viewed as a many-sided decision of operating policy calling for collective wisdom in reconciling research dreams, production feasibility, competitive pressures, and market acceptance.
>
> These qualitative considerations are usually focused on earnings, but often in terms of what is needed to preserve or enhance the earning power of the division as a whole, rather than incrementally in terms of how much added profits will come from the added investment. Thus, a car may be thought of as needing a new engine when its earning power (or market share) slips or is periled.
>
> These various facets can be viewed as adding up to a rate-of-return estimate, but this economic structure is obscured by the heavy overlay of business judgment and grand strategy.

If one recognizes what is probably the case, that the kind of decision which Professor Dean ascribes to the automobile industry is much more widely prevalent in industry, then the economist and the businessman are not far apart. The businessman appreciates that the more logically systematic approach to capital budgeting is desirable "because it forces orderly and complete consideration." [18] The economist recognizes the severe limitations of the practical applicability of his theoretically justifiable method of evaluating proposed investments. The neat numerical analysis with all its appearances of precision is often only the vehicle for a "seat-of-the-pants" decision, but at times it is a useful device for informing judgment at the other end of the anatomy as well.

2. A second consideration is related to this first. The notion of a clear-cut ordering of potential projects in terms of their projected rates of return is a logically necessary corollary of the profit-maximization motive to which most economists still subscribe. But if one accepts that businesses commonly work toward a profit target which is limited and definite, rather than seek a maximum which has no definition substantively, in a figure, but only procedurally, in the mechanics of the decision, then it may be that a relatively coarse sieve rather than a fine scale is all that is needed for the firm's purposes. The quantitative precision which is implied by the

[17] Joel Dean, *Capital Budgeting* (New York: Columbia University Press, 1951), p. 12.

[18] Connelly, *N.A.A. Bulletin,* June, 1960, sec. 1, p. 52.

discounting process may then give way to a more judgmental approach to the same conceptual schema.

3. If businessmen have tended to pay too little attention to the time factor in investment, it is probably equally true that economists have refused to accept as justified the businessman's high liquidity preference, even though this is his privileged judgment. It is, of course, true that numerous economic studies have referred to the high premium which business firms appear to place on security in the form of "excess" cash. The payback formula has been explained at least in part on this ground. Nevertheless, the two capital-budgeting approaches which economists have most vigorously defended, the discounted cash flow and present-value methods, reveal the economists' preoccupation with flows over time and exclude the businessman's desire for liquidity. While each formula discounts future receipts, it makes no place for a firm's premium preference to get its money back sooner rather than later.

A project which gives rise to small returns in the near future, building up very substantially in the more distant future, is discounted at the same objective rate as one which may return larger sums in the near term and virtually nothing later. If their present value is the same, or if their flows discount to the same rate, they are viewed as equally preferable. From the point of view of most businessmen, however, there would in fact be a clear-cut preference for the second investment, which yielded its cash returns more quickly. This is not because they fail out of ignorance to give adequate consideration to the future, but because their own subjective time preference—based on the uncertainty and riskiness of the future—leads them to that result.[19] The economist may question their judgment,

[19] Indeed, this attitude has been one barrier to the spread of long-range planning. Even in companies whose time horizons have lengthened and which now engage in five- to ten-year forecasting, or even longer, the risk and uncertainty factors show themselves in the effort to preserve options and alternative strategies as long as feasible. In some firms there has been an attempt to sort out types of investment and to ascribe different risk factors to them. Some investment decisions—major expansion plans, for example—require enough lead time before being brought to fruition that the first phases of capital spending cannot possibly show a return for more years than is permitted the more routine kind of investment. These "life-line" types of outlays, on which management believes the very future of the company depends, are allowed slower and lower rates of expected earnings than investments which are expected to add to profit but are in no sense "essential."

In one rubber company, investments for expansion and new products are expected to pay out 50 per cent "when the total amount of the appropriation request is $300,000 or less," but only 25 per cent "when the total amount of the appropriation request is over $300,000." A company official explained these dissimilar requirements by saying that "generally the appropriations involving higher amounts are considered of a more stable nature and pertain to activities which it is felt will have a long life, and are of a nature that over a fairly long period will work out to full advantage. Experience has shown that expenditures for the smaller amount quite frequently are short lived

but only in the same way that he might question consumer tastes. He would be on sounder ground in accepting their time preference and building it into his formulations.

One perceptive approach in that direction has been made by David L. Carpenter, who is at the same time on the staff of the analysis department of Johns-Manville Corporation and the economics faculty of Rutgers University. The "time-value method" which he has suggested [20] is derived in its essentials from the present-value approach, but instead of making use of a market rate of interest as the discount factor, it employs the firm's own subjective time-preference rating, which Carpenter calls its "time-value rate." To find the yield of any investment, however irregular its returns, he uses this time-value rate as the rate of discount to find total present worth of the expected flows. A regular annual (level) equivalent for this sum can then be derived, also in dollar terms. From this is deducted the level equivalent of recovering the original investment over the same period of time. The remainder is divided by the original investment to give the yield.

The significant contribution in this formulation is the use of the firm's own subjective discount factor, which may vary by type of investment. There is nothing to preclude a firm's imposing a time-value rate of 50 per cent on investments on which it now requires a two-year payback, for example. By being forced to examine whether in fact it does have so high a regard for liquidity, the firm may be driven to alter its time value. If, on the other hand, it chooses to adhere to what amounts to its liquidity-preference rate, competing investments could then be ranked by the present-value method, obtaining for the economist a recognition of the significance of the (discounted) flow of funds from the investment over its lifetime, but giving effect to the businessman's desire to recoup his investment within the time limit which he has arbitrarily imposed. The consequence would also be to make a normative analysis more descriptive of actual practice.

4. The economists' analysis of capital budgeting generally assumes that choice must be made from among competing projects. Most businessmen too speak as though the pressure of potential investment on capital funds is great and imposes the necessity for rationing. This assumption is valid in many instances. It is equally true, however, that it belies the fact in other

---

and not of the merit of appropriations for the higher amount." Eisner, *Determinants of Capital Expenditures,* p. 96. Whatever one may think of the logic, this double standard is characteristic of managerial efforts to classify investments by degree of risk and uncertainty. In some companies, the effort splays out into a number of standards and even *ad hoc* judgments.

[20] David L. Carpenter, "Time-value Method Improves Investment Yield Calculation," *The Controller,* October, 1960, pp. 461–467.

cases, though managers are sufficiently embarrassed to admit it that they maintain the fiction of many alternative projects competing for acceptance.

The increasing reliance on internal sources of funds for capital financing is itself a cyclical influence on investment outlays. In prosperous times firms realize profits which permit (one might almost say require) heavier capital expenditures. In harder times shrinking profit margins shrink the availability of capital funds as well. The increasing importance of depreciation allowances has provided a greater measure of stability, it is true, but retained earnings are still an important enough source of investment financing to introduce this cyclical effect. In the lean years the internal supply of capital funds may be sufficiently reduced to invoke a more searching evaluation of projects which in total exceed the available funds. But in the fat years the number of worthwhile projects may not be equal to the cash supply, leading either to a lowering of investment standards or to a build-up of cash which invites union officials to raise their demands, stockholders to become restless for a bonus dividend, and "raiders" to lick their chops.

The fact is that the supply of good ideas in some companies simply is not steady enough or pitched at a high enough level to create that competition for investment funds about which managements usually talk. This is not likely to be true of the largest corporations, which operate sizable research units whose function is to maintain such a flow of inventiveness. But in smaller and medium-sized companies whose research activities are limited and run more to styling and product redesign than to new developments (though no implication is intended that this is true of all smaller companies, or that productive research is confined to the large corporation), there often is no unit specifically charged with responsibility for creating or conceiving investment opportunities. The result is sometimes a trickle of ideas which fails to match the flow of available funds. In one highly reputed medium-sized company which was visited during the course of this study, an official confided that until that year the company's operating units had not used the sums earmarked for capital projects. In at least two years the corporation's principal subsidiary had put to work only 60 per cent of the amounts actually approved for it. This year, it was said, for the first time requests had exceeded the supply of funds, and for the first time rationing was needed. In previous years even projects below the company's stated "minimum" requirement could be accommodated.

Granted that this may not be a typical situation, there is good reason to believe that the practice of maintaining dividends at a steady rate and retaining for investment in the business all earnings above that level has in times of prosperity provided such ample internal sources of funds that managements have often accepted for their capital budgets projects which would be rejected by any market test, and, further, that in some companies (how many it is impossible to say) the discrepancy between cash and ideas has placed pressures on management to "discover" outlets for the former and substitutes for the latter. In such circumstances the need for careful project ranking and evaluation, as pictured in the economists' model, evaporates.

5. One outlet for cash accumulations is in the acquisition of other companies. An "excess" of money is not, of course, the only or even the principal reason for one company's buying out another. The desire to diversify and the difficulty of switching the firm's own management to a field with which it is not familiar is perhaps the most important motivation for this form of investment. A related reason is the desire to "buy up" a package of trained managerial talent as a necessary condition of expansion, even if the field is not a strange one. The fact is, however, that the market for small companies with promise whose need is genuinely one of insufficient capital (perhaps because they are at an early stage of development, when internal sources are still thin or nonexistent) has been a lively one in the postwar period. The assistant to the president of the Rockwell Manufacturing Company commented in 1957: "Since 1945 Rockwell has acquired sixteen companies. I have never tabulated the number of invitations to purchase that we have received, but I would estimate them to be close to 900. Of these 900 inquiries there have been about seventy that our management felt we ought to take a closer look at." [21]

A number of companies have assigned specific responsibility to a committee for searching out possible acquisitions. The urgency with which the search is pursued probably bears some correlation to the increase in internal funds without a concomitant increase in internal projects. This condition may not be a reflection of the lack of imagination of the company's management as much as a resultant of a period of rapid growth in a field which has definite limits to its possibilities for expansion. This set of circumstances provides the funds, limits the opportunities for their internal use, and drives management to look for external outlets all at the same time.

The purchase of a company will be based on an expectation of its potential earning power, to be sure, but it is exactly the kind of investment on which a precise rate-of-return estimate cannot be made. Management's judgment about what it can do with the company is likely to be more controlling than a quantified return on investment, even though a careful calculation of market potential precedes the judgment.

6. "Political" factors sometimes influence corporate investment decisions. Though understandably economists abstract from these in their models, top management cannot so easily do so. Influential backing may

[21] A. Clark Daugherty, "Acquisition of Companies," in *Marketing Research in Action*, NICB Studies in Business Policy, no. 84, 1957, p. 10.

lead to the selection of a poorer project over a stronger one. When competition for funds exists, figures may be manipulated to influence judgment; excessive claims may be made. "Claims for cost savings or added profits made to justify appropriations for a two or three-year period were added up. The total was found to equal four times the current profit of the corporation." [22]

In companies with numbers of plants or several operating subsidiaries common practice is for the capital budget to cover the company as a whole. In these situations ill feelings are sometimes engendered if one plant or subsidiary believes it is contributing a disproportionately large share of the corporation's profit but is receiving a disproportionately small share of the capital allocations. The capital projects screening committee defense that it is ranking all projects objectively is not likely to be received sympathetically, in view of the judgmental factors entering into the rate-of-return estimates. Under the circumstances plants and subsidiaries which are the heavy earners are likely to be given favored treatment in the capital budget, however that favoritism is disguised.

These six reasons, then, help to explain why in the field of capital budgeting business practice diverges from economic analysis—the business belief that judgment is more important than quantification when the basic data are weak, management's setting of a specific and limited profit target rather than a theoretical maximum, the economists' failure to give adequate recognition to the strong business preference for liquidity, the fact that the flow of ideas for new investment is not always so deep and turbulent as to require careful ranking of competing projects, the acquisition based on judgmental factors of whole companies as an outlet for investment funds, and the internal political pressures which cannot be ignored.

None of these reasons, it will be observed, marks a decisive conflict between the theory and the practice of capital budgeting. They deal largely with institutional modifications of the abstract model, lessening its sharpness and precision but leaving it, in broader and blunter outline, still representative of budgeting procedures toward which firms which plan their actions are clearly moving.

[22] Comment of a participant in an N.A.A. practices session, *N.A.A. Bulletin*, March, 1959, sec. 3, p. 25.

Chapter 13

DIVIDEND POLICY.
THE PROJECTED BALANCE SHEET

Dividend Stability

Next to the capital budget the most important determination affecting the projected balance sheet is a company's dividend policy. The distribution of dividends out of earnings is a major outlay decision which must be made recurringly, usually quarterly, and which involves the correlative calculation of how much of earnings will be retained for use in the business. While at times the decision may be *pro forma* and follow "automatically" from some predetermined policy, at other times (notably when the level of earnings has changed substantially) it requires a more deliberative approach.

The "policy" which companies adopt depends to some extent on the stage of their growth. Young companies which are experiencing growing pains are likely to conserve all revenues for use in the business and may run for years before paying their first dividend. "Growth" companies—a mysterious category which eludes exact definition, but whose names have somehow been divulged to the brokerage houses which compile lists of them—customarily trade on their shareholders' willingness to defer returns to the future by plowing back a very high proportion of their current earnings. "Mature" companies tend to fix on some level of dividends which is related to earnings and to maintain that rate with little variation over the years. "Dividend payments are based on both past earnings and future prospects. The plan is to set a level which it is expected can be maintained." Over the years, American corporations have, in the aggregate, tended to pay out between 55 and 60 per cent of net income.

The one consideration which appears to dominate management thinking in the matter of dividends, however, is the one suggested by the corporate official quoted above—stability. Maintenance of a level of payments through good years and bad is regarded as the mark of a "sound" company. A dividend which shareholders can count on is viewed with favor in the market.

The consequence of this overriding consideration is that some special reason must exist to justify a departure from the current dividend rate. After studying intensively the dividend policies of twenty-eight companies over a period of seven years, Prof. John Lintner concluded: "With the possible exception of 2 companies which sought a relatively fixed percentage pay-out, consideration of what dividends should be paid at any given time turned, first and foremost in every case, on the question of whether the existing rate should be changed." [1]

The specific dividend rate which is fixed on is almost always geared to the level of earnings, either past, present, or expected, or all of these. The relationship between dividend and earnings rates varies from company to company, however. In some instances there is a policy of settling on a flat sum, say $0.50 per share, and adhering to that payment unless there is special cause for change. The actual amount selected may be based on the level of payments in other companies, or it may follow from something like a "standard volume" concept—the rate of return which stockholders could reasonably expect over the years based on profits associated with the standard volume of output and sales.

In most instances, however, companies appear to base their dividend levels on some "target" rate of payout. "The target pay-out ratios varied from a low of 20 per cent to a high of 80 per cent, with 50 per cent the most common figure and most of the other companies aiming at 40 to 60 per cent." [2] The existence of a target rate does not customarily mean that the firm automatically distributes that proportion of earnings. It simply sets a kind of guide toward which management intends to move over the years. The caution which this approach suggests is due to the desire for a stable rate, and the policy of not moving up to a higher (or lower) level of payment until management is sure that the rate can (or must) be maintained. [3]

---

[1] John Lintner, "Distribution of Incomes of Corporations among Dividends, Retained Earnings, and Taxes," *American Economic Review,* vol. 46, May, 1956, p. 99.

[2] The same, p. 102.

[3] "This week . . . Capt. Eddie Rickenbacker announced that Eastern Airlines was doubling its annual dividend rate. One reason is the high depreciation charges, now running at about $25-million a year. That can take care of most of the capital needed for new equipment, so shareholders will get more of the company's earnings.

"Still, there is a hesitancy on the part of some managements to boost the dividend rate. It sets a precedent hard to break if cash should happen to become tight later on.

"So a good many companies will be reducing debt, rather than raising dividends significantly, in order to get rid of extra cash. Dow Chemical Co. has done just that." *Business Week,* Oct. 9, 1954, p. 44.

In effect this means that the company is always using a lagged earnings rate as the basis for its dividend actions. If it has as its target a 50 per cent payout rate, but is unwilling to distribute 50 per cent of this year's earnings until the next two or three years confirm that level of revenues can be maintained over the years, by that time earnings may have advanced still higher. The new dividend rate which would then be set would be based on the earnings rate of several years past, with the now higher receipts offering a margin of safety against the possibility that a profit decline would require reducing the dividend. Thus the desire for stability of payment ensures that the target rate can never be reached. The gap between the actual and target rates may never be closed, even with passing years, but existence of a target does serve to pull dividend rates along, with a lag, after profits (either rising or falling).

A few companies have adopted policies of distributing a fixed percentage of current earnings in dividends, however. One of these is Standard Oil of Indiana. "It is our Company's announced policy to pay out 50 per cent of estimated consolidated net earnings in dividends. For the past several years this has been done by means of a special dividend (in addition to the regular cash dividends) in the form of Standard Oil Company (New Jersey) stock, with equalizing cash payments in lieu of fractional shares, in the fourth quarter of the year."

Still other companies have adopted something of an intermediate position between the practice of distributing a flat-payment dividend, stable with the years, and a fixed percentage dividend, which fluctuates with earnings, by issuing an "extra" dividend in years of high earnings. The "extra" permits management to recognize stockholder expectancy of an increment when profits have been unusually good without modifying the basic dividend pattern whose stability it is dedicated to maintain.

Dividends as a Charge on the Company

The legal position of stockholders as the owners of the corporation has put them in a special position as claimant to the income of the firm. Despite this legal claim, in the large public corporation stockholders' dividends have become little different from other charges on the company. They are a cost to be met and managed in order to ensure the continued profitability of the firm. We may assume that, given its choice, management would always prefer to keep earnings in the firm rather than pay them out as dividends (except as the payment of dividends serves the purpose of opening up improved access to additional equity financing). Indeed, in flush years of the last decade, when some companies had embarrassingly large reserves of cash and were temporarily converting them into government securities until they could determine what else to do with them, the pressure was to find investment outlets rather than to distribute to the "owners."

Whatever dividend policy is adopted, then, is designed to satisfy this claimant group while preserving as large a share of earnings for internal uses as can decently be done. It is easier to understand management's attitude toward dividends if they are regarded in the same light as, for example, wages. Management is unlikely to squeeze them to a level which, in comparison with what other companies are doing, appears niggardly and ungenerous, any more than it would drive wages below some community level even if it could. At the same time, managements are unwilling to pay out all earnings in dividends, leaving it to the recipients to determine what they wish to do with them, any more than they would increase wages by as much as profits might permit.

The policy of relating dividends to earnings, but stressing stability, so that dividends are slow to follow profits upward, also provides management with a higher proportion of profits for retention in the business than its target payout rate might suggest. While it is true that the stability principle also serves to maintain dividend payments when profit levels slide, if the "stable" rate is set conservatively enough, the net effect, over the years, is still to keep actual payments below the "target." Moreover, to the extent the firm is geared in with the economy, the increases in retained earnings are concentrated in boom years, when typically managements are growth-conscious and investment-prone, and the decline in the amount of such discretionary funds comes in the lean recession years, when capital outlays are likely to be stripped down commensurately with lower current earnings. Thus the time pattern of accumulating surpluses in the corporate accounts tends to coincide, at least roughly, with management's time preference for making investment outlays.

Nor need managements live with an uneasy conscience that the stockholder is being given short shrift by such a policy. Reinvestment of earnings, if the investment is well advised, serves to raise the market price of shares, so that the stockholder may take his earnings over time as capital gains rather than in the short run as dividends.

In any event, the firm's dividend policy represents one other element which management must manage to achieve its budgeted objectives. It enters into planning via the projected balance sheet. Failure to achieve the operating profit which is set as target, coupled with a stable dividend policy, will require compensations elsewhere in the budget and have its impact on other items in the balance sheet. By reducing the amount of planned retained earnings, it will call for offsetting reductions in the assets column, probably in plant and equipment. On the other hand, maintaining a ceiling on dividends in times of rising profit levels opens up delightful possibilities for an expansion-minded management to contemplate—in the budget.

The Projected Balance Sheet

In arriving at the completed projected balance sheet, the capital budget and the dividend decision (with its correlative of how much of current earnings will be retained in the business) must be joined by certain other decisions. We shall note these only briefly. The important consideration is that the resulting statement of assets and liabilities represents part of the company's planning methodology, embodying as it does a picture in figures of the kind of company which management hopes to find at the end of the period, when plans will have been turned (more or less faithfully) into actions. No less than the projected operating statement does the projected balance sheet represent corporate objectives, though in this instance objectives relating to the basic plant and equipment and funds tied up in the business, rather than the specific production and marketing processes.

One decision affecting the financial state of the company on that future date for which the balance sheet is drawn concerns the depreciation policy which will be followed. From one point of view the depreciation reserves which are indicated in the balance sheet are simply a sanctioned method of segregating revenues in a special account, so that past depreciation decisions, like investments, represent a "sunk" or settled matter, affecting the balance sheet through their role in financing new investment but calling for no action other than making the best of them. Actually, however, depreciation decisions are not frozen but may be changed.

The significance of the depreciation decision lies in its effect on current and future tax-free flows. Choice of the depreciation policy (as between straight-line, years-digits, declining balance, and sometimes extraordinary acceleration) affects the distribution of tax-free dollars (because treated as cost) over time. The last three policies, for example, all bring a quicker recovery of original cost than does the straight-line method. The total sum of tax-free dollars recovered is the same under any method (within a finite time span), but when these can be segregated out of the income stream depends on the policy chosen.

The planned-for amount of working capital—cash, accounts receivable, and inventory—is generally related to the firm's projected level of operations. As production and sales increase, additional funds are needed to build inventories to a level appropriate to the higher rate of operations, to sustain the higher level of accounts receivable, and to maintain bank balances adequate for the expended activities. To a limited extent the needed resources will come from an increase in accounts payable, but most of them must be provided for by the firm itself. Failure to plan adequately for working capital needs is one of the most common failings of a growing business. Its higher level of operations may be pleasingly profitable, but profits may become more and more tied up in financing inventory and receivables, still without meeting all its cash needs. The projected balance sheet must take into account the levels of working capital which will be needed to carry the amount of business which is expected for the period.

Provision must also be made for the repayment of obligations, both short-term and long-term, though this is a matter too apparent to be overlooked (unlike working capital additions) and generally offering fewer intricacies than depreciation decisions, except at times when some form of refinancing is undertaken.

There are various guides to assist managements in planning their balance sheets for a future date, most of them designed to ensure that the several asset and liability accounts are in appropriate relationship to each other and to the level of the firm's activity. Some of these we noted in an earlier chapter, such as the current ratio, which is the relationship of current assets to current liabilities, average figures for which may be obtained for given industries as a basis for judging the appropriateness of the firm's own projections. Similarly, industry experience with other ratios may be compared with the firm's own calculations—current liabilities to net worth, total liabilities to net worth, funded debt to net working capital, fixed assets to net worth, sales to inventory, and so on. Such guides are only suggestive, however, since they relate to the historical experience of numbers of firms, whereas the logic of a particular firm's future planning may support a change from usual practice. Nevertheless, they do constitute reminders of what business experience has found to be desirable practice, and as such have their usefulness in appraising the acceptability of the financial condition which is proposed for the future.

Such balance-sheet projections may be made for varying planning periods, just as in the case of operating statements. The most frequent period is a year, but some firms prepare monthly balances over the year, and others draw up balance sheets for periods from two to five years in the future. Whatever the period, the end result is a snapshot of the firm as it is expected to look at the point in time, on the assumption that the operating plan and capital budget have been carried out as expected.

Chapter 14

THE PROJECTED FLOW OF FUNDS

The Cash Budget

The projected balance sheet indicates the planned-for relationship among assets and liabilities at some point in the future, as a consequence of the activities which are detailed in the projected operating statement and the investments which are proposed in the capital budget. The projected flow of funds is derivative from these statements and facilitative of the actions and programs which they contemplate. Sometimes called the cash budget, it outlines the cash movements which result from the planned-for operations and which, at the same time, are necessary if those operations are to be carried out as planned.

Within the firm two kinds of flows parallel each other and require coordination by management. One is the flow of real goods and services, the other the flow of money. Raw and semifinished materials and the services of men and machines flow into the enterprise, as the purchases of the business, and flow out in the form of goods and services which are sold to others. This circular flow of real products ties the firm into the real economy, but in order for it to continue, the firm must also be tied into the complex accounting system by which the debits and credits among people and businesses are recorded and transactions offset against each other—the money economy.

The System of Accounts

The system of accounts by which this is done, interfirm, is operated by the banking system of the country. Each business unit carries its account at one or more banks, maintaining some balance in that account. Each bank is tied (either directly or through correspondent banks) into community and regional clearinghouses. Each regional clearinghouse is tied into a national clearinghouse. Thus all the accounts of all business units are tied together in a single system.

As a firm purchases goods or services, it writes checks, which are debits to its account and credits to the accounts of those from whom it purchases. As it sells goods or services, it receives checks, which are credited to its account and debited to the accounts of those issuing them. Within the account of the business unit, its debits (the checks it writes) are offset against its credits (the checks it receives). Since the flows of real goods into and out of the business, and the parallel writing of checks, are not synchronous, however, there is usually some lead or lag of credits over debits. As credits lead, the firm's balance in its account builds up. As credits lag, its balance declines. The balance in the account, then, is the means of equilibrating the inflow and outflow of payments, which for convenience we usually lump under the general category of "money." At times when the in-payments lag seriously behind out-payments, the firm must add something to its balance to ensure that the two flows can be matched. Only as the firm manages its use of money to secure the continued equalizing of inflows and outflows over time, of all the payments it makes or receives (for whatever activities, whether or not related to immediate operations), can it continue to operate, or at a minimum can it continue to operate along the lines which it is pursuing.

If at some time its real activities swell, involving a heavy flow of out-payments which the incoming stream of credits is inadequate to match, it has several courses of action open to it. It may immediately curtail its activities and ask for a little time during which the continuing inflows will catch up with the reduced outflows. If it expects that the required balancing in the account will take place all right, but not until some foreseeable time in the intermediate future, it may arrange for a bank loan to tide it over until that time; the bank in effect agrees, for a fee, to let the checks which the firm's account cannot offset be offset against its own account, up to a stated amount. Or the firm may arrange from other sources to obtain funds which it can deposit in its account sufficient to take care of the lag in current receipts over current expenditures, over however long a period that condition is expected to obtain.[1]

The projected operating statement runs in terms of the real operations of the firm, its schedule of the quantities of materials and the number of people needed in order to produce the bill of goods which is to be shipped from the plant during the period. As to whether the credits and debits which arise from these activities will offset against each other in the firm's account, the operating statement only reveals how the total inflows relate to the total outflows at the end of that period. Similarly, the projected balance sheet deals only in totals for the end of the planning period, indi-

---

[1] The significance of this check-clearing method of tying the firm into the country's system of accounts has been most effectively developed by Charles A. Dice, emeritus professor of economics at Ohio State University.

cating (for the most part) how the credits will be obtained to match the outflows which will give rise to increased assets, whether in the form of inventory, accounts receivable, or capital investments.

This balancing of totals at the end of a given period is, however, only part of the problem of money management. The structure of credit is such that the system will not wait till the end of a firm's planning period to see if its offsetting of credits against debts will come out as it expects. The system is more skeptical and cautious: It requires that outflows be matched by inflows (or the difference made up out of the account balance) on a day by day basis. This necessitates foresight on the firm's part and gives rise to the other aspect of money management—the offsetting of debits by credits not only in total, at the end of a period, but continuously over that period.

Balance Sheet and Cash Budget Contrasted

The projected balance sheet (or a sequence of projected balance sheets) is often spoken of as the equivalent of, or one form of, the projected flow of funds. This conception is erroneous, however. It confuses a planning and an operating function. The projected balance sheet constitutes a state in which the business firm hopes to find itself at the date specified. It is not so much a financial statement as a statement of objectives, based in part on the operations which are planned for the intervening period (which give rise to projected changes in working capital and equity), as well as embodying a program for the future, in the form of its capital budget. The latter should, indeed, be considered a schedule supporting the projected balance sheet, rather than a separate and independent budget taking its place alongside the projected balance sheet.

The projected flow of funds, on the other hand, is purely an operating schedule. It embodies no plans of its own, other than how it expects to match credits against debits over the planning period, in order to permit the projected real operations and the projected capital provisions for the future to take place. It poses no targets independent of those which are posed for it by the other two planning statements. But its importance is not thereby denigrated, since without its facilitating function the plans embodied in the projected operating statement and balance sheet could not materialize.

Cash budgeting starts with the estimation of the flows of funds into and out of the firm, as called for by the operating and capital plans. The cash budget is not so much concerned, however, with the value of the activities called for by these plans as it is with the timing of the debits and credits to which they give rise. The purchases of materials needed for this month's production may not actually have to be paid for until thirty days following receipt. The sales of product affect the sum of accounts receivable, but they do not provide credits until checks for them have been deposited in the firm's account.

The job of estimating cash flows over the planning period thus is more than simply copying totals from the schedules underlying the projected operating statement and balance sheet. It requires the calculation of the impact of the firm's activities on its daily account balance. For this purpose statistical analysis may provide useful short cuts. On collections from customers, for example, experience will suggest what proportion of this month's sales will yield cash this month, what proportion will be paid next month, what amount two months hence, and so on. These proportions may then be applied to sales for that month in future cash-flow estimates; the seasonality of many activities makes it dangerous, however, to assume without testing that the same proportions will apply to other months as well.

Similarly with purchases of materials and subcontracted parts, the debit to the firm's account does not arise at the moment of receiving delivery of the goods but is dictated by the terms of the sale or customary relations. Statistical estimation may also be sufficient to determine the dates of impact on the firm's account balance.

Various methods for constructing a projected cash budget have been practiced, but their details are not of concern to us here. The one most frequently employed is probably the direct estimation of all anticipated expenditures and receipts. Noncash costs such as depreciation do not figure in such estimates, since they do not affect the cash balance. Other abbreviated methods have been devised, in general relying on short-cut estimation of categories of disbursements and receipts rather than the item-by-item detail of direct estimation.

Managing Cash Flows

Cash budgeting involves more than estimation of flows, however; it involves their management and control as well.

The objective of cash budgeting is to facilitate the real operations of the company, with their parallel movements of funds, by means of the smallest account balance necessary to make good any lag in the offsetting of credits and debits. The holding of cash in an account involves an opportunity cost; those funds could otherwise be loaned out for a return or invested in the company's own operations. At the same time, enough of a balance must be maintained to meet any lag in the matching of outflows with inflows, as a condition of doing business (that is, as a condition of being tied into the national system of accounts through which business is transacted). It is the job of the money manager, then, to budget in such a way that the latter objective is secured at minimum opportunity cost.

This objective is not made easier by the fact that the seasonality of some businesses, coupled with the periodical cycles of some flows (such as the quarterly payment of dividends), and finally the nonrecurrent payments associated with long-term investments often lead to violent fluctuations in the balance needed to provide for a lag in offsetting flows. The assistant treasurer of the Gulf Oil Company once reported that, in a recent year, the extremes in his company's cash position ranged from an excess of debits over credits amounting to $91.5 million during one month, followed, a few months later, by an excess of credits over debits of $34.6 million.[2] In some lines of business a smoothing of flows is more possible. "Some companies match up day-to-day inflow and outgo of cash so precisely that they can keep bank deposits almost constant through the year. American Telephone and Telegraph Co's average of cash and demand deposits through 1958 has varied barely $500,000 either way from $13-million." [3]

The timing of inflows to match outflows, or vice versa, can often be controlled. In part this comes about through convention or custom which business firms have arrived at through mutual agreement, such as the bunching of payments at certain dates during the month (typically the first, the tenth, and the twenty-fifth). A few companies time their disbursements more precisely by using time drafts rather than checks, directing a bank to make payment on a set date. Receipts by a desired date may be obtained by offering a discount for prompt payment.

Equally important, however, in balancing fund flows at the lowest opportunity cost, particularly in companies where flows are irregular, is the investment of balances which are unneeded now but will be needed later. By this device funds are made to earn a return even for the short term during which they are unneeded. The assistant treasurer of the Chesapeake and Ohio Railway is reported as saying that "cash forecasts make it possible to classify the investments in a portfolio according to the company's needs. For example, this might include a base of short-term highly liquid securities to provide against unforeseen contingencies; a much larger revolving fund in securities maturing up to six months—to take care of near-term cash deficits arising from dividend payments, payrolls, and taxes; and perhaps still another portion invested in longer-term and less liquid securities set aside for more distant needs." [4]

[2] John Shaw, "The Cost of Cash Handling and Mishandling," in *Control of Non-manufacturing Costs*, A.M.A., p. 91.

[3] *Business Week*, July 12, 1958, p. 121.

[4] *Business Week*, Apr. 16, 1960. The quotation is *Business Week*'s paraphrase of the assistant treasurer's statement.

Some companies have carried this policy of holding idle balances to a minimum to the point at which even an estimated one-day surplus will be put to work.[5] For similar reasons, they have reviewed company payment and receipt practices to reduce the time during which funds remain idle. The Gulf Oil official previously cited described to a group of managers several ways in which his company had accomplished this.[6]

> At one time, several of our divisional field offices requisitioned funds once or twice a week. After an examination of one week's cash reports, however, we found that the amount requisitioned was in excess of a total week's expenditures and that very often the largest portion of the cash advanced was disbursed late in the week. Other division reports were examined, and, as a result of our study, we put the offices on a daily cash requisition basis. Instead of seven transfers to these divisions each month, we are now making about 22.
>
> While I do not have a compilation of the exact savings effected in our working cash, I think a simplified illustration will emphasize the advantages: If 10 offices each required $500,000 weekly and requisitioned this amount for transfer each Monday, the corporation would be reducing its reservoir account by $5 million each Monday. By establishing daily remittances, the amount transferred would be $1 million each day. On the first day under this daily remittance procedure $4 million would be free, the next day $3 million, the third day $2 million, the fourth day $1 million. This adds up to the equivalent of $10 million free for one day, which, at 3 per cent interest, has a value of $833.33 each week, or a little more than $42,000 a year.
>
> Rather closely related to the hidden-loss item just mentioned is another example in which certain of our offices had periodic large payments to make and the practice had been to build up gradually, over a period of 15 to 20 days, sufficient local funds to meet these substantial payments. We recommended a change in the procedure and had the excess funds transferred to a Pittsburgh control account and invested. When the large payments were due in the field offices,

---

[5] The same article cited in footnote 4, above, reports: "One day last week Scott York of the Chesapeake and Ohio Ry. in Cleveland . . . telephoned a New York dealer in government bonds. York said he would like to buy some government securities if the dealer guaranteed to buy them back. This repurchase agreement—or 'RP'—had advantages for both sides: The dealer would have C&O's funds to cover some of his security transactions, while C&O would gain interest on its idle cash.

"The dealer agreed, and C&O took $1-million par value of Treasury bills, due June 30, 1960. Actual price paid for the bills was $991,145.83. The repurchase agreement was for a single day, so the next day the dealer paid C&O $991,250—netting C&O $104.17 in interest.

"Such transactions are standard operating procedure for C&O and many other large corporations. . . ."

[6] John Shaw, in *Control of Non-manufacturing Costs*, pp. 42–43.

the total funds were transferred back by converting securities to cash on the same day. In one instance, this particular utilization of the funds had a value of $4,000 a month.

In a large company with numerous accounts (Gulf maintains 1,300 accounts in 1,050 banks totaling $80,000,000 in working capital) one of the problems, and responsibilities, of cash budgeting is "knowing where the funds are at any time and why they are there." The larger companies often make regular analyses of their numerous accounts with a view to determining whether the balances are needed, or whether account activity reveals the existence of idle funds which can be put to work. The necessity of maintaining satisfactory relations with the banks at which accounts are maintained, however, sometimes acts as a restraint on the rigor with which balances are held to a minimum. A bank's analysis of the cost to it of the account's activity may be persuasive on management that some larger balance than its own needs would dictate should be left in the account, as a means by which the bank can satisfactorily cover its costs with a fair profit.

The strong drive for "security" on the part of most managers—the desire to ensure that their firm should not be caught unprepared by emergencies—has frequently been cited as explanation for the maintenance of cash balances which are excessive for the firm's operations. Increasingly, however, more sophisticated managers, particularly in the large corporations, are realizing that security can be preserved without sacrificing either earnings or liquidity, by the expedient of investing balances which otherwise would be idle in short-term paper. This requires, however, careful cash budgeting.

Sources of Funds

The preparation of the cash budget may reveal that the funds available are insufficient for the level of activity called for in the operating and capital plans. Even a tentative fitting together of the capital investment schedule with the operating schedule may indicate that to carry both at their planned amounts would make inadequate provision for working capital. In that event the list of capital projects may be pared; much more rarely a ceiling may have to be put on the amount of new business which can be accepted.[7] Short-term bank loans may be sought to finance an ex-

[7] As one example, however, Willis H. Briddell, vice-president in charge of operations of Charles D. Briddell, Inc., commented: ". . . after we have estimated how much and what kind of money is going to be needed, finding ways to provide these funds must be explored. As is well known, providing cash is easier at some times than others, and it may not be possible to find all that is desired. In such a case it may be necessary to alter course a little. Our 1953 sales forecast, for example, had to be

pansion of inventories and the amount of receivables, though in the face of a chronic shortness of cash even the largest firms may be driven to the markets for long-term funds to relieve them of the perpetual pressure which expanding sales, with their drain on working capital, exercise on capital investments which they intend to make. Both General Motors and General Electric floated debenture issues of $300,000,000 to add to their working capital at a time when their profit prospects had seldom been brighter. When a decision has been made to borrow, cash-flow planning will determine, as one company president expressed it, the "exact time" when it will be needed, to permit adequate preparation for its making and to minimize the period over which it will be carried.

At times a company may seek additional equity capital, a move which many managements resist since the cost of bonded indebtedness (which may be deducted as a business expense in computing corporate taxes) is often less than the "cost" of dividends to shareholders which must be paid out of after-tax profits. Nevertheless, the ease of securing funds in this manner for the large and profitable corporation makes it a tempting means of overcoming chronic cash deficiency: stock rights issued to existing stockholders may elicit enough buying interest to guarantee the issue.

Whether interest rates influence managements in their decision to borrow funds to finance operations as planned when internal funds are insufficient, or alternatively to curtail operations, has been debated by economists for years. Examples of both types of behavior can be found. An official of a food company says, "If you need money, you need it. And you go out to get it. The interest rate is unimportant when you need money." [8] But in other lines of activity the story is different. As contractors will testify, a high cost of money often leads to postponement or cancellation of building projects. It is probably a safe generalization, however, that high interest rates lead to a more careful scrutiny of spending plans when these cannot be wholly financed internally.

High interest rates are likely to have another effect on cash budgeting, particularly in those firms which have become conscious of the opportunity cost of idle assets. Slow collections are likely to be analyzed with a view to correcting the time lag, and inventory investment may be reviewed with an eye to possible reduction. As the financial vice-president of a metals producer commented, "the carrying of high inventories is expensive and with the present return on government bonds we would like to put as many

---

trimmed by about 10 per cent, and we put a ceiling of $4,000,000 on our 1954 estimate. Both these amended forecasts were lower than those made by the sales department." "How a Small Business Raised Cash to Expand Sales," in *Guides to Modern Financial Planning*, A.M.A. Financial Management Series, no. 104, New York, 1955, p. 39.

[8] *Business Week*, Feb. 27, 1960, p. 65.

of our inventory dollars as possible into short-term governments pending the need for these funds." [9]

Like the projected operating statement and projected balance sheet to which it is geared, the projected flow-of-funds statement may cover time periods of varying dimensions, ranging from a day to perhaps five years. Long-term investment planning typically calls for long-term financial planning. A decision whether to take accelerated depreciation, when this is available, for example, can make an enormous difference in the timing of the availability of funds for reuse.[10] Placing such a decision within the framework of cash needs and cash demands over the intervening period helps to clarify the ground for decision.

The plans embodied in the operating statements and balance sheets over the same period, however beautiful they may be, depend for their execution upon a firm's continuing to tie itself into the national system of accounts by meeting the indispensable condition that, daily, its account balance must cover any discrepancy between debits and credits. Plans remain paper without the facilitating medium of cash.

[9] S. M. Mathes and G. C. Thompson, "The Consequences of Tight Money," in The Conference Board *Business Record,* January, 1960, p. 13.

[10] "Last year, U.S. Steel charged $147.5-million for accelerated amortization. Had it charged regular depreciation—$30-million—instead, its cash flow would have been $80-million less. Federal income taxes would have taken $59-million and common dividends $20.7-million of the $118-million difference in the two accruals." *Business Week,* Oct. 13, 1956, p. 96.

Chapter 15

THE CORPORATE PLAN

The Units of Planning

Corporate planning is normally, or nominally, a process which commits the subordinate units of the enterprise to achieve certain objectives which are specified for varying periods of time, from the immediate present to a future distant by five years or more. The commitment may be affirmative, acquiescent, or imposed, depending on whether the subordinate unit has sufficient discretion to feel that its part in the plan has been reached by agreement with its superior, or whether plans for the unit have been made for it though it is accorded the privilege of commenting on the result (with assent expected), or whether its role has been handed to it to play without further discussion. Regardless of the degree of commitment by the parts to the whole, however, the plan—at least in most large corporations—is intended to tie together all phases of the company's activity in an integrated effort to achieve identified goals.

As was noted earlier, plans are usually drawn for periods of varying duration. The most commonly encountered unit of time is the fiscal year, generally dissected into monthly or quarterly segments. A longer-run (two-to five-year) plan has also become fairly standard in the larger firms. Beyond these time limits of comprehensive planning, partial planning may take place for lesser or longer periods. Some operations—the shops in a factory, for example—are governed by daily and weekly objectives. Other operations—the research and engineering division, for instance—may be looking ahead for from ten to twenty-five years. Planning horizons which are shorter or longer than the one- to five-year comprehensive plan are nevertheless geared into it in the sense that they must be consistent with it.

The units of planning are thus both organizational and temporal, operating units and time periods. Block by block they are fitted together to construct a "whole" which consists of a projected course covering all phases of the corporation's activity as far into the future as it seems reasonable to push any particular line of activity, with each unit (organizational and time alike) deriving its significance only from the contribution which it makes to the over-all design. That design is infused with and colored by the company's primary (profit) objective and its secondary and anterior objectives.

Because the relation of their contribution to the over-all design is frequently obscure to supervisors and employees in subordinate levels, the lower the unit in the organizational hierarchy, the more does the plan—the budget—stand as surrogate for the objective itself, so that "making budget" becomes the goal, instead of—as at higher levels in the business—the ends for which the budget simply stands as means.

As a consequence, the importance of the budget in integrating all phases of a company's activities and all levels of its operations is joined by its importance in providing a set of generally understood and (frequently) accepted standards on the strength of which any unit's performance can be judged. This dual aspect of the comprehensive budget makes it an instrument of such significance to the enterprise that only top management can make it effective. No top management which intended to put a comprehensive plan to work could delegate so important a decision to a staff planning unit, or a controller, or a budget director. To do so would be an admission that the plan was not in fact being taken seriously. Top line-management review and approval of the comprehensive plan is therefore a prerequisite to its effectiveness.

Top-management Review

The manner of this review varies from company to company. In some instances the president sits with a small high-level committee which has been responsible for pulling together all the data and underlying schedules on which the summary projections are based. He questions matters which are obscure or are of particular interest to him. He examines the basic assumptions of sales volume, price level, and product mix on which the projections are based. He weighs the profit projection in the light of the circumstances expected to prevail in his markets and in the economy at large. He relates the expected achievement of the time period under review to other time periods, longer or shorter, for which other plans may be in existence or in preparation.

In other cases the review is more extensive and may be spread over several weeks, as managers responsible for principal divisions or departments are called in to develop or defend their formulations. Sometimes the discussions are diffuse and undirected, intended mainly to convince the chief executive that serious effort has gone into the planning process and that his principal subordinates are satisfied with the expected results; he may also use the occasion to inform himself of his company's operations in greater detail and to become better acquainted with his personnel. But sometimes the review sessions are more intense and are designed to uncover where in the company lie the "bottlenecks" which prevent it from doing even better, and to which attention must be paid if future growth is to be made possible.

In some corporations the board of directors constitute a final reviewing authority, but seldom is it expected that they will give the comprehensive budget the scrutiny which the operating management accords it. More commonly they look to the final results of the plan as something of which they approve or disapprove on the assumption that the plan can be effectuated. A proposed budget is not often rejected by a board, but a board may at least ensure that its management does not suffer from complacency about the expected accomplishment.

The comprehensive plan consists, as we have seen, of three basic summary statements with their detailed supporting schedules. First, there is the projected operating statement, with its underlying sales budget (reflecting decisions on product or service line, product or service mix, and product or service prices, as well as marketing organization, inventory policy, and advertising program) and the resulting production schedules (based on a bill of materials and manpower for operations which have usually been put on a standard-cost basis, and incorporating period expenses drawn from flexible budgets after allowing for any changes in technological processes). Second, there is the projected balance sheet, which divides the expected profit between dividends and retained earnings, subsumes the capital budget, with its priorities of investment projects and its recommended means of financing them, and supplies a working capital budget, with its changes in inventory and accounts receivable. Finally, there is the projected flow of funds, indicating what account balance will be needed to offset any lag of credits behind debits in the course of the period's activity and revealing whether the cash component of working capital is adequate for the purpose.

These three projections together constitute the corporation's comprehensive plan, and each must be reviewed in the light of the others. The basic test which is applied is how close to target is the expected profit, a test which for most firms involves relating the net profit figure from the projected operating statement to the investment figure (total, gross or net, or net worth) from the projected balance sheet.

Concern with a firm's financial security frequently leads, too, to analysis of the probable impact on planned profit of changes which circumstances may require in the principal variables with which the firm works. Management may thus examine the consequence of a volume of sales different (higher or lower) from that expected. In this it is facilitated by break-even analysis. (In one survey, thirty-one of fifty companies reported that they made use of "a cost-volume-profit analysis regularly as part of the general process of preparing their budgets." ". . . By study of these relationships in connection with the budget, management can better appraise the profit plan which the budget represents." " 'The line executives are now in a better position to decide intelligently on their course of action if they are not satisfied with the goals indicated in our profit and loss budgets.' " [1]) Similarly there may be consideration of the effect on profit of possible price changes, shifts in the product mix, or direct-cost movements. The shape of these presumably less desirable outcomes may influence plans by introducing a more cautionary element, perhaps in planned investment, or a more strongly supported sales position, as through prior release of a product improvement or a stepped-up promotional campaign.

The seriousness of the review procedure is probably indicated, in a categorical sense, by whether it is customary for top management to accept the initial draft without amendment or with only minor modification. In view of the complexity and significance of a comprehensive plan, some more than perfunctory changes can be expected to result from a more than perfunctory review. A divisional controller of the Philco Corporation comments on his company: "Rarely can the first budget proposal be accepted. As a result, it is generally necessary that several successive reviews take place. We make quite a major thing of these reviews. High level executive attention is given on a serious basis, with all interested parties present, including each department head in turn." [2]

The changes which are made in consequence of such a review are more than a pushing around of figures. Behind each change in the figures there is a change of intended action or policy. A company official writes, "I think it is significant to note that in many cases action was taken because the forecast indicated that revenues and expenses were going to be at unsatisfactory levels."

There is, of course, no guarantee that the changes introduced will lead to any more satisfactory result than the original plan would have produced. The budget is not self-executing. Internally, it relies on a system of reports and controls designed to ensure conformity with its provisions. The assumptions concerning external conditions, the basic premises on which the document rests, cannot, however, be similarly controlled. A change in the economic climate, a shift in competitive positions, a modification of consumer tastes can render invalid the most carefully contrived projections, requiring an adjustment to changed circumstances. We turn now to this phase of business planning.

[1] *The Analysis of Cost-Volume-Profit Relationships,* N.A.C.A., pp. 22, 42.
[2] Bert E. Stromberg, in "Budgeting Policy and Practice in a Decentralized Company," *N.A.A. Bulletin,* October, 1957, sec. 1, p. 42.

Chapter 16

DEPARTURES FROM PLAN

The Relation between Plan and Action

The relationship between corporate plan and action has a common-sense simplicity which dissolves into complexity on closer inspection. A great deal of forethought goes into preparation of the comprehensive budget, which represents the attempted articulation of all phases of a complicated and often decentralized organization. The expenditure of time and effort is made only because it is believed that the focusing of all units of the organization on a common objective, in the achievement of which each must play an agreed-upon role, is a desirable prelude to action: The performance achieves its mark if each conforms to the script rather than extemporizes.

From this point of view the proximate objective of organizational activity is fulfillment of the operating plan. Presumably the behavior of each subunit of the firm is guided by the purpose of realizing the performance which it has helped to spell out in the master budget, and by which the success of its efforts will be judged.

The operating plan is normally geared to some longer-range profit target. In many instances, as we have previously noted, the target is quite precise. In other cases it may be looser, based on a "feel" from the firm's own experience and from the past performance of its rivals. Usually, however, no matter how it is derived, it has some standard by which the acceptability of the planned profit for the coming year may be judged.

Seldom will the operating budget's profit projection be identical with the long-range profit target. The latter is expected to be attained only by averaging the fat years and the lean. In any given year, then, we can assume that the budgeted profit will be either less or more than the long-run goal. It is, however, considered to be the best that can be done under all the circumstances expected to prevail. The firm may actually budget for a loss, but if so, it is only because—in the light of anticipated adverse conditions—a loss cannot be avoided, despite planning and replanning to cut down its magnitude.

Budgetary Control

As long as the assumptions and premises on which the operating budget is based remain approximately valid, the budget plan constitutes the basis for measuring and controlling behavior. This relationship of action to plan is based—as previously noted—on the reasonable expectation that an effort should be made to achieve the results which have been so painstakingly projected. Why plan if it is not expected that the plan will be followed? Thus *control* becomes an integral and essential aspect of the planning process—control in the sense of an organized and systematic effort to be currently informed on how closely action follows plan, and to do whatever seems to be called for to bring performance into line with plan. Without control in this sense planning is an exercise which has some intellectual usefulness but limited organizational significance.

For the purpose of controls, it is variances from plan which are signals to those in authority that corrective action is called for. In some identified respect—whether labor costs, inventory, promotional expense, or sales volume—the organization is going off the track, and unless it is brought back to the track it will not reach its destination. Variances constitute the red lights signaling to management, the engineer, that danger lies ahead unless something is done to meet the situation.

But this is by no means the whole story. Sometimes the plan itself must be changed rather than held to. Circumstances which could not have been foreseen at the time the comprehensive budget was prepared make it infeasible or undesirable to attempt to enforce, or control for, all its constituent parts. The premises on which planning was based are altered, so that the plan ceases to be realistic or effective. Now it is no longer the case that management is concerned with the achievement of the specifics of its original plan and with controlling the variances which appear. New plans must be substituted, and again management is guided by its long-run overall objectives in their preparation. In some instances, these may require only a modification of the existing budget. At other times, the change in the underlying situation may be sufficiently far-reaching to warrant starting the tedious process of preparing a master budget from scratch.

When some part or parts of the original budget are invalidated by unexpected and unfavorable events, what is needed is not "control" in the sense of attempted conformance to plan but compensation in the sense of an effort to offset the adverse circumstances. While management will lower its profit objective for the year only with the greatest reluctance, and under severe pressures, if the objective which it set for itself is to be approached, it must be by different means. "The original annual budget is the budget for the year, but because operations are not static, and economic conditions change continually, it is necessary to adjust the thinking which went into the annual presentation." If the bottom drops out of the market for one of the company's products, how can the sales manager be held responsible for achieving the sales goal he had previously set for his organization? If the union wins a bigger wage increase than had been contemplated at the time costs were computed, how will it be possible to "enforce" labor costs which had been based on an expected lower hourly rate?

In these instances variances from plan signal to management the need for doing something, as before, but now the something which must be done is not directed toward removing the given variance but toward offsetting its impact on the profit position. The action which is taken will almost certainly create other variances—deviations from plan—of its own, but these are planned rather than unexpected, and incurred in the expectation of having a beneficial effect on total performance. "Variances indicate changes from plan which in turn generate new plans and changed activity to obtain desired results."

Thus in one large food processing company sales volume falling short of that which had been projected flagged to management that action must be taken if the profit objective was to be realized. The repercussions were several. For one thing, the price of certain products was reduced. For another, the advertising budget of certain items was increased. The first action created a further unfavorable variance in the revenue account, the second gave rise to an unfavorable variance in the selling expense account, but both these "adverse" variances were created by intent. At the same time, steps were taken to improve the manufacturing cost side of the picture. Changes were made in a few products which lowered costs without affecting quality. Packaging expenses were reduced by changing package designs. The introduction of more economical administrative procedures and improved technological processes was accelerated. All these helped to create favorable variances. The result was to increase the volume of sales by 4.4 per cent over budget. The price reductions and expanded promotional program, which were the cause of the increased volume, held the increase in revenues to 3.3 per cent. But the benefit from spreading overheads over a larger volume, coupled with the cost-control programs in manufacturing, kept the increase in expenditures to 2.1 per cent over budget. The profit objective was thus overrealized.

Results are not always so happy. Sometimes the change in external circumstances may be severe enough to rule out any thought of "compensating" actions by management to achieve an original profit target. Plans are revised, but with more modest expectations. Performance may be tightened to prevent more of a profit slide than conditions demand, but despite the more strenuous effort only a poorer profit performance can be realistically planned for.

On September 29, 1959, we developed a total company forecast for 1960 of $75,000,000. As the steel strike wore on, it became evident to us that the effects of it were going to mean a permanent loss to the economy and hence to our company which would carry over into 1960, and so, about November 15, we lowered our expectations for 1960 to $72,000,000 and this became our official forecast for 1960. As is only too well written in history now it appears that the rosy forecasts for 1960 were somewhat over-blown. The plant and equipment expenditure rate did not come up as anticipated in the economic forecasts; the FRB Index fell short of it and in retrospect it now seems clear that everyone had much more inventory than the economists were telling us. About May 1, 1960, after our first six months was completed, we developed a new estimate for the total year 1960 at $68,000,000. Our incoming order rate has continued to weaken, however, and on August 1, 1960, it looked to us as though our year [would] come out closer to $61,000,000 and that is our estimate as we see it now with the year end one month away. . . .

We regard this overall result as an unsatisfactory result from the standpoint of the forecast. Of course, we adjusted as the year went off but even in preparing the second half budgets it now seems evident that we didn't adjust enough. The forecast at the beginning of the year was plainly too high. It seems we have a good deal of company in this. Actually we felt that we had taken a much more conservative forecast than some of the very rosy economic forecasts would have otherwise indicated our business would go to in 1960. We ourselves thought the steel strike was going to have a much more serious down dragging effect than many of the forecasts that we read. But now it seems that even so, we have over-forecast. While as I say we did make adjustments during the year, our final sales this year (acquisitions excluded) are going to come out about 15% below the final forecast made at the beginning of the year.

The invalidation of the premises on which the operating budget was based need not always reflect a change in external circumstances. Sometimes things go wrong within the firm, or timing is off. A vice-president for finance provides an example.

As an example of the ramifications of budget changes, it was anticipated in our original year's budget that a certain new product would be available for delivery to customers by mid-year and, on this basis, plans were approved to increase the staff of sales and installation specialists who handle this type of product. At the time of our first budget revision in March, a change in product development schedules made it apparent that this new product would not be available for delivery to customers before the end of the year. Accordingly, the plans to increase our sales staff were postponed and a number of other actions in connection with the introduction of this new product were rescheduled and re-budgeted. Certainly this is not an unusual situation, but occurs regularly. . . . It illustrates the manner in which periodic budget revisions are used to coordinate the various activities of a business and to guard against wasted or duplicated efforts.

A change in plans is not always in response to a deteriorating situation, nor does it always result in a worse performance than planned. Sometimes the reverse proves true. Circumstances which led management to contemplate a difficult year at the time the budget was prepared may turn brighter as the year unfolds. A poor profit showing (below long-run target) may be helped if market or competitive conditions improve during the year to permit an increase in product prices. An example is provided by the automobile industry. Senator Estes Kefauver, as chairman of a Senate Subcommittee on Antitrust and Monopoly, is questioning Theodore Yntema, vice-president for finance of the Ford Motor Company: [1]

> SENATOR KEFAUVER. Mr. Yntema, may I ask you to turn to what happened to your 1957 models in 1956. You have the figures there. I want to read this and ask you to comment on it.

> > On September 29, 1956, the Ford Motor Co. released its suggested price list for its 1957 models before any other member of the industry released their prices
> > Although rumors in the industry had indicated that prices would be increased 5 to 7 per cent, Ford announced an average price increase of 2.9 per cent, ranging from $1 to $104 on 1957 models. The heaviest increase fell in the lowest priced Ford cars. . . .

> That quote is from Business Week. . . .

> > On October 15, 1956, 2 weeks after Ford announced its price increases, Chevrolet division of General Motors announced its own price increases. The prices averaged 6.1 per cent higher than on 1956 models, ranging from $74 to $102.
> > The General Motors' price list was "warmly received by other car makers who, nearing their own pricing deadline, had to account for heavy investments in manufacturing and tooling changes but at the same time were concerned lest they over price their competitors."
> > One week following the announcement of Chevrolet's prices, the Ford Co. revised upward its 3-week-old suggested price list. The new list boosted the prices on 13 models and reduced prices on 5 others, bringing the Ford prices substantially in

---

[1] *Administered Prices, Hearings before the Subcommittee on Antitrust and Monopoly*, U.S. Senate, 85th Cong., 2d Sess., part 6, "Automobiles," pp. 2691–2693.

line with the Chevrolet prices. Besides bringing list prices in line with Chevrolet, Ford also brought dealer discount rates down from 25 per cent to 24 per cent, making it the same as Chevrolet's.

That is from Ward's Automotive Reports. . . .

How did it happen that 3 weeks later you decided to get your prices exactly in line with General Motors' prices?

MR. YNTEMA. Mr. Chairman, we did not get them exactly in line. I remember that very well, and I would like to tell you what happened. I wish you had been there and seen it. We came out in the beginning of the 1957 model year with a brand new car, the 1957 Ford, and that resulted in our getting before the year was out substantially higher registrations than Chevrolet.

That was a car that cost us a great deal more. It was a bigger car and a more expensive car. We were also engaged in an expansion program. There were some unusual costs involved. And I remember very well the Ford division studied the problem at great length. It came into the central staff and was reviewed as usual.

I remember going over it—and I cannot quote the detailed figures—but I remember quite well my opinion that the rise was not nearly enough to cover our costs, our increased costs, and I personally had violent objections to it. There was a great deal of discussion in the executive committee with respect to this matter, and there were persons with very strong differences of opinion.

I thought that we were making a mistake. . . . In spite of the increases in price, that one and the subsequent one, . . . our profit margins did not improve in the fourth quarter, and they continued to deteriorate during 1957, and I had personally thought we were making a serious mistake.

There were others who thought the same. The preponderance of opinion was, however, that we should not raise our prices by the amount of our costs because our competitor had a car that was in the third model year, and we thought it quite possible that they might shade very considerably. Our principal competitor came out with higher prices than we expected. We had a better product than they did. We knew we could beat them in the market with it. We wanted to make a decent profit, and so what we did was to raise our prices up to a point where we would still have a very substantial competitive advantage over them.

As it turned out, we did. We sold more Fords than they sold Chevrolets. I think if any one of you had sat in on the whole circumstance, that you probably would have done the same kind of thing. We were not covering our costs, even the two combined increases did not cover our increased cost, and this is not a matter of opinion. As I say, it was a very close decision in the first place as to what to do, and finally what we did was to revise it and to add something that still did not cover our total costs. Now, that is the whole story as it happened.

In cases like these, management's interest lies not in conforming to an original plan drafted in the light of what seemed possible at the time, but in seizing such opportunities as present themselves to raise the level of the firm's performance. Where the favorable opportunity is modest in its effect on the budget, the results may simply show up as overfulfillment of the original budget. But in circumstances where a substantial additional sales volume is possible, entailing substantially increased output, a whole new budget may have to be written.

Another example from the controller of a large food processing corporation illustrates that such a favorable change in external factors may require budget revisions even though the results do not conduce to a higher profit for the current budget year, as long as it promises more for the future.

> The original budget for this product called for a test market operation during Fiscal 1960, with a relatively small loss expected. As the year progressed it became apparent that test market results were favorable. Subsequent quarterly projections called for increasing sales volumes and revenues to expand the test market to a full scale introduction in several major eastern markets. Corresponding increases in Marketing expense were planned as the year progressed. The net effect of these changes was that the loss for this product was substantially higher than originally budgeted—the price of an acceleration in our rate of introduction for the product.

There is still another kind of situation which renders the "control" concept inapplicable. The comprehensive budget is the end result of corporate planning for the period in question, usually a year. As such it provides guidelines for all those in the organization, integrating the parts into an effective working whole. But the development of such a plan—to be made effective, let us say, on July 1 of each year—does not invoke a moratorium on management planning until it is time to prepare the next comprehensive annual budget. Planning is continuous. The results of continuous planning may not, indeed, affect the current comprehensive budget; they may relate to the period beyond it. But there is no necessary reason why this should be so, nor is there any reason why the existence of an operating plan should preclude management's introducing new lines of development before the current plan has expired.

The more energetic and imaginative the management, the more is it likely that new ideas or fresh activities the desirability of which, formerly only dimly or uncertainly perceived, has suddenly become clearly apparent, or the means for accomplishing which, previously vague and unclear, have now been found—the more is it likely that such ideas will come to fruition recurringly throughout the year. Why delay their introduction? An impatient and aggressive management will not be likely to accept the existence of a twelve-month budget as adequate reason for postponement. The plan must be redrafted to accommodate the new idea. "Most (budget) changes result from a change in plan made at the top management level. For example, a new advertising program to meet competition; or, to tie into a new product campaign; or, decisions to add a new function or enlarge an old one for some change in top management policy thinking."

No variances signal the need for or desirability of making such changes in the budget. These occur independently of performance, as a consequence of the fact that effective planning is continuous in nature, and the further fact that most top managements are impatient to implement plans which promise the sooner realization of long-range objectives. These actions create their own variances from the original budget—intentionally, and not simply with the intent of thereby facilitating achievement of the year's profit target, but because it is believed they will conduce to the company's future interest.

What the budget framework does, however, is to underscore the fact that in order to get coordinated action on some such front as a new product or a new marketing organization or program, at some point the planning process must extend into the budgets of all the related and relevant departments and units, whether as a modification of their existing budget or as an exception to it. If as a modification, then the new (revised) budget becomes the basis for control. If an exception, then the old (existing) budget remains effective in the unaffected areas, and retains its status as a standard by which the conformance of action to plan may be judged.

For one of several reasons, then, variances may arise which cannot be "controlled." The budget-plan itself is shown to be no longer workable—because the external premises on which it was based have changed, because actions taken in an effort to achieve profit targets in the light of changed circumstances create their own further variances, and because continuous planning generates internal changes which invalidate the original plan.

Budget Revision

In the light of the foregoing, it may seem strange that corporate opinions differ on the question of whether budgets, once approved, may undergo formal revision. One might reasonably assume that most managements would take for granted the necessity of altering the figures to conform to the facts, during the course of the period to which they apply, if adverse variances emerge and prove intransigent because conditions underlying the plan have changed. But such is not the case. The issue is not a trivial one. If revision is too readily accepted, the budget loses its incentive effect. Underrealization of target should prompt the unit facing it to intensify its effort. On the other hand, budgets which are missed by a wide margin may equally lose their motivating force and be branded as unreal; to provide a standard by which performance can meaningfully be measured, they must hold out the possibility of realization.

This critical question of whether or when to revise has been answered in a number of ways. There is general agreement, however, that even when revision is permitted, it is a step not taken lightly and is permitted only after earnest efforts to achieve budget have been made.

> In a large organization such as [ours], operating through hundreds of units located throughout the country, there are inevitably instances where a number of units do not perform according to plan for various reasons. In such instances, management action is taken at the appropriate level to define the problem and to obtain corrective action. In general, the effort is directed toward raising performance to the planned level. There is of course the alternative of reducing budgets to new performance levels, but this would be done in recognition of external influences rather than for the purpose of conforming a planned objective to a probable result.

The issue is not important in the case of minor variances, though the interpretation of what is minor varies, too, from company to company. ("Our plans always allow for a reasonable amount of fluctuation in results from forecasted levels." "Because we do not consider variances of less than 5% to be significant, no detailed analysis of such variances is normally prepared.") When variances pass beyond whatever level the management of a company considers tolerable, however, and persist despite pressures to correct them, the question must be faced whether to allow the original figures to stand or to modify them in the light of performance.

There are some managements which hold fast to an original budget plan:

> Our operating budgets, whether on the divisional and subsidiary level or on the consolidated level, are never revised during a fiscal period. Once established for a given fiscal year, they are used as a constant yardstick throughout that year.

> We never adjust our budget forecast downward because of poor performance. I suspect that if we were in the steel business [says this vice-president of a firm supplying printed business forms] and only operating at 50% of capacity for long periods, we would build a budget accordingly.
> It is our belief that the budget has more value if we do not adjust it. The comparison at the end of the year is more realistic if the

difference is properly analyzed and used as a guide in making the forecast for the new year.

Our management believes there are very few things that are non-controllable if you look at the problem on a broad scale, and we normally expect problems that might, in themselves, be considered non-controllable to be compensated for by improved activities in other areas.

In general, once our budget is established we do not change it during the year. This is particularly true in regard to sales volume.

We always measure performance against the original budget.

It is a rare occasion when we make any material revisions to our annual budgets. Much time, effort and analysis is devoted to the preparation of our annual budgets and once they are adopted their implementation entails commitments and courses of action which are not practical to deviate from materially within the period of time involved in an annual budget. It has been our experience that unless there occurs a major variance in forecast of sales no material revisions in budgeted expenditures are required. [This from the treasurer of a major distilling corporation.]

Much more common, however, is the compromise which takes the form of a terminological distinction. "Budgets" are held firm, despite variances for any reason, and original targets are held up to the operating personnel as the measure by which their performance will be judged. By this means the incentive effect, it is believed, will be retained. On the other hand, as a more realistic guide to top management, "forecasts" of expected performance—which in effect constitute unpublicized revisions to the budget—are prepared periodically. Thus, as one vice-president for finance explains, the term "forecast" is used to refer to the "periodically revised estimate of sales, earnings, etc., for the current year (the term 'revised budget' is not used here)."

We do not adjust budgets to new levels, but during the fiscal year monthly forecasts of year-end results are made with respect to revenues, expenses and earnings.

The budgets themselves are set annually, and are not revised for the entire year unless a very major change in uncontrollable costs takes place. We could almost say that annual budgets, once established, are never changed. Forecasts of net earnings, cash position, etc., are updated to show us where we are going for the remainder of the year.

Once the profit plan for the year is established, it is not changed in response to performance variance. The plan continues as the basis for measurement of performance throughout the year. Periodically, current forecasts of anticipated results are prepared to keep management informed of our current outlook. Likewise, operating budgets, which form the basis for the cost and expense sections of the profit plan, are not changed as a result of performance.

Our annual plan is built in the fall of the year preceding the plan year. Each major section of our organization develops a goal and a commitment for accomplishment, which, in turn, becomes a commitment for the company to the Board of Directors. While this plan basically remains fixed throughout the year, and comparisons are made each month of our performance vs. plan, major divisional heads are given the opportunity to submit revised estimates during the year of their latest estimate of profit contribution, taking into consideration those facts that have changed significantly or could not have been foreseen at the time the plan was developed. These latest estimates give corporate management a picture of where we are and how we expect to progress against the original plan, but original commitments remain firm.

We consider our budgets as a plan of operation and when circumstances arise which indicate the need for a change of plans, we take steps to make the necessary changes. These adjustments may be only in the form of conversations or memoranda between responsible executives. Our formal reports, however, retain the original budgeted amounts. On some occasions when a major down-turn in general business conditions has made it evident that our revenues will be substantially lower than budgeted, we prepare revised budgets in light of new conditions. Such revisions have generally been made during the first half of the year. However, we continue to report our operations in comparison to the original budgets and show the revised budget as a footnote so that management has two yardsticks of performance.

After receiving final approval, our annual budget which is made for a calendar year in advance by months does not change. Throughout the year it remains our goal. However, this does not mean that we do not recognize in our analysis variances resulting from changed conditions and factors not recognized in the preparation of the annual budget. . . . During the year, certain items are recognized as being substantial in effect on the results reported on our Statement of Consolidated Net Earnings or on the Profit Contribution Statements of our operating divisions. When approved by the divisions managers and the Controller, these items become adjustments to our budget for the remainder of the year. The budget, as adjusted for these items, we call our forecast for the remaining months.

We do not change profit plans during a given fiscal year. The original profit plan, or budget, is adhered to during a complete fiscal year and variations from this basic original budget are explained monthly at the budget review meeting. At the end of six months, and at the end of the third quarter of each year we do prepare new estimates for the year but these estimates are not used as measuring points for subsequent monthly variations. However, these estimates do give an up-to-date picture of the most recent thinking as to what will happen to profits and other planned items for the fiscal year.

Our annual budget is established in March of each year. Following that, on a quarterly basis, i.e., June, September, and December, re-estimates are made which serve to report the progress being made toward the attainment of the annual budget. The purpose here is to have the opportunity to take whatever corrective action may be required as soon as possible during the year. These quarterly re-estimates, however, do not replace the original budget as the target or goal for the year.

We feel that a constant revision of budgets weakens the idea of making a plan and doing all we can to achieve it. We, however, supplement each monthly performance report with a revised forecast for the year which is used as a guide to top management and the Board of Directors, but it is only when this figure varies considerably from budget that there would be any thought to revise the budget formally.

As the last comment above suggests, companies which normally retain original budgets as targets while revising forecasts as the basis for top management information and action may occasionally make a formal budget revision when the deviation from plan is marked. In this respect they merge into the group which adopts the practice of revising the budget only when there is so major a departure from it that it ceases to act as effective guide or control.

Operating budgets are revised only when significant changes have occurred in expenses or revenues. Labor contracts, major increases in the price of materials, or erratic adjustments in general business conditions affecting sales may result in a revision of our operating study, providing such changes are significant.

If unfavorable performance develops, we make every effort to improve operations and to attempt to meet original estimates. At the same time, we are realistic and adjust our forecasts to actual performance levels then expected during the course of the year. In most cases, we let original budgets stand, but for financial and top management guidance, provide a second "forecast" as a basis for evaluation.

Accordingly, it is not our normal practice to revise budgets during the course of the year. However, if variances of considerable magnitude develop, we may undertake semi-annual revision. Budget reviews are conducted quarterly, and normally we evaluate performance in terms of then current expectations. In general, we have found that original budgets prove to be at least as accurate as those made during the course of a year when pessimism may unduly reduce expectations.

Generally, our budget remains unchanged and serves as a yardstick for the year. Against this yardstick, actual results are measured monthly. All variations, whether favorable or unfavorable, in revenue and/or cost are analyzed and the reasons for the variations noted. Only in the case of unanticipated major changes in volumes to be transported [writes this vice-president of a pipeline transporting petroleum products] and those costs related directly to throughput levels, or extraordinary costs of an emergency nature such as other than routine repairs to pipelines or pumping facilities, are changes made in the budget.

There is no policy of scheduled revision of the original budget. As a practical matter, however, the budget is occasionally revised where actual circumstances are different enough to make the budget ineffective as an operating plan. This adjustment rarely occurs more than once a year, usually after five or six months. All income statement classifications (and most of the underlying detail) are estimated for the remainder of the year. The sum of that forecast and actual experience to date becomes the revised budget for the fiscal year.

When actual performance begins to vary, either in revenues or expenditures, from planned performance to the point where the plans can no longer be considered as operating guides, then we change the plans. This does not mean, however, that we would not make comparisons to the original plans at the end of a period; we do.

We do not make regular revisions to a fiscal year budget. We do, however, make regular revisions when conditions have changed to the extent that the value of the budget is endangered. We do make forecasts each month for the next three month period. These are used as a short range planning device.

We do not believe in periodic budget revisions once the annual plan has been approved. The budget is never revised because it cannot be achieved. The only condition under which the budget is revised is when it no longer serves as a planning medium for conditions as they actually exist.

Our normal procedure on budgets is as follows:
a. In December of each year, a master budget, covering every phase of the Company's operations, is prepared for the four quarters of the coming year.
b. At the end of each quarter, a profit and loss forecast only is prepared for the succeeding four quarters. For example, in March, the last three quarters of the current year plus the first quarter of the following year is forecast.
c. These quarterly forecasts are used to determine the direction

we anticipate going from the master budget plus a preliminary look at the following year. If these quarterly forecasts indicate any drastic change from the master budget, it may require a complete new master budget. If no drastic change is indicated, programs will be instituted in an effort to achieve the original master budget.

Our policy towards budget changes is as follows [writes the president of a major New York bank]: we effect such adjustments only in response to unanticipated changes in uncontrollable factors which will have a major impact on earnings. Specifically, these changes are generally made when a change in the prime rate occurs.

In contrast to those companies which seek to preserve original budgets, or which revise them only under considerable pressure, are those managements which make a point of frequent revision. In some instances this is at periodic intervals.

While forecasts do not need to be modified at the drop of a hat to reflect a projection of some isolated incident, they do require periodic revisions to reflect current trends which may reasonably be expected to continue. We revise our yearly budget the latter part of May and August. These revisions are computed on basis of actual results for the first four months and seven months, respectively, and the estimated volume of traffic [writes the president of a major Western railroad] for balance of current year, taking into consideration business conditions in general and the Government and our outside agencies' reports covering the estimated movements of grain and grain products in our territory.

The original Operating Budget for the coming year is prepared in December [explains the vice-president of an integrated gas system]. This "Original" budget is a refinement of the data incorporated in a preliminary estimate and includes updated information based on the most current thinking, again using gas requirements and supplies as shown by the long range budget.

A revised Operating Budget is prepared in May, incorporating actual figures for the months of January through April and revised estimates for the remaining eight months of the year including the gas requirements and supply levels budgeted in the new long range budget.

Monthly Operating Budget Comparisons are compiled showing the extent and reasons for variations from budgeted figures for both the month and year-to-date periods. The Budget Comparison compares actual versus original figures for the first four months of the year and actual versus revised budget figures for the remaining eight months. It also makes provision for indicating anticipated differences for the remaining months of the year to give effect to the latest developments.

[We] require quarterly revisions to the Budget of Earnings showing the most current quarter in detail, by months, and the remaining quarters in total. . . . As we progress through the year the revision to the most current quarter becomes the control budget against which actual results are compared.

In some companies revision is not only periodic but results in what may be termed a continuous budget—one which is always up-to-date and always extends into the future over the same time span.

> Our forecasts are made approximately every six months for the next year and a half or two years of operations. Thus we never operate for an entire year under one single forecast.

> The Budget Estimates are set up on a quarterly basis for a four quarter period (this provides planning for one year in advance). Each six months, the approaching two quarters are revised and then the forthcoming two quarters are originated.

> Our budget is revised quarterly not only to reflect changes which may be beyond our control such as the higher costs of raw materials but also to adjust to whatever conditions under management control have been brought about by management decisions in the previous quarter. Every quarterly change in the budget also results in its extension one year in advance so that at the end of each quarter, we have, in essence, a new budget for the next twelve months.

The use of flexible budgets constitutes one form of automatic if not continuous revision of plan, to adjust it to performance levels pending more calculated measures which may be undertaken to improve performance and attain original targets. Under flexible budgeting, expense budgets have been predetermined for any level of sales which eventuates. Actual revenues determine the permissible level of expenditures, for control purposes, regardless of any actions which may be taken to bring sales into line with original expectations. Especially in companies which believe there is little they can do to bolster declining sales is it likely that emphasis will be placed on a prompt flexible adaptation of costs to fluctuating volume. It is said of one steel company that foremen have been trained to respond to a decline in production with almost immediate layoffs. Manning tables are maintained indicating changes in required personnel for every 1 per cent change in output. This responsive action is stimulated in part by an incentive program which penalizes the foreman who delays in initiating layoffs; any failure to cut costs with volume is money out of his own pocket.[2]

Under flexible budgeting, the revenue and the expenditure halves are

[2] One might reasonably raise the question whether training foremen to control costs by such prompt personnel actions does not fly in the face of the unmistakable trend to convert hourly labor to a salaried basis and to treat salaried workers as a fixed cost (at least in the short run). This does not necessarily follow, however. A budgetary official in one of the more enlightened "little steel" companies suggested that the problem could be met in at least two ways.

1. Budgetary control of costs, under a system of flexible costs, requires planning—

treated differently. If revenues deviate from plan, the variance is measured by the original budget figures. At the same time the new (actual) revenue figures automatically introduce a new expenditures budget appropriate to the new sales level, and expense variances are measured by these new figures rather than the original cost figures. If the actual sales level is considered unacceptable, corrective actions may be undertaken. If these are successful, pushing sales to higher levels, the new sales figures once more automatically carry with them a revision in the permissible costs.

Flexible budgeting is extensively used by American corporations, and many companies which reported that it was their policy to hold fast to original budgets, regardless of performance, were implicitly (occasionally explicitly) assuming a flexible *cost* budget for control purposes. It is the sales or revenue budget, which in itself sets a target, to which they hold firm for incentive effects. Few managements consider costs to have been adequately controlled even if they are held to original budget figures, if the volume of output has declined.

Where costs are revised in this manner to adjust to the actual sales level developing, and where at the same time only a limited attempt is made to meet adverse variances from sales budgets, due generally to competitive restraints, the result is to conform the budget to actual performance. Under these circumstances the budget becomes useful to keep costs in line with revenues, coordinating the several parts of the operation, but it ceases to serve as a target or goal in the attempted achievement of which management expects to manipulate certain variables under its control.

> In general it is rather difficult to improve sales performance when we are falling below forecast because actually we are trying to achieve maximum sales every minute of every day anyway. I suppose that some companies select a certain segment of a market and are able to set their sales courses to some predetermined figure. We are in a number of very competitive industries and generally our sales goals are pretty much the maximum we can get within such competitive industries. Accordingly if we do not make [achieve] our forecasts there is little we can do to do much about improving the performance and hence the adjustment in the business falls in the area [of adjusting] the budgets to the new performance levels.

---

not callousness. Reductions in force can often be effected by proper attention to labor turnover; excess labor can be trimmed through normal attrition.

2. To the extent that turnover is inadequate to control costs, greater flexibility in the use of labor (a concession the unions can be expected to make in exchange for employment security) should permit transferring workers from direct production to indirect projects—not make-work, but necessary activities for which management would otherwise have to lay out additional funds if they were not handled in this manner. A "shelf" of such "private works" projects could be accumulated, he believes, just as with public works, to be undertaken during "rainy seasons."

On the basic question of whether to revise or retain original budgets, then, it is probably correct to summarize practice as follows:

Most companies revise sales budgets downwards and expense budgets upwards only with great reluctance, holding to original estimates as long as they retain any semblance of being achievable goals. When revision is necessary, it is often made in the form of a new "forecast" which is supplementary to the budget without replacing it. This reluctance to revise is in part due to a desire to motivate the organization to achieve as much as possible of the original objective and in part due to the considerable effort required to prepare a new comprehensive budget.

Downward adjustments in cost figures in line with lower revenues are commonly made through use of flexible budgets, as a necessary means of maintaining control over costs. Since variable costs can be predetermined to fit varying volume, they do not entail much of an effort to put into effect. These cost revisions do not, however, imply any change in the sales or revenue estimates, which are often retained as targets.

Some companies (probably an increasing number) are moving toward continuous revision and extension of budgets, so that the start of each "period" (a quarter, a half-year) sees a budget revised in detail for the coming period and in less detail for the remainder of the budget plan's perpetual time horizon. In these cases it is believed that revision is necessary to set realistic goals and to impose acceptable controls.

In general, managements seek to manipulate the variables within their control to bring adverse performance into line with budget. In highly competitive situations, however, budgets are likely to be brought into line with performance.

Relation of Revision to Control

The fact that budgets seldom remain firm for their nominal lifetime, and that the assumptions on which they are based are sure to be belied by the march of events, and that the planning process is more or less continuous and may be expected to project new dimensions into the shape of the current plan—none of these things invalidate the control function of budgets. They complicate their manner of use for this purpose and may even reduce their usefulness for this purpose, but it is unnecessary to view such instabilities in the plan as erasing the possibility of conforming corporate behavior to given objectives. As long as some plan exists, control consists in "a disciplined effort to follow a plan or explain deviations from it." [3]

[3] James L. Pierce, controller, A. B. Dick Co., "Budgets and People: A Positive Approach," in *Guides to Modern Financial Planning*, A.M.A. Financial Management Series, no. 104, 1953, p. 7.

The significance of variances from plan depends in part on the level of authority of the manager who reviews them. From the standpoint of the manager in whose unit it occurs, the variance always invites additional effort to make the original plan effective. Control over variances is an operating and localized responsibility. Inability to "make plan" requires explanation. From the standpoint of higher authority, however, variances may invite a replanning or rebudgeting of a major phase of the company's operations or of the totality of its operations. This is a centralized, not a localized, responsibility.

The comprehensive plan, it will be recalled, consists of a projected operating statement, a projected balance sheet, and a projected flow of funds. It may be assumed, at first inspection, that one effect of variances from the plan will be to unbalance these accounts. This is true only in a particular sense, however. As any accountant knows, the books of a company always balance ex post. A company can always cast up a balance sheet. Failure of revenues to materialize as expected, or an increase in costs above a planned level, will reduce operating earnings and will affect such balance-sheet entries as inventories and retained earnings. These outcomes, that is to say, affect the level and the manner in which the firm's accounts balance. They involve departures from the level and composition of the company's balances as planned, ex ante, in the comprehensive budget. It is not that variances unbalance the accounts but that they give rise ex post to a difference balance than had been planned ex ante.

Inflows and outflows must always meet somewhere and somehow as long as a company continues to operate—by the accumulation of debts or the using up of capital or a reliance on a general line of credit, or in some other manner. The important objective from management's point of view, however, is to make the level and composition of the balance come out where management would most prefer it, in the light of all the surrounding circumstances.

We may reasonably assume that the original projected budget constitutes such a favorable balance. It sets forth an end result—a target—which is viewed as being both feasible and desirable. When variances materialize, this simply means that the actual balance is something different from the one projected. But *some* balance exists—at some level and of some composition of inflows and outflows, assets and liabilities—since at any moment the firm is *always* "in balance." What is important to establish, however, is whether the balance of the moment ought to be accepted.

To do this requires a determination of whether the variances are of a kind which can be corrected (if adverse; consolidated if favorable) to permit retention and eventual accomplishment of the original target, or whether they are sufficiently intractable to require replanning. If the latter case, then management must substitute—in effect, if not in formal practice—a new budget, which is less favorable (if the variances were adverse) than the original projected budget but usually more favorable than the one which had actually emerged. We may call this the preferred balance.

This preferred balance becomes in effect the new projected balance from which—within the next time period—the actual balance can be expected to deviate. On the strength of the variances occurring, once again management will have to determine whether to seek to control performance to achieve the (once modified) budget as it stands or to revise further the budget to establish a new preferred balance. The fact that in many companies only at periodic intervals of a year is a new comprehensive budget formally adopted, with the more elaborate participative and review procedures described in earlier chapters, does not mean that in practice a "new" budget may not already have been adopted a dozen times (that is, monthly) in the intervening year. Repeatedly the actual balance may deviate from the projected balance, occasioning the drafting of a preferred balance, which (even if only informally, or at top management levels) becomes the new projected balance from which the actual balance will again deviate, perhaps giving rise to a new preferred balance, and so on successively. That these changes may occur piecemeal (as through flexible budgeting rather than by comprehensive revision) does not negate this frequency of change, any more than does the practice of labeling revisions by another name ("forecasts," for example).

We shall examine this continuing interplay between planning and action a little more fully after we take a look at the nature of the variances which are the proximate motivating influences, whether the consequence of external events that upset prior calculations, or internal decisions designed to offset external events, or management actions for which no previous allowance had been made. It is enough now to recognize that at any time, some budget (whether original or revised) exists by which performance can be judged, and deviations from which signal the need for either further control or further revision.

Revenue and Cost Variances

A "variance" occurs whenever an actual money item (receipt or expenditure) differs from the amount which had been expected and budgeted for that item. Thus every line entry in a comprehensive budget may give rise to a variance.

In terms of over-all performance, the variance about which most managements are especially concerned is in gross or net profit. Concentration on variances in such summary items frequently conceals variances in the individual line items which give rise to the over-all result, however. (". . . I have been surprised by the minor variation we have experienced between annual plans and actual results for the over-all company. Obviously there might be considerable variation for a particular product division, but the pluses and minuses average out so that the total variation of the over-all is comparatively small." "With respect to recent fiscal years, our actual revenue has been within 5% of the original forecast figure. While this has been true on an over-all basis, it has not been true with individual product lines wherein our forecast has deviated from actual performance by as much as, plus or minus, 30%.") For control purposes, it is necessary to go behind the summary or over-all figure to ascertain the effectiveness of the performance of the individual units or activities. That a poor performance in one division or department or shop or office has been offset by a superior performance in some other unit does not mean that the poor performance should go uncorrected or unattended.

The essence of control lies in tracing back the causes of variances as far as it is analytically feasible to do so. In some companies this form of analysis has become very highly developed so that it is possible, for example, to ascertain that 0.5 per cent of the 2.3 variance in the production costs of shop X is attributable to the below-standard yield of material Y, for the given volume produced.

In more general terms, we may say that profit variances are traceable to variances in revenues and expenditures, and that variances in revenues are chiefly resolved into variances in volume of sales, product prices, and product mix (with varying profit margins), while variances in expenditures are attributable to variances in materials costs (yield plus materials prices), in labor costs (efficiency plus wage rates), in manufacturing overhead expenses, and in selling and administrative expenses.

On the revenue side, the following comments by company financial officers illustrate the kind of variances encountered:

> Actual revenues (Net Sales) exceeded the budget by 3.1% reflecting a general pickup in business in most divisions not previously anticipated. This was offset by loss of revenues in two divisions due to lower prices and a fall off of volume of business in one division.

> In our last fiscal year, . . . actual revenues were 2.1% less than those budgeted. Sales of some of our principal products were higher than anticipated in budget while sales of other products were lower than planned. Price weakness in the industry where considerable overcapacity exists was probably the principal reason for actual revenues falling below budget. Some price increases anticipated in the budget were not realized and, in the case of other products, price pressure from competition brought lower net sales prices than expected.

> Actual revenues varied favorably from the budget by 4.4% due mainly to higher than planned sales of packaged air conditioning equipment. Causes of this increase were an abnormally hot summer coupled

with a high rate of residential construction. The favorable picture in residential construction caused, to a lesser extent, an above-budgeted volume pattern in residential heating equipment. Offsetting this increase was a slightly lower than budgeted performance in our capital goods businesses, notably the so-called "big air conditioning" and also our power generation equipment. The major cause of these deviations was selling price—as contrasted with physical volume.

Our most recent fiscal year operations resulted in net earnings being about 9% greater than forecast. Sales volume was about as planned but a selling price increase late in the year, which had not been contemplated, increased revenues above original expectations.

Our product revenues were 1.7% less than budget. .6% of this was because of a decrease in volume; 1.1% was because of lower prices. Both of these factors were the result of general trends in the industry.

Officials of two banks report on their company's receipts for a recent year:

With respect to our most recent fiscal year, actual revenues exceeded the original budget by about 7%. The higher revenues were due principally to interest rates moving up more rapidly than we had expected and higher loan volume due to deposits, mostly in the time category, exceeding expectations.

The tabulations below indicate the extent percentagewise by which actual revenues . . . for the calendar year varied from results which were incorporated in our Plan:

Interest earnings:	
Loans	+ 10.4%
Securities	− 16.0
Total interest	+ 4.1
Commissions from service functions	+ 9.5
Other operating income	+ 25.2
Total revenues	+ 5.8

An increase in the level of loans outstanding over Plan amounts, combined with a rise in interest rates, particularly in the latter half of the year, was responsible for the over-variation in loan interest income. To accommodate this higher level of customer borrowings, securities had to be liquidated and interest income from this source, as a consequence, was reduced below Plan expectations. Commissions from service functions substantially exceeded Plan, chiefly because of a much greater than expected volume of activity in the transfer and issuance of stock certificates of companies for whom we act as agent, and in large special jobs for corporations involving stock subscriptions, stock dividends, exchanges and the like which were not anticipated in Plan. While other operating income showed the largest variance percentagewise from Plan, the dollar amount involved was relatively small compared to interest earnings and commissions and deserves no special comment.

Two companies report product mix effects:

Gross Revenues (sales) were 5.79% below originally projected sales for the calendar year. The chief reason was that the forecast antici- pated a different product and size mix than was actually sold. Total tonnage was only 2.8% below the projection.

Our sales forecast came within a few percentage points of the actual situation. Due to an adverse product mix, our earnings results fell about 15% below the forecast.

Similar comments relating to expenditures variances provide an indica- tion of the range of reasons for costs falling below or rising above those budgeted:

Expenditures for the period were approximately 2¼% lower than originally anticipated. This was primarily due to lower than expected average prices paid for raw materials and certain packaging supplies, principally cans and cartons. In addition, an anticipated cost reduction program, started in 1958, produced greater economies than had been forecasted.

Operating expenses were less than budgeted by 3.2% due to a more favorable fuel purchasing position resulting from a lesser effect of a new miners' wage agreement on coal prices than expected, and an over-provision for the repairs to major equipment which had failed just prior to the start of the year.—*An electric utility.*

We experienced some extreme variances from budgeted costs in operations where radically new production methods were employed.

Expenditures exceeded budgeted expenses by a net of .78%. How- ever, the various expense classifications fluctuated from 1.03% under- expended to 3.50% overexpended. Variances were due mainly to minor changes or occurrences not anticipated when the budget was prepared.

Operating expenses were 3.4% over the original budget, due prin- cipally to the new wage agreement. It is the policy of the company to prepare the original budget each year without consideration of the wage increase that may be granted in the renewal of the union agree- ment. The original budget is revised after the union agreement has been signed and the new labor cost has been estimated.

Expenditures on a cash outlay basis were 10½% above original forecast for the following reasons:
(*A*) We advanced a portion of our capital expenditure program. This increased our cash outlay 2% over the total originally forecasted.
(*B*) Selling and warehousing expenses for the year were greater than anticipated resulting in a cash outlay 1.8% over that forecasted originally.

(C) Higher material and labor costs in manufacturing increased our cash outlay 1.9% over the total forecast, adjusted for the fact that sales were higher than anticipated and therefore outlays for material and labor were proportionately higher.

Expenses were 6% higher than those originally budgeted. The increase was due to a change in management's decision to spend more for new product promotion based on information developed during the year.

In the appendix to this chapter there is reproduced a relatively simplified analysis of budget variances experienced in the hypothetical operations of a company producing transformers. Here the attempt has been made to isolate, by functional responsibilities, the reasons for revenue and cost variances. The former is broken down by volume and product mix; price is not involved. The latter is analyzed in terms of yield and rate variances for direct labor, materials, and overhead.

Variance Reporting

In order for information concerning variances to be of value, it must reach the person who has the responsibility for the activity being reported on as quickly as possible following the emergence of any significant deviation from plan, and with enough information to indicate why the variance has occurred. Usually a more summary statement is also transmitted to the management person to whom he reports.

The frequency of reports varies with company practice. "Statements showing the actual incurrence of the cost as compared with the budgets are prepared on as frequent a schedule as is required in order that prompt remedial action may be taken. In some cases this is on a daily basis, others a weekly, bi-weekly, or monthly."

The accounting manager for a division of the American Can Company describes one reporting system for manufacturing operations as follows: [4]

> What we attempt to do is to provide production management with prompt reporting of performance in time for corrective measures. To accomplish this, a daily detailed record of machine activity and performance for each machine for each shift is developed. This can be called a daily machine log or daily performance report.
>
> It is the basic instrument of labor variance control available to the production superintendent and his foremen. It is available to him for his scrutiny early in the morning, usually before 9:00 a.m. Its purpose is to present to him, for the previous day, the actual production, the actual and earned machine hours, and the non-productive down-time for each machine for each shift. It is important to remember

─────────

* Victor Schmidt, "Constructing and Using a Flexible Budget for Manufacturing Cost Control," *N.A.A. Bulletin*, July, 1958, sec. 1, pp. 83–84.

that the performances calculated on this daily report are based on information approved by the superintendent or foremen at budget time. . . .

Although direct labor and machine performance can be controlled on a daily or shift basis, many of the expenses in the department or cost centers are budgeted and expensed on a period of time which is longer than a shift or a day. To provide production management with information to control these expenses, a weekly performance report is prepared, which is a summary of the direct labor reported on the daily performance reports and includes, in addition, indirect labor and other expenses which can be controlled on a period shorter than one month. . . .

As all responsible units receive daily or weekly reports, it becomes necessary to summarize this performance in monthly ones, eliminating detail valuable on a daily basis to a foreman but not required by a busy plant manager, and yet to furnish the manager with enough information so that he can intelligently appraise his operations and report to his superiors. . . . In comparison to a daily report, only a small amount of active control can be exercised by the information in the monthly report. However, we can tell the plant manager how his plant operated during the month and where there is a need for his attention.

The manager of the Ford Motor Company's budget analysis department describes the kind of monthly report which is provided in that company.[5]

In measuring profit performance on a month-by-month basis, attention is concentrated on forecasted performance for the coming four months rather than on historical performance, on the theory that there is still time to take action if forecasted performance is below budgeted levels. Each profit center submits a detailed variance letter along with its Monthly Profit Budget Performance Report. The data are significant only to the extent that they put price tags on management action. The real heart of the Report is the analysis of variance, which tells which programs paid off, which didn't and what Divisional Management is doing about the situation.

Variances are first broken out by element (revenues, costs, or assets) and then by causal factors such as sales volume, product mix, economic changes, design changes, sourcing changes, negotiated price changes, and efficiency. These variances are then identified with the specific management action or program with which they are associated.

Comparable reports of sales activity by product, by field office or region, and by time period are prepared for the benefit of supervisors at varying levels in the sales organization. In companies which have developed monthly projected operating statements, balance sheets, and fund-flow statements, comparisons of actual results with those projected are also cir-

[5] W. W. Booth, "Profit Control and Profit Measurement at Ford Motor Company," *Business Budgeting,* September, 1956, p. 13.

culated to top management personnel, both for the month just completed and for the year to date.

Corporate reporting increasingly has taken the form of "reporting by exception." "In reporting by exception we only highlight . . . those results or situations which are out of line by some standard which has been mutually established. Usually a reasonably small deviation is not pointed out, but any deviations beyond that standard are listed and commented on. . . . The difference between the standard and performance, with concise reasons for variance, is the information which is significant and which may be used as a basis for action." [6] "If proper standards, budgets, or forecasts have been established, the only items of major interest are those for which results have varied materially from that which was anticipated. If a job has been performed in the manner expected, the accountant has submitted enough information when he has reported this to the interested party or parties. There is no reason to take the time or effort or to burden the one responsible with detail on things which have gone in accordance with the plan." [7]

By systematic reporting, then, management at all the responsible and discretionary centers of activity within the firm has the variances from budget called to its attention—variances which may be attributable to internal ineffectiveness, or to external events which have altered the premises on which expected performance was based, or to managerial action designed to bring a faltering profit realization closer to goal, or to management decisions not necessarily related to the original budget at all but arising out of the planning function which is not dormant from budget to budget but continuous.

Appendix

ANALYSIS OF HYPOTHETICAL BUDGET VARIANCES IN A COMPANY PRODUCING TRANSFORMERS

"PROPOSED ACCOUNTING PROGRAM FOR HERMETIC SEAL TRANSFORMER COMPANY"*

PLANNED DIRECT PRODUCTION COST

The pre-determined direct production costs as shown in the Plan [Exhibit A, pages 324–325] on a unit basis are generally known as Standard Costs. As bases for control such costs include four planning elements:

[6] Cecil F. Adamson, assistant controller, Burlington Industries, in "Better Reports to Management," a paper delivered at the Nineteenth Annual Symposium on Accounting and Taxation, Chapel Hill, N.C., Oct. 23–23, 1958, pp. 9–10.

[7] Russell E. Larsen, assistant controller, American Steel Foundries, "Organizing around the Profit Motive: Theory and Application," *N.A.A. Bulletin,* January, 1958, sec. 1, p. 18.

* Prepared by W. J. Blood for Dresser Industries, Inc., and reproduced with their permission.

1. Planned Direct Labor Cost
   Expressed as rate per hour
2. Planned Direct Overhead Cost
   Expressed as rate per direct labor hour and determined from Production Department Direct Cost Budget
3. Planned Direct Material Content per Unit
4. Planned Production Rates per Unit

Standard unit costs used in the Profit Plan are developed from these planned elements as shown (in simplified form) [in] Exhibit B [pages 326–327].

(The reference to development of Standard Costs on a "unit" basis should not be interpreted to mean that every different item in the product line necessarily carries its own individual cost standard. Where a general product type includes numerous items varying slightly in specification one to another, cost standards may be developed on a "range" or "group" basis to reflect only significant cost differentials.)

BASIC COMMITMENTS IN THE PLAN

In this typical plan several commitments have been made, against which performance will be measured:

Sales is committed to the sales volume, mix and price which—at the predetermined cost—will deliver the planned variable margin.

Manufacturing is committed to achieving the pre-determined direct production costs.

Capacity Cost Centers are committed to certain levels of spending at various sales levels.

That these commitments are built from specific programs of action—and are not mere collections of numbers—should go without saying. Where the sales estimate assumes mix changes, penetration of new markets, introduction of new products, etc. etc., specific plans (including timetable and definite assignment of responsibility) must be laid. Planned variable margin factors should project cost improvement based on definite Cost Reduction (or Profit Improvement) programs in which areas of attack are specified and responsibilities assigned. Moreover, there must be adequate "machinery" for review of progress on these programs. In short, the Profit Plan—as a document—should be the end expression of the plan of action.

CONTROL FACTORS IN THE PLAN

A profit plan developed on the foregoing bases has incorporated into it well-defined measurement factors for virtually every facet of the business:

Variable Margin—

Sales plan documented by line or class of product with variable margins developed from standard costs. Actual sales, with costs developed on the same standard basis, will yield a comparative base from which variations due to volume, mix and price can be determined.

Direct Cost—

With standard unit costs available from budgeted expense and standard production data, actual production and cost data can be collected on a

EXHIBIT A

DEVELOPMENT OF TYPICAL PROFIT PLAN
(To Operating Earnings Level Only)

Sales Plan

Sales plan prepared by sales or marketing group, indicating expected sales by line, by month. Further breakdown by territory or major customer may be helpful. Prices are expected averages for each line.

Sales Plan

Product Line		Nov.	Dec.	Total Year
Transformers —Units		24,000	27,000	225,000
	Ave. Sell. Price	$ 8	$ 8	$ 8
	Sales Volume	$192,000	$216,000	$1,800,000
Networks —Units		9,000	12,000	200,000
	Ave. Sell. Price	$12	$12	$12
	Sales Volume	$108,000	$144,000	$2,400,000
Total Sales Volume		$300,000	$360,000	$4,200,000

Direct Production Cost Plan

Developed from pre-determined unit costs, applied to product line on an average basis in sufficient detail to give a good cross-section of the costs of producing each line. In this example it is assumed that each of the lines breaks out into 3 broad cost groups with average costs for each group as indicated.

Direct Production Cost—Based on Sales Plan

Product Line	Typical Mix			Nov.	Dec.	Total Year
	Group	Unit Cost	% of Total Load			
Transformers— A		$5	60%	$ 86,400	$ 97,200	$ 810,000
B		$4	20%	19,200	21,600	180,000
C		$5	20%	24,000	27,000	225,000
				$129,600	$145,800	$1,215,000
Networks — A		$8	40%	28,800	38,400	640,000
B		$6	40%	21,600	28,800	480,000
C		$7	20%	12,600	16,800	280,000
				$ 63,000	$ 84,000	$1,400,000
Total Direct Cost				$192,600	$229,800	$2,615,000

Capacity Cost Plan

Step budgets prepared for each capacity cost center and carried into Plan on a monthly basis consistent with Planned Sales Level.

Typical Capacity Cost Step Budget/Month

Sales Level ⟶	200,000	300,000	400,000
Engineering Expense Item			
Salaries	15,000	18,000	19,000
Travel	500	600	800
Supplies	500	600	800
Total Engineering Expense	20,000	24,000	26,000

Variable Margin Plan
($000)

Product Line	Nov.	Dec.	Total Year
Transformers—			
Sales	$ 192.0	$216.0	$1,800.0
Direct Cost	129.6	145.8	1,215.0
Var. Margin	$ 62.4	$ 70.2	$ 585.0
%	32.5	32.5	32.5
Networks—			
Sales	$ 108.0	$144.0	$2,400.0
Direct Cost	63.0	84.0	1,400.0
Var. Margin	$ 45.0	$ 60.0	$1,000.0
%	41.7	41.7	41.7
Total—			
Sales	$ 300.0	$360.0	$4,200.0
Direct Cost	192.6	229.8	2,615.0
Var. Margin	$ 107.4	$130.2	$1,585.0
%	35.8	36.2	37.6

Profit Plan Earnings Statement
($000)

	Nov.	Dec.	Total Year
Sales	$ 300.0	$360.0	$4,200.0
Variable Margin	107.4	130.2	1,585.0
%	35.8	36.2	37.6
Capacity Cost	$ 90.0	$ 101.0	$1,176.0
Operating Earnings	$ 17.4	$ 29.2	$ 409.0
%	5.8	8.1	9.7

Capacity Cost Plan

	Nov.	Dec.	Total Year
Planned Sales	300,000	360,000	4,200,000
Manufacturing Capacity Cost	24,000	27,000	300,000
Engineering Capacity Cost	24,000	26,000	300,000
Selling Capacity Cost	24,000	28,000	340,000
A & G Capacity Cost	18,000	20,000	236,000
Total Capacity Cost	90,000	101,000	1,176,000
% of Sales	30.0	28.0	28.0

comparable basis and evaluated to determine what costs should have been, whether variations are due to spending or efficiency and where such variations occurred (responsibility). The principal elements here can be reviewed daily from the standard cost base.

EXHIBIT B
TYPICAL DEVELOPMENT OF PLANNED DIRECT PRODUCTION COST BASED ON UNIT STANDARD COSTS

Under this arrangement spending rates are developed from production department direct cost budgets.

Standard production data is developed on an individual product basis or by some grouping of products if there are numerous items that essentially are homogeneous cost and market-wise. These production factors may be developed by operation or by department. They may be engineered or history-based— whatever is appropriate to the individual circumstances. As used for planning purposes these standards should be attainable under the conditions and with the efficiencies that are expected to prevail in the operation.

From these two sets of data — spending rates and production rates — the unit or group cost then is calculated. This unit cost then is used directly in the Plan (as in this example), or where there are numerous items in a line the average of a typical mix of items may be used.

Transformer Dept. Direct Cost Budget		
Planned Labor Rate/Hour 1.50	Annual Direct	Rate/
Planned Hours 300,000	Overhead	D.L. Hour
Indirect Labor	54,000	.18
Operating Supplies	24,000	.08
Machine Repairs	21,000	.07
Total Direct Overhead	$150,000	$.50

Standard Production Data Transformer — Group A		
Operations	Prod'n. Rate Man Hrs./Pce.	Material Allowance
Coil Assembly	0.4	2.50
Electrical Assembly	0.4	1.25
Finishing	0.2	.25
	1.0	4.00

Capacity Cost—

With the plan supported by detailed step budgets an actual versus budget comparison will show specific areas of deviation.

Development of a typical control reporting scheme tying back to Plan is dealt with in subsequent paragraphs with particular emphasis on the role of Standard Cost.

STANDARD COSTS FOR CONTROL

Formulated on the general basis outlined in the diagram, Exhibit B, standard unit costs serve not only as a profit planning base but as a specific framework for control and evaluation of manufacturing and sales performance.

The control aspects are best accomplished under an accounting set-up in which production is inventoried at standard cost (hence shipments costed at standard) and variations of actual cost from standard written off as an expense of the period involved.

For example, let's assume the following set of facts for the month of November:

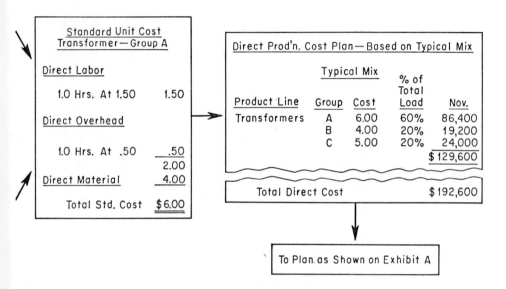

1. Shipments for the month were $320,000 at sales price.
2. The standard cost of those shipments was $200,000.
3. Only Group A Transformers were manufactured during the month (38,000 units were produced at $6.00/piece—standard value or total standard cost of $228,000).
4. Actual production cost for the month was $250,000.

These facts flow into an Earnings Statement as shown [in the diagram on page 328, Exhibit C].

VARIATIONS FROM PLAN

In the foregoing Earnings Statement can be seen two general variations from plan:

1. The standard variable margin generated by sales was $12,600 over plan.
2. The production operations exceeded standard cost by $22,000.

Before this information can be of any particular control use, however, it has to be developed in greater detail for each of the areas of responsibility: Sales and Production.

EXHIBIT C

TYPICAL FLOW OF DATA INTO EARNINGS STATEMENT

(To Variable Margin Level Only—With Variances from Standard Prod'n. Cost Carried as Cost for the Month)

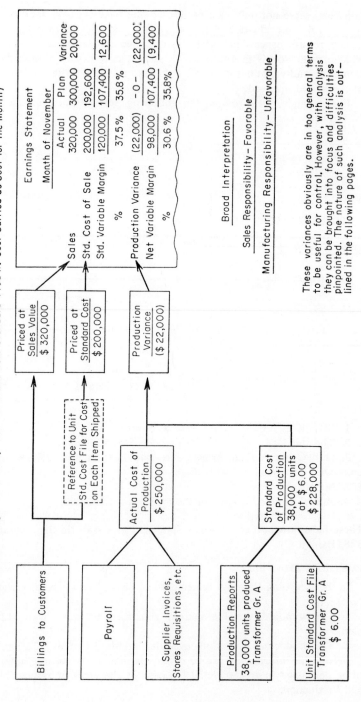

Earnings Statement

Month of November

	Actual	Plan	Variance
Sales	320,000	300,000	20,000
Std. Cost of Sale	200,000	192,600	12,600
Std. Variable Margin	120,000	107,400	
%	37.5%	35.8%	
Production Variance	(22,000)	- 0 -	(22,000)*
Net Variable Margin	98,000	107,400	(9,400)
%	30.6%	35.8%	

Broad Interpretation

Sales Responsibility – Favorable

Manufacturing Responsibility – Unfavorable

These variances obviously are in too general terms to be useful for control. However, with analysis they can be brought into focus and difficulties pinpointed. The nature of such analysis is out-lined in the following pages.

Priced at Sales Value $ 320,000

Priced at Standard Cost $ 200,000

Production Variance ($ 22,000)

Reference to Unit Std. Cost File for Cost on Each Item Shipped

Actual Cost of Production $ 250,000

Standard Cost of Production 38,000 units at $ 6.00 $ 228,000

Billings to Customers

Payroll

Supplier Invoices, Stores Requisitions, etc.

Production Reports 38,000 units produced Transformer Gr. A

Unit Standard Cost File Transformer Gr. A $ 6.00

SALES ANALYSIS

The sales and standard margin indicated in our statement were as follows:

| | ($000) | | |
	Actual	Plan	Variance
Sales	320.00	300.0	20.0
Standard variable margin	120.00	107.4	12.6
Percentage	37.5	35.8	

From this it is immediately apparent that sales dollar volume exceeded plan. Moreover, with the actual margin percentage higher than plan we see that sales mix was richer than had been expected. What we don't see, however, is the amount of margin from the increased volume nor can we tell whether the mix factor was between product lines or due to mix of items within a given line. We can determine those additional facts, having available the breakdown of actual and planned sales, and standard margins, by product line as shown:

Sales and Margin Detail

| Product line | Actual | | | Plan | | | Margin |
	Sales	Margin	%	Sales	Margin	%	Variance
Transformers ...	186.0	55.8	30.0	192.0	62.4	32.5	(6.6)
Networks	134.0	64.2	47.9	108.0	45.0	41.7	19.2
	320.0	120.0	37.5	300.0	107.4	35.8	12.6

Sales
% of Total

	Actual	Plan
Transformers	58.0	64.0
Networks	42.0	36.0
	100.0	100.0

From this detail we can immediately make these additional observations:

1. Transformer volume was off and mix was poor, yielding 30% versus the planned 32.5%.

2. Network volume was up and mix was good, yielding 47.9% versus the planned 41.7%.

3. High margin network sales commanded a bigger share of our volume than had been expected.

Although the dollar impact of these conclusions still is not really apparent, calculations can be made to show these effects and to give added meaning to the earnings picture as shown in the following statement.

Earnings Statement
Month of November
($000 Omitted)

	Actual	Plan	Variance
Sales	320.0	300.0	
Standard Variable Margin	120.0	107.4	12.6
Percent	37.5	35.8	

Standard Margin Variances due to:

Sales Volume		7.2
Mix Between Lines		1.8
Mix Within Lines		
Transformers	(4.7)	
Networks	8.3	3.6
Total Variance		12.6

The method of calculation yielding these variances is as follows:

Volume

Planned amount of margin for the month	$107,400
On the $320,000 actual sales the planned 35.8% margin would yield	114,600
Margin gain due to sales volume	$ 7,200

Here margins from actual and planned sales volumes are compared assuming the planned margin percent in both cases. By using the planned percentage all mix factors are eliminated and volume is the only consideration.

Mix Between Lines

In the sales plan we had expected transformers to comprise 64% of total sales and networks 36%; and margins of 32.5% and 41.7%, respectively, had been planned. If that pattern had held, the $320,000 in sales would have yielded the planned 35.8% overall margin, or $114,600

However, the actual sales split was different and, at planned margins, would appear as follows:

Transformers $186,000 at 32.5% = ...	$ 60,500
Networks $134,000 at 41.7% = ...	55,900
	$116,400
Margin gain due to favorable mix between lines	$ 1,800

(Effectively, this is the result of high margin network sales comprising 42% of total sales rather than the planned 36%.)

Mix of Items Within Each Line

Finally, you can see that the actual margin percentage on each of the lines was different than had been planned. This reflects the fact that the mix of individual items actually sold in each line was different than had been expected, as follows:

	Actual sales	Planned margin %	Expected margin	Actual margin %	Actual margin	Margin variance
Transformers	186,000	32.5	60,500	30.0	55,800	(4,700)
Networks	134,000	41.7	55,900	47.9	64,200	8,300
			116,500		120,000	3,600

While the presence of standard unit costs makes this type of sales analysis possible, this is only an historical use. Of perhaps greater importance is the fact that we have a tool for taking a look at future profitability in terms of order trends, potential profits in backlog, etc. In other words, by applying standard margin factors to orders and backlogs, we can see profit effects of changing sales mix as they are taking place, with an opportunity for shifting emphasis to improve the profit trend. Backlog analysis also is valuable as a forecasting medium.

Finally, the standard margin concept opens up a potential for setting sales incentives based on pre-determined profitability.

PRODUCTION ANALYSIS

In our example, we stated an unfavorable production variance of $22,000 resulting from:

Actual expenses for the month	$250,000
Less: Standard cost of the 38,000 units produced	228,000
Production variance	($ 22,000)

Broadly, there are two reasons why the actual cost can vary from standard:
1. The actual price or cost of labor, material and overhead items may vary from standard prices—such variations are referred to as *Spending Variances.*
2. The actual efficiency with which those cost elements are used in turning out product may vary from the efficiency assumed in the standard—these variations are referred to as efficiency or *Use Variances.*

Referring back to our unit standard cost for Transformer—Group A (see Exhibit B) we had indicated certain cost factors for that item, and we know from our production reports (Exhibit C) that 38,000 units were produced; thus the total standard cost for the month is comprised as follows:

Standard Cost of Production

Cost element	Standard factor	Units produced	Total standard
Direct Labor Hours	1.0 /unit	38,000	38,000 hours
Direct Labor Dollars	$1.50/unit	"	$ 57,000
Direct Overhead Dollars	$0.50/unit	"	$ 19,000
Direct Material	$4.00/unit	"	$152,000
Total Standard Cost	$6.00/unit	"	$228,000

Now let's compare that Total Standard Value to some assumed actual costs:

Cost element	Total standard	Total actual	Variance
Direct Labor Hours	38,000 hours	41,400 hours	(3,400 hours)
Direct Labor	$ 57,000	$ 63,000	($6,000)
Direct Overhead	$ 19,000	$ 21,000	($2,000)
Direct Material	$152,000	$166,000	($14,000)
Total	$228,000	$250,000	($22,000)

The variances at this point are in total by cost element and we have yet to determine the Spending and Use factors. These can be calculated as follows:

Direct Labor

Actual hours 41,400 at standard rate/hr. ($1.50) determines expected
spending for the actual hours worked $62,100
Actual direct labor cost was 63,000

Direct Labor Spending Variance .... ($ 900)
(At a cost of $63,000 the actual labor rate averaged $1.52/hr. compared to the standard of $1.50/hr.)
Actual hours (41,400) less standard hours (38,000) for 38,000 units
of production:
   3,400 hours lost at standard rate ($1.50) or Direct Labor Use
   Variance .... ($ 5,100)

   Total labor variances .... ($ 6,000)

Direct Overhead

Actual hours 41,400 at standard rate/hr. ($.50) determine expected
spending for actual level of activity $20,700
Actual direct overhead cost 21,000

Direct Overhead Spending Variance .... ($ 300)
Actual hours (41,400) less standard hours (38,000) for 38,000 units
of production:
   3,400 hours lost at standard rate ($.50) or Direct Overhead Use
   Variance .... ($ 1,700)

   Total direct overhead variances .... ($ 2,000)

Direct Material

A material spending (or price) variance will arise only if material purchases
and consumption are priced on a standard basis. When this is done the price
variances are determined as purchases are made, material is inventoried at
standard and the variance written off. For purposes of this example, let's assume
that the following has occurred:

Material item	Quantities	Standard unit cost	Total standard	Invoice cost	Variance
ABC	10,000	$.70	$7,000	$7,800	($ 800)
XYZ	14,000	$.15	$2,100	$2,000	$ 100
PDQ	7,000	$.50	$3,500	$3,800	($ 300)
		Total Material Price Variance			($1,000)

The Material Use Variance then is determined as follows:
Total actual material cost $166,000
Less: Price variances 1,000
                                              $165,000

Standard material use $152,000

   Material Use Variance .... ($13,000)

   Total material variance .... ($14,000)

In summary, we now can see that our Production Variance was due to:

	Spending factors	Use factors	Total
Direct Labor	(900)	(5,100)	(6,000)
Direct Overhead	(300)	(1,700)	(2,000)
Direct Material	(1,000)	(13,000)	(14,000)
Total	(2,200)	(19,800)	(22,000)

Beyond this it is most important to recognize that such variance determination must be made on as current a basis as possible and be tied down to specific product and departmental responsibility. This can be done daily in most instances. Finally, the direct labor and overhead spending variances must be detailed to the department and type of expense involved if effective control action is to be taken.

The diagram on the following page (Exhibit D) illustrates the flow of daily detailed reporting and build up to the month-end statement, using direct labor and overhead as an example.

SUMMARY STATEMENT

With gains and losses tied to sales or production responsibility, and analyzed, our earnings summary then presents this type of picture:

Earnings Statement
Month of November

	Actual	Plan	Variance
Sales	320,000	300,000	20,000
Standard Cost of Sales	200,000	192,600	
Standard Variable Margin	120,000	107,400	12,600
%	37.5	35.8	
Production Variance	(22,000)		(22,000)
Net Variable Margin	98,000	107,400	(9,400)
%	30.6	35.8	

Variances

Sales Responsibility		Production Responsibility			
			Spending	Use	Total
Volume	$7,200	Direct Labor	(900)	(5,100)	(6,000)
Mix between lines	1,800	Direct Overhead	(300)	(1,700)	(2,000)
Mix within lines:		Direct Material	(1,000)	(13,000)	(14,000)
Transformers (4,700)					
Networks 8,300			(2,200)	(19,800)	(22,000)
	3,600				
	$12,600				

When accompanied by appropriate commentary, and supported by more detailed analyses to lower levels of management, this framework provides a complete insight into actual variable margin performance compared to projections.

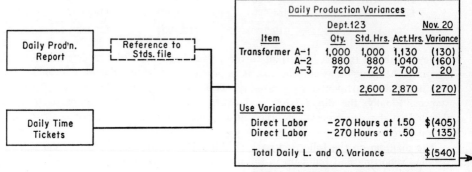

(Reported to Foreman or Dept. Head daily. Similar reports on Material Use also are prepared. Such reports usually find their greatest use in a Daily Production Meeting in which pertinent supervision reviews major variances to determine corrective action.)

EXHIBIT D

TYPICAL FLOW OF PRODUCTION VARIANCE REPORTING

Daily Earnings Summary

Production Variances

Date	Sales	Standard Var. Marg.	%	D.L.Use	Direct Od.Use
November 1	14,000	2,800	20%	(615)	(205)
November 2	12,000	3,600	30%	630	210
November 3	10,000	3,700	37%	(640)	(215)
November 4	16,000	6,080	38%	405	135
November 7	8,000	2,500	32%	(660)	(230)
November 8	12,000	4,800	40%	630	210
November 9	10,000	3,700	37%	(640)	(215)
November 10	14,000	4,900	35%	615	205
November 20	16,000	6,400	40%	(405)	(135)
Total Month	320,000	120,000	37.5%	(5,100)	(1,700)
Plan	300,000	107,400	35.8%	-0-	-0-

(Summary to Division or Company management daily. Depending on organization, this daily summary may go to one level of management and a weekly recap to the top company executive.)

Earnings Statement

Month of November

	Actual	Plan	Variance
Production Variance	(22,000)	-0-	(22,000)
Net Variable Margin	98,000	107,400	(9,400)
%	30.6%	35.8%	

Production Variances

	Spending	Use	Total
Direct Labor	(900)	(5,100)	(6,000)
Direct Overhead	(300)	(1,700)	(2,000)
Direct Material	(1,000)	(13,000)	(14,000)
Total	(2,200)	(19,800)	(22,000)

Departmental Direct Cost Budget
(41,400 Actual Hours)

	Std. Rate	Budget	Actual	Variance
Direct Labor	1.50	62,100	63,000	(900)
Indirect Labor	.18	7,500	7,800	(300)
Operating Supplies	.08	3,300	3,400	(100)
Machine Repairs	.07	2,900	2,800	100
Total Direct Overhead	.50	20,700	21,000	(300)

Total Spending Variance		(1,200)
Use Variance: 41,400 Actual Hrs. Vs. 38,000 Std.: (3,400) Hours at $2.00		(6,800)
Total Department Variance		8,000

(In detail, as above, to Dept. Head; summary of all departments to higher management.)

Chapter 17

CORPORATE ACTION IN RESPONSE TO VARIANCES

Reactions to Variances

For whatever reasons variances emerge, when they emerge they call for recognition and action. The appropriate action depends on the nature of the variance. No particular problem presents itself, for example, when a variance requires only the attention and application of the person immediately responsible (and perhaps his superior) in order to remove it. Perhaps a production inefficiency has brought the cost of some operation above standard, but it is taken care of when the foreman spends an hour with the operative reviewing where the difficulty arises. Or possibly sales in Peoria have fallen off by 10 per cent, but this is made up for when the district sales manager applies pressure to the local sales force which has been a bit slack of late.

If variances cannot be so readily corrected, however, and if the budget plan is to have any meaning, some special effort is required. The situation calls for reexamination in order to determine what action is called for. If sales are falling below the budget figures and cannot be brought back by pep talks or warnings, or if costs have persistently been out of line with budget despite repeated efforts to hold to standard, either management must accept the inferior performance, lowering its budgetary sight, or it must adopt new tactics to meet the deteriorated situation.

If the decision is to "do something" to improve profit performance, the choice of tactics is likely to be *ad hoc* in nature. Managements can—and many times do—play the situation "by ear" or "by the seat of the pants" or "off the top of the head" or from some other anatomical vantage point. Sometimes the decision is based on a consensus emerging from a committee of ears or seat pants or cranium tops. It is also possible, however, to classify variances, to examine the characteristics of the categories, and

336

to draw some conclusions about what kinds of action may be appropriate to each category.

Variances are simply changes in the actual flow of funds within the company relative to those which had been projected. If costs in shop A are above standard, this means that more money is flowing out in payment for that operation than had been expected. If the sales of product X in Atlanta are higher than had been forecast, this means that more money is coming into the firm as a consequence of that activity than had been counted on.

These changes in fund flows—the pluses and minuses of income and outgo, relative to budget—sometimes offset each other, at least partially. Thus a poor sales performance by one product may be offset by an above-budget sales showing by another product, or a high-cost operation may be offset by one which shows unexpected efficiency. ("Actual results for the year were within one percentage point of the original plan. This close relationship between plan and actual was accomplished, however, with larger percentage fluctuations between major divisions of the company. It is our policy that the overall commitment for the company to the Board of Directors will largely be accomplished—sometimes by making adjustments in divisions where performance is good to compensate for poor performance in other divisions, so long as these adjustments do not have adverse longer term implications. Generally speaking, our goal is to have our profit plan be accurate within 2%, while we expect variances for each major division to be no larger than 5%. Expenditures, therefore, could vary from original plan even though our final profit goal was attained. . . .")

At other times, however, income changes in one unit of the firm are not offset in another unit, or are not offset sufficiently to make much of a difference. Indeed, variances may be cumulative rather than offsetting. The rise in costs over budget in one shop finds its parallel in other shops, and outflows for the firm as a whole increase. A number of the major products in a firm's line sell poorly, and the firm's total revenues take a tumble.

Whether a variance is offset or nonoffset depends on the level from which one is surveying operations. A variance which is not offset within a shop may be offset at the level of the plant. From the viewpoint of the foreman of the shop within which it occurs, it constitutes (let us say) an above-standard cost which he must explain to his superior and which he must attempt to control; but from the viewpoint of the plant manager it appears as a budget lapse which, while unfortunate and subject to correction, is not serious because it is counterbalanced by a cost saving elsewhere in the plant, so that the level of over-all plant costs, on which the projected budget balance in part depends, is maintained. Similarly, the variances in a plant's operations may be offset at the level of a corporate subsidiary, while the variances in a subsidiary may be offset at the corporate (consolidated) level.

The offsetting of income variances does not stop here, however. From the standpoint of the economy as a whole, variances which emerge within one firm may be offset elsewhere in the economy. Variances may be offset *between* firms, just as within them. Firm A has a lower sales achievement than projected, but firms B and C are doing better than they had hoped. If profits are down at the Jones Co., they are up at the Smith Co. This offsetting of income flows between firms may occur between firms in the same industry (one automobile manufacturer sells fewer cars and another sells more), or it may go on between firms in different product lines (people spend less on clothing this year, but more on travel). The fund flows between firms are altered because consumers have shifted their preferences. Over-all levels of spending, or of GNP, may show a stable growth pattern, but within the aggregate there is a good deal of churning of income flows to and from individual firms.

As in the firm, however, so in the economy it may be the case that the changes in flows in one firm or sector are not offset in other firms or sectors. All sell less. Reduced inflows in one industry are not offset by heavier selling in others. Or all sell more, and the increased income in one firm is not at the expense of income to rival firms. Similarly with costs: Wage rates and materials prices may rise for all firms (outflows increase) or decline concomitantly. The phenomena of recession and inflation may be described in terms of nonoffsetting income flows.[1] The offsetting or nonoffsetting character of corporate variances at the level of the economy has significance for what the individual firm does about its own budgetary problems.

A firm's reaction to variances depends (1) on whether they are adverse or favorable; (2) on whether they are offset at some level (within the firm itself, within the industry, within the economy); and (3) on how the variances, as well as any attempts to correct for them, affect the firm's network of relationships—that complex of relationships which at the start of this inquiry we likened to a spider's web or a frosted windowpane or a kaleidoscope, with lines running off in all directions to a large family of other firms and individuals with whom it maintains ties of differing importance.

If the variances within a company are favorable, managements are likely to take a relaxed attitude toward them. If the favorable variance is short-run and accidental, it constitutes a windfall gain. If the result of longer-run factors which are likely to bring continuing benefits (an expanded market for some product, so that sales can be expected to grow faster than had been expected, or a change in workflow or materials handling that cuts costs), the improved experience will be built into next year's budget and

[1] Elaboration of this approach is given in my *A General Theory of Economic Process*, chap. 16.

the favorable variance, while not accidental, will disappear in the same manner as though it had been. We shall further examine management reactions to favorable variances shortly. For the present let us confine our attention to adverse performances.

In the case of an unfavorable deviation, the whole nature of the budgeting process creates an expectation that something should be done about it. If the variance has been offset within the firm, however, so that underperformance in one respect has been counterbalanced by overperformance in another and the over-all target is approximately realized, the pressure for corrective action is relieved. An energetic and ambitious management might still press to improve the below-budget operation, so that the total profit showing would be better than planned, but in most instances the effort would not be so insistent. If adverse variances are not internally offset, however, so that the profit target is missed by more than the tolerable amount, then they constitute, collectively, an incentive to *top-management* corrective action. Except in cases where the cause is, unmistakably, internal inefficiencies, the first step is to check the profit performance of other firms.

If profit performances by firms which it considers rivals, as well as by other neighboring firms, show no clearly defined movement up or down, this suggests that the difficulty lies within the firm itself and is unrelated to what is happening in other firms. Its unfavorable profit showing may be due to a slump in its sales or a rise in its costs, resulting in lesser inflows to or greater outflows from the firm, in ways to which its competitors or neighbors are not, apparently, subject. These changes in its flows may be offset by compensating movements in funds elsewhere in the economy, but if so these offsetting flows are sufficiently diffused that they cannot, in this assumed instance, be traced or correlated.

Except as the *aggregate* flow of funds rises or falls abnormally (a condition which we have hypothesized is not present in this case), changes in income within a firm may be presumed, by definition, to be offset elsewhere in the economy. But if there is no clear *pattern* of offsetting discernible to the firm, the variances which it has experienced are viewed by it as random effects of the system, not directly attributable to the actions or accomplishments of any rival firm. Corrective action need not therefore be directed against some competitor or competitors which are besting it in market performance, and which are the cause of its misfortune, but relates primarily to its own internal performance.[2]

[2] The idea which I am trying to express here could be conveyed much more precisely by use of the concepts which I employed in *A General Theory of Economic Process*. What I am saying is that the firm's adverse profit showing is, presumably, not attributable to commensal competition (that is, from those which are supplying the same services or performing the same functions as it is doing), though it may be attributable to symbiotic competition (that is, from those with whom it is linked in a complementary functional relation, such as labor unions and materials suppliers).

The kinds of corrective actions which a firm may safely undertake, in the case of variances of this "random" type, are any whose effects will be regarded in the same light by its rivals—that is, as "random," not directly affecting their own profitability. Thus neither is the variance itself viewed as the result of some provocative action by a competitor, nor is the corrective action which is taken viewed by competitors as provocative. The kaleidoscopic shifts in the network of business relations are viewed by any of the firms involved as the result of chance rather than design, of localized rather than general interest, from the point of view of both firm A which experiences the variance and firms X, Y, and Z which observe what it does to correct the variance.

Nonprovocative Reactions

The class of variances as well as of corrective actions of which this is likely to be true are those dealing with cost. As previously noted, any variance (change in fund flow) will necessarily have its offsets somewhere in the system except in those circumstances when flows are generally increasing (growth or inflation) or decreasing (recession or deflation). Thus adverse cost variances in one firm mean a greater outflow of funds (to workers, to supplier firms, to capital providers), which can then be spent on goods and services in the discretion of those receiving them, to the benefit of those firms from which they purchase. Correction of these adverse (higher) cost conditions implies a drying up of these "extra" receipts which other firms have been enjoying.[3] But these shifts in the flow of funds among companies are so diffused that their cause is not directly traceable or attributable to the actions which the Frank Smith Company or the General Motors Corporation has taken in trying to correct its cost variances.

Even if the effects of one company's actions on other companies could be so traced, there is a range of behavior which managers permit each other to engage in which is sanctioned, viewed as "acceptable" or "permissible" or "reasonable" in the light of the code of conduct prevailing. Actions outside these limits, however, would be regarded as "offensive" or "unfair" or "cutthroat" and would be subject to whatever retaliatory reaction recommended itself. Even in the generally permissive area of costs, for example, a firm which was experiencing an adverse profit performance because of

---

In correcting its "internal" problems, it may very well have to direct aggressive or retaliatory actions against the latter, though not against the former. Since these concepts have not found acceptance in the literature, however, I have refrained from introducing them into the text, with the accompanying elaboration which that would require.

[3] The company which has corrected its adverse cost conditions now has more funds which it may itself distribute, to the benefit of a different set of other firms; the shift in fund flows is thus again offset.

high costs would be frowned on, and its actions invite retaliation, if it sought to lower costs by depressing wages to a level substantially lower than prevailed elsewhere in the industry. (Rivals would demand that the union with which they dealt take more effective action against such a "sweatshop" employer, or they would discipline it within their trade association, or they would more readily accept a raising of the legislated minimum wage to a level above that paid by the "exploiting" firm.) Such a situation is most uncommon, however. In general, a firm's efforts to deal with a high-cost operation are considered its own internal affair. The cost variance itself is considered "random" by the firm, and efforts to correct it are similarly regarded by its competitors.

The president of one corporation provides a good example of this kind of variance and the corrective actions taken:

> Actual sales revenue for the fiscal year varied 1% from the original forecast. Expenditures varied 30%. The reasons were practically entirely due to manufacturing problems of inefficiency and quality, resulting in overtime, extra help, and overhead items. In other words, we had to produce more than our budgeted production in units, to obtain budgeted sales revenue.
>
> The only actions specifically taken were in attempted changes in methods of production to alleviate the problems stated above. This meant bringing in new supervisors, the use of an engineering consulting firm, and the trying out of some new machinery. The other action required was that we had to delay some of our planned investment program, because we were not generating enough profits under our reinvestment formula.

No threats to their positions could be seen in such actions even by the most suspicious of competitors. Other examples of such efforts to meet cost problems come ready to hand. "Major cost reduction programs were installed in two mills which were experiencing high costs." "With overall expenses higher than forecast, principally in the area of fuel costs, a continual effort was made to reduce this variation by good control of operations and the addition of more efficient generating units when economically justifiable." In the category of materials costs, efforts may be redoubled to purchase in more advantageous quantities, to reduce the amount of spoilage or scrap, to control more critically for the quality of supplies. With respect to the use of labor, word will go out that foremen must avoid overtime except where absolutely essential, machine down-time allowances will be controlled more rigorously, indirect labor will be watched more carefully. Overhead, administrative, and selling expenses will be reviewed, even though they may be within budget allowances, in the possibility that excess costs in other categories may be offset there. ("An unbudgeted increase in wages of 5% was absorbed by under-runs in other expenses.")

The possibility of offsetting rising costs in one category by cost savings in other areas is systematically exploited in some companies. In the Minnesota Mining and Manufacturing Company, for example, a division manager reports: "There is no adjustment made in profit targets for current changes in raw material costs, labor costs, or in any other cost factors. It is our company objective that these cost changes should be compensated for through increased productivity in manufacturing operations rather than to change the profit objective of the division." [4]

The director of management analysis for Capital Airlines commented to a conference of businessmen that his company attempted to offset cost increases by improved performance over time. "Knowing that January . . . is going to exceed budgeted unit costs establishes a target for offsetting unit cost economies in later months through schedule and operation revisions which must be planned 30 to 90 days before accomplishment." [5] Cost increases coming in the late months of a budget year can obviously not be easily offset within that same year; since budgeting is in reality a continuous process, and planning periods are simply arbitrary time divisions, this is not a material consideration, however.

In other instances an adverse cost variance, if the consequence of an increase in material or labor prices which is expected to continue, may be met by raising the price of the product. An "increase in selling prices for one of our products to cover higher than planned raw-material costs," or increases to cover the higher labor costs brought on by a wage bargain, are common enough when demand conditions permit.

Cost control efforts by one or more companies can, of course, put pressure on its competitors to do as well in order to maintain as good a profit showing. This kind of rivalry is regarded as so nonprovocative, however, that businessmen scarcely conceive of it as rivalry at all. To the uninitiated it is always a cause for surprise to discover how freely one firm will disclose to its competitors cost-cutting efficiencies which it has pioneered. As we have already noticed in an earlier chapter, one source of information available to a firm that runs into a difficult production problem is another firm in the industry which is known to be good at that sort of thing. It is not only visiting "productivity teams" from abroad which have been exposed to American industry's best practices, but visiting managers and teams from among one's own rivals. Trade associations and management societies are continually mounting conferences on technical problems, at which officials of selected companies give considerable detail on how "things are done" in their establishments. There are, of course, limits to such revelations, but they embrace a wide territory of interchange of technical knowledge.

[4] C. W. Walton, "Company and Division Planning and Control," *N.A.C.A. Bulletin*, October, 1956, sec. 3, p. 312.

[5] G. E. Park, in "Evaluation of Operations by Management," *The Controller*, August, 1959, p. 362.

In general, then, a firm's attempts to overcome an adverse budget performance by reducing its costs of operation are unlikely to excite a reaction from competitive firms. The effects of such corrective actions are dispersed too widely in the economy to be of concern. In the exceptional event that such efforts lead to production innovations, the benefits will in time be spread to all who are interested. A low cost of production is not a goal which, when realized in one firm, makes realization more difficult or less feasible in others.

Provocative Reactions

Let us now move to a second class of cases. If a firm which is encountering an adverse profit variance finds that the profit performance of its immediate rivals shows a generally upward movement, this suggests, even though it does not establish, that the difficulty lies within the firm but is (contrary to the previous case) directly related to what its rivals are doing.[6] There is an indication that the downward shift in its own income flows is being offset by an upward shift in income flows to its competitors. Since any offsetting effects of costs are not so readily attributable, as we have just noted, it is with respect to sales that this competitive offsetting is most discernible.

When adverse variances are considered to be the *consequence* of offsetting shifts in fund flows, originated outside the firm from identifiable sources, they invite a responsive reaction. The offsetting shift in sales revenues may be considered to be due to a price action by rivals, or to their promotional activity, or to some change in their product line. It is in one of these three areas that a responsive reaction must be made. But an attempt to correct an adverse profit variance by action in one of these three areas, if successful, will for exactly the same reason invite further reaction from its rivals, and even before its effectiveness is established may evoke retaliatory action in anticipation of possible success. Unlike the field of cost reduction, actions designed to increase sales are viewed with concern by competitors. Unlike cost reduction which can be a goal for all to achieve, the increased sale of a product is usually made at the expense of others. Unlike the case

---

[6] It does not establish this as fact since it is never possible to trace conclusively the shifts in consumer expenditures. A producer of high-priced television sets may be selling fewer not because its rivals are selling more but because people in the income brackets to which it had formerly appealed are now spending more on tape recorders or hi-fi equipment or live theater or travel. On the other hand, expenditures in these categories may have risen because people were spending less not only on television sets but also on clothes, and so on. There is always the possibility, of course, that one firm may be experiencing serious production-cost problems precisely (coincidentally) at the time that its competitors are solving all of theirs, leading to discrepant profit movements which, however, would be quite obviously *causally* unrelated.

of actions intended to correct adverse profit variances by improving production performances, other firms are sensitive to and suspicious of efforts to correct profit variances by expanding sales.

For this sequence of action and reaction to be set in motion it is not even necessary that a firm suffer an actual decline in profits or sales over previous levels. The decline may be from levels which had only been projected, not experienced, but if the projections were based on an expected maintenance of a previous share of a market or a share to which the firm believed it should be able to make good its title, the variance would nevertheless be viewed as important. It is thus evident, and not at all surprising, that the circumstances under which firms are likely to attribute a causal relationship to offsetting flows of rival firms (profits moving in the opposite direction from their own) is the classical case of oligopoly.

When there is a large number of competitors, the chances of some firms moving up while others decline are more to be expected, and the offsetting flows, as in the case of costs, are more diffused and less attributable. Corrective actions are less likely to be regarded as a reply to the identified initiative of competitors or to be taken in awareness of possible retaliation which they may provoke. In the case of monopolies, actions designed to stimulate sales can be taken without fear of possible retribution, since no near rivals exist. (Thus an official of a utility which had suffered a loss in revenue due to a strike affecting the major industries which it supplied with power wrote: "Because the Company had surplus power due to the decline in its industrial load, it temporarily sold some of its surplus at a reduced rate to neighboring utility companies. No changes were made in the price of electric power or natural gas to customers on a firm basis." Such a two-price "dumping" operation could be carried out because there were no competitors whose markets it was undercutting or which could undercut its markets.)

It is preeminently in the case of oligopoly (which, without respect to size of firm, is probably the most common case) that profit variances may be *attributed* to the offsetting flows in rival firms, when the latter materialize, and corrective action *directed* to a firm's product, promotional, or price relations with its rivals. It is in the case of oligopoly that projections based on previous market shares are usually regarded as targets to be vigorously defended against identifiable close rivals. It is with respect to oligopoly that defensive reactions by a firm experiencing the adverse sales variance, even if designed only to regain an historic market-share position, are the more likely to arouse retaliatory reactions from its rivals, since there is always the danger that the effect of such corrective actions may not stop with the historic share.

When a firm attributes its adverse profit variance to the fact that somehow a rival or several rivals have forged ahead of it, capturing some of its actual or expected market, its response must take the form of an improved product, a stepped-up promotional effort (including, as one possibility, improved marketing and distributive arrangements), or a price reduction. While these may be used in combination, they are commonly regarded as substitutes for each other. The action taken may be in kind with the presumed cause of the adverse profit showing: A product sold by a rival, which consumers appear to favor, may be met by a hastily effected product improvement; the reduced "visibility" of the firm's product (either in advertising media or on dealer's floors or shelves) relative to a competitor which has expanded its advertising budget or nurtured its dealer relationships may be countered by "beefed up" programs along these same lines; a lower price tag on a rival's product may lead to a matching price cut. But rather than such responses in kind, a firm whose profits are down when its competitors are prospering may choose to bring out an improved product as an answer to another firm's lower price, or to promote more vigorously its always-well-regarded product against an innovation by competitors, or to reduce its price as an effective counter to either innovation or promotion elsewhere in its industry.

There is no necessary reason, however, why a firm experiencing a poor sales and profit performance need attempt to answer so directly those firms which it regards as the cause of its troubles. Suppose a rival's promotion of a product coincides with the falling off in sales, in this firm, of a product which is a substitute, so that a cause and effect relation may be imputed. It does not inescapably follow that the firm must meet this competition in any one of the three ways which are open to it. Its primary goal is some target rate of return on sales or investment, an aggregate profit. A specific share of some particular market is at best a secondary objective. An alert management, watching its position in a given market deteriorate, might decide that the investment required to hold that position would bring less of a return than if put to use in building up its position in some new and developing market into which it had moved or was about to move. If a price cut by a rival was diverting sales and reducing revenue and profit, management might conclude that a matching price cut would lose more than could be gained through any recapture of sales, so that its best strategy would appear to be to leave price where it was, accepting the smaller revenue from that product, but to raise prices on another product line in which it occupied a superior position (particularly if the price increase could be timed to coincide with a product change which contributed nothing additional to cost).

The one thing that is inescapable, however, is that whatever response is provoked by the revenue variance, survival of the firm dictates that it be in the product-sales arena. If a firm's sales revenues slide, its long-run future cannot be assured by any amount of cost-cutting, even though such an effort may win it its target profit in the short run. The challenge must sooner or later be met on the field of sales. But this necessity introduces a dilemma. The firm must respond to an adverse revenue variance (offset at the level of the industry or the economy by increased sales on the part of rival firms), and for its own survival it must respond in the selling field. But such a response is just what is likely to elicit a reaction or retaliation from its rivals. This is the inevitable dilemma of competition. It can be met in part, but only in part, by learning the limits within which its sales actions will not provoke reaction, and the types of initiative it may undertake which will not result in "progressive" retaliation (that is, a tit-for-tat response). The objective of a firm which is seeking to recoup a deteriorated competitive position is to adopt a sales strategy which has a maximum effectiveness vis-à-vis the consumer and a minimum provocation of business rivalry.

Sales Strategy

Of the three possible lines of sales strategy, product innovation or redesign is probably most suited to achieving this objective. While it lends itself to a rival response, it does not foster progressive retaliation, since it takes time to modify or develop a product. One response to a revenue variance (offset in rival firms) is, then, the accelerated introduction of a product in the preparatory stages. "Competition introduces an entirely new item to the public which catches your firm's research and development department flat-footed, so to speak, and forces a 'crash' program to issue a similar product within a very short time." [7] "We undertook some 'crash programs' in certain areas of new product development and in certain promotional developments."

As part of this manipulation of the product line, some products may be dropped as well as added. A food company reports as an action taken "specifically in response to variances from the original budget the dropping of one of our new products because it failed to live up to originally budgeted sales and profit levels." Another company writes: "One division was sold during the year. . . . Volume levels (and profits) had never met expectations but optimism continued to prevail. In 1959 when expectations again were not materializing it became expedient to dispose of this operation." Dropping an unprofitable product line may improve the percentage return on investment, but it does not help the dollar profit position, unless it had actually been producing a loss.

A bolstering of the promotional and marketing programs supporting existing programs also promises to be effective on consumers without necessarily arousing "enemy" firms. There are several possible lines of attack

[7] F. W. Fehr, " 'Surprise' Products and Budgeting," *N.A.A. Bulletin,* December, 1958, sec. 1, p. 14.

here. One which is gaining increasing attention is detailed market analysis. The reason why sales have declined in one city may be quite different from the reasons for a decline in other communities. In the Mercury Division of the Ford Motor Company, for example, a so-called "X-ray study" is made whenever sales lag in a locality. Any factor which may have a bearing on Mercury sales is isolated and examined by a team of analysts. Capital Airline's director of management analysis describes the practice in that company: [8]

> The Marketing Department sets a sales quota for each station for each month. This is always somewhat higher than the operating budget for sales. Management Analysis breaks this quota down into weekly segments based upon past experience for the month involved and we measure station performance, week by week, against this sales quota. . . . The 18 largest stations . . . contribute 89 per cent of our total sales while the other 35 contribute only 11 per cent. (Individually, the contribution of the smaller stations to total sales is insufficient to make top-management attention necessary and these are watched by the Marketing staff.)
>
> [The chart on page 348], "Quota Per cent and Variance," shows the 18 top stations in detail with the others lumped in one line. This chart is for the full month of January and opposite each station's code name is the per cent by which it varied from quota and the thousands of dollars of the variance. . . . When this chart is shown on a weekly basis, top management is in a current position to demand reasons for sales lags and Marketing is in a position to know which stations require investigation. This investigation of all phases of the delinquent station's sales effort gets under way immediately. It may take the form of headquarters staff assistance to the local sales organization through special calls on customers, revision of advertising schedules, inspection of adherence to reservations and ticketing service standards, checking for abnormal local market conditions or perhaps all these. This does not mean that a correction can always be made. Sometimes the failure is due to an unpopular schedule pattern versus that of a competitor and time is required to revise it. . . .

A second line of attack is in the area of selective promotion.

> In the current fiscal year one of our newer minor products has fallen behind sales forecast. In an effort to regain sales volume, promotional efforts are being altered from budget plans and additional funds are being switched from other products. Another minor product line, which does not have the (same) margin as the first product, is also below sales forecast. In this instance promotional expenses are being reduced by the same degree as profit contribution in an effort to maintain the same earnings result.

[8] G. E. Park, *The Controller,* August, 1959, p. 362.

QUOTA PER CENT AND VARIANCE

Target: 100.0   Period: Jan. 1–31

		(000)			(000)
ATL	101.3%	$ 5	MSP	101.0%	$ 3
BAL	90.6	8	MSY	157.8	58
BHM	123.1	22	NYC	122.7	301
BUF	92.8	30	ORF	96.2	7
CHI	106.5	76	PHL	102.6	10
CLE	101.9	11	PIT	102.2	16
YIP	100.4	3	ROC	104.0	8
GRR	76.3	33	DCA	89.0	98
MIA	98.6	6	Other	96.1	37
MKE	109.9	22	Total	103.5%	$316

An enlarged promotional campaign for one of our products was undertaken in the fall of the year when it became obvious that shipments were going to fall short of the budget.

The variances from forecast indicated the need for corrective action. . . . A portion of the institutional advertising, part of a long range program, was deferred. However, increased promotional efforts were made in those specific areas of our business where physical volume had decreased.

Response to sales undervariance in the first quarter was . . . an extensive promotional program in the 2nd quarter to obtain a higher sales base, not only to offset 1st quarter undervariances, but also to improve sales for the balance of the year to offset increased costs of the promotional program.

A stepped-up sales offensive may take the form of improved customer service. A company which supplies the oil and gas industries with equipment and services for exploration, drilling, and production reported that, owing to failure to achieve planned sales, "Sales efforts in the oil fields were intensified in order to increase market share and to meet sales targets. Price changes were made in line with changing competitive patterns and greater emphasis was placed on broadening services offered to enable us to fully service a given drilling project."

Special inducements ("deals") may be offered without actually cutting price.

During the year monthly management meetings were held at which the Vice President in charge of each Division of the Company accounted for variances in the operations over which he had jurisdiction and presented proposals for corrective action on adverse developments. Such corrective action included:

(*a*) Trade deals to stimulate the sale of certain products.

(*b*) Price schedules revised upward or downward where studies indicated that such action would have a favorable effect on net profit.

(*c*) Advertising programs were revised and the accent shifted from product to product as circumstances warranted.

(*d*) Sales effort was stimulated in certain lines by the use of contests and prizes among the sales force.

In the same category, retail establishments may introduce trading stamps. Producers may make use of coupon "introductory" or "trial" offers.

One further avenue for improving sales through promotional efforts lies in expanding dealer outlets or upgrading dealer contacts and services. "Several wholesalers (were) added . . . during the year in an effort to extend and improve our distribution system. Expansion abroad was actively pursued." None of these approaches is likely to evoke retaliation from rivals, though some may elicit reactions taking the form of comparable efforts. Generally speaking, however, this is an area of activity in which rivals are not likely to be provoked unless the action taken turns out to be unusually effective.

In addition to product change and promotional effort, the third possible line of action open to a firm which seeks to recoup a sales position which rivals seem to have eroded is in the sensitive area of price. An earlier chapter noted the influences operative in the setting of prices on the basis of which sales revenues were originally calculated. We observed there the reliance on a markup over standard cost at standard volume adequate to achieve the target return on investment, as the point of departure for price determinations, with these accounting prices then manipulated depending on the competitive and market position of the individual products in the line, always with the hope that downward adjustments which competition might seem to require would be compensated for by upward adjustments on other items so that the over-all target return on investment would be preserved. If rival offerings and consumer responses set limits to management's discretion, from one point of view, they also may be viewed as directing management's attention to those areas where, because their control is weaker, managerial discretion has more latitude.

As the operating year unfolds, it may become evident that particular price decisions on which results were premised are not tenable in the light of competitive action and market behavior. Projected sales fail to materialize. Prices may then be further manipulated in an effort to come closer to short-run target realization than do the results of current performance, and to preserve the firm's market position for long-run goal achievement. In this event, managements sometimes resort first to *sub rosa* price cuts in the form of increased dealer discounts, price quotations at less than customary markup, freight absorption, overseas dumping, the shaving of "extras" (as in the steel industry), and other such concessions, usually made on an individual customer basis.

The reason for the clandestine nature of such price cuts is to be found in the business attitude toward price cutting as an instrument of competition. Although the literature of business professions and trade associations contains frequent reference to the advisability of considering any order which returns something over variable costs and thereby makes a contribution to period costs (and the direct costing system of accounting implicitly stresses that possibility), almost all such statements are modified by warnings of the adverse consequences which may follow from indiscriminate resort to price concessions. The most widely advertised bugaboo is that they may lead to a crumbling of the whole price line, as other customers learn of the favored treatment and press for equal consideration and rival producers or distributors learn of the competitive practice and move to meet it.[9]

Since price cutting so often starts with *sub rosa* concessions to individual purchasers (and may get no further), and since it is important for competitive firms to be alert to what covert price actions their rivals may be taking to gain a bargaining advantage, most companies resort to "intelligence" activities to find out. A survey conducted by the *Harvard Business Review* suggested that perhaps only 5 per cent of 1,500 companies replying to a questionnaire gathered no information on competitors, though the reporting was spasmodic or informal in a majority of cases.[10] The most prevalent instrument for gathering information seems to be a company's network of salesmen, who are often instructed to report back findings. A sales manager writes: [11]

> You must . . . make every effort to learn from our customers and other normal sources in the trade what our competition is doing at all times in your market. To maintain our trade position, it is imperative that Armco have this information and every effort must be made to obtain it, provided that it is not obtained from our competitors themselves, either directly or indirectly through some arrangement with those competitors.

[9] "The true value of marginal business taken at 'contribution' prices can be appraised only in the light of the long-range effects on other prices." Keller, *Management Accounting for Profit Control*, p. 400.
"Does a price concession on new or modified products result in weakening the regular market price for the normal output by encouraging pressure from others to get the same concession . . . ?" "Will the added sales hold present and new regular customers, or merely attract 'good-time Charlies'?" Gardner, *Profit Management and Control*, pp. 181, 182, 184.

[10] "Industrial Espionage," *Harvard Business Review*, vol. 37, November–December, 1959, p. 8.

[11] Letter from the general manager of sales, American Rolling Mills Company, to district sales managers, reproduced in *Administered Prices*, part 8, p. 4614.

A high official of a cement company illustrates the practice: [12]

> A report of a cut price is received from one of our salesmen. This immediately leads to an investigation as to whether it is a general reduction or an isolated case. If the former, the matter is immediately referred to our president and authority to meet the reduction comes at once. If it is an isolated case, all the circumstances are reviewed by our president and chief sales executive and a decision made on the basis of the probable effects on our volume of business. In many cases, a cut price by one competitor would lead to similar action on the part of others so that the decision to meet it would be forced upon us.

The president of a supermarket chain reported to a group of interested managers: [13]

> We . . . subscribe to a private service which provides a continuous price audit of all major competition in our field. Every week we receive a report showing what each major competitor is charging for each of several hundred different commodities. In addition, of course, we conduct our own private surveys.

Such "comparison shopping" is common in the retail field.

As one obtains widespread corroboration of these "intelligence" activities (it would be too strong a term to brand them "espionage," though in particular instances it appears to approach such a category), he is struck by the contrast between the secrecy in which initial price actions (at least reductions) are often shrouded and the openness with which technological and organizational advantages are exposed to competitors. This peculiar mixture of a closeness of commercial information and a free exchange of technical information is partly explainable in terms of a business ethic which assumes that prices should remain stable [14] (so that revelation of one's departure from that state of grace is withheld partly in fear of retaliation but also partly in embarrassment) and that costs should steadily decline (so that to help a competitor is to preserve the industry's morality and invite not retaliation but reciprocity later).

Nevertheless, circumstances arise under which open price cuts appear to be no longer avoidable. Almost always the reason given is "to meet competition." "In some instances where market conditions indicated the possibility of heavy loss of volume, prices were lowered to meet competitive conditions. The policy has been to maintain prices and not to upset the market

[12] G. Clark Thompson, "How Industry Prices Its Products," *The Business Record*, June, 1947, p. 181.

[13] Claude W. Edwards, president, Alpha Beta Food Markets, in "Meeting the Cost/Quality Challenge," *Ends and Means of Modern Management*, A.M.A. Management Report 30, New York, 1959, p. 111.

[14] "Stability of prices is a condition under which industry prospers." Albert Bradley, *N.A.C.A. Bulletin*, Jan. 1, 1927, sec. 1, p. 433.

with frequent changes." A price reduction not designed to meet competition is normally scheduled in the budget plan as part of a longer-range program to expand a product market, without concern over whether rivals move to meet it, and is seldom specifically in response to an adverse revenue variance. "Prices of certain products were reduced during the year both as a result of competitive activity and in an effort to increase our market penetration. Prices were not increased in an effort to recover forecasted profit because of the intense competition in the industry."

In general, then, price as a means of removing revenue variances (offset in rival firms) is used in instances where those rivals have already undercut the firm's price. The reduction is in response to an action already taken by competitors hoping to achieve a temporary advantage or as part of a longer-run plan of market penetration. Only with reluctance does a firm openly initiate a reduction in the market price of some product line in an effort to rebuild shrunken sales, since it can realistically expect that its more profitable competitors will quickly move to match its actions, leaving all worse off than before and the firm itself worse off than its competitors. As long as it has reason to believe that its rivals have not clandestinely cut their listed prices, it has no reason for concluding that its declining revenues are traceable to competitive price relations, which remain as before. The firm is more likely, and probably correctly so, to look to relative product designs and marketing patterns for the cause of its misfortune.

Cost Reactions to Revenue Variances

As previously noted, when unfavorable sales variances materialize at the same time that rivals show offsetting gains, the long-run interests of the firm dictate that the problem should be met in the selling field. To fail to do so jeopardizes the security of the company in its present product markets. The impression of retrogression may also injure it in its relations with capital suppliers and stockholders, conceivably loosening management's hold on the corporation. Cost-cutting measures are no real solution to such a situation. Nevertheless, although no solution, there are several understandable reasons why firms frequently respond to revenue variances (offset in competitive firms) by attempted cost savings.

Flexible budgets provide a weapon for curbing direct labor and material costs as volume declines; they are less effective in controlling variable period expenses. For this purpose *ad hoc* cost reduction programs may be necessary. "This year . . . we have initiated an expense reduction program to bring our commercial, technical and administrative expenses more in line with the level of sales realized. We established targets for savings in each of the variable accounts, such as Travel and Entertainment, Telephone and Telegraph, etc. We postponed some personnel recruitment until next year."

A second reason for reacting to a revenue variance by attempting to cut costs lies in a company's need to conserve cash. While cash outlays fall with cash receipts, they do not fall proportionately. Fixed and continuing expenses continue to drain the company of its cash, and efforts to meet this drain by controlling outflows come naturally from financial management. Capital investment projects make particularly inviting targets.

> With the failure to achieve planned revenue and with costs staying up, our cash position, though relatively good, was not as planned. As a result, all proposed investment outlays were given a very thorough perusal with regard to certainty of performance. Some of a generalized improvement nature were postponed indefinitely and others, though pointing to a specific avenue of gain, were deferred until evaluation could be more clearly defined.

> We have a system of budgeting capital dollars and a semi-formal system of ranking the forecast projects in their order of importance. In the event the forecast net earnings are substantially above or below forecast, the capital improvements program would be altered to fit our cash generation picture. As a matter of fact, there is one rather large capital outlay that is being considered for the current year that will definitely not be approved unless the results of operations do live up to our forecasts.

> In the oil business, the most flexible financial aspect is found in capital expenditures. If properly controlled, capital expenditures may be quickly curtailed or even shut off, as conditions require. That is why [our company] budgets this type of expenditure more formally than any other phase of its business.[15]

A third reason for trying to brake, through cost actions, the impact on profit of a revenue slide is the desire to maintain a relatively stable record of earnings. A smooth earnings curve conveys a sense of corporate soundness in a way which an erratically fluctuating one does not.

These three reasons for cost control in the face of a revenue decline—to keep variable period expenses in line with volume, to conserve cash, and to stabilize the earnings record—obviously overlap and reinforce each other. Equally obvious, they are all short-run measures, constituting no answer to the underlying problem which can be met only by actions affecting the

---

[15] In reporting on his investigation of surveys of business planning, Prof. Irwin Friend reported that "A change in the sales outlook was by far the most important single factor mentioned by businessmen as the reason for a significant modification of investment plans, though apparently moderate changes in the sales outlook did not significantly affect capital programs." "Critical Evaluation of Surveys of Expectations, Plans, and Investment Behavior," in Mary Jean Bowman (ed.), *Expectations, Uncertainty, and Business Behavior* (New York: Social Science Research Council, 1958), p. 192.

revenue side of the ledger. To the extent that the management of a company believes that the latter correction will take time, and particularly if it is dependent on the development of new products, then cost responses to revenue variances may be all that is possible in the short run. In a figurative sense, the company marks time (conserving cash and bolstering earnings through control of expenditures) while it waits the development of the new products or the opening of the new fields which will restore its lost profit position. "Since company backlog indicated a continuing decline in military business during the year, promotional activities were increased. . . . Other action taken included increased emphasis on cost reduction, greater research and development effort and acceleration of a planned diversification program into non-military fields."

The vice-president and treasurer of a chemical concern reports that in the year just past "our earnings results fell about 15% below the forecast." He comments:

> Our most important activity to improve our earnings is in our research program. We have stepped up our research and development activity considerably during the past several years, both to enter new fields of operations and to improve our present line of chemical products and find new fields for their use. . . . Similar to many other industries, we have been experiencing a price squeeze, both from local and foreign competition. Since it is very difficult to increase prices, we are making a concerted effort to improve our products as well as our methods of manufacture. This requires, as stated before, a certain amount of additional research expense plus new equipment. During the current year our capital expenditure program—partly for addition of new product lines, but mostly for improvement of present product lines, will more than double the [previous year's] outlay.

Replacement of the weak members of the product family is a process which often cannot be accomplished within the current budget year. "Product changes in design, material or function require considerable time in development and testing. In our industry, short-term business fluctuations do not trigger sudden product changes." In the meantime, cost control eases the firm's financial plight.

Cost Reactions to Nonoffset Variances

If a firm experiences an adverse profit variance and finds that the profit performance among its immediate rivals, in its product markets, shows a generally downward movement, like its own, and particularly if it finds that this profit decline is characteristic of business generally throughout the economy, this suggests that its difficulty lies outside the firm and is related to what is happening in the industry and in the rest of the economy.[16] The slack within its own operations is not offset by increased activity in other firms which are viewed as rivals. All firms (or most firms) are suffering from the same malady, so that generally speaking no profit variance is offset elsewhere.

Since the reason for this misfortune is not peculiar to the firm but is shared by its competitors as well (and perhaps business generally), there is little which the individual firm can do of a corrective nature. The underlying conditions which give rise to its adverse profit showing can be corrected only with the passage of time or by governmental intervention. Nevertheless, it faces the problem of lasting out the spell of bad weather. There is therefore a compulsion to "do something" about the situation.

Even though it cannot itself correct circumstances which are general, the firm can act *as though* the situation was particular to it and take the appropriate action. Just as in the case of revenue variances attributable to offsetting revenue increases in rival firms, so now may a management try to improve its short-run profit position by cost cutting, even though this constitutes no solution to its problems.

> [In] 1958 and 1957, the textile industry experienced depressed economic conditions which were reflected in the earnings results of this Company. In 1958, net earnings were 15.2 per cent less than anticipated in the Original Budget while in 1957, earnings were 21.9 per cent under the Original Budget estimate. As this was a relatively prolonged period of reduced earnings for this company, it was necessary to emphasize programs for the reduction of costs and for the curtailment of expenses. These programs included deferring of maintenance expenditures, reductions in promotional expenditures for some products, the use of substitute materials and concerted efforts for better plant efficiencies. These were combined with increased sales promotions for other individual products, the development and marketing of new products, the utilization of incentive selling programs and, in general, remedial action in all selling areas.
>
> Expense savings programs were instituted throughout all the selling, administrative and general expense classifications. Where possible, expense items were either eliminated completely or delayed to a future period.
>
> In line with the reduction in cash resulting from reduced earnings, some minor revisions were made in the timing of large investment outlays.

---

[16] The suggestion is not conclusive, since influences may be mixed. A firm may be troubled not only by a general recession but by that as well as circumstances and conditions peculiar to it, in a proportion difficult to identify. Its decline may be measured relative to its rivals in an effort to establish the difference, but it is not always possible to find rivals which can be considered reliable standards. Nevertheless, without being overly precise, the comparison certainly suggests the conclusion.

The controller of a grain company provides another illustration:

> During the fiscal year, . . . our gross margins were below budget
> by 14%. For approximately a year and one-half, we have seen de-
> pressed agricultural prices, specifically for broilers, eggs and hogs.
> Feeders of these particular types of livestock are our principal cus-
> tomers. Reduced production on the part of the feeders has, in turn,
> resulted in a reduction in our feed business. It has also resulted in
> reduced feed business for the entire industry. . . .
>
> Below budget performance during the current year, as well as in
> the latter part of the preceding fiscal year, motivated us to give serious
> thought to a cost reduction program which we inaugurated. The aim
> of our program was not a temporary reduction in cost because of a
> poor year, but could better be described as a long-range house clean-
> ing, or reviewing our operations, weeding out the unnecessary and
> giving increased impetus to the worthwhile. The ever-increasing level
> of wage rates makes it imperative that more effort be put behind labor
> efficiency improvements. This we have done! We have also examined
> carefully all Service Department and fringe type activities to ascertain
> to the best of our judgment that they are required or are operating at
> the required level.

An official of another company affected by the doldrums in agriculture
reports:

> We have had two separate reductions in expense budgets, affecting
> all divisions of the company except Research, as a result of our failure
> to attain our budgeted sales volume. These have not been large enough
> to offset the loss in net profit as a result of the lack of sales, but they
> have materially helped in that direction, and have also kept us from
> building up expenses at levels which we could not sustain next year.
> Further, we have instituted additional cost reduction programs which
> include, among other things:
>
> 1. A basic switch from first class to coach air travel.
>
> 2. A daily report to the Executive Vice President on all long dis-
> tance phone calls over three minutes.
>
> 3. A new requirement that all expense accounts be additionally
> reviewed by one organization level higher than previously.
>
> 4. A statement of policy that, except for direct labor and replacement
> of terminations, there will be no new hires without advance approval
> of the Executive Vice President.
>
> 5. A review of our trade association memberships, with the thought
> in mind of reducing our expense in this area.
>
> 6. We are also looking into the potential savings of self-insurance
> in several areas. In addition, we have delayed capital investment in the
> way of new buildings in some of our subsidiary companies, we have
> moved an additional portion of our manufacturing facilities . . . to
> . . . Tennessee (where labor rates are lower), and are now in the

process of dividing our marketing activities into three major product lines. This latter move will take a good part of 1961 before it is completed, but we expect to achieve a greater sales effort through specialization of our sales force.

Another example comes from the president of a steel company.

The current year [1960] has been one of gross uncertainty inasmuch as the steel business has developed contrary to the expectations of all of us. . . . Our business has shrunken some forty-odd per cent below our original estimates, which were very carefully prepared by our Sales and Administrative departments back in November and October of 1959. It is rather apparent, in our opinion, that the reason for the tremendous shrinkage came about by the fact that everyone had a great deal more inventory than they anticipated because the integrated mills as well as the cold mills got back to work at capacity [following the steel strike] a great deal faster than anyone had anticipated plus the fact that a number of major industries in the country anticipated a larger volume of their end products than actually developed, therefore, under good, sound management, it was necessary for everyone to reduce inventories, thus, the basic industries, such as steel, felt the drop-off almost immediately.

Since a budget is the fundamental management tool used by the vast majority of sound American companies, it becomes necessary to change these budgets in accordance with the things that happen during the year.

We did change our promotional activities by reducing our advertising schedules in certain markets that our Sales Department knew we were unable to acquire any additional business even with a stepped-up program because of the inventory situation. Therefore, this schedule was cut very substantially. . . .

In times such as these, cost reductions are absolutely essential, and we put all of our methods engineers and production control people to using all of the ingenuity at their command to increase productivity and thereby reduce costs. This is a continuing program but in times of distress, it is even more important than under normal operations when it is strictly a routine day-in and day-out matter.

An interesting case is provided by an official of a company supplying the housing and construction industries.

Actual revenues were down 11% from our original forecast. The principal reason was that construction generally was down lower than we had forecast. This was particularly true in the home building market which affects our cement business and seriously affects our gypsum business. Overall expenditures were approximately 9% lower than forecast. However, there was a wide variation depending upon the type of expense. For example, Costs of Products Sold and Operating Expenses were down somewhat over 12%, whereas, selling, administrative and general expenses were down approximately 5%. The first type of expense would normally follow quantity production although from the percentage, you can see that there was an effort to reduce operating expenses. In the case of selling, administrative expenses, etc., a large portion of this was due to expense control measures. The following action was taken as a result of decline in revenues and profits. In the first place, we revised our entire forecast since it became obvious that the overall industry sales would be down and that we would not be able to increase our share of the market sufficiently to maintain our previous sales forecast. Reduction in quantity sales, of course, in some instances automatically increased unit expenses. Prior to the start of 1960 we had stepped up promotional activity in anticipation of higher competitive business during 1960 and now that some efforts have accrued from that activity, we are considering the possibility of eliminating some types of promotional activity particularly those directly related to immediate sales. There have been no price changes except minor fringe changes in order to meet competition. There have been no important product or service changes.

There has been an intensive program which is still going on and probably will go on throughout this year at the very least, in cost reduction on three lines:

1. Further emphasis on an already started program toward longer term cost reduction. This includes such additions toward further automation, streamlining of department operations, etc.

2. Immediate cost reduction programs geared to particular plants and production departments. This includes complex problems such as analysis of utilization of production machinery to direct and simple cost reduction such as layoffs of personnel.

3. Revision of administrative and selling practices including streamlining and increasing efficiency of these administrative departments.

The reduction in sales and profits in our forecasts thereof [has] changed both the level and timing of our investment outlays although timing has been a more important consideration than level. In effect we have postponed some capital outlays and have slowed down others. This is, of course, directly related to cash flow of the corporation. Personnel recruitment has been affected in that except for replacement it has slowed down considerably. The level of our dividend payments has not changed and is not expected to change since our payout has been only about half of overall profits and only about one-third of our overall cash flow.

Another firm whose product line is geared to residential construction reported more drastic action in the face of declining revenues.

We do, of course, annually forecast our anticipated sales volume and budget expenditures by classification against income in such a way as to provide a planned profit at the rate of projected sales.

We also enter our actual results against budget on a monthly basis and on a periodic basis we re-forecast our sales in the light of results obtained to that date.

Our particular problem is complicated by the fact that our sales are tied in directly with new residential construction and, therefore, are subject to cyclical as well as seasonal variations, which can not be readily determined in advance. For example, this year we experienced a very slow first half and, therefore, on the basis of past performance we were rather confident that our third and fourth quarters would, to some extent, offset the slow start. This year, however, we just didn't get the boost in activity which we expected and as a result found that we had delayed too long in adjusting expenditures to the level of sales, which will be significantly less than anticipated.

We did re-forecast our sales in April and in so doing had reduced considerably our original forecast figure for the year, but the adjustment was, unfortunately, not as great as it should have been because of our anticipation that business would pick up substantially as the construction season got into full swing.

During the second quarter we began to be really concerned about the sales outlook for the year, and I set a deadline of July 15th for taking a completely new look at our projections.

When that date was reached it was evident that sales for the year were going to be off significantly; therefore, we re-forecast on the most conservative basis we could envision. After doing so, we developed a new projected profit and loss statement which in this particular case indicated that a loss would be incurred, and then planned and put into effect very severe restrictions on expenditures. Our objective was to produce a profit at the end of the year in spite of a sales decline and this meant, of course, that the profit would have to be produced from curtailed expenses.

In this connection the following moves were made:

1. Salaries of $10,000 or more per year were reduced 10 or 15% on a voluntary basis. Restitution with interest to be made at a future date at the discretion of the president, and salaries to be restored to the previous levels at the earliest possible time.

2. The direct labor force was laid off to the extent needed to bring production in line with inventory reduction objectives.

3. Certain managerial functions and activities were combined to permit the termination of a number of salaried employees.

4. All expense classifications were reviewed, re-budgeted, and this data along with weekly performance data was made available to all department heads and managers.

5. Stringent controls over cash expenditures were instituted so that we would be sure to have available sufficient cash to pay our seasonal bank borrowings. These controls took the form of setting planned cash objectives which if attained will build up the full amount needed to pay bank indebtedness. As one example, we developed plans to go

to our suppliers for extended terms of payment on some mutually satisfactory basis.

6. We took an interim physical inventory and planned the disposition of slow moving items.

7. We sought out and employed from the outside an experienced production superintendent and an experienced salesmanager to take the places of persons with lesser capabilities.

8. We put our product planning and development people to work on items which could be brought to the point of sale much quicker than those which they would normally work on.

9. We closed down certain manufacturing departments which were determined to be adding to expense rather than contributing to profit.

10. We transferred certain people so as to minimize the problem of round pegs in square holes, while at the same time putting greater emphasis on short term sales improvement and long term cost reduction.

Whereas in the past we have been going through the motions in connection with periodic appraisal of budget performance we have now scheduled such appraisals on a quarterly basis and have set the specific dates for a year in advance.

Revenue Reactions to Nonoffset Variances

There are some actions which a firm can undertake in the selling field in seeking to meet a poor profit position due to shrinking revenues, at a time when its rivals are similarly affected. As in the case of sales activities taken to remedy declining revenue offset in competitive firms, these may elicit imitation or retaliation, short-circuiting their effectiveness. Nevertheless, some types of actions are less likely to evoke such reactions or to lead to progressive retaliation, and even if followed may still leave the firm (and sometimes its competitors) better off than before. Such actions are particularly of the type which gear a product or marketing strategy to the needs of customers which have themselves shifted under the impact of receding economic activity and personal incomes. An example is provided by a biscuit manufacturer which reported these actions in the 1958 recession:

> *Changes in promotional activity.* Changed slant to consumer value; i.e., weight, retail price, etc. Turned promotional emphasis to staple commodities such as Saltine Crackers, excluding luxury crackers.
> *Product line changes.* Oriented Research and Development program to deliver quickly smaller packages with lower retail price opportunity. Developed line of sandwich cookies of medium quality, packaged to offer genuine and unusual value to consumers.

Such product-line and promotional efforts, as we have noted, are least likely to arouse the enemy to respond, but the inevitable uncertainty about their effectiveness is also likely to make them less attractive to the hard-pressed firm which is urgently seeking to improve its cash position. Such a firm is often driven to flirt with something which it—as well as its rivals —would prefer to avoid: price reductions. This action taken while its competitors are holding their price line will probably increase the inflow of needed cash, and there is always the hope that the increase will continue long enough to provide the required cash injections if it is able to hide its action from its rivals or at least avoid calling attention to it.

Professor Alfred Oxenfeldt of Columbia University, appearing as a panelist before the Joint Economic Committee, provided a nice statement describing the firm in this circumstance.[17]

> An unsystematic study of announced price reductions during the present and the last recession suggests that the most important cause of price reductions these days is that a competitor has already reduced prices. Thus, to explain a general price reduction for a product requires that one seek out the firms which were the first to reduce price and account for their actions. The result is the *"weak link"* explanation for price declines.
>
> Price reductions during recession generally are initiated by firms that have been very hard hit by the business decline. They may have suffered a larger reduction in sales than most firms in their industry due to accidents of product mix or because they did not have as popular a "line" as their rivals at the time the recession developed. Or, they may be firms with the lowest financial liquidity—or with the largest obligations coming due. Sometimes the "weak links" are firms whose managements are prone to panic under pressure; they may be executives of low intellectual caliber who are unwilling to reason through the consequences of their price actions. We do not consider as "weak links" those firms which hope to divert business from many rivals without stirring them up to retaliate or those that hope to "beat their rivals to the punch" and make a minor "killing" before the others do something to protect themselves. The "weak link" is a firm that is, or imagines itself to be, in danger of being driven out of business or of sustaining extremely heavy financial losses or of suffering a loss of standing (as, for example, a loss of a high credit rating or a reputation for uninterrupted dividends) that is extremely valuable to continued operation.
>
> Under such circumstances, the management of a stricken firm will almost always feel compelled to take some action that promises speedy relief. The only policy that is clearly intolerable at such times is that the firm do nothing to save itself. One of the most potent and speedy sales promotion devices is a price cut.

[17] Alfred R. Oxenfeldt, "Cyclical Implications of Private Pricing Policies," in *The Relationship of Prices to Economic Stability and Growth* (compendium of papers submitted by panelists appearing before the Joint Economic Committee), 85th Cong., 2d Sess. Mar. 31, 1958, p. 465.

However necessitous actions of this type may appear to the firm which institutes them, the business community has unhesitatingly condemned them. However understanding a businessman may be of the circumstances which prompt a hard-pressed fellow to such behavior, the behavior itself is not condoned. A kind of business morality regards price cutting as at best a questionable yielding by weaklings to external pressures and at worst an unethical practice. William S. Kemp, a past president of the National Association of Cost Accountants, has said:

> In periods of depression or decreased sales due to overproduction it has been the practice of many to cut the sales price and accept business at cost or less in order to offset or reduce the loss in overhead expense. While this practice under keen competition is to be expected, it is a selfish policy and detrimental to business as a whole. All methods of forced sales, when a legitimate demand for the produce does not exist, are bad practice and only prolong the time necessary to get back to a reasonable relation between supply and demand.[18]

The appendix to this chapter reproduces an unusually lucid statement prepared during the depression of the 1930s by the president of a trade association, setting forth the rationale for the compulsory use of cost as a basis for price with the objective of "rationalizing" the manufacturing and distributive sectors of the economy. The philosophy represented by that statement—that price cutting in response to sharp bargaining by the buyer in the face of necessitous circumstances impinging on the seller is reprehensible and calamitous—lies behind "fair trade" and "nondiscriminatory pricing" legislation.[19]

---

[18] In "Budgets and Pre-determination of Costs," *N.A.C.A. Bulletin,* July 15, 1926, sec. 1, p. 823. Mr. Kemp goes on to say: "The attitude of the United States Government toward trusts, consolidations and the exchange of information between trade associations in the past has done much to foster ignorant and unfair competition and overproduction. There are now hopeful signs that business organizations may consolidate and that associations may legally exchange trade and statistical information.

"Under these changed conditions and with the progress that is being made in the standardization of production and distribution, it is hoped that a reasonable control of production will result. If such conditions can be brought about they will do much toward the stabilization of sales prices, labor employment and returns on invested capital."

[19] The attitude of the business community toward maintenance of a sound and stable price structure parallels very closely the attitude of labor toward wage maintenance as against wage cutting in the face of business adversity. In the following quotation from Prof. Henry C. Emery, "Hard Times and the Standard Wage," appearing in the *Yale Review,* vol. 17 (1908), pp. 266–267, the term "standard price" could readily be substituted for "standard wage." Time has not affected the validity of his observation.

"What they [Emery was speaking of unionists, but in the present connection we might substitute management] dread most of all is a reduction of wages, not so

Nothing—not even union "excesses"—arouses managerial spleen more than the specter of the business community being subjected to the depradations, uncertainties, and "inhumanities" consequent upon competition which borders on price warfare. The textile industry has frequently been pictured by businessmen themselves in the same terms that a theologian might use to describe the pitiable and wretched end of the evil and unjust man. For example: [20]

> Buyers shop among textile makers for the lowest price. Textile mills shave pennies and fractions of pennies from the price so they can sell more of their product. Prices are often cut to the loss level to keep a mill running. When a mill fails, another manufacturer may buy it [for] a fraction of its cost. This lowers his overhead so he can reopen the mill, produce textiles at still lower costs, and cut prices further. The result is frequent bankruptcy. . . . In this competition, the goal of most companies is to survive. In the daily struggle to stay alive there is little money, time or energy left for efforts to get a wider market or a better product.

When the firm which is the weakest link in a given market gives way to the pressures on it to raise cash to match its outflows and cuts prices, it is difficult to prevent a general caving in of the price line. Even though the total capacity of the company which is responsible for this result is only a fraction of the total market, so that if all other companies held fast to their price position they could not, collectively, lose many sales and such as they did lose would be distributed among them, so that individually no one firm need expect any large defection of buyers, those companies which themselves were none too strong would hardly reason so self-reassuringly. There is no guarantee that sales which were gained by the price cutter would be taken randomly from the rest of the field. Suppose other companies were also shaving prices clandestinely? The "resolute" firms might find their

---

much because they unreasonably refuse to make any sacrifices when the whole community is suffering, but because they believe, and they think they know from experience, that a reduction of wages once made is very difficult to restore. . . . When the manufacturer cannot pay standard wages and run full time at a profit, let him curtail his production, let some men be discharged, but let the level of wages continue intact."

"Fair trade" or "resale price maintenance" laws are designed to prevent cut-price retailing of branded products. "Nondiscriminatory pricing" legislation is intended to prevent businesses in strong bargaining positions from forcing price concessions from suppliers, at the expense of weaker rivals. The former laws seek to hold the price line for the benefit of the small-firm seller, just as the latter seek to do for the benefit of the small-firm buyer. Most legislation of these and related types, both Federal and state, came into existence as a consequence of the Great Depression.

[20] *Profit, Performance and Progress* (New York, American Telephone and Telegraph Co., May, 1959), p. 11.

revenues suddenly drying up, with lost markets hard to recover. Even the hardiest of firms might conclude that their very strength made it possible and desirable to teach the price-cutting management, and others like him, a lesson by moving quickly to remove his advantage, matching him cut for cut, and perhaps even a little better.

We have already observed that even in normal times most firms benefit from some form of "intelligence network" in acquiring information on the price actions of their rivals. The need is intensified when the setting is one in which all firms start from a generally deteriorated revenue position, in the midst of an industry-wide or economy-wide recession. For self-preservation it is necessary for every firm to be keyed to what its rivals are doing. There is no way of avoiding the ill effects of covert price concessions by enemy firms except by alert reporting and intelligence activity, permitting reaction as considered necessary.

Reporting and informational activity is not useful solely with respect to price cuts, however. It is as necessary and as widely used at times when rising costs are poaching on profits and inviting consideration of price advances as a means for remedying a generally adverse situation (profit variances in one firm nonoffset in others). Under such circumstances there is a penalty for the firm that initiates a price increase if its rivals do not follow, but there is gain for all if they move prices up concurrently, while avoiding collusion. The following is a paraphrase of the comments of one corporate controller in the chemical industry:

> In a competitive industry "intelligence systems" are really the foundation of company price policy. We may have increased costs and feel that a price increase is justified. We are aware that our competitors are likely to be similarly situated. But any one company faces the danger that if it raises its prices the others will not follow. Even if only a few hard competitors do not follow there is the fear of trouble, the fear that they will take a company's business away from it. Companies of that kind—which take advantage of a firm that starts a price rise after costs have gone up—are not just tough competitors, they are unscrupulous. They are taking advantage of companies which have made perfectly justifiable price increases.
>
> I can remember one company in our field which raised prices when the industry clearly thought this was necessary, only to have the others hold back to see what would happen. When another company put on a campaign to win the customers of the firm which had raised its prices, that company had to retract its price increase and the whole industry suffered as a consequence.
>
> The intelligence systems keep the reports coming back as to competitors' price quotations, costs, and operating problems. Quarterly and annual reports are studied carefully. Degree of capacity utilization is a key figure. If this gets high for the industry, price increases can

be given serious consideration. When it gets low, look out for discounts from list and also some price declines in the list itself.

The intelligence activities of firms relate, then, not only to *competitive* behavior under conditions of recession or inflation. They are also required to organize "compatible" or "orderly" price behavior among competitors when the time comes that it is desirable for an entire industry to move up or down the price ladder in competing with other industries for its share of the consumer's dollar. Some means of effecting consensus is needed to avoid turning a downward movement into a rout and an upward movement into a fiasco which leaves some courageous firm in an exposed position from which it can only retreat with injury to itself.

In order to settle such questions of whether there should be a general price movement in an industry, up or down, and if so of what magnitude, over the years firms have devised means of signaling and reading intent without actually taking joint actions which would be illegal. Most of these industry conventions can be put under the general category of "price leadership," but this is a more complex phenomenon than the simple name would suggest. An oil company executive has said: [21]

> The so-called price leadership in the petroleum industry boils down to the fact that some company in each territory most of the time bears the onus of formally recognizing current conditions. . . . [It is] always in danger of taking a step with which competitors will not agree, with the penalty for misjudgment a sharp reduction in profits unless the misjudgment is rectified at once. In short, unless the so-called price leader accurately interprets basic conditions and local conditions, it soon will not be the leading marketer. Price leadership does not mean that the price leader can set prices to get the maximum profit and force the other marketers to conform.

The price leader is not typically some firm which, because of its size, is able to dominate an industry and therefore to take price actions for its own benefit which other smaller firms either are obliged to follow (in the case of price declines) or are only too happy to follow (in the case of increases). The price leader is an instrument for the industry, a bellwether, whose function is to study the situation at time of price restiveness to try to ascertain the industry consensus. When the leader is convinced that a price movement is called for, it formalizes the matter and signals the timing by initiating the action itself. If it has performed its study function well, the rest of the industry, or most of the industry, will follow suit, thus putting the stamp of approval on the price decision and making it effective. If it has misjudged

[21] S. A. Swensrud, vice-president of the Standard Oil Company of Ohio, testifying before the Temporary National Economic Committee, *TNEC Hearings,* 1939, part 15, p. 8436.

the situation and other firms do not follow, it must usually rescind its action (if it has been to raise prices) or recalculate the impact of its action on its profit position if it has lowered prices (as in the Ford case, cited earlier).

It is misleading to speak of the price leader as though it were always the same firm and always the largest firm in the industry. The largest firm must usually sanction (conform to) a price change to make it effective throughout the industry, but any other firm may take the initiative if it believes the time is ripe and no one else is making a move. Indeed, there appears to be a growing preference for spreading the leadership function around the industry, to avoid any impression of collusion or dominant control. Moreover, for public relations reasons the largest firm in an industry often hesitates to take the initiative in raising prices, though it would welcome and follow the action of a smaller rival.

What conclusions may one draw from all the available evidence of the importance of price as an instrument for improving company performance in the face of adverse variances of profit from the budget plan—when these are either offset or nonoffset in rival firms (that is, when competitors are either avoiding or sharing the misfortune)?

On the whole, price seems to have relatively limited value for this purpose. A firm's product prices can seldom be advanced to improve an unfavorable profit position unless it has a product sufficiently dissimilar from other products on the market as to have no close substitutes and, at the same time, sufficiently wanted to confer on it a measure of price inelasticity. This is most likely to be the case in the stage of the life cycle of a new product when it is meeting with a growing momentum of acceptance; but this is precisely the time when most firms prefer to reduce the new product's price, to gain for it a wider market. Prices may also be advanced without fear of loss of sales to competitors if the occasion is ripe for a price leader to take the field up with it, in a concurrent price movement. But this takes preparation and time.

The most likely short-run use of price to meet an adverse profit showing is to win new business with *sub rosa* price cuts. Whatever contribution the additional business makes to the firm's revenues over its marginal costs improves its position. It undertakes such a course, however, in the knowledge based on experience that such cuts are likely to come to the attention of its competitors, who will follow suit, putting pressure on the industry's whole structure of prices and thereby perhaps deteriorating its revenue position still further. It may be willing to run that risk, however, in the belief that if it fails to use lower prices as a bargaining tool to gain more business, it will simply be forgoing an advantage which a rival in like circumstance will seize, and in the further belief that, if other firms face the same worsening situation as confronts it, the whole industry structure of prices is going to be subjected to irresistible pressure in any event.

A firm is likely, however, to resist open reduction in its price list until the situation is sufficiently clarified (distressed) to encourage a price leader (or a weak link) to take the industry down with it. The longer such action can be postponed, the more favorable its own position vis-à-vis the trade, since it can continue to resort to secret concessions as a lure to new business. The open price reduction is likely to come only after covert reductions have become so widespread and have taken such a number of forms as to threaten industry stability. The same oil official testified: [22]

> The major sales executives of all companies watch carefully the number and size of the subnormal markets. . . . If the number of local price cuts increases, if the number and amount of secret concessions to commercial consumers increase, if the secret unpublicized concessions to dealers increase, it becomes more and more difficult to maintain the higher prices. . . . Finally, some company, usually the largest marketer in the territory, recognizes that the subnormal price has become the normal price and announces a general price reduction throughout the territory.

The mechanics of a price increase are similar, but operate in reverse.

> Price advances may be either local increases which represent a reversal of a previous price reduction or a general price advance. Local price advances come about when dealers' struggles have spent themselves. The salesmen, therefore, constantly gage the attitude of dealers. All companies serving the particular territory are anxious to raise the price in the subnormal market, but the leading marketer in the territory is naturally most anxious to get the price up because the territory is more important to him than to the other companies. But the local manager of the leading company does not know whether his competitors are ready to advance the price. He fears that they may seize upon any price advance by him as an opportunity to gain volume at his expense. He therefore asks his salesmen to gage the attitude of competitors through the reports of the customers as to actions and comments of the salesmen of competitors. Finally, the local manager for the leading company decides that the decrease in the ambitions of dealers and competitors makes possible a price advance in the local area.

Under the circumstances it is easy to understand why so many managements have product prices on their mind—they constitute a variable which

---

[22] S. A. Swensrud, vice-president of the Standard Oil Company of Ohio, in *TNEC Hearings,* 1939, part 15, p. 8433. The subsequent quotation is from the same testimony, p. 8434.

is critical to successful corporate performance and one which must be watched carefully—but it is also easy to understand why they do not regard prices as a readily manipulable variable for the improvement of a poor profit showing. Like sin, prices are important and must be consciously considered, but played with only at one's risk, and then with great exercise of caution; they are most tempting to a manager precisely when his defenses are weakest, but the possible penalty of the act committed—whether clandestine and discreet or brazenly open—is a constant deterrent.

Reactions to Favorable Variances

While favorable variances tend to create few problems for management, they cannot simply be dismissed with expressions of joy. They too require thought.

The master budget is a statement of the flows of funds expected within the company due to projected rates of activity. As such, its parts are proportioned to each other. As changes develop in certain respects, these affect their relationship to the rest of the firm's activity and necessitate accommodating changes. Favorable variances no less than adverse may require budgetary revisions to retain correct proportioning. Otherwise the budget would resemble a sculpture whose creator had started out to fashion, let us say, the figure of a little girl, but forgetfully had provided the bust of a mature woman.

The lore of business is filled with examples of growing firms which, in the flush of a better sales volume than had been expected, expand their operations without regard to the adequacy of working capital—after all, each sale returns a profit—until suddenly they are brought up short by an overextended position. Obligations which cannot be postponed are not fully covered by quick assets; bankers regard with disfavor a loan application from a management betraying such unseasoned judgment; equity capital is unavailable without sacrificing control at a bargain price. For the same reason the literature of business provides cases of companies which had to refuse orders and hold to a given volume of sales out of a lack of additional working capital. In other words, the original budget plan had to be maintained as representing the best proportioning of the parts to the whole which was possible under the existing circumstances.

Admittedly, these are extreme examples, and not many firms are required to go through the traumatic experience of turning down sales, though a good many have at times faced the necessity of giving such late delivery dates as effectively to say No to a prospective customer. Nevertheless, the element of proportioning a budget does require paying attention to favorable as well as unfavorable deviations from the budget plan.

On the cost side, a favorable variance that repeats itself calls for analysis in an effort to consolidate a possible long-run improvement in productivity. It does not normally, however, entail the kind of problem which, if unattended to, creates future difficulties. Usually only favorable variances on the sales side do that.

As sales volume increases and inventories are drawn down, production must be revised upward. Commonly a budget revision providing for this is made through the flexible budget, which gears production costs to production levels. But no similar automatic provision is made for the necessary increase in inventories and accounts receivable. These must be consciously allowed for, and the amounts so tied up in working capital must find their way into a revised budget.

In so far as additional sales bring higher unit profits (as fixed costs are spread over larger volumes), the cash generated frequently creates a liquid condition even after these accounts have been increased as necessary. The funds flowing into the firm accumulate initially in the working capital accounts, as cash or accounts receivable, and in so far as the cash receipts are in excess of what is needed for the expanded production, it is management's decision how they shall be used. "Whenever actual performance is more favorable than budgeted performance, the increased revenue goes into current assets to be used at the discretion of Management. It may be used for debt retirement, capital investment, or other timely purposes."

Among other timely purposes for which companies have used surplus cash have been the purchase of securities, the acquisition of other companies, or "fringe benefits." ("Probably one result of the better-than-expected year was the decision of management to air condition our Main Office at a cost of approximately $3,000,000. This is one item in our capital budget which might have been delayed had the year been less successful.")

In some companies certain uses of funds, other than production, expand proportionately with sales. Advertising expenditures and research outlays are sometimes budgeted on a percent-of-sales basis and rise with revenues.

Not all actions which increase the sums of cash in the company are favorable. While normally a reduction in costs is looked on with approval, this is not necessarily true of failure to use capital appropriations. If appropriations are underspent not because the capital project has been secured more economically but because delays in completion or technical problems have been encountered, cash may accumulate but the variance cannot be called favorable.

Finally, the unplanned prosperity which descends on a company when sales increase but inadequate attention has been given to useful ways of investing the surplus cash often has the effect of loosening the lines of budgetary control. Adverse cost variances are looked on more tolerantly because offset within the company. Requests for above-budget or out-of-budget authorizations are approved with less scrutiny. Wasteful practices get their start and may persist until some future recession forces a belt tightening. It takes exceptional strength of character to operate under flush conditions in the same manner as under normal or straitened circumstances, even for the impersonal corporation.

Variances and Flows

"Offsetting" and "nonoffsetting" occur with respect to actual flows of funds. All the economic units in the system are tied together by the flows which they generate and which they receive, and it is changes in the magnitude of these micro-flows of which we can say they are offset at a higher level of aggregation by some compensating change in income flow in another unit, or nonoffset if that should be the case. "Variances," however, are not—or are not necessarily—changes in actual income flows, but deviations from *expected* flows. The actual flows into and out of a firm might remain constant at some level, but variances from budget nevertheless arise if the firm had projected an increase or decrease in its activity. In the preceding analysis, however, variances have been discussed as though they were identical with actual flows, so far as inducing action by management is concerned. Is there a cause here for possible confusion?

If a shift in income was in the process of taking place (upward or downward), involving an offsetting of actual flows among firms, and if this shift was properly anticipated and provided for in budgets, no variances would emerge. But offsetting would have taken place nonetheless. Again, does treating these two as equivalents not lead to possible error?

No error or confusion should result as long as one maintains the perspective of the individual firm, which is the point of view which has been adopted throughout this study. If a shift in actual income which had already taken place or was about to take place had been recognized and provided for in a firm's budget, presumably that budget incorporates too whatever actions it proposes to take in the face of such shifts in its flows. From the standpoint of this firm, then, it is the variances from the budget which are important for it to watch and which motivate its reactions. At least, this is the case as long as the budget is effective; if circumstances should alter—including further shifts in actual flows, either offset or non-offset—requiring a budget revision, once again the firm's new budget would take into account the effect of such changes on its plans, and once again it would watch for variances from budget as a signal that further control or revision was needed.

Moreover, the management of any firm sees only the actual income flows in the other firms on which it looks out, as these are reported in quarterly or annual statements. It has no knowledge of other firms' budgets. It is actually only with respect to the firm from inside which we look out that we treat variances as equivalent to shifts in actual flows.

From that viewpoint, the treatment of these two admittedly different concepts as similar not only is not material, but emphasizes the significance of the planning process. To the extent that deviations from plan are treated as though they were changes in actual flows (an adverse variance the equivalent of a decline in revenues, even though revenues may have been maintained, the only decline being from a projected income), to that extent are the reactions to variances likely to be of the pattern here described—behavior triggered off by a variance as signal. To the extent that variances are not treated the same as changes in actual flows, the former concept ceases to be relevant, and we are left only with changes in actual flows as the stimuli to management action, involving no confusion, apparent or analytical.

The first case (variances and changes in actual flows treated as equivalent) represents firms which are at the planning end of the planning–no planning spectrum. They emphasize attempted control over operations to such a degree that any deviation from plan requires explanation and, following explanation, either control (correction to plan) or revision. The second case (variances not accorded the same motivating force as a change in actual income flows) characterizes firms at the other end of the spectrum, tending more to react to changes imposed on them that to attempt to impose their own control over change.

Actually, as we noted in an early chapter, most firms fall somewhere between these polar extremes. Probably most firms would not treat variances with the same urgency or respect that they would an actual shift in flows, and few would ignore them. Some would accord them greater attention than others; some would be more willing to waive variances, or some part of them, as reflecting hope rather than what might or should have been made real. ("In respect to our most recent fiscal year, we budgeted an extremely large sales increase—in the neighborhood of a 40% increase. While we had an increase of approximately 30%, this left us with a deficit of 12.9% from our originally budgeted figure. I would say, as far as reasons go [writes this president of a rubber company], we were over-optimistic." How much of a variance from the original sales figure increased by 40 per cent over the previous year would have been accepted as "over-optimistic" and how much of it would have been treated as equivalent to a downward shift in actual flows is the measure of where this firm would fall on the planning–no planning spectrum.)

Every firm is faced with the problem of determining whether failure to realize its projected sales or to maintain its planned costs is due to poor performance or unrealistic estimates. If poor performance, then the variance represents income lost and from the standpoint of the firm should be treated as a shift in actual flows. If unrealistic estimates, then nothing has been lost and the variance can be treated perfunctorily. But a firm which takes its budget planning seriously will seldom treat its estimates so lightly. It will *tend* to treat variances from them as equivalent to a change in actual flows.

Summary

Let us pause to survey the ground we have covered, in which an attempt has been made to lay out the relationship between plan and action in the business firm. We can perhaps best summarize our findings in a series of propositions.

1. The operating plan, with its short-run profit objective, is geared to the long-range profit goal. The planned profit for the coming period may fall below or be set above the expected long-run profit target. It is viewed as acceptable—a desirable objective—only in the light of the circumstances expected to prevail. It is even possible that a loss may be budgeted, and operations resulting in that loss considered an achievement, but only in the sense that under the economic conditions foreseen it would require a performance as good as that which has been carefully planned in order to prevent losses from going higher.

2. The budget is not regarded as a plan to be faithfully followed but as a control against inferior performance. All deviations from plan must be analyzed and explained, but only unfavorable variances require an effort to conform to the plan.

3. "Control" (the use of budget as a standard for judging the quality of performance, and an accompanying attempt to "make budget") is not *possible* when the premises on which it was based change adversely to a degree which invalidates the budget as plan. In this case performance will necessarily be inferior to plan and cannot be "controlled."

4. Control is not *desirable* when the circumstances which had been foreseen (the premises on which the plan was based) change for the better. In this case, performance can be made superior to what had been planned and should not be "controlled" by the original plan.

5. Control is neither possible nor desirable when management, on its own initiative, introduces new conditions geared to achievement of long-run objectives, which it prefers not to delay until the start of a new budget year. In this case performance will be different from what had been projected as a consequence of the fact that planning is a continuous and not a periodic process.

6. Management always faces a question whether the changes in conditions, for whatever reason occurring, are substantial enough to invalidate a carefully constructed budget and to require substitution of a revised

budget. Particularly in the case of adverse deviations from plan is it difficult to determine whether to attempt to hold to plan for its incentive value or to revise targets downward to make the plan more effective because more enforceable.

7. Every firm, recurringly, however, faces the necessity to revise its plan because of a change in circumstances, either externally or internally introduced. As the actual balance deviates from the projected balance and cannot be brought back to course, changes are called for resulting in a plan which is expected to lead to an outcome different from both that originally projected and that presently occurring. This "preferred balance" in effect becomes the new projected balance, from which actual performance sooner or later again deviates, again requiring revision and a new (preferred) plan, and so on indefinitely. The firm moves into the future by a series of planned steps.

8. Thus at any moment of time *some* plan may be said to be in existence (or in the process of being brought into existence) which serves as a control over actual performance. Whether the original plan (still valid) or a revised plan (when changed circumstances invalidate the original), there is always some standard for judging performance. Or to put the matter another way, a plan always provides the basis for control until it is revised.

9. Variances signal the necessity for either control or revision. Which is necessary cannot be ascertained until variances are analyzed. Increasingly, variances are highlighted by a procedure known as "reporting by exception," which reduces the amount of detail flowing to higher authority by confining it to (or focusing on) those respects in which the plan has not been realized.

10. A "variance" constitutes any departure from a budget projection, either in a summary total or in a detail of a schedule. "Profit variances" (deviation from target) are the resultant of variances in the two broad categories of revenues and costs. Cost variances typically stem from variances in factor prices or productivity, revenue variances from product prices and volume. In general, remedial action designed to control for or correct cost variances is presumed to be a firm's own internal affair, having no significant repercussion on other firms. Similarly, the firm experiencing the cost variance does not normally attribute it to the action of any other firm. Both cost variances themselves and corrective actions taken with respect to them are thus usually "nonprovocative," in the sense that they do not elicit retaliatory actions directed against business rivals. They are not viewed as the effects of a cause which lies in another firm.

11. Revenue variances are more difficult to handle. Attempts to correct for them are more likely to be provocative, since the action of one firm in respect to product design, product price, or marketing will have a seem-

ingly more discernible and attributable effect on its rivals. Nevertheless, where revenue variances appear to be offset in other (rival) firms, direct action in one of these three fields is inescapable if a firm is to survive. It can only exercise discretion and caution in an effort to minimize the provocation. When revenue variances occur without apparent offsetting in rival firms, that is, where there is a movement of sales revenues upwards or downwards which extends to the industry or to business generally, corrective action taken with respect to revenue variances is likely to be relatively ineffective. The cause of the variance runs deeper than a product relationship to a rival or rivals, and attempts to meet it on that ground will probably lead only to further general deterioration of the situation.

Effective corrective action must come from some force acting on the general circumstances affecting all firms, and such a force can be supplied only by some external agency such as government. To the extent that an individual firm can improve its sales appeal relative to rivals (usually in the price field) without its rivals being aware of this fact, it may, however, reduce its revenue variances at the expense of rival firms (treat a nonoffset variance as though it were an offset variance). In doing so, it runs the risk of retaliation. At times of nonoffsetting revenue variances, all firms would usually be better off if collectively they could avoid intensified competition for the smaller volume.

12. "Price leadership" is a phenomenon whereby rivals are able to make an orderly price movement downward, in time of recession, or upward, in time of inflation, without competitive dangers to members of the industry. It is designed primarily to strengthen the position of the industry as a whole at a time when its share of GNP is being threatened, though it may be used at other times, though less effectively since it is more difficult to determine whether consensus is possible.

13. Revenue variances creating a profit variance may always be "corrected" by actions taken with respect to costs rather than sales, since any action which provides a net increase in revenues or a net decrease in costs will have a favorable effect on profits. If the basic problem is in the area of sales, however, efforts to beat down costs have no genuine corrective effect; they are palliatives at best. At times when revenue variances are nonoffset in other firms, this may be the most effective action possible, but when intended as an answer to revenue variances which are offset in rival firms it is an illusory tactic unless intended only to buy time until more fundamental changes can be made on the revenue side.

14. Most firms generally pay less attention to the effect of favorable variances on budget or view favorable variances as a cause for revision of the operating plan. Commonly, surplus revenues are allowed to accumulate in working capital. They are sometimes also employed to extend the firm's capital investment schedule.

Corporate Plan, Corporate Action, and the Economic System

The value of budgeting as a planning process is evident enough. Even if events do not unfold as expected, the direction of management's attention to the future has value in itself. Similarly, the value of budgeting for cost control purposes is evident, particularly as this is expressed in standard costs incorporated into a system of flexible budgeting. (In the words of the vice-president and controller of one of the nation's major banks, "The knowledge that actual expenditures will be compared with the Plan, and that accountability must be clearly and convincingly established when variations develop between actual and Plan results, alone exerts a very salutary effect on keeping expenditures within Plan limits.") From an economist's point of view, however, the real interest lies in something which combines elements of both planning and control, where the value of the budget is not so evident but must be established.

Budgeting implies something more than forecasting. It involves the planned manipulation of all the variables which determine the firm's performance in an effort to arrive at some preferred position in the future. To this end a number of drafts of proposed budgets may be made and discarded as unsatisfactory or unacceptable, until one has been drawn which seems feasible in execution and desirable in planned result. Nevertheless, it is too much ever to expect that the future will develop exactly as planned. There are too many elements affecting the outcome over which management has little or no control, too many assumptions on which the planning process rests which require a prophetic vision which management cannot put on the payroll (although some prominent firms in France are reported to have hedged their statistical bets by hiring, at fat fees, the services of a highly regarded card reader). The consequence is that budget revisions are required from time to time if the budget is in fact to serve as a guide and a control. Each of these, like the original, is an effort to arrive at a preferred position.

The manipulation of variables in advance, on paper, if it is to be more than an intellectual exercise, implies a belief that at least certain of these variables can in fact be controlled as planned, or that certain of these variables can at least be partially controlled. If the plan is expected to provide an outcome superior to what would have been gained through simple response to external ("market") pressures, there is an underlying assumption that the company can in fact control, within some limits, the variables of markets, men, and money on which the planned performance rests. An element of control is implied not only over and through the budget, but over the firm's environment as well.

The suggestion which is offered here is that budgeting constitutes a continuing attempt to explore the meaningful limits within which such control can be exercised. The firm's planning horizon extends into the indefinite future, but the uncertain horizon line is given sharper definition by fixing on a definite long-range planning period of up to five years (sometimes longer). Within this span shorter operating periods are delimited, customarily a year, within which operational objectives are given greater specificity but always with a view to their contribution to the longer-run objective. Even within the operating year revisions occur monthly, quarterly, semiannually, or spasmodically, over which fragments of time the approach to the year's target can be given even greater provision. Over this whole range of time, from the immediate present to the periodic revision, from the operating year's goal to the long-run objective—throughout this continuous always-extending time stream, management probes the limits of its control over its environment.

That probing serves two functions. It helps to establish the reasonableness and the ambitiousness of the goal itself. It helps to establish the feasibility of the plans for achieving the goal. Over time, the plans are pushed and pulled and molded not only by management but also by the market and by competitive forces, which force the plans—undergoing continuous revision—into a logical mold and a meaningful cast, stripping them of their impracticalities and vagaries, imposing on them the limitations, and exposing to them the potentialities, of experience.

In the short run, it may not prove possible to exercise a high degree of control over the market and competitive forces which largely shape the operating year's outcome. Many managements stress that the sales program has already been planned to maximum advantage, and except for a little more pressure on the sales force here or an accelerated introduction of a new product there or limited experimentation with price changes which are hoped to be nonprovocative, there is not a great deal which can be done significantly to affect the year's outcome. On the outgo side, costs can be controlled a little more tightly, but for a firm which has already carefully budgeted its costs, the results are not likely to make the difference between a successful and an unsuccessful corporation. These limitations on adapting corporate behavior to changing circumstances in the short run are probably somewhat exaggerated, but they probably also reflect a considerable measure of validity.

The importance of budgeting—the continuous process for replanning the firm's path into the future—lies primarily in using the experience of the short run as guide to the longer run. The probing and testing of current operations disclose the respects or areas in which managerial discretion is excessively limited, suggests other respects or fields in which managerial freedom is greater to manipulate the economic environment to the firm's advantage. A management which year after year persisted in operating with product lines and production techniques and marketing processes which revealed themselves as offering little leeway in accommodating to changing circumstances, but forced management simply to react to change, would be gaining little from its experience. The firm which analyzes the variances from its current operating plan to ascertain if the reasons for variance can be controlled, and if not why not, is put in a better position for adjusting its future planning along lines which give it greater discretion. As the president of a large retail and mail-order company remarked, "[Our] consolidated budget, which is revised semi-annually, is composed of many individual budgets. . . . Operation of the budget must be quite different from companies whose operations are much more concentrated. In our case more emphasis is placed at the local level on immediate responsive action to budget variances. Consolidated variances will affect our long range planning but only after deliberation of the causes by the executive committee."

This pattern is probably more general than the respondent believed it to be. The short-run significance of budget variances is more on the control side—an attempt to hold costs in line with operations. The long-run significance of budget variances is on the planning side—constituting information on the feasibility of certain actions, the desirability of others, the likely reaction patterns of rivals, and so on. The market, by the process of compelling budget revisions, forces the budget plans into a consistency and compatibility with the underlying economic pressures and influences which cannot be controlled or evaded.

Management plans, and in doing so presses on the limits of the forces which bound its discretion. The market—a collective noun for all the individuals and institutions engaged in financial transactions—acts, and in so doing places limits on management's discretion. The pressures of management on the market, and of the market on management, determine both the firm's budget plan and the variances from it. Over time, management constantly probes for the areas where market control is weakest. Over time, market action sooner or later reasserts its influence. The extent to which the management of any firm profits from the periods when the market's grip on its profit-seeking activities is lightest and most permissive is in part determined by the effectiveness and imaginativeness of its planning—and also, perhaps, not a little by chance.

Appendix to Chapter 17

REASONABLE COST-PRICE RELATIONS*

The only approach to price stabilization which is possible among manufacturers in a highly competitive market arises from the similarity of costs and a general recognition of the level at which loss begins. It works through a sort

* From "Setting Sound Selling Prices," by Nelson B. Gaskill, president, Lead Pencil Institute, N.A.C.A. Bulletin, Apr. 15, 1933, sec. 1, pp. 1188–1194, 1197, 1198–1199.

of protective instinct. Other than that, each manufacturer lets some part of his volume go, on one pretext or another, at a loss or at an insufficient margin of profit. He seeks a higher profit rate on the balance of his sales. Particularly as sales volume tends to concentrate in the hands of large dealers, this counterbalance of profitable and loss prices becomes intricate and delicate. The more intricate it becomes, the more susceptible it is to the threat of a sudden competitive price change, and when price rather than an established consumer demand determines sales volume, these price changes become more rapid and more severe.

The only foundation for a sound selling price in manufacture and distribution presupposes a uniform method of computing selling prices, with a strict requirement that the same elements of cost and of profit be taken into consideration at their proper, individual rates. For instance, suppose there were an absolute requirement operative over the whole of a particular industry, that the minimum selling price permitted any individual manufacturer at least equal the return of all costs; that by reason of a uniform accounting system, there was a common understanding as to the computation of cost. While the individual minimum prices might differ, yet each of those competitive selling prices would be soundly constructed. There could occur no displacement of one manufacturer using a sound selling price by another using an axe.

Unfortunately this supposition has now no foundation in fact. Manufacturer selling is a highly agile opportunism. It needs a seismograph to record its past and a crystal gazer to foretell its future. As a man said to me the other day, "You can't run this business on an ideal basis. If you do, you will go broke." This man is no more deficient in ideals than he is lacking in intelligence, as his competitors will admit. Business men do not like this situation but they are individually helpless under it, since there is no procedure open by which it can be controlled through collective action. In some occult manner, this state of affairs is supposed to promote the public welfare.

It would be fortunate if this were the complete outline of the practical objections to a soundly conceived selling price structure, but the worst is yet to come. If we assume that the conditions required for sound selling prices obtain in the manufacturing group, the second phenomenon awaits attention. This is the complete breakdown of functional distinctions and the disregard of functional service costs in the field of distribution. To make this clear to you, it will be necessary to take a hypothetical case.

We will suppose that John Jones, a bright, young, college graduate with no business traditions or experience but with some capital, decides to go into business. He will make what are known as shelf goods. We will suppose that he is equipped with the most modern plant and machinery, a production engineer, a cost engineer, an advertising manager and a sales manager. He is all ready to toot the whistle and start the wheels going round. He summons all his engineers and managers and tells them to work out a sound selling price, estimate a sales quota, calculate a production schedule, a sales dollar, a cost dollar and have them all ready for him next Monday morning. At that point some one asks him whether his price is to be based on the wholesaler or the retailer and then the trouble starts.

We will suppose he decides to go the traditional road and bases his price on the wholesale transaction. By some process he arrives at the conclusion that the wholesaler needs 15% of his selling price and the retailer needs 25% of his selling price. So he takes his own sound requirements as 60% of the proposed price to the consumer. He calculates 100% as his list price and quotes the wholesaler at 40 off list. We will assume a good demand for his product. For the time being, his carefully selected wholesalers sell the retail trade at 25% off list and retain their full margin of 15%. We will assume another miracle, namely, that the retailers do not cut the full list price but stand on their margin of 25%.

But into this Paradise comes Satan in the form of a large retailer. Not a fat man but a chain store, if you like. He talks in terms of carload lots, large volume of sales, no selling cost, nationwide distribution and quick turnover. While we are assuming miracles we might as well assume another. This large retailer asks only the wholesale terms, 40% off list, as a quantity discount. He gets the goods and he has quite a margin to play with. He can undersell the retailers buying from the wholesalers by about 15% before he begins to trench upon the normal retail margin of 25%. This is where the assumption of miracles must stop. This retailer has nothing to gain by maintaining the list price and has no intention of maintaining it. The greater the reputation the commodity has as a nationally advertised brand, the more certain it is to become a cut-price "loss leader" in the hands of this large distributor.

Now let us follow events backward. This particular oversize retailer cuts the price to the consumer. The effect upon other retailers of the commodity is immediate. They come back upon the wholesaler for a price which will enable them to meet this competition. The wholesaler passes the demand back to the manufacturer, and unless the manufacturer can create by advertising a consumer demand strong enough to force the wholesaler and his retailers to handle the commodity at an insufficient margin or at a loss, his price structure breaks down, no matter how soundly it is constructed.

While he is wrestling with this problem Mr. Jones' Paradise is invaded by seven other devils. To him appear the purchasing agent of a large corporation, the manager of a buying syndicate of retail stores, the manager of a voluntary chain of retail stores, a contract jobber, etc. They sing one siren song though in divers tones; quantity buying and no selling cost, quick turnover and national distribution.

If Mr. Jones sells the consumer direct it must be on terms better than the retailer would give, else the purchasing agent has no justification for his existence. This is a wrong to the whole distributing trade. It sucks their life blood, a current which comes to them from the volume of consumer sales. Finding their volume declining, they are more than ever apt to seek to recover volume through cut prices. The buying syndicate, which merely negotiates for prices, places no orders. The member stores get the advantage of prices on quantities they do not sell and thus reap a margin with which to play. The manufacturer is saddled with the cost of selling each one of them. The members of the voluntary chain gain a similar position and the contract jobber, with no overhead that is recognizable, plays hide and seek with the lot. This incoherent derangement is shot through with secret discounts, rebates, advertising allowances, commissions to salesmen, free deals and what have you.

As sensible men, you will doubtless say that no sensible man would do all these things. You would be surprised! But let us suppose another miracle. Mr. Jones gets fed up with all this and goes back to a strict wholesale basis. Then he discovers that a great many wholesalers are also operating retail establishments, and he has the same problem to meet in another form.

So far we have seen only the problems that arise out of Mr. Jones' own actions. Let us throw in a few active competitors to make the picture completely haywire. We will give Mr. Jones credit for tying up the best wholesalers in the chief distribution centers, by exclusive dealing arrangements. So at least some of his competitors are compelled to drive directly at the retailers. Now unless the list prices of these competing manufacturers are much the same as Jones' and they preserve the same differentials as Jones by selling their retailers at 25% off list, Jones' retailers are shot as full of holes as a Swiss cheese. These competitors selling the retailer direct will retain the wholesaler's 15% margin to cover the added cost of selling the retailer, and they will have nothing to gain by not selling at least 30% off list. They do so and a new resale price level is created. Jones can reduce his price or increase his advertising appropriation but either one puts a kink in his sound selling price.

I think it can be written down as a law of price making that the validity of a sound primary selling price depends upon its projection through to the consumer by distributive agencies rendering the same functional service and incurring the same elements of functional costs. It is the underlying body of service costs equally encountered by all the distributive agencies involved, which carries through to conclusion the manufacturer's basic element in the ultimate consumer price. Of course, the violation of this law is destructive of the sound pricing of the distributor whose service cost is ignored when his function is disregarded. Sales to the retail trade direct, at prices which do not include the wholesaler's differential, wreck the wholesale trade.

In my opinion, this loss of recognition of functional service costs and their relation to a sound system of selling prices from producer to consumer, is a part of the confusion which was created in the mad rush for an increase in sales volume. This was a phase of the mass production movement, the search for lower costs to make lower prices to move an ever-increasing volume of production. Manufacturers naturally became obsessed with the one element of quantity in sales.

In the earlier days of our industrial development, the ordinary course of distribution was manufacturer to wholesaler to retailer to consumer. The jobber acted as a safety valve, handling seconds, odd lots, obsolete goods, excess inventories and the like. The significant fact is that the *quantity* buyer was characteristically the wholesaler or the jobber. The quantity discount and the wholesaler's trade discount were one and the same thing. Quantity buying by the retailer began with the department store but the merchandising operations of these stores were so limited that the quantity discounts received by them passed almost without recognition or notice. Then came in rapid succession the mail order house, the chain store, the buying syndicate and the voluntary chain, all retail operations. But they claimed and received as *quantity* discounts, the equivalent of the *trade* discounts formerly given for a *different functional service,* and the cost of this short-circuited functional service was thrown back upon the manufacturer.

Naturally, the distress of the wholesaler under these conditions is extreme. He has either largely passed out of the picture in those parts of the country where the large retailing systems have become established or he has become by force of circumstances, a retailer also. This mistaken use of the quantity discount is now in an acute phase. Retail stores are banding together in voluntary chains. At least one of them now numbers more store members than the largest corporate chain. It is a contest for the appearance of the greatest quantity of sales as a basis for the largest quantity discount. The manufacturer is caught in a snare of his own devising. The drive upon him for price concessions is enormous. Chain must meet chain, the voluntary chain must meet the corporate chain and vice versa. The independent must meet them both.

As mass retail buying comes to dictate price terms to the manufacturer, it also throws back on him the costs of the wholesaling service. The manufacturer's prices go down and his costs go up.

If anything is needed to give a spicy flavor to this dish, we have only to add the supposition that Mr. Jones is primarily interested in nationally advertised, standard brands which encounter a number of lower-priced private brands being offered for sale at lower prices.

This is a rather impressionistic picture of the deranged distribution system into which the manufacturer's sound selling price must go. I do not think it surprising that the manufacturer, or for that matter the dealer, should regard selling price as capable of no scientific improvement. Selling price is not static but fluid, it is not stable at any level nor is it constant with reference to a margin for profit. Net profit is a matter of average selling prices which are dictated by circumstances over which neither the individual manufacturer nor distributor has any control.

I assume that when you speak of sound selling prices, you are thinking of selling prices which, while not necessarily constant in amount, are at least always constant in relation to cost return and the necessary profit margin. Unless he has or can secure for his commodity a sufficiently strong consumer demand and avoid the flagrant, price-cutting distributors, the individual manufacturer can hardly hope for any better price-making methods than those which are thrust upon him by his competing manufacturers and by the different functional types of distributors.

I assume further, that you are not so much interested in a better pricing method for the individual as in the possibilities of the systematic use of better pricing methods both by manufacturers and distributors. If you are thinking in these terms, the implication is that you are thinking of production and distribution as a procedure capable of being organized, systematized and made subject to the statement of governing principles and rules. I beg you to note that if you are even beginning to think in these terms, you have abandoned the dogma of an unlimited freedom of competition as the source of the public welfare. You are thinking in terms of an orderly procedure, under the control of some established principle, directed at a perceived objective instead of a helter-skelter cross country race in which the only rules are that the fittest will survive and the Devil get the hindmost. If you have gone so far in your thinking, you have necessarily come to the point where objection, economic or legal, to what is commonly known as "restraint of trade" is untenable. You will, on the contrary, perceive the necessity for some very decided restraints upon the unbridled liberty of competition because you will be thinking of a regulated competition, the coordination of personal actions to produce a desired result. . . .

. . . if we are thinking in terms of a restatement of economic policy so as to permit the better price making with all that that entails, I submit that the governing principle should be the control of selling price by the requirement of the return of cost as the minimum below which, except for some necessary concessions, the individual selling price may not go. This is in effect, to trace the national calamity back to its beginning, in the loss-taking individual transaction and commence the reconstruction at that point.

Suppose we apply this rule to the two phenomena which now practically obstruct the systematic computation and use of better selling prices. First we will suppose the rule to be applied to the manufacturing group. Naturally this presupposes a uniform cost accounting system. It is more than likely that as each of these manufacturers for the first time comes face to face with a collection of all his costs, properly spread over his production volume and their relation to unit price with all margin requirements, so stated that each unit sold would return its due proportion of gross profit and gross margin, he would have heart failure. His successor would find quite a range of competitive prices. The pressure on all elements of waste, loss and non-productive activities would be immediate and enormous as well as effective. Everything would be subjected to the acid test of measurable return of cost. Competitive prices would no longer depend upon financial strength to sustain loss but upon ability and efficiency stated in terms of sound selling prices. The quality of the product would return to the sales argument. All that any manufacturer would have to fear from a competitor would be either a lower cost and marginal requirement on an equivalent commodity or an equivalent price on a better commodity. That is all he ever ought to be called upon to meet. . . .

If . . . we close the limit of manufacturer price concessions by his cost requirements and this prime cost plus the distributor's costs becomes his *resale price minimum,* the distributor stands on a parity with the manufacturer with an established, irreducible cost.

As between retailers of the same commodity in the same trading area, there will be conflict unless differences in resale prices represent only differences in overhead and operating costs. Difference in cost subsequent to prime costs of the delivered commodity becomes a legitimate competitive advantage whereas differences in the prime cost of the commodity become unjust discriminations. As no retailer is entitled to the true "trade" discount which belongs to the wholesaler, all secret discounts, rebates, concessions and allowances not for measurable and measured service, go by the board. Here we must take the quantity discount all apart. We must see it as a cost which is to be returned.

The value of a quantity discount, strictly speaking, is measurable as the present value of a future payment, the relief from interest and storage charges, possibly a lessening of delivery charges if the seller makes delivery. In other words, in the light of the stated principle, the allowance of the quantity discount is the payment to the buyer for the assumption by him of certain charges which otherwise would be borne by the seller. It is a recognition of and a payment for certain functional services and costs and the amount of these is the limit of the quantity discount. In excess of this amount, it is a price concession and an improper price discrimination. The quantity discount must be reduced to its true terms as a return of cost.

In coming to the question of selling the wholesaler and the retailer, one faces a stark and grim alternative. Because their functional service is different, their costs are different. To make one prime cost to both types of distributor, the selling price would have to be calculated on the wholesaler. To this base, we suppose the wholesaler adds 15% and the retailers to whom he sells, add 25%. The retailer buying direct at the same price as the wholesaler, adds 25% and undersells the other retailers by 15%. The manufacturer's selling price will be forced down to the level fixed by the direct buying retailer, simply because the wholesaler's function has been thrown back on the manufacturer and its cost is not expressed in the retailer's selling price. On the other hand, if the manufacturer's selling price is calculated on the direct sale to the retailer, the wholesaler is wiped off the map.

Now here is the stark alternative. If sound selling prices both for manufacturers and distributors are not a delusion, never to be realized, the wholesaler must go and the selling price system must be based on the retailer sold direct or there must be a classification of distributors according to the function served with an established trade discount or differential between them. This differential would have to be observed in all sales to the retail trade direct or such sales be prohibited. The wholesaler-retailer, the retailer-wholesaler, the buying syndicate would have to become one thing or the other.

Chapter 18

BUDGETS AND ORGANIZATION

The Budget as a Contract

In its earliest applications, budgeting in business firms took the form of expense control. Operations and units were held responsible for staying within cost limits which often if not usually were imposed on them by some higher authority. In this form budgeting had relatively little impact on corporate organization.

As budgeting took on its present complexion and was converted into an instrument for business planning, certain organizational consequences followed. The data needed to prepare a plan concerned both sales and production; coordination of functions required considerable detail, and usefulness of the plan placed a premium on reliability. More and more people in the organization became involved in the supplying of the data needed. Moreover, planning lost much of its point if it was not accompanied by control and the analysis of variances, but these could be made meaningful only if the individuals on whom they depended admitted a responsibility for them. Otherwise a foreman whose shop performance fell below standard could short-circuit the whole planning and control process by insisting that the standards were "impossible" or "unreasonable," or a district sales manager who did not make his quota could excuse his behavior—to himself as well as his superior—on the ground that the quota had been "unrealistic" to begin with, as he had said at the time.

Acceptance of a responsibility for accomplishing a budgeted level of performance almost necessitates the participation of the supervisor affected (at whatever level) in the setting of the budget task. Recognition of the desirability of this procedure was helped along by several concurrent developments. One was that in the post-World War II period when budgeting was gaining more and more attention by top management officials, supervisory talent was relatively scarce, so that individuals were encouraged to assert their "rights" and refuse to accept imposed responsibilities which seemed unfair. Criticism that a shop was turning in a poor performance was more likely to be met with a response (thought if not spoken), "If you think you can get someone else who can do the job better, go ahead," than in the preceding depression-ridden decade.

Moreover, the rise of labor unions, with their insistence on a greater participative role in determining standards, set something of a precedent. Could the company do any less for its supervisors and managers? Finally, the "human relations" approach to management and the development of a more sophisticated "organizational theory" had its impact on upper levels of management in this period. For all these reasons, then, there was a relatively widespread and prompt recognition of the necessity for involving in the budget-preparation process all levels of supervision and management on whom the budget relied for fulfillment. In the words of one company's budget manual:

> The budget allowance bases are established on the postulate that authority and responsibility go hand in hand, and therefore those responsible for operating according to the standards established have an opportunity to partake in its construction and to approve it. Any revisions to be made in the original budget bases are referred to the persons who originally compiled the specific data, for their consideration, comment, and approval.

The *quid pro quo* that went along with this right of participating in determining the performance for which a supervisor or manager would be held responsible was that the performance agreed on ex ante was to be viewed as a kind of "contract" or "commitment" on his part. Thus pressures for job performance were not to be applied to him except as the level of performance had been voluntarily assumed, but the pressures were considerable to make good on the performance to which he had "committed" himself.

The point at which this general conception of the budgeting process has tended so far to break down most frequently has been at the level of the first-line supervisor or foreman. In the setting of standard costs, for example, industrial engineers may have more to say than does the foreman. At the time that new processes or products are being standardized, the foreman can often exercise some degree of influence on the result, but with a turnover of foremen the new supervisor typically confronts a table of standard costs on the basis of which his budget performance will be computed—and to which his "agreement" is expected—although he will himself have had little or nothing to do with their determination. Frequently a shop's budgeted costs are prepared by a representative of the controller's office or a higher level of production management and submitted to a foreman for his "approval."

In explanation, budget officials report that it is difficult to get foremen to work with budgets. Foremen regard them defensively and often seek to write in a level of costs high enough to provide themselves with "protection." The notion of flexible budgets is one which they frequently resist, since a reduction in personnel is neither pleasant to make nor easy to accommodate. The idea that some period costs should be treated as variable downward with declining volume is one which is particularly resisted.[1] In some companies which have managed to create a favorable "climate of opportunity" for first-line supervisors, sometimes by giving them a share in or at least special recognition for cost-saving results, foreman participation in the budgetary process (both planning and control phases) has been spontaneous and enthusiastic. On the whole, however, this remains a problem area.

Authority in Relation to Budgeting

At least from the level of departmental management upward, however, participation in budget planning has become a standard means of ensuring responsibility in performance. But one other ingredient has been necessary to a recipe for responsibility. It is not only important that a manager consent to accept responsibility for a projected result; it is also essential that he have control over the factors on which that result depends. If the production manager is made responsible for the cost of the goods sold but actually has no authority in the purchase of raw materials other than to provide specifications, that authority being lodged with a purchasing agent,

[1] One budget director has worked out a standard approach to this problem. He starts by asking a foreman to budget his present level of activity as he thinks it should ideally be carried out. This usually results in some minor modifications of present expenditure levels which the foreman is willing to admit could really be made without affecting production. Then the budget director asks the foreman to estimate his costs at a level of production perhaps one-third higher than current. The foreman has no reluctance to increase his manning table not only in the direct labor categories but also with respect to indirect labor. With some discussion on the size of these increases, the budget director acquiesces as to their probable reasonableness. He then asks the foreman to estimate his costs for a level of production perhaps one-third below current output. If, as often happens, the foreman reduces direct labor only, leaving indirect labor relatively untouched, the budget director is in a position to inquire, for his own information, if it wouldn't be true that just as indirect labor had to be increased in going to a higher level of production, it could equally be decreased when going to a lower level. The foreman is usually driven to admit the reasonableness of this principle of a reversibility of indirect costs, and the discussion is then placed on a basis of magnitude. When agreement is reached, the budget director has secured from the foreman his own "voluntary" estimates of costs at three levels of production. These give him the fixes necessary for fitting a rough curve on the strength of which a flexible budget can be adopted—and agreed to—for levels of output within a range which is likely to cover most contingencies.

then however willing he may be to accept responsibility for seeing to the fulfillment of budgeted costs of production, he will in fact be unable to control certain particulars on which costs depend. The effort to see to it that a manager of a unit has control in fact of those elements going into his budget has had its impact on corporate structure and organization: [2]

> If the operation of a budget reveals that there are some limitations upon an executive's responsibility for the costs with which he is charged, it probably means that some limitations have also been placed upon that executive's freedom to act within his department, upon his authority in the organization. Responsibility for costs should follow the lines of responsibility for operations. When questions arise about cost responsibility, they are usually symptoms of imperfect organization. Therefore, if we improve our cost control by making cost responsibility more explicit, we will, at the same time, establish more clearly the lines of authority and responsibility with respect to the company's operations and ultimately we will improve our organization.

Out of this effort to accompany cost responsibilities with cost authority came the definition of a "cost center" as an operating unit sufficiently distinct from other units that in those matters for which it shouldered budgetary responsibility it likewise assumed operating authority. Sales or distribution centers could similarly be identified. A company was composed of a number of such centers or units plus an overlay of centralized responsibility for investment, financing, product-line development, engineering, and so on.

Sometimes but not always a cost center or a sales center might be equivalent to a department. A number of centers would compose a division (based on functional, product, or geographical lines). Several divisions might add up to a subsidiary, and several subsidiaries would form the company. Thus along with unitization of the organization for direct budgetary responsibility went its divisionalization as a means of both centralizing and decentralizing oversight of the budget, at appropriate peaks of control.

Centralization came as the division put together the budget recommendations of the centers or units of which it was composed, making these consistent with each other. The same process was repeated at higher levels, as a subsidiary integrated the divisional recommendations, and the corporation consolidated the subsidiary budgets into a master budget. Decentralization came by placing responsibility for preparation of initial budget recommendations, and defense of variances from official budget, at the several operating levels.

[2] K. C. Tiffany, vice-president in charge of finance, Burroughs Adding Machine Co., "At the Threshold of Events: The Services of Budgeting as a Management Guide," *N.A.C.A. Bulletin,* January, 1950, sec. 1, p. 596.

With its relatively late arrival on the corporate scene, business budgeting was certainly not responsible for what is recognizable as the typical hierarchical form of organization. What it did do was to help in the process of rationalizing the lines of accountability and authority.

Each unit of the organization was tied into a larger organizational unit through a budgetary relationship. Each supervisor committed himself to fulfillment of a responsibility whose significance derived from its relationship to all the other responsibilities which were simultaneously being assumed by other supervisors, the total complex adding up to a planned performance which had the top authority's stamp of approval. At any point in this system a supervisor was free to take actions, within the scope of his authority, even though these created variances from his part of the plan. In doing so, however, he must be prepared to justify his actions (rationalize the variance) to the next level of authority, whose budgetary responsibility too had been affected by the variance-creating action. He must report the "exceptions" to (deviations from) planned performance and explain these. Sometimes the exceptions might be attributable to forces over which he had no control (a rise in material prices, for example), but whether or not this was the case he must keep his superior informed of the reason for any significant departure from budget.

Budgeting thus constituted—in principle, at least—no managerial straitjacket, binding a supervisor or manager to conform to some predetermined standard of performance. The budget did not deprive the supervisor of his authority. It constituted, in effect, his own statement of intent and his own commitment to a planned over-all result, but it left him with all the authority which he required in order to fulfill his operating responsibilities. In the exercise of that authority he might find reason to depart from plan, but he now would do so with clearer knowledge of the effect of his action on the performance of other units and with the understanding that he must be prepared to defend the reasonableness of his action.

Decentralization

This sort of corporate organization is most suited to a functional form of organization. The production function is built up from a number of cost centers. The distributive or marketing function is built up from a number of sales or distribution centers. The planned profit results from the effective coordination of these two major functions (and other ancillary functions) at the top administrative and planning level.

With the growth in the size of corporations, however, and their change from a single-product to a multiproduct base, the job of coordinating functional lines of authority has posed on top management a task of almost unmanageable proportions. The consequence has been to push corporations, as they grow, in the direction of new forms of organization. In these the budget has played an important part.

The technique which has been most widely employed has been to convert from a functional to a product-group basis for structuring the organization. When corporate divisions are organized in this fashion, both the cost centers and distributive centers related to the particular product group (and only that product group) come together at the divisional level to compose a "profit center." Each such center is, very roughly, the equivalent of a separate business, headed by its own "top" management, with its own profit plan or budget. Divisional management is responsible not for producing a certain bundle of goods at a given total cost, or for selling a total bundle of goods for a given total revenue, but for producing a profit of given magnitude (as spelled out in its budget). As conditions change and variances emerge, its authority extends to taking whatever actions may seem desirable or necessary to achieve the planned profit performance, or to come as close to plan as possible. All the stages of preparing the budget, reporting on performance, and revising the plan in the light of performance which we have examined in previous chapters are its responsibility, for the products under its supervision.

Under this form of organization the amount of coordination which is required at the peak corporate level is significantly reduced. Top corporate management keeps an eye on how closely the profit centers are coming to achieving their budgets, but no intervention or action is required except under unusual circumstances, when a profit center gets into difficulties serious enough to require top-level assistance. The attention of corporate management is thus freed to focus on over-all and long-range planning, in particular the planning of new product lines.

An official of American Steel Foundries summarizes this development in his own company: [3]

> Some years ago, our top level organization consisted of a president, vice presidents in charge of sales, manufacturing, and engineering, a treasurer, a controller, and a secretary. Naturally, if a problem was one of manufacturing, it was the manufacturing vice president's responsibility. If it was one of sales, it was the responsibility of the sales vice president. In other words, each of these top level people, with the exception of the president, was responsible for a particular function of the company, but it was necessary to go up to the president before encountering an individual truly responsible for the profitability of the enterprise or of any of its operations. Under this type of organization, which was prevalent then (and is still too prevalent today), too many decisions had to be made in the president's office. It was

[3] Russell E. Larsen, "Organizing around the Profit Motive: Theory and Application," *N.A.A. Bulletin*, January, 1958, sec. 1, pp. 16–17.

humanly impossible for him to make all of these decisions on as broad a groundwork as is possible under the form of organization that we have today. . . .

As a result, today our entire business is organized along operating lines. I use the word "operating" in its broadest sense to include sales, manufacturing, engineering and accounting. Each division has a general manager who reports to a line vice president. Each general manager is, in a sense, the president of a company. He is held responsible for the entire operation as a board of directors would hold the president responsible for the entire company operation. In this situation, the profit motive is uppermost in his mind. He has his own organization to work with and each of these organizations, as a result of breaking the company up in divisions, is smaller and more closely knit. The profit motive is pushed further down in the organization and spread all through it. Each general manager is able to clearly define the responsibilities of each of his direct subordinates and see that they do likewise for their subordinates. By careful attention, responsibility is assigned in such a way that accountability is much easier to attain. Communications within groups of smaller size are better and, as a result, everyone understands better the objective of operations and the plan of how to get there. Constant association of the manufacturing head, for example, with the general manager and with the other department heads develops in him an over-all business viewpoint and makes him more conscious of the profit motive than was possible without such constant association. This diffusion through the company of conscious profit motive is the key to our improved organization.

The Case of Minnesota Mining and Manufacturing

Another example of decentralization of corporate operations to profit centers is provided by a division general manager of the Minnesota Mining and Manufacturing Company.[4]

Since 1946, 3M's once horizontal management structure has been decentralized into the present vertical management structure until today 3M is composed essentially of a large number of aggressive and rapidly growing small companies, each operating essentially in a separate business field. Each operates almost independently, with the guidance and flexible control of a top management group which provide counsel, services, suggestions and operating capital. Today 3M has 36 separate and different product divisions, each a separate business unit and each a separate profit control center. . . .

Each 3M product division is a self-contained business unit. Each has its own management team, headed by a general manager. Each

[4] C. W. Walton, "Company and Division Planning and Control," *N.A.C.A. Bulletin,* October, 1956, sec. 3, pp. 309, 311, 312, 313.

has its own technical organization, manufacturing organization and sales organization. It may operate a number of manufacturing plants scattered throughout the U.S. on a decentralized basis, to achieve optimum production costs and provide improved customer service. Its sales organization operates nationally and may specialize in specific markets or customers served. Each division is assigned a division engineer, a division purchasing agent and a division controller, each of whom have appropriate staffs required to service the division. The assigned staff specialists report directly to staff heads of staff vice presidents in St. Paul but work closely on essentially a 24-hour-per-day basis with the division. . . .

The general managers of operating divisions or subsidiaries, report directly to group vice presidents. General managers of divisions have complete autonomy within their divisions, subject, of course, to over-all company policy. . . .

First and foremost of the control mechanisms used by 3M is the establishment between company management (the management committee) and division management of profit targets for each of our 36 major divisions. These profit targets are expressed as a per cent of sales and are based on a review of the history of the division, markets to be served, competitive conditions in the market, unique contributions through technology (or patents), and return on capital employed for each division. In a new division or newly-acquired subsidiary, a planned approach to the ultimate profit target is provided by establishing a progressive target over a period of 3 to 5 years to gain experience and permit establishing the ultimate profit target on a sound and factual basis. . . .

Second, division profit targets are supplemented by a current year forecast of sales, costs and profits. When reviewed and approved by top management (in a joint meeting of division management with the management committee), the current year forecasts become the division operating plan for the current year. . . . With expense and profit histories as a guide, each general manager and his staff determine how much money may be allocated (or forecast) for spending in the year ahead for people and materials in each area of the division, including manufacturing, research and development, sales, engineering, purchasing, accounting, etc. The division controller plays a key part, and works closely with all key division heads in the preparation of these forecasts, including the preparation of an anticipated profit and loss statement for the coming new year.

Because of conditions prevailing at any one time, it is obvious that not all current division forecasts will result in the profit target for their respective divisions. This is recognized by 3M top management, but the division forecast does give top management an opportunity to review the current conditions affecting division operations, which may preclude reaching the target objectives currently or, in other instances, may make it possible for a division to exceed its profit target. . . .

Whenever, in the opinion of our management committee, circumstances warrant, the general manager of a division may be called into the [top management quarterly] meeting for a discussion of his division's problems. . . .

Once per year, at the president's annual review, usually in January, each division meets with the management committee to review the past year's division operations, to present the division forecasts of sales, costs, and profits for the coming new year and to obtain the management committee's seal of approval on such forecasts, which thereafter become the division's operating plan for the forthcoming year. Projected capital expenditures for the division are normally reviewed with the management committee at the time of the president's review. These projected expenditures are not presented at this time for final approval of top management, but rather to apprise management of the potential requests for capital which may be made within the near future.

Other Examples of Decentralization

In a quite different line of activity, the Ford Motor Company has likewise made use of the "profit center" approach.[5]

Organizationally, Ford breaks down into four main pieces: top management; the central staffs that service top management and maintain functional consistency among counterpart activities in the operating activities; the Administration Committee, which makes day-to-day policy decisions for the Company; and the 16 operating Divisions that are referred to as "profit centers."

Each Division or "Profit Center" is set up like a smaller counterpart of Ford Motor Company. It is headed by a General Manager who, in his own domain, has virtually all the authority and prerogatives of the senior executive of an independent company. The Divisions have their own staffs, committees, and operating activities—the plants. The 16 Divisions, of course, vary as to size and organizational complexity, the largest being many times larger and more complex than the smallest. Some of the Divisions with a number of plants have carried the delegation of profit responsibility a step further and established the plants as individual profit centers. -

Regardless of size, profit centers at Ford share these characteristics:

1. Decentralized Operating and Profit Responsibility—The General Manager is given full responsibility for operating the assets entrusted to him, and is held accountable for their operation at a satisfactory profit.

[5] W. W. Booth, "Profit Control and Profit Measurement at Ford Motor Company," *Business Budgeting*, September, 1956, p. 12.

2. Physical Separation of Assets—Some are dispersed, others are concentrated and hard to separate. For example, 6 Divisions have a total of 15 plants in the Rouge area at Dearborn.

3. Product Separation—The better-known end-product Divisions of Ford number less than half of the Company's total Divisions and employ less than 40% of the total Company work force. Separate Divisions manufacture such items as metal stampings, automatic transmissions, engines, steel and miscellaneous automotive parts.

4. Separate Financial Statements—Each Division has its own income statement and balance sheet, as if it were an independent business.

5. "Arms-Length" Dealing Between Divisions—Goods are not transferred at cost between Divisions; they are bought and sold at competitive terms and prices. A shipment from one Division to another is billed and paid for as if it were a transaction with an outside vendor or customer. This means intra-Company prices negotiated on the basis of competitive "outside" prices or, when these are not available, on the basis of a competitive cost plus a competitive profit margin.

6. Financial Controls Tailored to a Profit-Center System—Cost controls and measurements are primarily important to the extent that they give some clue to the underlying causes of an unsatisfactory profit condition. If profit performance is satisfactory, central staff will ordinarily not question divisional cost performance—although the Divisional General Manager will of course want to clean up the situation to maximize profits.

The decentralized organizational structure of General Electric is also well known. "Authority has been pushed down the line. Each of the hundred operating departments became a small company, in effect. Its head is the boss. Within a loose framework of policy, he sets his own budget, raises and lowers his own prices, can spend up to $200,000 of capital. If the money goes for better plant, however, it must pay for itself in two years." [6] The controller of Philco Corporation comments: "Philco manufactures and sells a variety of products for the home, for industry, and for the armed services. Organizationally, because of the size of the business and its varied activities, Philco has followed a decentralized concept of operations.

[6] A.T.&T., *Profit, Performance and Progress,* 1959, p. 47. Of these department general managers a GE official has said: "The job guides of these men call for them to submit each year a well-documented budget for the next year's operations. At the same time, they must submit a ten year forecast of the operations of their respective businesses as to volume, the introduction of new products, major development expense, personnel needs and organization plans and inventory and facility requirements. In other words the basic product, facility and organization *structures* of the business are developed on a "10 years—forward" basis, every year." Robert Paxton, in *Planning, Managing and Measuring the Business,* A Case Study of Management Planning and Control at General Electric Company (New York Controllership Foundation, 1955), p. 7.

Nine separate, autonomous divisions have been established and each of these divisions is organized almost as a separate company." [7]

The controller of a food processing and distributing company reports: "We have upwards of 20 major operating divisions, each of which prepares its own operating budget. The over-all picture is obtained merely by adding the operating budgets together." In a producers-goods company the controller writes: "The corporation serves its markets through three basic divisions. . . . The divisions in turn consist of twelve major operating companies doing business internationally with plants, mines, mills, offices and licensees virtually world wide. . . . To cope with this complex we have developed a rather highly refined business budgeting or profit planning program. Each of our companies develops an Annual Profit Plan supported by detailed plans by product line and market area, and further based on departmental budgets, standard costs, etc." The vice-president for finance of a major news and entertainment medium states: "The various business activities of [the company] are organized into eight divisions, each headed by a division president. The annual operating goals for each division for the coming year are translated into a profit budget. The budgeting process within each division is a pyramiding of the individual goals and objectives of each management level within the framework of the objectives of the division. Completed divisional budgets are then submitted to Corporate management for approval, and then consolidated into a total budget for the Company."

The "profit center" approach does not, however, do away with functional breakdowns and cost and distribution centers. It simply terminates these organizational hierarchies at lower levels in the over-all corporate structure, by having them report to divisional management rather than top management. These infradivisional functional groups are, as before, judged by budgetary performance which is limited to either a cost or revenue standard. Divisional profit centers, however, are judged by a budgetary performance which is based on both cost and revenue management and which is summarized in an over-all profit figure, to be compared with the year's budget plan and a longer-term profit target. [8]

[7] Ernest E. Bareuther, "Budgeting Policy and Practice in a Decentralized Company," N.A.A. Bulletin, October, 1957, sec. 1, p. 31.

[8] ". . . accountability of the lowest level of the organization cannot always be measured in terms of profit. For example, the unit foreman will undoubtedly have to be measured on the basis of his manufacturing results, since he has had little or nothing to do with sales policy and probably has had little or nothing to do with the choice of the particular class of product which he is called upon to produce. . . . It would appear, at this level in accountability, that cost control is the most that can be expected, and it is on this basis that performance must be measured. . . . Likewise, the salesman may have to be judged solely on the volume of business he

Potentialities of Decentralization

The whole budgeting procedure with which this study has been concerned has as one important consequence the fact that it permits corporate growth to occur without necessary loss of efficiency. The neoclassical school of economists believed that the one sure curb on the expansion of any company was a marginal cost curve which was bound to rise, sooner or later, due to the inability of all factors to increase proportionately; and that the factor which, of all factors, was most certain to be the limiting one was management. More labor and more capital might be added in equal doses, preserving their proportionality, but management—particularly the top-level entrepreneurial type of management—by its very nature had to remain fixed, or relatively fixed, thereby eventually leading to diminishing returns: The job of overseeing the expanding firm would require management to spread itself thinner and thinner, becoming less and less effective, until rising costs would put an end to its growth.

The process of budgeting, with its potentialities for decentralization, no longer makes this expectation so certain. At a minimum, it increases very considerably the size to which a firm may grow before diminishing returns set in. The weight of detail under which it was believed that top management's effectiveness would be smothered has been distributed to others farther down the organization; the necessity for close supervision has been lightened through the concepts of budgetary responsibility and management by exception. Nor has the process of growth led to an authoritarian structure, blighting individual participation through a self-imposed necessity of keeping a tight rein on a sprawling complex; on the contrary, as we have already seen, opportunities for meaningful participation in the planning process have been opened up to lower levels of supervision in the preparation of operating and long-run budgets. While a theoretical "final authority" rests somewhere in the management structure (with the president or with the board chairman usually), its significance for corporate operation has become less and less. Recommendations for action get pushed up through the budget preparation process, from virtually any level within the organization, and are more likely to receive attention and approval when formal provision is made for their consideration in a planning stage (periodically recurring). "One of the primary intentions influencing the design of the Westinghouse Planning Program has been to create a framework of basic company objectives and policies, within which division managements can

brings in." Larsen, *N.A.A. Bulletin*, January, 1958, sec. 1, p. 15. The author of this article, then assistant controller at American Steel Foundries, advised efforts to make both foreman and salesman aware of their impact on profits, however.

plan and work, with broader independence of action than is otherwise possible. Without such a framework, greater centralized control of division activities is necessitated." [9]

This potentiality inherent in the budgeting process of limiting the demands on the top-management function by spreading the responsibility for planning and control throughout the organization is perhaps most fully realized in the profit-center approach. Under the functional form of organization, divisional managers are less inclined to be guided by the company's profit objective than by the special interests of production, or sales, or finance, or whatever their functional responsibility may be. Production may plump for runs in lot sizes which are large enough to be economical and convenient to schedule, regardless of their impact on inventories (which are then likely to range from excessive to insufficient, in order to accommodate scheduling needs); the sales division will seek more frequent runs in order to keep inventories fat enough to meet any possible customer demand; finance will strive to keep inventories low, to avoid tying up working capital, without adequate consideration of either scheduling or selling problems. Only top management can resolve such functional conflicts. But with the development of profit centers the divisional managers now take over the top-management job of coordinating the functional outlooks of their subordinates. They no less than top management are now motivated by the over-all company profit target rather than particularized functional responsibilities. In some instances it may even prove possible to push such general profit responsibility one step lower in the hierarchy (to a product manager under the product-group or divisional manager). "As a consequence, when the profit motive is instilled far down the ladder, many more decisions can be made, and made intelligently, at a relatively low level in the organization. This frees lines of communication for other matters, frees higher levels of the organization to consider other still more important problems and, at the same time, to develop individuals for more important jobs in the organization." [10]

Problems of Decentralization

Decentralizing budgetary and profit responsibilities is not, however, a perfect answer to effective corporate management. It carries with it problems of its own. One of these is the difficulty of determining the appropriate profit performance of each of the "autonomous" divisions. What rate of profit should be considered acceptable from division X, and what rate from

[9] Mark Cresap, "Long-term Planning," *Advanced Management,* January, 1953, p. 36.

[10] Larsen, *N.A.A. Bulletin,* January, 1958, sec. 1, p. 14.

division Y? A minimum rate can be imposed on all, but should not some divisions be expected to return more than the minimum?

A further problem arises in determining with what assets a division will be charged (or with what proportion of common assets) in calculating a rate of return on its investment. Recognizing that capital assets differ in age between older and younger divisions, how shall depreciation be treated in measuring the value of assets? What proportion of the costs of common or central services shall be charged to the profit center? These problems are important not only because divisional managers will be judged in terms of their relative profit performances but also because certain capital expenditures must be judged not by their own isolable expected rate of return but by the rate of return of the division to which they are expected to make a contribution (although not a specific and identifiable contribution). Thus capital funds will to some extent be allocated according to the relative profitability of divisions. One company reports: [11]

> When profit planning was started it was necessary to devise some standard to measure the performance of the various divisions. The company decided to use return on assets employed. Assets employed include cash, receivables, inventories, fixed assets minus depreciation, and in some divisions, capitalized tools. The company had to make certain decisions both on receivables and cash because finance is centralized and receivables in many instances entail intra-divisional transactions. It was decided that both cash and receivables would be calculated at a specified per cent of sales. The specified per cent for receivables is higher than the specified per cent for cash.

Whatever decisions along this line are made, however, it can be expected that some divisions will benefit more than others. "Equity" is a matter of judgment and point of view, not of logical imperative.

A second thorny problem concerns the degree of independence or autonomy of the profit center. This is important from two points of view: From that of top management, the question is vital in determining how much in fact it has been relieved of detailed supervision; from that of divisional management, the issue is significant in affecting the degree of responsibility it feels for the division's performance. Although the most lyrical statements in praise of decentralization speak of divisional managers as "independent businessmen," usually a cautionary note is introduced by prefacing that phrase with the adverb "almost." But how much is almost? If divisional managers are "practically" independent, then what function does top management perform (other than the holding-company function of deciding whether to keep or sell the operation)? If divisional managers are not in fact independent, however, then neither can they be said (by way

[11] Sord and Welsch, *Business Budgeting,* p. 150.

of either praise or blame) to be wholly responsible for their profit performance.[12]

This problem of autonomy, or independence, or control, is intensified in
those instances when top management, entranced with the advantages to be
gained from pushing a profit incentive as far down as possible in the organization, has set up pseudo profit centers. These are units which are admittedly set up on functional lines, so that their supervisors have no control
over the related functions which are necessary to a completed business transaction, but for which "profit and loss" statements are prepared by a combination of imagination and oversight.

One company whose manufacturing operations are geared to a departmental breakdown provides an example. A manufacturing department,
which is composed of perhaps fifteen to twenty sections and is roughly
synonymous with a product line, is the planning unit. A monthly profit-and-
loss statement is prepared for it and goes to top management, presumably
to inform it of relative product-line profitabilities. This is not a profit-and-
loss statement of a profit center, however; although it shows actual sales for
the month, the department has no control over the sales force and no discretion about price concessions which may have been agreed to; although
it shows the standard costs for direct materials and labor and indirect expenses connected with setup and operation, it also includes administrative,
selling, and engineering expenses over which the department has no say but
which are allocated to it on the basis of the ratio of its standard conversion
and setup costs to the total of such costs for the plant. Whatever value it
may have to top management in indicating the contribution of one product line as compared with another, it does not establish the department
as a center whose supervisor has discretionary control over all the elements
affecting the profit-and-loss statement.

Internal Pricing

Some managements have attempted to meet the problem posed by this
situation by contriving "internal" or "shadow" or "transfer" prices at which
a producing unit of a company "sells" its output to the sales units. Thus

[12] In the study by Sord and Welsch, p. 67, ten of thirty-four companies interviewed
reported that "divisional, subsidiary, or plant managers have FULL authority and
responsibility for their operations in a manner similar to a separate company, except
for broad over-all policy, control, and appraisal of results"; thirteen said that such
managers have "CONSIDERABLE authority and responsibility and are expected to develop operational plans (and control procedures) in detail, subject to continuous review and approval by centralized management." Three other companies were reported as relying on some "combination" of these two approaches, while the remaining eight operated under a budgetary but not a profit responsibility.

both units are provided with a gross sales figure from which they may deduct their cost of sales to arrive at a profit. The same device may be applied to a processing sequence, with one shop or section turning over its production—at a transfer price—to the next shop, which carries production one step further before passing the product—at a transfer price—to the next unit, and so on until the completed good is turned over to the sales department. Thus presumably it is possible to establish every functional unit within the company as a profit center.

A former budget director for the Allen B. DuMont Laboratories summarized the system used at that company: [13]

> The manufacturing division sells to the sales division at an agreed-upon price which, besides covering the cost of materials, labor and overhead, must also include in its overhead charge an amount to cover interest on investment. This is a monthly charge of one-half of one per cent of the total cost of fixed assets and inventories used in manufacturing. Finished goods are not included as they become the property of the sales division immediately upon completion.
>
> The sales division is broken down by product managers—one for each group of products requiring a similar type of effort. Industrial television, for example, is under a separate product manager since industrial applications of TV require field engineering and are sold through channels entirely different from those of any other products. Transfers from manufacturing become finished goods in the sales division and cost of sales on the sales profit-and-loss statement as they are sold. The sales division profit-and-loss statement picks up the usual deductions and allowances, selling expenses, advertising, commissions, and freight. In addition, it is charged for development engineering based on engineering development orders.
>
> Finally, interest on investment is provided for. Here, as in manufacturing, the rate charged is one-half of one per cent each month for receivables and finished inventories. Interest on investment is a means of distributing the corporate office costs. The advantage of this method is that it places an incentive on reduction of inventories. The corporate office, in turn, must hold its costs below the aggregate of interest charges made to all the divisions. . . .
>
> The preparation of separate profit-and-loss statements for manufacturing and for sales has the effect of setting up each group as if it were in business for itself. Where excess manufacturing costs previously were buried in cost-of-sales figures in a composite statement, the sales group can now scrutinize the transfer prices readily. Frequently it sends its field engineers into the factory to determine whether certain tight specifications need be so tight, and whether change of design or

[13] Thomas S. Dudick, "How an Electronics Manufacturer Sharpened Cost Responsibilities," *The Controller*, February, 1960, pp. 53–54 and 60.

use of substitute material is indicated. In the past, the sales department might have been tempted to sell merely to increase volume, without regard to the profitability of the items or size of the resulting
production run. Now it makes certain that the items which are sold
will have sufficient margin to realize an adequate return. Likewise,
the sales department realizes that the factory must be kept loaded
with optimum production runs in order to keep transfer prices competitive.

The manufacturing manager is also more conscious of performance
because he realizes that his results will be clearly spelled out in a
separate statement. It is true that standards and variances from standard accomplish the same type of control and constitute an important
analysis function in the controller's department. But being responsible
for results on a profit-and-loss statement which is scrutinized not only
by the officers of the company but by the board of directors as well,
creates an aura of responsibility not readily attainable through reporting by conventional methods.

The vice-president in charge of sales for Ditto, Inc., explains that the
major tool on which his company relies for the achievement of sales quotas
is "a simple profit-and-loss statement for each of our branches and sales divisions which is designed to provide them with the same type of operating
data which they would use if each were an independent business. This
profit-and-loss statement shows total sales less cost of goods sold and local
expenses, arriving at a net profit for each outlet." He discusses mechanics
and results as follows.[14]

The most important and difficult step in preparing such a statement
is to arrive at some intra-company factory or transfer prices on which
the theoretical cost of goods sold by each branch can be based. In
general, our transfer prices are roughly equivalent to prices quoted by
manufacturers in the duplicating industry to jobbers who, in turn,
sell at wholesale and/or retail as we do. Obviously, setting such prices
is not an accurate science; furthermore, they are always subject to
modification in detail, if not in basic structure.

We intended that such price determination should be subject to
negotiation between the sales division and the manufacturing divisions
(and perhaps negotiation is really too polite a word to cover all
facets of this procedure). However, all free price determination is
subject to pressures in the marketplace, and we so intended here—
particularly insofar as such pressure would be constructively used by
the manufacturing divisions to pare costs and otherwise "stand up"
to competitive efficiency as it developed. . . .

It may seem strange to some that a simple profit-and-loss statement

---

[14] Lawrence A. Watkins, "Assigning Profit Quotas to the District Sales Manager,"
in *Increasing Profits on the Marketing Dollar*, A.M.A. Marketing Series, no. 100,
New York, 1957, pp. 42–43.

such as this could create many basic changes in the attitudes, objectives, and achievements of a sales organization; yet this has certainly been the case in our company. Our local branches are staffed by men who are professional salesmen. The branch managers are, by and large, the most experienced and successful salesmen. Like all salesmen, they have been at least 99 per cent "volume minded": They have directed all their energies toward achieving ever-higher volume levels throughout their business careers; furthermore, they have been encouraged in this singleminded pursuit of volume by their superiors.

We all know that volume itself does not automatically produce profits. However, until the field sales force is provided with some other criteria for measuring the results of its efforts, it is extremely difficult, if not impossible, to direct its efforts along any other lines.

These simple profit-and-loss statements provide such criteria, and they have in themselves started to redirect the thinking of our men. It is most gratifying to ask one of our branch managers how things are going, as I did not long ago, and have him reply that things are going fine—that profits are up 20 per cent! In this particular case it happens that the profit improvement is being achieved without any significant change in the volume levels: It is the direct result of more efficient branch operation. Rather than concentrate solely on volume, this man has directed his efforts toward obtaining *more profitable* volume, and at the same time has also reduced his local expenses. The 20 per cent increase in profits from his branch is the inevitable result.

Major companies such as General Electric, General Motors, and Socony Mobil have also made use of transfer prices between profit centers within their own organizations. A variety of devices have been employed for determining the prices at which products (partially or wholly completed) are transferred. Where comparable products are available from other companies, "competitive" or "market" price has been used. In the major meat packers, for example, transfers between slaughtering plants and branch houses (the latter handling sales) are made on the basis of the "going carload market" as reported in the price sheet of the *Daily National Provisioner*. Credits and charges are made in the central office. (Electronic data recording equipment is now being installed which will permit information on carload sales prices to be obtained minutes after a sale is made.)

In instances where "market price" is less easily ascertained, perhaps because of product differentiation, internal prices are sometimes negotiated. Negotiations may also be undertaken not simply to match competitive prices but to beat them, as an inducement to a selling division to take more output.[15] If agreement cannot be reached by direct bargaining, re-

[15] "To illustrate, let us consider the case where the producing division has excess production capacity available and would therefore be willing to take a smaller profit. In such a case the manager of the producing division could go to the manager of the

sort is sometimes had to arbitration. "In order to keep interdivisional prices in line with the market, a pricing committee consisting of a representative each of the supplier and customer divisions meet weekly or oftener if necessary. If these two representatives cannot agree, a decision is made by a member of the central raw materials purchasing staff." [16]

In the absence of any comparable product markets, a formula approach may be used. This may be full cost plus a standard "profit" markup or marginal cost. Sometimes the transfer price is determined by subtracting from the selling price the costs of completion plus a "normal profit."

Because of the arbitrary elements introduced into the process, concerning which a supervisor has little to say, these efforts to convert units which might normally function as cost or selling centers into full-fledged profit centers have not been wholly successful. Some managers have questioned the attempt to push the profit concept into uses where its applicability is dubious if not specious. A controller writes: [17]

> The need, however, for setting up divisions of a company for profit evaluation is best served where the manager is required to produce profits only to the extent that his operations are controllable by him. As operations of subdivisions become more dependent upon related subdivisions in a company or are allocations of costs or selling price, the need for carrying profit evaluation to the net profit level decreases. As a matter of fact, in a study on "Centralization vs. Decentralization," published in August, 1954, by the Controllers Institute of America, it is said, "No evidence was found that decentralized profit and loss statements are more effective than decentralized responsibility statements in promoting profit consciousness." It may be observed, therefore, that, in those areas where grave doubt exists as to the ability of the subdivision unit manager to control the operation measured by profit, it might be well to consider the development of a less expensive but equally effective method, such as budgets or sales forecasts, to do the job of effecting profit control.

---

selling division and say to him, 'I'll charge you only 80 per cent of the selling price on such-and-such a product [instead of a standard 83 per cent] because I'm anxious to utilize some excess capacity and to keep my trained crews on the job.' The manager of the selling division would receive, in effect, a 20 per cent commission for his selling effort rather than the 17 per cent." C. I. Keelan, office methods specialist, Johns-Manville Corporation, "Some Unusual Devices for Reducing Office Costs," in *Control of Non-manufacturing Costs,* A.M.A. Special Report 26, New York, 1957, pp. 110–111.

[16] *Accounting for Intra-company Transfers,* N.A.A. Research Series, no. 30, New York, 1956, p. 26.

[17] Paul A. May, controller, Mine Safety Appliance Co., "The Need for Profit Evaluation for Sub-divisions of a Company," *N.A.A. Bulletin,* September, 1957, sec. 3, p. 29.

Similarly,[18]

> When the budget is approved, the various segments of our management team know that, to make their planned contribution to the company's earnings, they must not exceed budgeted costs. They know that they can make an extra contribution to company earnings by bettering their planned budget performance.
>
> We think that, for us, this is a far better program than one which arbitrarily establishes markups over cost as a basis for determining contribution to successful management. Since each division plans its own operation, we think the challenge is far more productive of effective management than would be the case under a division or departmental profit procedure which would require an arbitrary spread, with which the various members of the team might not agree. Some ingredients are purchased locally at the plants, others are purchased by staff purchasing managers and then allocated to the plants on a basis that produces the greatest company-wide advantages. Occasionally, this policy penalizes a particular department in a way for which it cannot be held responsible. It is our belief that, to over-emphasize profit particularly when it must be artificially allocated is not in our company's best interest.

The fact is that the impact of the budget planning process on corporate organization is still making itself felt, and budgetary uses and effects in decentralized operations are one area which still requires exploration, experimentation, conceptualization, and refinement. In the matter of internal pricing, for example, one authority has suggested that component parts of a company cannot be judged as though they were entities, and different procedures may be required for the internal purposes of at least partially dependent units from those which are suited to the external relations of a wholly independent company.[19] An example of the sort of thing which might be found desirable internally, though unsuited to external business relations, would be the use of two prices for the same transaction.[20]

Nor should it be assumed that the effect of budgetary practice on corporate organization and structure need be solely in the direction of decentralization. One major meat packer is now puzzling over how it can effectively integrate its many historically quite independent profit centers into a more cohesive system in a way which effectively realizes the potential of central planning; recognizing that its present subunits, however independent in

---

[18] Oscar H. Curry, vice-president, administrative planning, Campbell Soup Company, "Budgeting: The Art of Planning and Cooperation," *N.A.A. Bulletin,* September, 1958, sec. 1, p. 72.

[19] Joel Dean, "An Approach to Internal Profit Measurement," *N.A.A. Bulletin,* March, 1958, sec. 1, pp. 5–12.

[20] As suggested by Allan R. Drebin, "A Proposal for Dual Pricing of Intra-company Transfers," *N.A.A. Bulletin,* February, 1959, sec. 1, pp. 54–55.

their present behavior, are functionally dependent on other units in the company, how can it best coordinate their activities without robbing them of initiative?

Further Organization Effects of Budgeting

It was previously noted that the consolidated budgets for some corporations constitute merely the summation of divisional or subsidiary budgets. In these instances decentralization is virtually complete at this level. It seems quite probable that in such companies one future development will be along lines which explore a more meaningful relation of each of these major components to some planned over-all result to which they are expected to contribute. In the absence of such an effort the organizational function of the superstructure is inescapably called into question. If it is solely an ownership relationship, then little argument against divestiture can be raised, if the state, as a matter of policy, seeks to prevent "undue" accretions of market power. On the other hand if some organizational contribution to operating efficiency is the rationale, this can better be planned for than left to haphazard and *ad hoc* determination.[21]

[21] The rise of the product manager is an interesting phenomenon which appears to have some relationship to the growing use of budgets. His role seems to have been developed most effectively in those companies which produce a number of products in the same functional unit, so that constituting a division as a profit center, on a product line or group basis, is not very feasible. At the H. J. Heinz Company, for example, there is a functional divisional organization, since each of its food products ("varieties") is produced in a number of plants, and each plant produces a number of varieties. The company is, however, obviously interested in the relative profitability of its products and recognizes that particular varieties may require special attention. For purposes of profit planning it therefore makes its projections on the basis of variety lines (which are really product groups rather than individual products).

In order to cut across a system which organizes activity by function and planning by product line, the company has appointed product managers. For organizational purposes they report to the vice-president of marketing, but actually they cross the (functional) divisional lines, pursuing, wherever it takes them, the problems associated with making their particular product more profitable. They become, in effect, staff advisers or "consultants" to the functional divisions. Controllership Foundation, *Management Planning and Control: The H. J. Heinz Approach,* pp. 87–94.

Similarly, Kaiser Aluminum maintains a product manager for each of eight basic types of mill products. "The product manager performs a staff function, acting in direct liaison between mill production and our field sales organization." Raymond G. Boyd, in *Materials and Methods of Sales Forecasting,* A.M.A., p. 201.

The device of the product manager is an interesting case where decision making gets diffused within the corporation, without following formal lines of authority. The distinction between line and staff is preserved to avoid indecision or lack of decision, but practically the decisions get made by a number of people coming at the

A related question has been lurking in the background of much of the previous discussion. If budget planning, with the decentralization of a corporation into a number of nearly autonomous profit centers, makes possible the growth of a firm both within its present fields and also by expansion into more and more areas of activity not necessarily related to each other, and with growth uninhibited by the requirement on the part of top management to concern itself (actively and continuingly) with anything more than major financial matters, will we have to face more effectively than we have in the past the issue of limits on private organized power?

---

same problem from a variety of directions. These decisions get written into the budget, or budget revisions, and become the "constitutional" operating authority of the units affected.

Chapter 19

STANDARDS OF PERFORMANCE

Comparisons

A budget—whether long-run or short-run—constitutes a plan for achieving certain objectives. By analysis of variances it also serves as a means of appraising performance in the light of those objectives. The objectives which most managements have set themselves relate to profit—a return on sales, a return on total assets, or a return on net worth. (Sometimes there are also secondary objectives such as market share.) Many companies pose quite specific profit objectives for themselves: long-run profit targets for the company as a whole, expressing a minimum toward which every profit center of the company is expected to move; long-run profit targets for each major division, but differing among divisions, which each is expected to achieve within some prescribed period; short-run profit goals, for company, for major subdivisions, or for both, expressing how much of—or how much more than—the long-run profit target can be achieved in the current year.

How are such budgetary goals determined? What leads the management of one company to pose a 20 per cent return on investment as the purpose which should motivate its efforts, while another company bends its efforts to secure a 5 per cent return on sales? Why is top management satisfied if one product division earns 8 per cent, but dissatisfied if another earns 12 per cent? If managements seek a "satisfactory" profit, on what basis do they decide whether it is satisfactory?

The answer is comparisons—comparisons with other companies, comparisons with a company's own past, and internal (intraorganizational) comparisons.

The comparisons which are made may be of some over-all profit figure. A company may rank itself relative to other companies in terms of return on net worth, for example. If it is located near the top of the ladder, it has reason to feel better satisfied than if it falls near the bottom. Since a single ratio expresses a static relationship, it may, however, be more interested in whether its return on net worth has been moving up or down over the last decade, and how this historical performance compares with the performance of other companies. Or it may compile the return on investment contributed by each of its profit centers to determine the effect of each on the corporate profit showing.

There is no "logically objective" standard by which a company may judge itself, however. Even after making such comparisons, it has no basis for asserting that its performance (or that of any of its reference companies) is good or poor in any definitive sense. It has no way of determining a theoretical or hypothetical standard of excellence with which it may compare itself.

In addition to some summary profit measure, a firm may also examine on a comparative basis particular aspects of corporate performance which affect the profit result. A return on assets, for example, is derived from the two ingredients of the rate of profit on sales and the turnover of capital. Not satisfied with ascertaining that its profit performance was fourth in an industry, a firm might want to check its rate of profit per dollar of sales (which might be revealing of the need for more adequate cost controls) or the number of times it was able to turn over its capital during the year (which might indicate the need for an expanded sales effort). In either event, comparisons with other firms of these two measures would suggest why its profit ranking was fourth.

Further breakdowns of operating and balance-sheet data, relative to similar data for other specific companies or averages for a number of companies, would be revealing of areas of strength and areas of weakness. How does its labor cost per dollar of sales compare with other companies? What of its occupancy expense, advertising costs, bad debt losses? How does the ratio of sales to receivables show up alongside competitors? Its current assets to current liabilities, its total liabilities to net worth, its funded debt to net working capital?

The choice of the companies which are to serve as measuring rods is obviously important. A management can always make itself look either good or bad—relative to some other management. There are four likely choices: comparisons with a given "industry" or "line of activity"; with selected competitors; with all business firms (or all firms of a given size class) or with selected (usually "well-managed") firms from among the general business population.

Industry comparisons are based on the premise that the same general conditions face all firms being compared, so that a reasonable basis exists for presuming that the experience of one is relevant to the experience of all. Some business analysts go further and assume that in any given line of activity there exists something comparable to the economists' "normal rate of profit," which a person comes to identify by familiarizing himself with the industry's characteristics. "Within certain limits there is a natural gross profit in every line of merchandising and manufacturing. By natural gross profit it is meant that under ordinary business conditions staple materials and merchandise in any given standard line can be acquired and sold at about the same cost and price by those in that line who possess about the same amount of ability." "If one is familiar with what might be called the normal proportions that particular items of expense should bear to net sales in a specific line of business activity, like the normal relations between balance sheet items, it becomes evident when a particular expense is excessive." [1]

Even on this definition, the natural or normal rate of profit varies by degree of managerial ability. ("If there are 100 manufacturers in a certain type of business, some will be found with greater ability than others; also some may have insufficient capital, so that the gross profit may be greater or less in certain plants than in others, and the average gross profit of the hundred will not be as large as the "natural profit" of those possessing reasonable ability and capital." [2]) Managements which prefer to set high standards for themselves therefore tend to compare themselves with the best of their competitors. Some firms become tagged as the "leaders" of an industry and set a profit target at which other ambitious managements continue to shoot, year after year.

The fuzziness of definition of an industry sometimes makes comparisons with its so-called members little more meaningful than comparisons with broad sector categories, such as manufacturing, mining, retailing, or wholesaling. Or a manager may believe it is more meaningful to compare his company with other companies of comparable size (in terms of sales, assets, net worth, number of employees, or some other criterion), irrespective of industry, than it is to gauge his performance relative to all firms in a given industry, irrespective of their size. Or an industry leader may prefer to test its mettle against the whole field (in which it can expect to find some performers doing better than itself) rather than to lapse into complacency because it consistently does better than its competitors in a given line of activity. For any or all of these reasons, some managements compare their results with the population of business firms generally, or with all business firms in a certain size range.

Just as an ambitious management does not usually judge the quality of its performance by the average of all companies in an industry, neither does it generally use the average of a total business population as any standard. Such a management would normally refer its own results to the results of "well-managed" business firms. One corporate official has said: "There is sufficient evidence in published corporate reports that the type of industry

---

[1] Foulke, *Practical Financial Statement Analysis,* pp. 505, 496.
[2] The same, p. 505.

does not determine the return on capital employed which may be expected in that industry. Companies with high, average, and low returns are found in every industry. The return achieved is the result of management, and no company should feel that its return is satisfactory until it is in the upper quartile of all companies." [3]

Comparing business performances is, of course, a treacherous undertaking. Historical results come out of a combination of continuing and one-time, of general and particular influences, and it is not always easy to determine which should be viewed as relevant. Comparisons always relate to the past, while the logic of events may dictate change. These are problems inherent in comparative analysis. Other problems are peculiar to comparisons among business firms, where accounting dissimilarities complicate the procedure. Research and development which are expensed in some companies may be capitalized in others, affecting the return on investment measure. The treatment of long-term leases affects asset-liability ratios. Inventory valuations may be on a direct costing or absorption costing basis. The treatment of depreciation varies among companies. Accounting totals may also hide underlying differences. Cost variations between two companies in the same line of business may be due to a different product mix rather than to different production processes or productive efficiencies.

These limitations on the value of comparisons are real enough, but they do not constitute grounds for abandoning the effort. Experience constitutes the only basis for judging the quality of a performance, and the use of experience as a guide necessitates comparison—with others, with one's own past.

Sources of Comparative Data

The sources of comparative data on which a firm can draw are numerous. The Securities and Exchange Commission and the Federal Trade Commission jointly publish a Quarterly Financial Report for Manufacturing Corporations which summarizes uniform financial statements from a systematic sample of all manufacturing enterprises, except newspapers. Estimates are provided for 15 profit-and-loss and 32 balance-sheet items, as well as 46 operating ratios, for each of 31 industry groups and 13 asset size categories. The Federal Trade Commission also publishes, irregularly, the rates of return on investment, before and after taxes, for approximately 500 "identical" companies in 25 selected manufacturing industries. Rates of return

[3] Keller, *Management Accounting for Profit Control,* p. 317. Keller goes on: "However, there is evidence that companies which have a very small percentage of an industry do not usually realize a high return. There is also evidence in some industries that the average return for the industry is low and only a very few companies are achieving a high return."

for the four largest companies in each industry are also reported. The Federal Reserve Bulletin regularly publishes quarterly figures on sales, profits, and dividends of large corporations, by sector, in aggregate dollar terms as well as percentage of change. The United States Department of Commerce and the Small Business Administration have helped to circulate figures compiled by a variety of agencies.

Among more specific sources of information is Robert Morris Associates, which engages in ratio analysis for more than 140 lines of business on behalf of more than 800 banks and 2,500 individuals who compose its membership. Dun & Bradstreet publishes annually a series of ratios for 72 lines of business in manufacturing, wholesaling, and retailing fields. Credit associations frequently make studies of a related nature. Trade and industry associations compile operating statistics on member firms, without identifying any member; some of this information is quite detailed, particularly in the area of costs, where the labor costs of particular operations may be shown in tabular form, or the total costs of other operations, such as labeling or packaging.

Large manufacturers (of drugs, cosmetics, candy, and so on) are frequently sources of comprehensive information on the operating characteristics of retail stores in their respective fields. The publishers of certain trade magazines make a point of compiling operating data (*The Progressive Grocer* or *Printers' Ink* or *Drug Topics,* for example). University business schools or bureaus of business research frequently organize data for a region, sometimes for particular industries; the Harvard Graduate School of Business Administration has become especially well known for its data on department stores. The firm itself is the source of detailed operating statistics on its various units, functions, and branches, once it is conscious of the value of such information.

Significance of Comparisons

Such comparisons provide some basis for setting long-run targets. On the strength of knowledge of what other firms have been able to accomplish in fact, a management may pose a goal for its own organization which is reasonable in the sense that other companies have been able to achieve it. Similarly, in the light of its own accomplishments in the past, the firm can set its sights for the future. The arbitrary selection of a target because others had been able to do that well would make little sense, however, unless based upon more detailed analysis of why they had been able to do better, with accompanying efforts to improve the firm's own performance where it is found to be inferior to that of the reference companies. The determination to rack up a result at least as good as and possibly a little better than the firm itself already had to its credit is meaningless without an examination of the respects in which both the organization and its environment may have changed.

Since a long-run target allows time for correcting weaknesses and building on strengths, this provides further basis for justifying even an ambitious goal as "reasonable." There is no necessary expectation that it be gained in the current year, even if there is pressure to achieve it within the next three to five years. (We have noted in previous chapters that some companies require division managers to lay out the program by which they propose to realize such a long-run target, year by year.) There is no sense of the unreasonableness of a long-run target even if the company falls far short of it during the present operating period due to general business conditions or factors more particular to it, as long as there is ground for a continuing expectation of that level of performance *on the average,* over a period of years.

The short-run target presents more of a problem, however. To what extent should present conditions and circumstances be treated as excusing a below-average performance? To what degree should a shortfall be viewed as evidence of the organization's inability to cope with its problems? There is no objective basis, and little of an ex ante comparative basis, for determining how much of a profit (how much less than the "average" performance expected, how much more than the long-run target) should be viewed as acceptable in the short run. About all that a firm can do is to budget and plan its forthcoming quarter or operating year as effectively as it can, in the light of the externally determining factors (market and competitive conditions expected) and its internal characteristics (product line, technology, and organization as given at the moment).

Ex post it will be able to get some judgment of the effectiveness of its performance by comparison with what others have done. Ex post, analysis of the reasons for variances from its own budget or for a performance inferior to other firms may suggest significant changes which should be made over time. But ex ante, in the planning of its upcoming year, the firm has little by way of bench mark to guide its thinking. It can only do and redo its budget plan until it is satisfied that it is making the most of its resources under the conditions given and expected.

The use of profit targets thus has its impact primarily in the long run, when it holds up some reasonable expectation of what profit a company ought to be able to earn if it operates as effectively as it itself or some other companies have in the past, perhaps adding a little more on by way of optimism and encouragement. Performance short of target encourages examination of the major determinants of profit performance over which the firm has control—its lines of activity, its production processes, its locations, the structure and quality of its organization—but about which it can do little so immediately as to affect short-run profits. Its profit performance over the years, and that of other firms, will help to establish its own expectations, its own views on what achievement levels are to be considered feasible and satisfactory. In this sense the external factors over which it has no control will, over time, help to mold its goals. But both these external and internal determinants of profit expectations relate principally to the long run. The short run may be one of those plus or minus periods that go to make up the average or that fluctuate around a trend. But minus or plus by how much will not be revealed by any amount of comparative analysis, either with other companies or with the firm's own past.

The fact that reference firms have earned 20 per cent on capital in eight years of the last ten, and that this firm earned the same amount for the last two years, though not as much previously, may give some basis for setting that level (or a little more) as a long-run target. These facts will condition the firm to strive, in its budget planning, to come at least as close to a 20 per cent return in the coming year as it possibly can. The facts as given, however, provide little basis for believing that the firm should make 20 per cent its actual target for the next year. As a long-run goal, it will be achieved only if in some years more is earned to compensate for the years that are lean. Is next year likely to be a lean year or a fat? Should the budgeted profit be higher or lower than the long-run target? How much higher or lower? Comparisons provide no answer.

Thus targets relate primarily to a time horizon long enough to permit a firm to act on the variables under its control. (In the short run, then, as we observed in examining the nature of a firm's responses to variances, the principal adjustments a firm can make in meeting deviations from budget are sometimes only of production and costs to sales, as under a flexible budget. Other actions are likely to be quite limited in their effect, except as they involve the acceleration of the end stages of some long-run adjustment such as the introduction of a new product.) Measures to meet basic changes in the firm's external environment, which could not have been or at least were not foreseen far enough in advance to have taken the indicated action, require time to be worked out and made effective. In the meantime, a below-target result may have to be accepted as the best performance possible, even though unacceptable as a long-run level of performance.

To be sure, over time the experience which molds expectations may itself change. With changes in the institutional environment it may be found that whatever actions are taken with respect to the variables under management's control, a profit target which once seemed reasonable and attainable is now out of reach and therefore out of date. The long-run target itself must be moved up or down. The area of latitude permitted to the individual firm may be less (for most firms, which have become integrated into the environment) or greater (for a few innovating and opportunistic firms which are not anchored in an institutional past and which are free to "wheel and deal" in ways not contemplated by others).

Comparisons and Incentives

The purpose of targets, and of comparisons of a firm's own performance with its past performance or with the results achieved in other companies, or of one plant's record relative to the record of other plants in the same company, lies in a presumed motivational effect which targets and comparisons have. A firm is inspired to realize a goal or to do as well as or better than others. There is, however, an ellipsis in the argument. Targets or comparisons have a stimulative or emulative effect only if there is some reason why the people in a firm choose to regard them as incentives. There are many firms of whose personnel this is not true. If their profit performance is twenty-fifth in the industry, or at the low end of the spectrum in the local community, they are not therefore stimulated to try to do better. There must be some additional reason which prompts management and work force to try to do better.

That incentive is sometimes provided by a profit-sharing approach, either formal or *de facto*. A *de facto* profit-sharing arrangement comes about when the people connected with a company develop an expectation, which is usually satisfied, that their own rewards will rise with the profitability of the company even though no formula is followed. "Ability to pay" is the basis for remuneration and is so recognized both by the firm and its people. This approach is sustainable as a continuing policy only in firms whose profitability permits above-average wage and salary scales. Ability to pay as an incentive wage policy has no long-run effectiveness in struggling firms.

Where individual standards of performance (based on comparisons) are provided, they sometimes motivate behavior by planting a fear of failure. The basis for the fear may be simple exposure to one's fellows and one's superiors as ineffective, injuring one's position of esteem and possibly his chances of advancement. It may even raise the specter of possible discharge for incompetence or transferal to a less desirable assignment. Standards of performance which are taken as personally applicable may also stimulate efforts to achieve or surpass them simply as a means of proving one's worth to one's self and to others. This may be as true of the rank-and-file workman as of the company president. The performance which others have achieved in the past, or elsewhere, becomes a mark which spurs an effort to surpass it.

But in some companies something else is at work. In a previous chapter we have already encountered a new organizational device which in recent years has become quite widely adopted in the large corporation, providing built-in pressures for improved performance. This is the department of industrial engineering (or an office by some similar title) whose sole function is to suggest new production efficiencies, improved technologies, superior financial procedures, better ways to select and use manpower, and so on. People in this department are themselves under continuing pressure to prove their own value by coming up with profitable suggestions for change. In many instances they comb the industry, or related industries, for practices which others have found to be beneficial. They constitute a technical intelligence staff whose function is always to find a better way.[4]

From one point of view, then, it is unessential (even though helpful) that operating people be stimulated to do a better job by the device of posing a target or comparing their performances with others. It is enough that there are people in the organization whose job it is to find out how the better performance can be achieved, what improved techniques of producing, selling, financing, or accounting are available by which a gain in efficiency can be made, what methods have contributed to the superior achievement in these fields by other companies (whether or not direct competitors).

Of companies which rely heavily on this built-in pressure for improvement, one is almost tempted to say that the maximization process, after all, applies. But the two are not quite the same. There is no suggestion here that the one best way has been found in all the numerous aspects of business operation, or that indeed it is even discoverable. The implication is more modest. In these companies there is simply a continuing search for improvements—a search which is more selective, less embracing, less demanding, and more feasible than "maximization" implies. Market pressures may not be adequate to compel a General Motors or a General Electric to some theoretical minimum cost, even in the long run. Personal motivations to gain the maximum dollar of profit which current knowledge makes possible may not be the driving force of top management, again even with due regard to some presumed long-run measure of profit. But built-in organizational devices for permitting—and even pushing—the company to do better (better than it has done, better than others) constitute the institutional substitute for personal profit motivation, just as the search for more replaces our old belief in the search for most.

----

[4] "The historical standard has been very helpful in showing the trend of our performance; the market standard tells us what others are doing; but neither is a good measuring stick for what our performance should be in our own particular situation. So we turned to engineered standards for both our office and field operations." Carl W. Schoepfle, supervisor, field work measurement, "Use of a Measurement and Standards Program," in "Improving Managerial Performance at the Cleveland Electric Illuminating Company," *Organizing for Effective Systems Planning and Control,* A.M.A. Special Report 12, New York, 1956, p. 155.

Chapter 20

SUMMARY AND CONCLUSIONS

Business budgeting is the method by which a firm plans its performance. It does so by projecting into the future, for various time intervals, operating statements which detail the financial magnitudes of the firm's activities which are planned for the intervening period, balance sheets which indicate the composition of assets and liabilities resulting from and facilitating those activities, and flow-of-funds statements which reveal the relative magnitudes of total cash flows in and out of the firm in a way that establishes the bank balances needed to accommodate them. These three sets of statements are supported by underlying plans and schedules which collectively constitute the rationale for the financial results expected. These detailed plans in turn are based upon internal and external conditions given or anticipated.

This planning process starts from projections of the sales expected of the firm's given or planned line of products, at estimated prices. From this are derived the schedule of production (for sale and inventory), the estimated period costs (some fixed, some variable), and the direct costs, the last usually figured on a standard-cost basis. To these manufacturing costs (the "cost of goods sold" of the typical income statement plus the cost of production for inventory) must be added the costs, mostly of a period nature, of administration and selling.

The profit resulting (usually computed as a rate of return on assets or sales) is reviewed for its acceptability in the light of the conditions expected to prevail. A number of budget-plan variations may be attempted before the result is considered satisfactory under the circumstances. When the plan is approved, we have the projected operating statement.

Planned profits are divided between distributed dividends and retained earnings. Retained earnings take the form either of current assets (working capital, such as cash, receivables, and inventory) or of capital investments. The capital budget is prepared in the light of the expected longer-run operations of the company, often tailored to the funds made available by current operations. In some instances a firm will add to its assets and liabilities by

415

outside financing. In either event, a method of rationing capital among com peting projects must be used, usually the payback period, or the internal rate of return, or the present worth. Now we have the projected balance sheet.

At any point in time funds flow into the firm, generally from the sale of goods or services, but also from earnings on property or short- or long-term financing (credit or cash). Funds also flow out of the firm, usually as the cost of producing goods or services but also for dividend payments and investment. Over any given period—indeed, at any moment of time—the sum of inflows exactly matches the outflows. A company's books are always in balance, even if it is in arrears in its payments. Red ink balances books no less than does black ink.

But at some levels or with some compositions of the balance the firm is no longer viable. Creditors are unwilling to hold debt of given magnitude, employees are unwilling to work unpaid, stockholders demand some return on their investment. It is not enough that a firm's inflows and outflows be in balance; they must be in balance at a level and with a composition that permits the continuity of the firm. In a planning sense, they must also be in balance at a level and with a composition that permits the achievement of the operating results projected. To accomplish this, a firm must plan its inflows and outflows so that there is always cash and credit enough on hand to carry the level of operations wanted. Over a substantial part of a planning period the funds generated from sales plus normal trade credit may be enough to accommodate the total outflow necessitated by the given level of operations. But at certain points in time (recurring perhaps monthly, perhaps seasonally) operations could not continue at these levels without a further infusion of funds. The bank balance, which smoothes out temporary discrepancies between inflows and outflows, permitting them to balance at the level and with the composition which is appropriate to the firm's activities, must be built up for the purpose. A projected flow-of-funds statement indicates when bank balances must be built up and by how much.

The purpose which motivates this business planning is not profit maximization in the theoretical sense of some ascertainable point of most return. The objective is commonly some quite specific rate of return on net worth, total assets, or sales. The standard typically owes its origin to comparisons with the firm's own past performance and to comparisons with the performance of other companies. It is more applicable to the firm's long run than to its short-term operations. Some companies are quite content with low-level targets. Others are more ambitious and demanding.

The short-run operating budget itself constitutes the short-run objective, even when the profit expected falls below the company's target. This is because the latter is not necessarily expected to be achieved every year, dependent as it is on external forces such as consumer tastes and general economic conditions. The best that management can do is to plan its operations as effectively as possible to come close to its target under the conditions expected to prevail. The operating budget thus becomes, in the next planning period, surrogate for the long-run profit target.

The company analyzes variances from the budget plan in order to take corrective action as needed. In some instances the deviation from plan can be righted by further application of effort or by removing some impediment to efficiency. In other instances the variance is more intractable, and special action is called for. In the short run, the principal adjustments which are possible are in controlling production and costs in line with sales, within the framework of a flexible budget. Other possible courses of action are price discounts or advertising programs to promote sales, intensified effort on selective (more profitable) products in the product line, and accelerated introduction of new or redesigned products. These latter actions, intended to spur sales rather than control costs in line with reduced sales, are most likely to be effective when a firm is suffering competitively (falling behind its rivals) and least likely to have an impact when its industry or business in general is suffering a decline.

A declining competitive position and persistent adverse budget variances can be adequately dealt with, however, only in the firm's longer-run planning (periods beyond the current operating year). The principal strategic variables with which it must work are product planning and introduction, new and improved technological systems, and improved organization (the latter referring not only to structure but to quality of personnel).

Planning implies discretion, which economists over the years have tended to remove or reduce in their formulations by emphasizing competition and the market as controlling forces, superior to the individual firm. Planning implies control, but economists have emphasized the constraining forces of the environment, which push individual actions—whatever their motivation or target—toward specifiable outcomes. The fact is, however, that both discretion and external limitations on discretion are present, and the mix of these two necessarily varies from business to business and from time to time. Business budgeting and planning attempt both to enlarge the area of business discretion and initiative and to capitalize on whatever measure of these assets is already enjoyed. Competitors and society at large tend—sometimes *intend* and at other times act unintentionally—to limit business discretion. But neither can ever eliminate the other.

It is this interplay between individual firm and environment which provides the economist's real interest, as the increasing attention paid to oligopoly suggests. There is relatively little subtlety needed in analyzing the hypothetical situations of pure competition or pure monopoly, but a great deal of conceptual ingenuity is needed to analyze effectively conditions of interdependence between firm and environment.

The environment principally exercises control over the individual firm by constantly whittling down special position, through such instrumentalities and agents as rival firms, inventors, and (to use Professor Merton's expressive term) social "influentials," who help to modify or mold tastes. Indeed, it would be safe though dogmatic to assert that special position is *always* lost over time. But at the same time, new special positions are always in the process of being created, as the innovator and entrepreneur seize upon elements of social change to turn them to their own advantage.

This entrepreneurial function may be exercised anywhere in the economy, in a small one-man shop or a giant corporation, in a one-plant firm of several hundred employees or a corporate empire with a dozen major operating companies flying its banner. It is less likely to arise in ongoing operations, which have had time to become too encrusted with tradition and intrenched privilege and personal status and organizational personality to make radical shifts in response to suddenly perceived possibilities.

But this carries no connotation that ongoing and established companies are incapable of seizing the new chance. The firm which is organized on a decentralized, multicenter basis can simply add another—quite new—operation to its empire, providing it with the financial support that the ongoing operations make possible. The firm which is alert to the possibilities inherent in change can build into its organization units engaged in research and development.[1]

A related aspect of the budget planning procedure is that by making the budget a coordinating device it permits a devolution of authority to subordinate units (profit centers), whose results constitute a demand on top management's limited time and attention only at time of budget preparation or when results depart significantly from budget.[2] The consequence is to

[1] The fact that few large corporations have effectively exploited such units is no indication that it is organizationally impossible. One of the problems yet to be overcome is the centralization of decision making about the use to be made of centrally administered research and development groups. One interesting experiment which I am still waiting to see some corporation undertake is to set up its "R & D" operation as a profit center, which will undertake assignments on contract from other arms of the company (conceivably from noncompeting companies as well), but which would be entirely free to engage in any line of research its director and research staff chose to follow. It would sell the results which emerge either to its own company or (if its company rejects them) to any other management it can interest. Like any other profit center, it would be judged by the earnings on its operations. The rationale behind building such a profit-making research unit into the firm would be to put pressure on a firm's top management to think outside of familiar routines (should it let some new development go to another company for exploitation?) and give greater assurance that ideas do not get bottled up by the unwillingness of a top management to become interested in something too novel or too remote from its traditional paths.

[2] The 1961 conspiracy trial in the electrical industry, resulting in the sentencing to one-month jail terms of a number of high-level executives for participation in flagrantly illegal activities of which the corporation presidents professed no knowl-

make possible a growth in size of the organization which would be effectively impossible under centralized control.[3] Whether the further growth of our largest firms is desirable, for reasons relating to the organization of economic power on such a scale, becomes a problem posed all the more sharply. If there are grounds for believing that at some point further aggrandizement is undesirable, we can place less reliance on internal limitations to stop expansion at that point. Size itself ceases to act as a brake on further growth as effectively as we once believed.

There remains only a valedictory comment. For many generations economists have tended to focus on price decisions as being the crux of micro analysis, the analysis of the behavior of firms and households. The interrelationship of prices determined the allocation of resources and the distribution of proceeds. Without repeating here the arguments which I have adduced at considerable length elsewhere,[4] I should like simply to restate my conviction that much is to be gained by reorienting micro analysis to the same interest in income flows which characterizes national income (macro) analysis. The principal questions to be explained in micro analysis are why and how the incomes of households and business units change size and direction. In the shift of competitive fortunes among business firms, in the changing tastes and aspirations and capabilities of members of households, the incomes of some units rise and the incomes of other units fall. Some of these shifts are offsetting, implying a redistribution of resources among the household and business units of the economy. The business unit (like the household) which experiences an unfavorable change in its income flows may attempt to correct the situation by actions which seem appropriate to the circumstances. It can take steps to remedy the adverse effects on discretionary income (undistributed profits, in the firm) by makeshift means in the short run and more fundamental measures in the long run.

At other times the changes in income flows in some units do not encounter offsetting flows in other units. The changes are cumulative, upward or downward, leading to recession and possible deflation, or to growth and possible inflation.

---

edge, raised important questions, however, of whether "management by exception" or "management by results" is enough. Top management cannot shirk ultimate responsibility for the character of its organization, even if it has delegated operating responsibility as a matter of principle.

[3] Informed speculation sometimes suggests that decision making in the future will become more and more centralized, with computer installations doing most of the work. Every man is entitled to his own view of the future. My own is that while this may be true of certain types of decisions (financing, for example), it will not be representative of the whole range of business decisions. Computers will undoubtedly become increasingly useful in budget planning, but I do not look for them to take over the planning and control process.

[4] *A General Theory of Economic Process,* especially chaps. 16 and 18.

It is thus changes in income flows which are critical both to individual units and to the economy as a whole. It is the relation between flow changes within and between units (their offsetting or nonoffsetting character) which provides the analytical link between micro and macro analysis. Price, important though it is in explaining changes in flows, becomes demoted in importance, taking its place as only one influence (albeit a major one) on the flows which affect the realization or nonrealization of the firm's (and household's) projected balance.

To the extent that one subscribes to this view of the central importance of income flows in economic analysis does it become desirable to become better acquainted with the institutional mechanisms by which such flows are channeled, and to explore the extent to which intent (planning) is attempted in the control of such flows, and to examine the interrelationship between such attempted control and environmental limitations on it. It seems likely that the budget (expressive of anticipations and intentions) may become as useful an analytical concept to economists in understanding the firm as it has proved a functional device to management in administering it.

INDEX